History, Memory and Public Life

History, Memory and Public Life introduces readers to key themes in the study of historical memory and its significance by considering the role of historical expertise and understanding in contemporary public reflection on the past.

Divided into two parts, the book addresses both the theoretical and applied aspects of historical memory studies. 'Approaches to history and memory' introduces key methodological and theoretical issues within the field, such as postcolonialism, sites of memory, myths of national origins, and questions raised by memorialisation and museum presentation. 'Difficult pasts' looks at history and memory in practice through a range of case studies on contested, complex or traumatic memories, including the Northern Ireland Troubles, post-apartheid South Africa and the Holocaust.

Examining the intersections between history and memory from a wide range of perspectives, and supported by guidance on further reading and online resources, this book is ideal for students of history as well as those working within the broad interdisciplinary field of memory studies.

Anna Maerker is Senior Lecturer in History of Medicine at King's College London. Her work on the material culture of medicine and science and on the history of expertise includes *Model Experts: Wax Anatomies and Enlightenment in Florence and Vienna, 1775–1815* (2011).

Simon Sleight is Senior Lecturer in Australian History at King's College London. His research interests include urban life in the past and the evolution of youth cultures. Recent publications include the co-edited collection *Children, Childhood and Youth in the British World* (2016).

Adam Sutcliffe is Professor of European History at King's College London. He is the author of *Judaism and Enlightenment* (2003), and the co-editor, most recently, of *Philosemitism in History* (2011) and *The Cambridge History of Judaism, Volume 7: The Early Modern World, 1500–1815* (2018).

History, Memory and
Public Life

The Past in the Present

**Edited by
Anna Maerker,
Simon Sleight and
Adam Sutcliffe**

Routledge
Taylor & Francis Group

LONDON AND NEW YORK

First published 2018
by Routledge
2 Park Square, Milton Park, Abingdon, Oxon OX14 4RN

and by Routledge
711 Third Avenue, New York, NY 10017

Routledge is an imprint of the Taylor & Francis Group, an informa business

British Library Cataloguing in Publication Data
A catalogue record for this book is available from the British Library

Library of Congress Cataloging in Publication Data
Names: Maerker, Anna Katharina, editor. | Sleight, Simon, editor. | Sutcliffe, Adam, editor.
Title: History, memory and public life : the past in the present / edited by Anna Maerker, Simon Sleight and Adam Sutcliffe.
Description: London ; New York : Routledge, 2018.
Identifiers: LCCN 2018002019| ISBN 9781138905832 (hardback : alk. paper) | ISBN 9781138905849 (pbk. : alk. paper) | ISBN 9781351055581 (ebook)
Subjects: LCSH: Public history. | Memory—Social aspects. | Collective memory. | History—Psychological aspects. | History—Philosophy. | Historiography.
Classification: LCC D16.163 .H58 2018 | DDC 900—dc23
LC record available at https://lccn.loc.gov/2018002019

ISBN: 978-1-138-90583-2 (hbk)
ISBN: 978-1-138-90584-9 (pbk)
ISBN: 978-1-351-05558-1 (ebk)

Typeset in Galliard
by Keystroke, Neville Lodge, Tettenhall, Wolverhampton

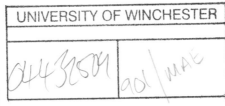

Printed and bound in Great Britain by
TJ International Ltd, Padstow, Cornwall

Contents

Illustrations

Figures

Table

Notes on contributors

Frank Bongiorno is Professor of History at the Australian National University and was previously Senior Lecturer in Australian History at King's College London. He is the author of *The People's Party: Victorian Labor and the Radical Tradition 1875–1914* (1996), *The Sex Lives of Australians: A History* (2012) and *The Eighties: The Decade that Transformed Australia* (2015). He is also co-author of *A Little History of the Australian Labor Party* (2011).

W. Fitzhugh Brundage is the William B. Umstead Professor of History at the University of North Carolina at Chapel Hill. He is the author of *The Southern Past: A Clash of Race and Region* (2005), *Lynching in the New South* (1994) and the forthcoming *Civilizing Torture: Reconciling American Democracy and Torture* (2018).

Laura Gowing is Professor of Early Modern History at King's College London. Her books include *Common Bodies: Women, Touch and Power in Seventeenth-Century England* (2003) and *Gender Relations in Early Modern England* (2012).

Toby Green is Senior Lecturer in Lusophone African History and Culture at King's College London. He is the author of *The Rise of the Trans-Atlantic Slave Trade in Western Africa, 1300–1589* (2012), and most recently (as co-editor with the late Patrick Chabal) of *Guinea-Bissau: Micro-State to 'Narco-State'* (2016).

Peter Heather is Professor of Medieval History at King's College London. He is the author of *The Fall of Rome: A New History* (2005) and *Empires and Barbarians: The Fall of Rome and the Birth of Europe* (2009). His current project focuses on the evolution of medieval European Christendom.

Eureka Henrich is Research Fellow in Conflict, Memory and Legacy at the University of Hertfordshire and Honorary Associate of the Menzies Centre for Australian Studies, King's College London. Her publications include 'Museums, History and Migration in Australia', *History Compass* (2013) and *History, Historians and the Immigration Debate: Going Back to Where We Came From* (2018), co-edited with Julian M. Simpson.

Tom Lodge is Professor of Peace and Conflict Studies in the Department of Politics and Public Administration at the University of Limerick, Ireland. He is the author of several books on South African politics and recent history, including *Mandela: A Critical Life* (2006) and *Sharpeville: An Apartheid Massacre and its Consequences* (2011).

Anna Maerker is Senior Lecturer in History of Medicine at King's College London. Her work on the material and public culture of science and medicine includes *Model Experts: Wax Anatomies and Enlightenment in Florence and Vienna, 1775–1815* (2011).

Ian McBride is Foster Professor of Irish History at the University of Oxford. He is the editor of *History and Memory in Modern Ireland* (2001), author of *Eighteenth-Century Ireland: The Isle of Slaves* (2009) and co-editor of *The Princeton History of Modern Ireland* (2016).

Keir Reeves is Professor of Australian History and Director of CRCAH at Federation University Australia where his current research investigates the intersections of history, heritage and memory. Recent books include the co-authored collections *Anzac Journeys: Returning to the Battlefields of World War Two* (2014) and *Reviewing the AFL's Vilification Laws: Rule 35, Reconciliation and Racial Harmony in Australian Football* (2017).

Simon Sleight is Senior Lecturer in Australian History at King's College London and Adjunct Research Associate at Monash University in Melbourne. His recent publications include 'Plasticine Cities: On Young People and Historical Urban Morphology' in Griffiths and von Lünen (eds), *Spatial Cultures* (2016), and a co-edited volume, *Children, Childhood and Youth in the British World* (2015).

Adam Sutcliffe is Professor of European History at King's College London. He is the author of *Judaism and Enlightenment* (2003), and the co-editor, most recently, of *Philosemitism in History* (2011) and *The Cambridge History of Judaism, Volume 7: The Early Modern World, 1500–1815* (2018).

John Tosh is Professor of History at the University of Roehampton and Visiting Professor at Birkbeck, University of London. His main research area is the history of masculinities in nineteenth-century Britain, and he has also published extensively on historiography. *Why History Matters* (2008) argues that good citizenship requires critical history and that historians have a social obligation to provide that in accessible, practical form.

Introduction

Memory, public life and the work of the historian

Adam Sutcliffe, Anna Maerker and Simon Sleight

What is the use of history? Amid the dizzying transformations of our digital present, on what terms is the past still worthy of our attention, as teachers and students, and worthy also of public support, whether through general interest, institutional policies or funding? The relevance of history as a source from which to predict or extrapolate the future is a particularly uncertain basis for the justification of the subject. Nonetheless, some historians today discern trends that do not bode well for their discipline. According to one recent argument, in today's present-focused age we seldom look either backward or forward, having lost faith both in the national narratives that used to shape our sense of the past and in the utopian visions that provided us with a vista to the future. In consequence, 'Clio, the aging muse of history, seems to be fading into the twilight' (Sand 2017: 261–2).

Our contrary contention in this volume is that a reflective and nuanced approach to the past is today as vital as ever, and that historians need to hone their skills as the key mediators of this reflection and nuance to the wider public. There has indeed been a decline in the authority of traditional 'kings and queens' or 'great presidents' history, which dominated the public and scholastic presentation of the subject into the late twentieth century, laden with hoary anecdotes and reverential detail about the lives of past elites. Such narratives remain popular among some, but they compete for attention with other accounts of the past. New interpretations of the past now often focus on non-elite perspectives, the diversity of lived everyday experience, or on alternative perspectives on controversial and troubling historical episodes. These various faces of history are all present in the public consumption of the past, which takes many forms. History today is relayed and explored not only through education and reading, but also at historical sites, in television and film, through monuments and rituals, via radio, podcasts, and online resources and interactions, and in public and private debates over how the past has shaped our present, and how it might provide resources for shaping the future.

The past has always been an instrument of power, most often used to naturalize and justify the existing social order. It has also played a very important role in providing inspiration, identity and focus to movements challenging the status quo, in the name of women, the poor, and religious, ethnic or sexual minorities.

In today's fragmented and fast-changing media landscape the presence of the past, and its use and contestation, are more dispersed and diverse than ever before. Trained historians must therefore be similarly agile in renewing their public role. Unchallenged professorial authority may indeed be fading into the twilight, but the importance of historical expertise and sophisticated analytical skills in our public debates about the past seems, if anything, to be greater than ever.

In recent decades historians have paid increasing attention not only to what happened in the past, but also to the uses of the past: the instrumentalization, contestation and suppression of particular accounts of the past in successive presents. This turn has been heavily influenced by the boom in the study of memory across the humanities and social sciences since the 1980s. A new interdisciplinary field of 'memory studies' has emerged, drawing heavily from philosophy and from literary, cultural and psychoanalytic theory, as well as from sociology, anthropology, geography, cognitive science and other disciplines. There is now an immense literature in this area, as well as several books that offer a broad survey (Radstone and Schwarz 2010; Erll 2011; Tota and Hagen 2016). Historians' changing interests have also been spurred by the increased expectation that scholars should seek to engage broader audiences and to bring their expertise to bear on the challenges of the present. This has drawn them into another burgeoning interdisciplinary field, also now with its own extensive literature: museum and heritage studies (Corsane 2005; Anheier and Isar 2011; Waterton and Watson 2015).

The past is clearly central both to memory and to heritage. However, these fields have to a large extent detached themselves from history, becoming independent areas of study in their own right. Memory studies today has a strongly theoretical bent, while heritage studies is more applied and vocational in focus, paying close attention to the multiple practical issues raised in the conservation and presentation of heritage sites and materials. The interdisciplinary skills nurtured in these areas have contributed immensely to our understanding of the complex psychic texture of the past, and of the professional skills and subtleties of thought that can enhance the presentation of the past to the public. What, though, is the place of the discipline of history in these broader debates? The core skills of the historian, in interpreting evidence and understanding change, should surely be important in all forms of reflection on the past. In relation to memory and public life, though, these skills must be deployed with sensitivity and humility, alongside attentiveness to the varied and sometimes raw responses of the general public to the past. In this volume, building on earlier work by historians, we will explore this intersection between history and memory (Cubbitt 2007; Tumblety 2013; Hutton 2016). Our central question is: what is the role of historical expertise and understanding in public life today?

The omnipresence today of digital technology, and the never-ending procession of video clips and social media posts that it offers us, readily creates the impression that our era is unprecedentedly absorbed in the present. While this may in some sense be true, it is certainly not the case that the rise of digital media has heralded an era of collective amnesia. On the contrary: the amassing of data, including the digitization of historical records, most of which are increasingly easily searched, relayed and adapted, has made it possible for the past to be injected into current conversations in a wide range of innovative ways. Memories can now be almost instantaneously shared across the world, generating new forms of digital commemoration and mobilization that are only just beginning to be analysed by scholars (Reading 2011, 2016). Technological change has accelerated and intensified the globalization of memory: traditional patriotic narratives of the past now compete for attention in a landscape in which alternative historical connections across space and time can be communicated and accessed with unprecedented ease.

History is most vividly present where its consequences are most painful or controversial. The legacies of colonialism, slavery and war profoundly shape the social inequalities of our world, and the most profound differences in the stories of the past we prefer to tell ourselves. In countries grappling with the immediate aftermath of long periods of violent internal conflict, such as Northern Ireland or South Africa, addressing the clashing narratives of the past of different communities is a major challenge. More broadly, though, the pain caused by the violence of the past continues to be keenly felt by many people, and to play a fundamental role in their understanding of their place in the world. What and how we remember is therefore often particularly important for minority groups – ethnic, religious, racial, linguistic or sexual – for whom memory plays a central role in their collective identity and sense of social or political recognition. All of us, however, are equally confronted with the challenge of acknowledging and attempting to learn from the most troubling episodes of history, such as the world wars, genocides and totalitarian regimes of the past century.

Historians are stakeholders in these debates simply as citizens. They also have a particular contribution to make to them, as skilled and thoughtful interpreters of the past. Many would argue that trained historians, including university students of the subject, have a responsibility to participate in these public conversations, in a spirit of fair-mindedness, sensitivity and respect for empirical accuracy. The rise of memory studies has roughly coincided with a recent boom in history publishing, with a number of professional historians since the 1990s reaching large audiences with what Peter Mandler has described as 'popular yet serious' history books (Mandler 2002: 135). It is certainly desirable that the expertise of historians should be communicated to the public directly, clearly and when appropriate also entertainingly. However, historians also need to stimulate public reflection on the ways that the past is consumed and remembered. This requires not only historical knowledge and interpretive nuance, but also the ability to explore and engage with the political and emotional investments of different groups of people in different accounts of the past. The teaching of history is now increasingly nurturing both skill sets. This volume, which emerges from a core undergraduate module on 'History and Memory' that we have taught very successfully for almost a decade at King's College London, seeks to further this development, and to contribute to preparing future generations of historians to think sharply and communicate nimbly at the triple nexus of history, memory and public life.

Our volume is divided into two sections. The first, 'Approaches to history and memory', encompasses seven essays that together survey and explicate the most important methodological and theoretical issues in the field. These essays range widely over questions of place, race, language, mobility, nation and authority in the articulation of memory in public life. The second section, 'Difficult pasts', moves in a sense from theory to practice. The six chapters in this section each explore a different case study, ranging from the First World War in Australian memory to slavery and its legacies in the American South, and from the politics of Holocaust memory to the diversity of queer memory. These studies are informed by the methodologies and issues discussed in the first section, and further illuminate their significance in relation to some of the most intensely discussed and contested topics in contemporary historical memory. The terrain covered by both parts of the volume is complex, but our contributors have aimed to be as accessible as possible, avoiding unnecessary jargon while also offering a vigorous interpretive analysis that will be stimulating both for newcomers and for experts on their topic. The remainder of this Introduction offers a succinct overview of the key concepts and questions addressed by the volume as a whole, by treating each of the key terms of our title in isolation: first memory, then public life, and finally the role of the historian in relation to both.

Memory

When we use the word 'memory' today, we are likely to be referring not to a mental faculty, but to what resides on our desktops or, even more ubiquitously, in our pockets. 'How much memory have you got?' This question, which would have been met with perplexity not so long ago, can now be readily answered by almost all of us. Whatever the number, in gigabytes, that we give in response, we can be sure that before too long it will be insufficient for our needs, which will signal that it is time, if we can afford it, to buy a new phone.

In the premodern period, in stark contrast, memory was mostly considered not in material terms at all, but as an art and a practice. The use of mnemonic devices to commit knowledge to memory was a valued rhetorical technique both in the ancient world and in medieval and Renaissance Europe. The famous 'memory palace' technique, by which sets of ideas are committed to memory by associating them with a sequence of vivid spatial images, is mentioned by Cicero (106–43 BCE), and its origins were attributed by the Romans to the Greek poet Simonides (c. 556–468 BCE) (Yates 1966; Hutton 1993: 27–36; Carruthers 2008 [1990]; Rossi 2000). For more practical matters of record, such as land title, medieval European society moved from a reliance on memory, often validated by artefacts such as swords or other heirlooms, to the use of written records, which by the start of the fourteenth century was firmly established in English governmental practices (Clanchy 2013 [1979]).

In early modern Europe, humanist historical scholarship emerged as an important genre, but it was to a large extent imitative of the ancient chronicle tradition. Antiquarian in spirit, these historians sought to record what was most significant, but with little self-consciousness about the process of selection that this inherently involved (Burrow 2007: 299–319). Only in the eighteenth century, with the sweeping philosophical narratives of writers such as Voltaire, Hume and Gibbon, did the crafting of reflective, argument-driven accounts of the past emerge. Beyond these elite scholarly circles, the texture of memory is something to which we have relatively little access. Among the literate, practices such as diary-keeping and letter-writing – early technologies of memory – encouraged the self-fashioning and archiving of individual life stories. Collective activities such as walking along the boundaries of a community or a traditional processional route reinforced customary memories among the population more generally. Overall, though, remembrance of the past was not a leading concern of the European eighteenth-century public sphere.

The political, social and economic upheavals of the late eighteenth and early nineteenth centuries – the 'age of revolutions' – brought with them, several historians have argued, a widespread shift in the experience of time. The American and, even more so, the French Revolution ushered in rapid and radical transformations that had previously been almost unimaginable. 'News' circulated with unprecedented rapidity and vigorous debate. This increasing consciousness of political drama was coupled with a rising awareness of economic and technological change, which many writers in the Romantic era described as the eclipse of an old world of stability and tradition by a new, fast-changing order that inspired mixed and complex feelings in them. The term 'nostalgia' had been coined in the late seventeenth century by a Swiss physician to describe a yearning for home among soldiers kept away from their familiar Alpine environment. In the Romantic period, though, nostalgia became a much more prevalent phenomenon, as people from all social classes looked back to a past they believed was lost for ever, and could only be captured in memories tinged with melancholy (Boym 2001: 3–18; Fritzsche 2001, 2004; Koselleck 2004 [1979]: 222–75).

Memory, then, has a deep history, which historians can excavate and explore (Berger and Niven 2014). Self-conscious reflection on the nature of memory, in ways that can be directly connected to the development of the modern field of memory studies, stretches back less far: the roots of this field lie in the late nineteenth century. A key early stimulus was the work of the French philosopher Henri Bergson (1859–1941), who was fascinated by the nature of the human experience of time and thought. In his *Matter and Memory* (1896), Bergson dissected the difference between the unconscious form of memory, as 'motor mechanisms', and the conscious form of memory, as recollection of a moment in the past. His favourite example of this is the distinction between the ability to remember something (such as poem) by heart, and the memory of the effortful act of learning those words. It is this latter form of memory that interested Bergson. The perception of memory, he argued, is a complex temporal manoeuvre: a drawing of a moment from the past into consciousness in the present, which is constantly rolling into the future (Bergson 1911 [1896]: 86–105, 170–94; Ansell-Pearson 2010).

Bergson's interest in the experience of memory in the present strongly influenced both literary and psychological approaches to the topic in the twentieth century. The novelist Marcel Proust (1871–1922), in his celebrated seven-volume novel *À la recherche du temps perdu* [*In Search of Lost Time*], explored the ways in which memories could be involuntary and powerfully prompted, for example when his narrator tastes a piece of madeleine cake he has dipped in his tea, and feels a wave of 'delicious pleasure' which he only much later realizes was because the taste had reminded him of Sunday morning childhood teas with his aunt (Wood 2010: 116). The psychoanalytic theories of Sigmund Freud (1856–1939) centred on the psychic handling of memory: traumatic memories, he argued, were repressed in the unconscious mind. The labour of psychoanalysis was to coax these memories back into consciousness and to decode and dissolve their traumatic meanings, with the aim of enabling a life of greater happiness and self-understanding. In his *Psychopathology of Everyday Life* (1901), Freud argued that lapses and errors of recall almost invariably had an unconscious significance ('Freudian slips'), and that seemingly banal memories were sometimes imbued with psychic significance because they served as a 'screen memory', behind which was hidden something traumatic and repressed. Although psychoanalysis as a system for understanding the mind is today dismissed by many, Freud's core ideas have percolated into our common assumptions about the workings of memory, and have been particularly important for historians interested in how difficult memories can find expression in indirect and surprising ways (Terdiman 1993: 151–343; Freud 2003 [1901]; Rothberg 2009: 12–14).

Not until the second quarter of the twentieth century did scholarly attention focus on collective, as opposed to individual, memory. This turn is associated above all with the French sociologist Maurice Halbwachs (1877–1945). A student of Bergson who was also greatly influenced by the founding father of French sociology Émile Durkheim (1858–1917), Halbwachs' central insight was that all individual remembering takes place in a social context, using the linguistic and symbolic resources of that milieu. Even when we remember alone, we can only communicate our memories using language, which is inherently social in nature. Halbwachs' emphasis on the social determination of human inner life was in part shaped by his personal experience. His family, like Durkheim and his parents, had lived in the eastern French provinces of Alsace-Lorraine, which were annexed by Germany following the Franco-Prussian War in 1871. Halbwachs' parents chose to move to Reims, nearby but still in France, where Maurice grew up, his family patriotically affirming a French identity despite remaining close to German culture. After the First World War Halbwachs took a post in Strasbourg, the principal city of Alsace, which was then restored to France, and it was there that he wrote his earliest pioneering work on collective memory. His most famous study of the inscription of collective memory in the urban landscape focused on Jerusalem, where the historical perspectives of successive waves of inhabitants and invaders were inscribed in the local topography. One wonders, though, whether this study, published in 1941, was also for Halbwachs in some sense a 'screen' confrontation with the more traumatic (for him) historical layering of Alsace, which at that time was once again annexed to Germany (Halbwachs 1992 [1925/1941]: 193–235; Apfelbaum 2010).

The First World War profoundly fractured national traditions of memory and mourning. Over the long nineteenth century European and colonial cities had been adorned with statuary proudly honouring military leaders who had led their forces to victory. The immensity of the loss of life in the Great War demanded a different register. The war memorials that were built in the heart of towns and villages across Europe and beyond after the 1914–18 war typically remember the fallen soldiers of the community in a quiet and egalitarian fashion. While still placing them within a traditional idiom of heroism and sacrifice, these memorials are places of shared mourning rather than national glory (Winter, J. 1995: 78–116; Inglis 1998). After the Second World War more names were added to most of these monuments. However, the vast loss of civilian life in that war and in other later twentieth-century conflicts has displaced the centrality of the soldier in the memory of war. This 'democratization of suffering', as Jay Winter has put it, has prompted new and more inclusive forms of historical remembrance (Winter, J. 2006: 282). The public commemoration of the losses and atrocities of war is today not only the most emotionally intense field of collective memory, but also often the forum for the most complex debates over the relative merits of different forms and practices of remembrance.

The final two decades of the twentieth century witnessed a 'memory boom', as scholars in a range of disciplines discovered the subject. There were several interrelated reasons for this. A generation after the end of the Second World War, there was by the 1980s a readiness to confront the horrors of the conflict, including and perhaps especially the Holocaust, which had been largely eclipsed since 1945 by preoccupations with post-war recovery, domestic consumerism and the realigned antagonisms of the Cold War. In the 1980s this ideological conflict began to crumble, before suddenly disappearing in 1989, when the collapse of communist regimes brought to the fore numerous tensions and strands of memory that had been frozen, taboo or inaccessible for decades. In the West, a long period of sustained post-war economic prosperity and broad political consensus faltered in the 1970s, ushering in a more polarized and uncertain political mood in the 1980s, in which a wide range of voices were now distinctly audible. The liberation movements of the 1960s and 1970s – second-wave feminism, the gay and lesbian rights movement, Black Power, and the anti-colonial and civil rights struggles – were by the 1980s breaking through into the mainstream, and challenging dominant assumptions about whose histories should be taught and commemorated. The memory boom was also related to the impact of postmodernism, which posed a philosophical challenge to the authority of traditional history. Changing technology, too, played a role: advances in digital data storage and transmission with the emergence of the personal computer and email allowed 'witnessing' to expand both in reach and in range of content (Winter, J. 2007: 373). The late twentieth-century turn to memory was, then, a heady moment. A new diversity of approaches to the past had emerged, challenging the methodological self-confidence of the historical discipline in ways that troubled many of its practitioners (Klein 2000; Winter, J. 2001; Appleby et al. 1994; Hutton 2016: 1–20).

The 'post-' ideas – postmodernism and postcolonialism – profoundly shaped the intellectual mood of the late twentieth century, and were fundamental influences on the turn to memory in this period. In his chapter in this volume Toby Green focuses on postcolonialism, showing how it emerged in the 1960s when decolonization was at its peak, a range of counter-cultural movements were strengthening in the West, and both in newly independent nations and across African and Asian diasporas there was a desire to challenge the dominance of Eurocentric cultural and historical perspectives. Postcolonialism, he shows, was indebted to the postmodern critique of the 'master narratives' of Western thought, which postmodern thinkers challenged in a range of ways, such as through the French philosopher Jacques Derrida's method of 'deconstruction', which highlighted the linguistic uncertainty and instability of texts which had generally been taken to have a firm, authorially controlled meaning. However, Green highlights the key distinction between postmodernism and postcolonialism: whereas postmodernism was a challenge to the authority of Western thought from within, postcolonialism challenged the dominance of the West from without, and sought to establish an alternative to it. Historical facts were very important in postcolonial thought – the key issue was to challenge the emphasis on certain facts at the expense of others. Green exemplifies this through an exploration of the issues raised by the commemoration of the bicentenary of the British Abolition Act of 1807, which banned the Atlantic slave trade. The official British narrative in 2007 emphasized the moral leadership of the British, and the heroism of abolitionists such as William Wilberforce. In the Caribbean, in contrast, and also for black British and other critics in the UK, the vast human costs of slavery, and the huge profits that accrued to British slave-owners, both of which continued after 1807, seemed more salient. In this case study we see very clearly how the insights of postcolonialism continue to challenge and to expand the ways in which we remember and represent the past.

The turn to memory was accompanied by a turn towards place as an object of study. In this regard the huge French collaborative project led by Pierre Nora on *lieux de mémoire* (sites of memory) was extremely influential (Nora 1989, 1996–8). In his chapter, Keir Reeves discusses Nora's work, elucidating the distinction Nora drew between 'real' community memory ('*milieux de mémoire*'), which he believed died out in France around the 1970s, and the didactic expression of national memory through *lieux de mémoire*. Reeves notes that Nora has been widely criticized for his focus on national memory, but explores the wide variety of ways in which historians and interpreters of heritage have used his concepts to think imaginatively about the intersections of memory, place and the public at sites of historical commemoration. Surveying a wide range of sites across the world, from Australia and Cambodia to the British Channel Islands and the United States, Reeves shows how complex these dynamics of memory can be, and how important it is for historians to be attentive to the responses of visitors to sensitive sites of memory, and to the ways in which their emotions and actions continually reshape the meanings of these landscapes.

The topographic enshrining of national memory has its roots in the nineteenth century, which was the formative period of European nationalism. In our next chapter, Peter Heather explores the ways in which the development, in this period, first of linguistics and then of archaeology laid the intellectual groundwork for nationalist ideologies. The archaeological argument – based most fundamentally on the interpretation of pottery types – that Europe had long been populated by distinct and rival cultural groups was quickly co-opted into late nineteenth-century nationalist agendas, and enshrined within the patriotic school curricula of the rapidly expanding state education systems of the period. In the aftermath of fascism, which took this perspective to its extreme, there was a strong counter-reaction: from the 1960s onwards, supported by new anthropological approaches and reinterpretations of material culture, archaeologists and historians increasingly emphasized the malleability of cultural identities, which displaced the earlier assumption that waves of invasion explained changes in European place names and styles of material production. This account of the past also readily found political support, particularly from the European Union during its period of peak expansion and optimism in the 1990s. Heather's analysis shows how the interpretation of the history of the first millennium CE has long been, and remains, a key domain for the formation and contestation of the deep structures of European collective identities. Similar structures of argument have been equally important beyond Europe – for example in shaping notions of 'tribal' identity in Africa, or in the forging of nationalist traditions in new nations such as Israel (Zerubavel 1995). This field is also of heightened resonance in contemporary Europe, as the place of migration in human history continues to be rethought, against the backdrop of conflict-driven refugee emergencies on a scale not seen since the Second World War (Heather 2009).

Nationalist interpretations of the past tend to take culture for granted, seeing it as the natural expression, and indeed content, of an individual's inherent and essentially fixed identity. British people, for example, do British things. For scholars of memory, in contrast, culture is in no sense straightforward or unchanging: a thriving sub-field of 'cultural memory' has emerged, devoted to exploring the ways in which cultural heritage is recorded, transmitted, enacted and lodged in human consciousness. This tradition draws early inspiration from the German émigré art historian and collector Aby Warburg, who was devoted to the study of the transmission of classical culture, through all channels but particularly through the successive reinterpretation of iconography (Gombrich 1986). Aleida Assmann has developed this focus on transmission, drawing a useful and influential distinction between those aspects of the past that we actively remember, such as by choosing to display them in a museum (which she terms 'the canon' of cultural memory), and those forgotten but not lost traces of the past, which we store for possible access in the future ('the archive') (Assmann, A. 2008, 2011 [1999]: 119–32). In related work, the Egyptologist Jan Assmann has emphasized the importance of the transmission of core cultural texts and practices in shaping and sustaining the sense of distinction between different cultural identities. The self-image of a culture, he argues, is based on the sustenance of its core heritage. This takes a different form in each cultural tradition, but is generally based around a set of canonical religious texts, hermeneutic or embodied rituals, or other practices of memory transmission that are held to be most precious in that culture (Assmann, J. 1995, 2011 [1992]: 111–41).

Memory's twin, inescapably, is forgetting. What is the cultural significance of forgetting, and what is the relationship of history and historians to it? Drawing together Nora's sense of the loss of collective memory in the modern era with Jan Assmann's emphasis on the centrality of religion in cultural memory, Yosef Yerushalmi's reflections on the place of memory in the Jewish tradition highlight the distinction between history and memory. The commandment to remember is fundamental to Judaism, but in the modern era most Jews have grown increasingly distant from this sense of shared memory. As a Jewish historian of the Jewish past, Yerushalmi has no remedy to offer, but insists that historians should nonetheless seek to make the past memorable and meaningful (Yerushalmi 1982: 81–103). The intensified pace, scale and sensory impact of modern urban life, and particularly the rapid transformation of our built environments, has been associated with the erasure of the past and the rise of cultural forgetting (Connerton 2009). Forgetting, though, can also have positive consequences, particularly as part of a process of reconciliation and forgiveness. The various forms of forgetting have been analysed by the philosopher Paul Ricoeur, who contrasts in particular the dangers of 'escapist forgetting', such as the tendency by the victors of history to forget the history of its victims, with the value of 'active forgetting' in the context of forgiveness. Such forgiveness should not erase the traces and records of the past, but it moves us beyond its emotional burden of guilt, and as such, he argues, it is 'a way of healing memory and of completing its period of mourning' (Ricoeur 2011 [2006]: 480; see also 2004 [2000]: 412–506).

In some ways we seem more conscious than ever of the presence of memory in our lives. Marianne Hirsch's influential concept of 'postmemory' was originally conceived to capture the sense of many children of Holocaust survivors that their lives have been haunted by complex inherited memories that they only partially understand. It has, though, been widely applied in other contexts to explore the transmission of the past, and particularly traumatic or concealed pasts, to subsequent generations (Hirsch 1996). On the other hand, the fast-developing sciences of memory may soon lead us into a new era in which pharmacological treatments will be available to enable 'therapeutic forgetting'. Experimental attempts are already underway to use such techniques to treat American military veterans suffering from post-traumatic stress disorder (PTSD). What, we must ask, will it mean for the future of memory, and indeed human identity, if we become able with relative ease to edit or even erase our mental store of memories (Winter, A. 2012: 257–72)?

More immediately, what is the future of memory studies? It may be that the 'memory boom' has already peaked, and that challenges and conflicts of our millennium, emblematically irrupting into consciousness with the terror attacks of September 11, 2001, are shifting our intellectual priorities to new terrains (Rosenfeld 2009). Alternatively, the study of memory may continue to diversify and to re-energize itself, stimulated in particular by the continually changing ways in which social media and other forms of digital communication and archiving are used to explore, represent and experience the past (Bond et al. 2016). Whatever the prognosis, history will remain a prominent element of human mental life, and the interpretation of its legacy will continue to be, by turns, controversial, confusing and painful as well as fascinating, illuminating, liberating and even joyous. Historians, as trained specialists in the interpretation of the past, will continue to have a key role in guiding and enriching these interpretive processes. They therefore need a rich understanding of the dynamics of memory that shape those processes – and also, no less critically, of the matters on which the remainder of this essay will focus: the public landscape in which memory takes place, and the possibilities and pitfalls of their role within that landscape.

Public life

The past is present in public life in many different ways, as commemoration, education and entertainment. Audiences encounter history through a wide range of formats, from museum displays, memorials and live performances to historical novels and television documentaries and dramas. Some forms of public engagement with the past are highly participatory, such as genealogical research, which has been greatly facilitated and boosted by digitization and the internet, or historical re-enactment. Exploring the past is of course central to tourism. In Britain, the stately home remains the classic destination for a family 'day out', while 'living history' museums have proliferated across the world: notable examples include Colonial Williamsburg in Virginia, USA; the Historical Village of Hokkaido, Japan; and the Beamish Open Air Museum in North East England. How, though, can historians map, evaluate and most productively participate in this great diversity of public experiences of the past? In parallel with the rise of public interest in history since the 1960s, professional historians have increasingly sought to engage – both as contributors and as critics – with the many forms of history in public life.

This involvement has led to the development of 'public history' as a recognized professional field in its own right. Public history emerged in the United States in the 1970s, with the foundation by the pioneering scholar Robert Kelley of the first degree programme in the field, at the University of California, Santa Barbara, followed by the establishment of the journal *The Public Historian* and the U.S. National Council of Public History (Graham 2001). The early public history movement captured the energy generated at that time by the impact on the historical discipline of the rise of women's history and black history, which had brought forward perspectives on the past that had until recently been marginalized or overlooked. Inspired by this expansion of the purview of their subject, public historians investigated the relationship between the professional discipline and the general public, and asked how ordinary Americans engaged with the past (Rosenzweig and Thelen 1998). Their work questioned whether there was a 'right way' to approach history, and challenged the widespread elitism of the discipline. In Britain in the 1970s the History Workshop movement emerged, in which a leading role was played by Raphael Samuel and other left-wing historians outside the academic mainstream. Espousing similar goals to the early public historians in the United States, History Workshop promoted 'people's history' as a collaborative and public activity (Schwarz 1993).

Today, undergraduate and graduate programmes in public history have been established not just in the US, the UK and Australia, but also in Germany, Italy, India, China, Poland, Ireland and the Netherlands. The U.S. National Council of Public History defines its field as 'the many and diverse ways in which history is put to work in the world. In this sense, it is history that is applied to real-world issues.' As such, public history is practised by a wide range of professionals and amateurs, including 'historical consultants, museum professionals, government historians, archivists, oral historians, cultural resource managers, curators, film and media producers, historical interpreters, historic preservationists, policy advisers, local historians and community activists'.[1] Public historians have now firmly established their intellectual credentials, institutional niche and textual canon (Kean and Martin 2013). However, the relationship of public historians to the general public, and to the political, institutional and commercial structures that mediate public engagement with the past, continue to be areas of considerable debate and controversy.

The concept of 'heritage' has been a key focus in these debates. In his classic work *Theatres of Memory* (1994), Raphael Samuel noted the 'nomadic' nature of heritage: the term, he suggested, 'travels easily, and puts down roots – or bivouacs – in seemingly quite unpromising terrain. . . . It sets up residence in streets broad and narrow, royal palaces and railway sidings, canalside walks and town hall squares. . . . It attaches itself to an astonishing variety of material artefacts' (Samuel 2012 [1994]: 205). For Samuel, this 'inflation' of meaning could have a positive, egalitarian effect, as the notion of heritage, and the sense of value with which it was associated, was extended to cover environments and artefacts that had previously been considered 'beneath the dignity of history', because they were too mundane or too recent to be worthy of serious attention (Samuel 2012 [1994]: 208). Samuel stood against a vocal group of critics who denounced the 'heritage industry' as conservative, escapist, superficial, commercial and nostalgic (Wright 1985; Hewison 1987; Cannadine 1990; Lowenthal 1996). For David Lowenthal, the ubiquity of heritage in late twentieth-century Western society was highly problematic. Rather than inviting critical engagement with historical truth, he suggested, the celebration of heritage asks us to exalt 'rooted faith', privileging tribalism over reason in the manner of a 'quasi-religious cult' (Lowenthal 1996: xiii–x, 1–3, 250). Ultimately, these divergent judgements on the 'heritage industry' hinged on different views of the general public. Samuel was optimistic about the public's ability to engage with the past in an active and emancipatory way, whereas Lowenthal was pessimistic, commenting that 'lack of hard evidence seldom distresses the public at large, who are mostly credulous, undemanding, accustomed to heritage mystique, and often laud the distortions, omissions, and fabrications central to heritage reconstruction' (Lowenthal 1996: 249).

These debates have continued unabated in our new millennium, with increasing attention to the ever-changing impact of digital technologies on the public relationship with the past. 'Digital history' has become a new area of study, with the uses of social media, historical gaming, the incorporation of genetic mapping into online genealogical research, and the power of computer-generated imagery (CGI) and virtual reality to create extremely powerful immersive evocations of the past (both accurate and not), all attracting the interest of historians (De Groot 2016: 67–104, 117–22). According to Sharon Macdonald, heritage plays a highly diverse and agile role in Europe's contemporary 'memorylands'. While it remains an important anchor of traditional national identities, she sees heritage being used in various ways to facilitate the emergence of new multicultural, transcultural and cosmopolitan articulations of memory and identity (Macdonald 2013: 162–215). However, David Lowenthal has recently extended his extensive earlier critiques of the function of heritage, arguing that 'today the past is ever more comprehensively domesticated', no longer approached as an unfamiliar foreign country, but as a tamed and sanitized past rendered less and less distinct from the present (Lowenthal 2015: 594). Beyond an enduring contrast between optimistic and pessimistic perspectives, these debates also highlight differing views on the politics of professional engagement with heritage. Whereas some scholars seek primarily simply to understand the changing dynamics of popular engagement with the past, others believe it is important to interpret those engagements with supportive empathy rather than condescension, while still others see their role as trenchant critics of the commercial interests and other structural forces that shape the consumption of the past in the contemporary world.

Precisely what, though, is 'heritage'? The utility of the concept perhaps rests in part, as Samuel suggested, in its flexibility. However, its slippery nature has also, as Emma Waterton and Steve Watson have recently observed, left contemporary heritage studies an 'unsettled field' (Waterton and Watson 2015a: 1). Beyond this wider conceptual uncertainty, definitions of heritage also differ across disciplines and domains of practice such as archaeology, museology, and history (Schofield 2008). Most theorists of heritage today agree that it is more useful to consider heritage as a process, rather than as a stable array of objects, places or activities (Kirshenblatt-Gimblett 1998; Hall 1999; Harvey 2001; Smith 2006; Moody 2015). Debates over the definition of what constitutes heritage have raged since the 1980s; many historians, and even more heritage professionals active in the everyday presentation of the past to the public, feel that it may be more fruitful to focus instead on more practical matters.

'Heritage' is now a sizeable sector in most Western economies, supported by state funding as well as private enterprise. It is therefore not surprising that recent scholarship has turned to questions about practice, highlighting how heritage management as a profession and practice is 'the particular product of a particular historical trajectory in particular social and cultural contexts' (Fairclough et al. 2008: 1). A key example investigated by historians of Britain is the historic country house as a popular site of heritage tourism. At the height of the early 'heritage debate' David Cannadine denounced 'the plague of country-house nostalgia', which he saw as wilfully blind to the exclusions and privileges that used to govern access to these magnificent spaces (Cannadine 1990: 100). In contrast, Peter

Mandler has rejected the view of the English country house as the static embodiment of class privilege. Visitors to stately homes, he argues, often regard them critically rather than reverentially; rather than standing as unchanging monuments to British deferential nostalgia, country houses, 'created and valued by humans, must, like humans, evolve to survive' (Mandler 1997: 415–16, 418). Over the past two decades the presentation of grand residences, by the National Trust and other custodians in Britain and elsewhere, has indeed evolved, with the opening of 'below stairs' spaces portraying the lives of domestic servants proving extremely popular with visitors (Barker 1999: 205–8; Evans 2011).

Heritage is also a legal category. Various institutions have the power to designate spaces or buildings as 'heritage', but at the international level this is most significantly vested in the World Heritage Committee of UNESCO, which has designated over 1,000 sites around the world as 'World Heritage Sites'. UNESCO also identifies and seeks to protect 'intangible cultural heritage', which it defines as 'the practices, representations, expressions, knowledge, skills – as well as the instruments, objects, artefacts and cultural spaces associated therewith – that communities, groups and, in some cases, individuals recognize as part of their cultural heritage'.[2] These international definitions and designations have an important impact on the management of heritage sites and activities across the globe (Schofield 2008; Harrison 2015).

The question of what is designated and valued as heritage – and thus which pasts should be remembered in public – is brought to the fore by Eureka Henrich's chapter in this volume, on the public remembrance of human migration. Henrich uses a range of international case studies, from the United States, Australia and France, to investigate how public narratives of migration have been constructed for the present. She highlights how these narratives typically attempt to portray a shared collective memory, which may be at odds with academic historians' desire to acknowledge the complexity of the past. Museums and memorials of migration, she shows, are used in the present to support democratizing efforts in post-imperial multicultural societies, and to acknowledge the contributions of different communities to the national story. For Henrich, 'heritage' is a key concept for understanding historians' relationship to public representations of the past. The very term (and also equivalent words in other languages, such as the French 'patrimoine' and the German 'Kulturerbe') suggests an acknowledgement of some form of value, be it cultural, economic or political. It denotes things worth preserving for the future, which may be spaces, objects or stories. In the context of the institutional memory of migration, Henrich explores how certain things acquire the status of heritage, and how this is influenced by present-day values and power structures. The designation of 'heritage', despite its claim to eternal status, is, she reminds us, highly context-dependent and subject to historical change.

Heritage moves, with migrants, across vast distances – but it is also sedimented in specific locations. In our next chapter, Simon Sleight makes use of the concept of the palimpsest to capture the nature of cities as sites of memory. Like a palimpsest – a multilayered manuscript that still contains traces of earlier over-written texts – the city contains layers of historical fabric, hidden or half-hidden, beneath the surface. Sleight uses three 'prism cities' – Hiroshima, Berlin and New York – to analyse the relationship of the built environment to urban public memory. Crucially, he highlights how the importance of city spaces as sites of memory may be as much about forgetting as about remembrance. Cities, Sleight shows, are frequently spaces for official articulations of shared heritage, such as statues of individuals deemed significant in civic or national history. These sites often become symbolic focal points at moments of political change, for example with the toppling of statues erected by previous regimes. The scars of history leave voids in the urban fabric, which create shared challenges for both public memory and urban planning: the destruction of New York's Twin Towers, and the subsequent redevelopment of their site, is the most prominent recent example of this. The city may also act as the backdrop to performances of memory: parades, historical re-enactments and rituals of commemoration. Importantly, the city's palimpsestic nature means that it is always host to many co-existing narratives, often reflecting the presence of different communities within the city.

At both the national and the civic level, history is marshalled in the public sphere to promote a 'usable past', in keeping with the outlook and aims of those in power. Public memory is most frequently shaped by states in order to foster a particular sense of national identification and pride (Anderson 1983). Our next chapter, by Anna Maerker, explores this in more detail, looking at the role of 'great man' narratives (including the occasional 'great woman') in academic and popular histories of science and in science museums. Maerker reminds us that appeals to the past may be instrumentalized not just by nations, or by communities who share ethnic or gender identifications, but equally by professional groups. She shows how diverse actors, from the Academy of Sciences in eighteenth-century France to exiled Poles in the United States during the Second World War, have used stories of individual genius as sources of national pride. These narratives have been used as inspiring models in science education, and also to establish a shared identity for science as it developed into a profession, and a powerful basis for its cultural authority in modern society. However, both critical academic perspectives on the conceptual challenges of biography and practical issues with the use of heroic figures in museums and popular histories highlight that a focus on heroic individuals in history may be problematic both for academic historians and as a form of public history.

The place of heroism and patriotism in public history has been particularly bitterly contested in relation to the memory and presentation of warfare. Public historians engaged vigorously in the most intense controversy in the modern history of the Smithsonian Institution, which occurred over plans to mark the fiftieth anniversary, in 1995, of the end of the Second World War. The National Air and Space Museum, part of the Smithsonian on the National Mall in Washington, DC, planned an exhibition for that year around the *Enola Gay* – the plane that dropped the atomic bomb on the city of Hiroshima. The symbolic meaning of this aircraft, however, was highly contested: an important element in a proud victory for some, but a focus of horror for others. Heated public debate over the exhibition drove the Smithsonian to cancel it, deciding instead to display the *Enola Gay* away from the main museum, and with very little historical contextualization (Linenthal 1996; Moody 2015: 120–1). The memory and representation of slavery, at Colonial Williamsburg and in relation to many other sites and contexts, has also been an extremely charged area of controversy in the United States, with many public historians committed to addressing the silences and obfuscations that surround 'the tough stuff of American memory' (Handler and Gable 1997: 102–15; Horton and Horton 2006). In the second year of the Trump presidency, as this book goes to press, these issues are perhaps more politically central then they have been for decades. Public history today without question pressingly demands the attention of the historian.

The role of the historian

Public history emerged in the 1970s as a critique of mainstream academic historians, who were seen as locked away in their ivory towers, largely disdainful of the general public and too often ignoring 'real world' issues. There is, though, a longstanding tradition of professional historians seeking to promote deeper public understanding of the complex forces shaping society. For Britain, Peter Mandler has outlined the early efforts of historians, especially the celebrated Cambridge academic G. M. Trevelyan (1876–1962), to broaden the constituencies addressed by historical scholarship (Mandler 2002: 70–7). Building on Trevelyan's ideas, from the 1960s the remit of social history – or 'history from below' as popularized by the trailblazing left-wing historian E. P. Thompson (1924–93) – embraced both new historical subjects and ever more varied recipients. Thompson's career took in adult evening education, painstaking archival research on non-elite history, university lecturing and prominent campaigning for nuclear disarmament. In his best-known work, *The Making of the English Working Class* (1963), he called for the rescue of the lived experiences of his historical subjects from what he famously termed 'the enormous condescension of posterity' (Thompson 1991 [1963]: 12). Twenty years later, when the European peace movement was at its height, he took to the main stage at the Glastonbury music festival in Somerset to address the crowds on the rich creativity of what he called an 'alternative nation', past and present.[3] Elsewhere, the radical French historian Michel Foucault appeared frequently on television in France in the 1960s and 1970s, as well as acquiring a sizeable international public following (Chaplin 2007: 106–44). While the criticisms levelled at the historical profession by the first generation of public historians certainly had much legitimacy, their new field also built upon the earlier impact of these high-profile historians.

As John Tosh argues in the opening chapter of this volume, selected historians have since the mid-nineteenth century also sought to engage those outside the academy on policy matters, and to enhance what would only much later be called 'public memory'. Historians have 'a special competence and a special responsibility' in this field, he insists: through their work they correct mistruths and puncture myths. Taking to task misinformed or deliberately disingenuous public figures who play fast and loose with the past is only half the story, though; historians also possess the creative capacity to supplement short-sighted perspectives with wide-angled, richly textured visions. In this respect historians can look back to some illustrious antecedents: in Edwardian Britain, for instance, he notes that two couples, the Webbs and the Hammonds, drew on historical sensibilities to offer informed commentary on contemporary social issues. Tosh uses three case studies to explore the contributions made by historians to public memory: the place of Bosnia in European memories of conflict; the memory of the British Poor Law of 1834 and its deployment in later political debates about public welfare; and the relationship of the colonial history of Rhodesia to controversies over land ownership in its postcolonial successor state, Zimbabwe. Taken together, these examples demonstrate the range of ways in which historians are able to mediate usefully between public memory, history and government policy.

The second half of our volume, titled 'Difficult pasts', in a sense takes its cue from Tosh's approach, in that it consists of six case studies, each of which explores a key and contrasting domain of public memory, and the ways in which historians past and present have engaged with its particular challenges and controversies. The seven chapters in the first half of the book together offer an overview of the central debates, theoretical foundations and methodological approaches of historical engagement with public memory; these six case studies demonstrate how that toolkit is used in practice. These chapters are, inevitably, incomplete in their collective coverage. Had we been able to extend the volume, we might have added fuller discussion of the enduring silences and evasions of European historical memory in relation to the legacies of imperialism, or to the suppression in France of the complexities of occupation and collaboration in the Second World War, which have been analysed influentially by Henry Rousso as 'Vichy Syndrome' (Rousso 1994 [1987]). The confrontation of Central and Eastern European populations since 1989 with their communist past, and the partially similar issues of collaboration, ideological revision, collective identity and traumatic change that this historical reckoning has raised, is another area on which a rich literature exists (Mark 2010). However, these issues also emerge, in different guises, in our six examples, which together offer a broad survey of the diverse ways in which history and historians feature in the key debates, conflicts and identity formations of our contemporary world.

The First World War, as we have noted above, was a key threshold in the history of modern memory. In this respect its impact was immense not only within Europe, but also beyond. In Britain's imperial dominions, participation in battle served to elucidate generational understandings of nationhood (Sleight and Robinson 2016: 1, 7). Seen in this light, Britain's imperial 'children' had come to aid the 'motherland', and whether through the shedding of blood at Vimy Ridge (featuring Canadian troops in 1917) or at Gallipoli (involving Australian and New Zealand soldiers in 1915), these nations had purportedly 'come of age'. Frank Bongiorno's chapter in our volume examines the history of Australian commemoration of the First World War, setting his case study in international context. In contrast with Britain and France, where staggering losses at the

Somme, Verdun and Ypres foregrounded tragedy as a commemorative refrain, resilience and nation-building characterized Australian – and also Turkish – early responses. Bongiorno charts the origins and shifting fortunes of what is now a national day in Australia: Anzac Day, which on 25 April each year commemorates the landing of the Australian and New Zealand Army Corps on the Gallipoli peninsula. Using the concept of 'postmemory' to help explain the reinvention of Anzac Day since the 1960s, he also explores the role of politicians in amplifying various features of Anzac mythology to suit their own agendas. The chapter also looks at the place of Anzac memory in Australia's relations with both Britain and Turkey, and evaluates the sceptical perspectives of many Australian historians towards the prominence accorded to Anzac as a keynote of national commemoration.

Since the 1990s historians have become increasingly involved in attempts to address entrenched divisions over the interpretation of the past in communities emerging, or seeking to emerge, from periods of internal conflict. Alert to deliberate or unconscious attempts to 'hide one set of memories behind another' (Winter, J. 2007: 383), historians have sought to excavate these contested memories, sometimes in a quasi-therapeutic mode, while also challenging simplifications, contributing factual accuracy and nuanced interpretations, and whenever possible bringing antagonistic communities towards an empathetic understanding of each other's perspectives. In his chapter on the divided memory of the 'Troubles' in Northern Ireland, Ian McBride argues that since the 1998 Good Friday Agreement, which brought to an end three decades of political violence, the politics of memory has assumed greater significance, as 'war by other means' between the Protestant unionist and Catholic nationalist communities. This conflict about the conflict has centred on how to describe it – terrorist campaign or anti-colonial struggle? – and on who should be considered its primary perpetrators and victims. McBride analyses the delicate linguistic and procedural compromises that have enabled Northern Ireland's 'consociational' form of government to function since 1998, despite there being no resolution of the core issues that divide the historical memories of its two communities. Various initiatives have tried to promote reconciliation, truth recovery, and 'healing through remembering', but, despite some notable achievements, these projects have also encountered significant obstacles and a high level of public scepticism.

Debates in Northern Ireland have often looked to post-apartheid South Africa as a possible model for how a post-conflict society might most productively address its recent past. In our next chapter, Tom Lodge examines the activity and impact of South Africa's Truth and Reconciliation Commission (TRC), which was established by President Nelson Mandela in 1995, following the country's first democratic multiracial elections the previous year. Seeking to forge a shared national narrative of South Africa's traumatic recent past, the Commission placed particular value on the public witnessing of painful memories. Truth-telling was linked to reconciliation and nation-building, within a legal framework influenced by Christian ideals of forgiveness in which multiple notions of justice were in play. There were initial high hopes that the work of the TRC would promote reconciliation in the 'rainbow nation', but its work also met with much criticism. Lodge explores how this conciliatory historical narrative has shaped the reconstruction and reinterpretation of the most important *lieux de mémoire* of apartheid, and reflects on the challenges that face South Africa's continued grappling with the legacies of its violent and racist past.

Race is also central to our next chapter, in which Fitz Brundage surveys the elaborate fashioning and intense contestation of historical memory in the American South since the end of the American Civil War in 1865. Recent events in Charlottesville, Virginia, where in August 2017 a violent 'Unite the Right' rally gathered in defence of a statue of Confederate general Robert E. Lee, have brought this struggle over memory to the fore of American and international public consciousness. (At the time of writing, *The New York Times* is among those news organizations keeping track of removed, threatened and protected Confederate monuments.[4]) Offering a much-needed deep historical perspective on these issues, Brundage shows how southern elites have since the mid-nineteenth century promoted a romanticized notion of a cohesive regional culture. Noting comparisons with South Africa and Australia (where controversies regarding memorialization have also flared), he examines how certain historical narratives have been amplified and others suppressed in the construction of white southern identity. He also considers the persistence of alternative traditions of memory among southern African Americans, sustained through public ceremonies, in oratory and in black schools. Only in recent years, Brundage argues, have southerners begun to fashion a pluralist public culture in which both black and white historical memories are acknowledged.

Surely no pasts are more difficult than those involving genocide. In recent decades the Nazi Holocaust has come to occupy a uniquely prominent place within global memory, as the primary example and yardstick of atrocity. Ranging widely, Adam Sutcliffe's chapter explores the history and politics of Holocaust memory, charting its changing significance and varied uses in the United States, Europe (in particular Britain, Germany and Poland), Israel and elsewhere. He explains why there was little attention to the Holocaust as a focus of memory until the 1960s, and why there was a dramatic boom in Holocaust memory in the 1990s, immediately after the end of the Cold War. His chapter also explores the immense impact of reflections on the Holocaust on the wider fields of historical memory, trauma and memorialization, and on historians' debates over the methodology and ethical purpose of their discipline. More than for any other historical event, there is a widespread yearning for the Holocaust to teach us something; to yield a usable lesson for the future. However, Sutcliffe argues, many diverse and contrasting lessons have been drawn from the Holocaust, shaped by different contexts, perspectives and political agendas. Today, not least in relation to the continuing Israeli–Palestinian conflict, the politics of Holocaust memory are if anything more contested than ever.

The final chapter of our volume addresses a past that is difficult in a very different sense. LGBTQ (lesbian, gay, bisexual, trans and queer) history has also been scarred by persecution: gay men were among the groups targeted by the

Nazis. The core challenges of this field, however, are conceptual and method-ological. What does it mean to explore and memorialize the history of sexual or gender identities that have only relatively recently been identified as such? And how can these perspectives, which have long been silenced, marginalized or kept profoundly private, be restored to the historical record? Laura Gowing charts the emergence and rise of queer history and memory, considering the theoretical models that have shaped it, and assessing how LGBTQ public history has been produced in relation to political exigencies, community dynamics, and both collective and individual desires. She examines the place of queer public history in landmark legal cases in the advance of sexual equality (in which historians have participated as expert witnesses), as well as with regard to key locations such as monuments, museums and country houses, community collective memory and the digital realm. Through this diversity, she argues, queer memory of the past is currently flourishing as never before, although its recognition and incorporation within wider public history remains limited and precarious.

The duties of academic historians are many and varied, encompassing teaching, research, administration and sustaining the professional life of the discipline. Do they have time also to engage in public life? And if they do, is anybody listening? Despite these professional pressures, public history is thriving. There is a vast range of ways, as the essays in our volume show, in which historians contribute to the enrichment of the public understanding of the past, and to our collective confrontation with the challenging and contested memories it has bestowed upon the present. In much of the world, including across the Anglosphere, universities and governments have recently begun to place increasing value on the participation of historians in public life. Historians also now increasingly contribute to contemporary policy debates. In the UK, the *History & Policy* initiative, which seeks to connect historians with policy-makers, has thrived.[5]

The role of historians is not, however, to provide our governments with straightforward and readily applicable 'lessons of the past'. For Matthew Grant, the influence of history on policy is best conceived 'not as a lamp illuminating the path ahead, but as a red man on a pedestrian crossing – requiring us to stop, look both ways and only proceed when safe to do so' (Grant 2017: 243–4). A sense of public purpose is central to how many if not most historians understand their role in society. This has been defined in more detail by public historian Alix Green as 'a moral, methodological and intellectual impetus for working in ways that contribute to public life and societal good', in the furtherance of which the historian's 'toolkit' – practised skills in analysing social relations, patterning time, weaving and mapping context, evaluating and integrating evidence, and persuading audiences – can prove extremely valuable in a policy context (Green 2016: 3, 65–85). Historians' contributions to public life also extend far beyond their involvement with policy debates – working with government bodies, pressure groups, charities, think-tanks and trade unions – and their cultural work, with museums, galleries and historical sites. Historical thinking and writing, as our contributors in this volume show, can also make a crucial contribution to public life: by deepening the quality of public discussion, bringing new or marginalized perspectives to public attention, unsettling cosy assumptions, and challenging sloppy invocations of the past in public debate.

Let us end our discussion closer to home. Each year academic historians welcome new students of history to their campuses. The education of these individuals is our first responsibility, and collectively these practitioners of history represent our most important public. Learning with these students is not a one-way process; instead we seek to establish a community of enquiry in which we teach and we guide, while our students also help us – and each other – to attain a richer and more nuanced historical understanding. As we prepare our students for public life beyond the gates of the university, it is vital that we encourage critical reflection on the role of history in the world, and on the skills and insights that a historical training brings to public deliberation on the place of the past in the present. We hope that this volume will assist students – and others – in becoming more keenly and critically attuned to the uses of the past, as well as to its emotional significance and the means by which it is variously manipulated, overlooked, harnessed and celebrated.

Notes

1 http://ncph.org/what-is-public-history/about-the-field/ (accessed 3 September 2017).
2 https://ich.unesco.org/en/convention (accessed 3 September 2017).
3 An excerpt of Thompson's Glastonbury speech can be found here: www.youtube.com/watch?v=MdPwZMyb1sM (accessed 4 September 2017).
4 See www.nytimes.com/interactive/2017/08/16/us/confederate-monuments-removed.html?mcubz=0 and http://edition.cnn.com/2017/08/15/us/confederate-memorial-removal-us-trnd/index.html (accessed 4 September 2017).
5 See www.historyandpolicy.org/ (accessed 4 September 2017).

References

Anderson, Benedict (1983) *Imagined Communities: Reflections on the Origin and Spread of Nationalism*. London: Verso.
Anheier, Helmut, and Yudhishthir Raj Isar (eds) (2011) *Heritage, Memory & Identity*. London: Sage.
Ansell-Pearson, Keith (2010) 'Bergson on Memory', in Susannah Radstone and Bill Schwarz (eds), *Memory: Histories, Theories, Debates*. New York: Fordham University Press, 61–76.
Apfelbaum, Erika (2010) 'Halbwachs and the Social Properties of Memory', in Susannah Radstone and Bill Schwarz (eds), *Memory: Histories, Theories, Debates*. New York: Fordham University Press, 77–92.
Appadurai, Arjun (1996) *Modernity at Large*. Minneapolis, MN: University of Minneapolis Press.
Appleby, Joyce, Lynn Hunt and Margaret Jacob (1994) *Telling the Truth about History*. New York: W. W. Norton.
Assmann, Aleida (2008) 'Canon and Archive', in Astrid Erll and Ansgar Nünning (eds), *Cultural Memory Studies: An International and Interdisciplinary Handbook*. Berlin: Walter de Gruyter, 97–107.

Assmann, Aleida (2011 [1999]) *Cultural Memory and Western Civilization: Arts of Memory.* Cambridge: Cambridge University Press.

Assmann, Jan (1995) 'Collective Memory and Cultural Identity', *New German Critique* 65: 125–33.

Assmann, Jan (2011 [1992]) *Cultural Memory and Early Civilization: Writing, Remembrance, and Political Imagination.* Cambridge: Cambridge University Press.

Barker, Emma (1999) 'Heritage and the Country House', in Emma Barker (ed.), *Contemporary Cultures of Display.* New Haven, CT: Yale University Press, 200–28.

Berger, Stefan, and Bill Niven (eds) (2014) *Writing the History of Memory.* London: Bloomsbury.

Bergson, Henri (1911 [1896]) *Matter and Memory.* London: George Allen & Unwin.

Bond, Lucy, Stef Craps and Pieter Vermeulen (2016) *Memory Unbound: Tracing the Dynamics of Memory Studies.* New York: Berghahn.

Boym, Svetlana (2001) *The Future of Nostalgia.* New York: Basic Books.

Burrow, John (2007) *A History of Histories.* London: Penguin.

Cannadine, David (1990 [1981/83]) 'The Stately Homes of England', in *The Pleasures of the Past.* Glasgow: Fontana Press, 99–109.

Carruthers, Mary (2008 [1990]) *The Book of Memory: A Study of Memory in Medieval Culture,* 2nd edition. Cambridge: Cambridge University Press.

Chaplin, Tamara (2007) *Turning on the Mind: French Philosophers on Television.* Chicago: University of Chicago Press.

Clanchy, Michael T. (2013 [1979]) *From Memory to Written Record: England 1066–1307,* 3rd edition. Chichester: Wiley-Blackwell.

Connerton, Paul (2009) *How Modernity Forgets.* Cambridge: Cambridge University Press.

Corsane, Gerard (ed.) (2005) *Heritage, Museums and Galleries: An Introductory Reader.* London: Routledge.

Cubbitt, Geoffrey (2007) *History and Memory.* Manchester: Manchester University Press.

Erll, Astrid (2011) *Memory in Culture.* Basingstoke: Palgrave Macmillan.

Evans, Siân (2011) *Life Below Stairs in the Victorian and Edwardian Country House.* London: National Trust Books.

Fairclough, Graham, Rodney Harrison, John H. Jameson Jnr. and John Schofield (eds) (2008) *The Heritage Reader.* London: Routledge.

Freud, Sigmund (2003 [1901]) *The Psychopathology of Everyday Life,* trans. Anthea Bell. London: Penguin.

Fritzsche, Peter (2001) 'Specters of History: On Nostalgia, Exile, and Modernity', *American Historical Review* 106: 1587–618.

Fritzsche, Peter (2004) *Stranded in the Present: Modern Time and the Melancholy of History.* Cambridge MA: Harvard University Press.

Gombrich, Ernst (1986) *Aby Warburg: An Intellectual Biography.* London: Phaidon Press.

Graham, Otis L. (2001) 'Robert Kelley and the Pursuit of Useful History', *Journal of Policy History* 23: 429–37.

Grant, Matthew (2017) 'History and Policy', in Tracey Loughran (ed.), *A Practical Guide to Studying History.* London: Bloomsbury.

Green, Alix R. (2016) *History, Policy and Public Purpose: Historians and Historical Thinking in Government.* London: Palgrave Macmillan.

Groot, Jerome de (2016) *Consuming History: Historians and Heritage in Contemporary Popular Culture*, 2nd edition. Abingdon: Routledge.

Halbwachs, Maurice (1992 [1925/1941]) *On Collective Memory*, ed. and trans. Lewis A. Coser. Chicago: University of Chicago Press.

Hall, Stuart (1999) 'Whose Heritage? Un-settling 'The Heritage', Re-imagining the Post-nation', *Third Text* 49: 3–13.

Handler, Richard, and Eric Gable (1997) *The New History in an Old Museum: Creating the Past at Colonial Williamsburg*. Durham, NC: Duke University Press.

Harrison, Rodney (2015) 'Heritage and Globalization', in Emma Waterton and Steve Watson (eds), *The Palgrave Handbook of Contemporary Heritage Research*. Basingstoke: Palgrave Macmillan, 297–312.

Harvey, David C. (2001) 'Heritage Pasts and Heritage Presents: Temporality, Meaning and the Scope of Heritage Studies', *International Journal of Heritage Studies* 7: 319–38.

Heather, Peter (2009) *Empires and Barbarians: Migration, Development, and the Creation of Europe*. London: Macmillan.

Hewison, Robert (1987) *The Heritage Industry: Britain in an Age of Decline*. London: Methuen.

Hirsch, Marianne (1996) 'Past Lives: Postmemories in Exile', *Poetics Today* 17: 659–86.

Horton, James Oliver, and Lois E. Horton (2006) *Slavery and Public History: The Tough Stuff of American Memory*. New York: The New Press.

Hutton, Patrick H. (1993) *History as an Art of Memory*. Hanover, NH: University Press of New England.

Hutton, Patrick H. (2016) *The Memory Phenomenon in Contemporary Historical Writing*. New York: Palgrave Macmillan.

Inglis, K. S. (1998) *Sacred Places: War Memorials in the Australian Landscape*. Carlton, VIC: Melbourne University Press.

Kean, Hilda, and Paul Martin (2013) *The Public History Reader*. Abingdon: Routledge.

Kirshenblatt-Gimblett, Barbara (1998) *Destination Culture: Tourism, Museums, and Heritage*. Berkeley, CA: University of California Press.

Klein, Kerwin Lee (2000) 'On the Emergence of Memory in Historical Discourse', *Representations* 69: 127–50.

Koselleck, Reinhart (2004 [1979]) *Futures Past: On the Semantics of Historical Time*. New York: Columbia University Press.

Linenthal, Edward T. (1996) 'Anatomy of a Controversy', in Edward T. Linenthal and Tom Engelhardt (eds), *History Wars: The* Enola Gay *and Other Battles for the American Past*. New York: Henry Holt.

Lowenthal, David (1996) *Possessed by the Past: The Heritage Crusade and the Spoils of History*. New York: The Free Press.

Lowenthal, David (2015) *The Past is a Foreign Country – Revisited*. Cambridge: Cambridge University Press.

Macdonald, Sharon (2013) *Memorylands: Heritage and Identity in Europe Today*. London: Routledge.

Mandler, Peter (1997) *The Fall and Rise of the Stately Home*. New Haven, CT and London: Yale University Press.

Mandler, Peter (2002) *History and National Life*. London: Profile.

Mark, James (2010) *The Unfinished Revolution: Making Sense of the Communist Past in Central-Eastern Europe*. New Haven, CT: Yale University Press.

Moody, Jessica (2015) 'Heritage and History', in Emma Waterton and Steve Watson (eds), *The Palgrave Handbook of Contemporary Heritage Research*. Basingstoke: Palgrave Macmillan, 113–29.

Nora, Pierre (1989) 'Between Memory and History: Les Lieux de Mémoire', *Representations* 26: 7–24.

Nora, Pierre (1996–98) *Realms of Memory: The Construction of the French Past*, 3 vols, ed. Lawrence D. Kritzman, trans. Arthur Goldhammer. New York: Columbia University Press.

Radstone, Susannah, and Bill Schwarz (eds) (2010) *Memory: Histories, Theories, Debates*. New York: Fordham University Press.

Reading, Anna (2011) 'Memory and Digital Media: Six Dynamics of the Globital Memory Field', in Motti Neiger, Oren Meyers and Eyal Zandberg (eds), *On Media Memory*. Basingstoke: Palgrave Macmillan, 241–52.

Reading, Anna (2016) *Gender and Memory in the Globital Age*. Basingstoke: Palgrave Macmillan.

Ricoeur, Paul (2004 [2000]) *Memory, History, Forgetting*. Chicago: University of Chicago Press.

Ricoeur, Paul (2011 [2006]) 'Memory–Forgetting–History', in Jeffrey K. Olick, Vered Vinitzky-Seroussi and Daniel Levy (eds), *The Collective Memory Reader*. New York: Oxford University Press.

Rosenfeld, Gavriel (2009) 'A Looming Crash or a Soft Landing? Forecasting the Future of the Memory "Industry"', *Journal of Modern History* 81: 122–58.

Rosenzweig, Robert and David Thelen (1998) *The Presence of the Past: Popular Uses of History in American Life*. New York: Columbia University Press, 1998.

Rossi, Paulo (2000) *Logic and the Art of Memory: The Quest for a Universal Language*. London: Athlone.

Rothberg, Michael (2009) *Multidirectional Memory: Remembering the Holocaust in the Age of Decolonization*. Stanford, CA: Stanford University Press.

Rousso, Henry (1994 [1987]) *The Vichy Syndrome: History and Memory in France Since 1944*. Cambridge, MA: Harvard University Press.

Samuel, Raphael (2012 [1994]) *Theatres of Memory: Past and Present in Contemporary Culture*, 2nd edition. London: Verso.

Sand, Shlomo (2017) *Twilight of History*. London: Verso.

Schofield, John (2008) 'Heritage Management, Theory and Practice', in Graham Fairclough, Rodney Harrison, John H. Jameson Jnr. and John Schofield (eds), *The Heritage Reader*. London: Routledge, 15–30.

Schwarz, Bill (1993) 'History on the Move: Reflections on History Workshop', *Radical History Review* 57: 203–20.

Sleight, Simon, and Shirleene Robinson (2016) 'Introduction: The World in Miniature', in Shirleene Robinson and Simon Sleight (eds), *Children, Childhood and Youth in the British World*. Basingstoke: Palgrave Macmillan.

Smith, Laurajane (2006) *Uses of Heritage*. London: Routledge.

Terdiman, Richard (1993) *Present Past: Modernity and the Memory Crisis*. Ithaca, NY: Cornell University Press.

Thompson, E. P. (1991 [1963]) *The Making of the English Working Class*. London: Penguin.

Tota, Ana Lisa, and Trevor Hagen (eds) (2016) *Routledge International Handbook of Memory Studies*. London: Routledge.

Tumblety, Joan (ed.) (2013) *Memory and History: Understanding Memory as Source and Subject*. London: Routledge.

Waterton, Emma, and Steve Watson (eds) (2015) *The Palgrave Handbook of Contemporary Heritage Research*. Basingstoke: Palgrave Macmillan.

Waterton, Emma, and Steve Watson (2015a) 'Heritage as a Focus of Research: Past, Present and New Directions', in *The Palgrave Handbook of Contemporary Heritage Research*. Basingstoke: Palgrave Macmillan, 1–17.

Waterton, Emma and Steve Watson (2015b) 'The Ontological Politics of Heritage; or How Research Can Spoil a Good Story', in *The Palgrave Handbook of Contemporary Heritage Research*. Basingstoke: Palgrave Macmillan, 21–36.

Winter, Alison (2012) *Memory: Fragments of a Modern History*. Chicago: University of Chicago Press.

Winter, Jay (1995) *Sites of Memory, Sites of Mourning: The Great War in European Cultural History*. Cambridge: Cambridge University Press.

Winter, Jay (2001) 'The Memory Boom in Contemporary Historical Studies', *Raritan* 21: 52–66.

Winter, Jay (2006) *Remembering War: The Great War between Memory and History in the Twentieth Century*. New Haven, CT: Yale University Press.

Winter, Jay (2007) 'The Generation of Memory: Reflections on the "Memory Boom" in Contemporary Historical Studies', *Archives & Social Studies: A Journal of Interdisciplinary Research* 1: 363–97.

Wood, Michael (2010) 'Proust: The Music of Memory', in Susannah Radstone and Bill Schwarz (eds), *Memory: Histories, Theories, Debates*. New York: Fordham University Press, 109–22.

Wright, Patrick (1985) *On Living in an Old Country: The National Past in Contemporary Britain*. London: Verso.

Yates, Frances A. (1966) *The Art of Memory*. Chicago: University of Chicago Press.

Yerushalmi, Yosef Hayim (1982) *Zakhor: Jewish History and Jewish Memory*. Seattle, WA: University of Washington Press.

Zerubavel, Yael (1995) *Recovered Roots: Collective Memory and the Making of the Israeli National Tradition*. Chicago: University of Chicago Press.

Part I

Approaches to history and memory

1 Historical scholarship and public memory in Britain

A case of oil and water?

John Tosh

What is the connection between history and public memory? At first glance the question appears to be straining at an over-worked distinction. If the role of historians is to interpret the past to the present, they can hardly be indifferent to how their work is received by the public. As for the public, how else can they 'remember' the past – especially the past that lies beyond their own life span – except by drawing on the resources of historical knowledge?

Yet public memory and history are more often seen to be separated by a yawning gulf. 'Public memory' is the creature of contemporary culture. It draws on a limited range of memorable historical material to support political values or cultural identities in the present. It becomes lodged in the public mind through a combination of elite dispositions and popular recall. It lays claim to a timeless authenticity, independent of evidential controls. The standing of academic history, on the other hand, stems from the rigour of its scholarship and from standards that have little resonance with the lay public. Historians claim to follow the internal logic of their subject, rather than subordinate it to a servicing role. Whatever topical resonance their work has is the by-product of scholarly research rather than its governing rationale. The exponents of public memory tend to turn these virtues upside down: the history that professional historians research and write is disparaged as 'academic' in the strict sense that it is pursued in the academy for a specialized audience of professional historians and their students. Thus while public memory is manifestly part of common culture, academic history is in danger of being dismissed as the gratification of an intellectual coterie. In Britain in the 1990s, this critique of academic history was fervently put forward by Raphael Samuel, and equally passionately rebutted by David Lowenthal (Samuel 1994; Lowenthal 1996).

Neither of these polemical positions is constructive. They foreclose on an important debate that should be taking place about the social utility of historical scholarship. At issue is how we interpret the concept of public memory itself. In its current guise as reinforcement for current cultural identities it allows little scope for the work of professional historians. This means that the light that historical scholarship can cast on topical issues of great moment is obscured. Yet logically there is no reason why the findings of such scholarship should not take their place in public memory. There are important instances of public recognition that this is so, for example in relation to the Holocaust, where popular understanding has drawn heavily on the findings of historians, mediated though the mainstream media. Another recent example of particularly immediate relevance to Britain is the study of the Atlantic slave trade and its abolition in the early nineteenth century. The social utility of history is lost sight of if it is treated as antithetical to public memory. My purpose in this chapter is to consider the case for enlarging our definition of public memory, and in so doing to elaborate the role of historians as bearers of socially useful knowledge. The argument is developed with prime reference to Britain, where public memory has attracted a great deal of scholarly attention in recent years, but readers might bear in mind that France and the USA would make equally revealing studies (see bibliographical guide).

Definitions of public history and public memory

Definition is critical, because in the context of memory studies the usage of 'public' is imprecise and inconsistent, despite the cultural significance now routinely accorded to public memory. The term is most commonly applied to the version of the past promoted for public consumption by the public authorities: an officially promoted history, or a form of 'civic remembrance' (Burgoyne 2003). Public history is associated with the state, and even more with the nation, since national consciousness is largely founded on a shared view of the nation's past (whether of victories or of steadfastness in defeat). The ideal is a consensual view of the past, enthusiastically endorsed in society at large. Public memory in this sense is one of the principal cultural supports for a stable polity. Its most visible forms are the commemorative monument and the public ceremony: for example Remembrance Day in Britain, or Bastille Day in France. The tie between public memory and the public places where it is enacted is certainly a close one (Nora 1989; Casey 2004), but public memory is also sustained by a variety of media, typically television, popular works of history and school textbooks.

Confusion is sometimes caused by eliding public memory with other related categories, particularly 'social memory' and 'collective memory'. Both these terms are commonly applied to the entire range of representations of the past that inform popular consciousness. Public memory is included in that broad sweep, but it is important not to lose sight of its distinctive features: its bearing on politics, its manipulation by the state and its more formal articulation (Cubitt 2007).

This kind of high-profile public memory carries the marks of its emergence in nineteenth-century Europe, when representative national assemblies became a defining feature of the modernizing nation state. These institutions conferred legitimacy on the governing class, but potentially they also offered a window of political opportunity to groups at odds with the national project. Hence the priority given by the political authorities to entrenching prescribed versions of the past in their populations. Expanding literacy rates and universal schooling provided the means to do so (Hobsbawm and Ranger 1983).

This might be described as the 'monolithic' approach to public memory. It carries the assumption that everybody thinks in the same way about the past, or ought to do so. It has certainly not disappeared from political discourse today. In Britain, educationalists on the political right from time to time espouse an ultra-prescriptive history curriculum, designed to restore a unitary public memory (Phillips 1998). Their efforts have met with little success. In Western societies since the 1960s there has been a decline in respect for the state and its claims to cultural hegemony. Public monuments are more likely to be viewed with indifference, rooted in historical ignorance. Trafalgar Square, with its parade of naval and military heroes in stone and bronze, is a case in point (Schwarz 2005). Yet it may be that what has declined is not public memory as such, but a particular rendition. Trafalgar Square is a monument to Britain's imperial past which today is soft-pedalled in political discourse. In its place has arisen a more pluralistic public memory, reflecting the aspirations of a range of political interests.

Today public memory is better regarded as the hegemony of one take on the past among many. One measure of political maturity is the range of competing interpretations of the past which find public expression in a given polity. The state has no monopoly of public memory, because collective interpretations of the past are no less essential for other communities that demand a public presence: groups defined by ethnicity, gender, religion, sexuality, and so on. All of them require a public memory as a precondition for cultural cohesion and social action in the present. This is why it makes sense to identify a second category of public memory, one that expresses an alternative politics (like the labour movement) or an alternative identity (based for example on ethnicity or gender). For this reason John Bodnar distinguishes a 'vernacular', as opposed to an 'official', form of public memory (Bodnar 1994). The uneasy relationship between 'official' and 'vernacular' is what endows public memory with its dynamism and its mutability. Official memory has frequently been contested by oppositional groups and ideologies. Thus the militant suffragettes, reviled in their own day as deluded extremists, are now firmly established in the approved national story of development towards a full representative democracy.

The example of Bosnia

An initial example may serve to explain the different ways in which public memory and historical scholarship address the needs of the present. The outbreak of the First World War was precipitated by the assassination of Archduke Franz Ferdinand, in Sarajevo, the Bosnian capital. It is well known that his assassin, Gavrilo Princip, was a young Serb motivated by irredentist anger against Austrian rule. But the date of the assassination reveals an additional dimension. 28 June was the most important date in the Serbian national calendar. It commemorated the battle of Kosovo Polje in 1389, when the Serbs were roundly defeated and their kingdom absorbed into the Ottoman Empire. Defeat can sometimes be a more potent national symbol than victory, and so it was in Serbia. Memory of the battle celebrated the valour of the Serbs in the face of adversity, and it reminded them of the lands that had once been ruled by their king and should now be part of 'Greater Serbia'. This was public memory in the service of an idea of the nation.

The national enemy was no longer the Turks, but by invoking so clearly the memory of Kosovo Polje Princip was stoking the fires of Serb expansionism (Clark 2013).

Some 80 years later, Bosnia was once more a flash-point of conflict. The future of what had recently been Yugoslavia was being fought out in the first overt military conflict in Europe since the end of the Second World War. Bosnia was the victim of attack by the Serbs, and their siege of Sarajevo attracted particular concern. In these circumstances the French president, François Mitterrand, made a surprise visit to the city in 1992. At some personal risk, his journey was widely taken to be a humanitarian mission. But the timing indicated another purpose. Mitterrand arrived in Sarajevo on 28 June. He was making the point that, just as the assassination of Franz Ferdinand had unleashed world war, so the current conflict in Bosnia held out the danger of a wider conflagration (Braunstein 2001). But his message proved in vain. Hardly anyone picked up the significance of the date – certainly not the press. Eric Hobsbawm summed up the episode by concluding 'the historical memory was no longer alive' (Hobsbawm 1994: 3). There was no longer a public understanding of how the First World War had started, or of the cautionary significance of that precedent. In pointing out that public memory had failed, Hobsbawm was referring not to a partisan or exclusive interpretation, but to the stock of validated knowledge about the past that may help people to understand their world. The argument of this chapter is that historians have a special competence and a special responsibility in the field of public memory in this second sense.

(Academic) history and memory

As the case of Franz Ferdinand's assassination demonstrates, public memory is not just a feature of contemporary society. The term may be a recent coinage, barely present before the 1990s, but it pinpoints a phenomenon to be found in many of the past societies that historians study. Discerning whose interests were served by public memory, how and when the emphasis shifted from one set of values to another, tells historians a great deal, not so much about the remembered past, as about the political culture and the collective mentality of the society that was ordering its memory in this way (Hobsbawm and Ranger 1983). Thus in seventeenth-century England celebrations were held every year to mark the anniversary of Elizabeth I's accession (17 November). This expressed not only gratitude for a Protestant deliverance in the past, but an anxiety about the threat posed by Catholic powers in the present; the Gunpowder Plot (5 November) was commemorated for the same reason (Cressy 1994). In the late nineteenth century great care was taken to mould public memory in Britain according to an imperial agenda, based on an uncritical pride in colonial expansion and an inflation of heroic reputation (Mackenzie 1986; Castle 1996).

When it comes to public memories current today, the approach of historians is somewhat different. Like public memory in earlier periods, the images of the past that ordinary people today imbibe from the media provide evidence of current values and prejudices. But as 'live' memory such images also stand in the way of more accurate and more useful historical knowledge. Through its perspectival distortion and errors of fact, most public memory obscures the relation of past and present. For historians it is therefore a cardinal principle that public memory should not be uncritically accepted as 'history'. As one gate-keeper of the discipline has put it: 'history is precisely non-memory' (Bentley 1999: 155). Indeed one of the few practical applications of their discipline on which most historians are agreed is that popular myths of the past should be dissected. Theodore Zeldin (1981) likens it to the eye-surgeon's task in removing cataracts. Peter Burke says it is the business of historians to bring to light the skeletons in the cupboard of social memory (Burke 1989: 110). Historians approach this task with a certain relish. When in the 1980s Margaret Thatcher sought to dignify her political programme as a return to 'Victorian values', historians recognized the danger of public memory being reordered along highly partisan lines. In a range of publications they attacked her misrepresentation of class, wealth creation and poor relief in nineteenth-century Britain.[1] By the 1990s the popular mythology surrounding Winston Churchill was considered by historians to be ripe for demolition. His inspirational leadership in 1940 remained more or less intact, but historians like John Charmly portrayed a deeply flawed individual, prone to costly errors of strategic judgement, and wedded to a completely outdated and reactionary vision of British society. These defects had been overlooked for several decades because the Churchill of legend offered some kind of consolation for the painful decline of power which Britain was experiencing at that time (Charmley 1993).

The reason that these instances of public memory can be branded as 'myth' lies in their governing rationale and their method. It is not difficult to understand why so many historians have argued that in both respects memory is antithetical to history. Historians, they say, are committed to representing the past in all its complexity, its contradictions and its moral ambiguities. What their studies yield is reflective understanding and critique, not ammunition for a partisan position. Public memory, on the other hand, starts from an agenda grounded in the present, and this leads to a single perspective, imposing a spurious continuity on the past (such as an undifferentiated centuries-long 'national spirit'). For its evidence public memory draws on an incoherent assemblage of materials that may include historical fiction, journalism and visual remains, while historians submit the evidence of the past to methodical analysis. According to this charge-sheet, public history is not a tissue of fabrication: there is usually a kernel of demonstrable fact. But it is selected according to present-day requirements and detached from its context of time and place.

Historians in general do not claim that their work is free of present concerns (indeed there is a highly sophisticated debate about the ways in which the present not only can but *should* inform historical scholarship). Their critique of memory is based on its prioritization of present requirements, to the point where any sense of historical reality is lost. Our collective past seems to depend on 'backward projections' of current perceptions of identity (Cubitt 2007: 200). As David Lowenthal puts it, 'History differs from memory not only in how knowledge of the past is acquired and validated but also in how it is transmitted, preserved and altered' (Lowenthal 1985: 212). Pierre Nora is even blunter: 'Memory is . . . a bond tying us to the eternal present; history is a representation of the past' (Nora 1989: 9). In a much-cited article Nora positions memory as the enemy of history, because it expresses collective values rather than scholarly findings, and because it elides the past with the present. Nora makes the point that memory flourished best in pre-industrial societies with limited literacy. With their passing, memory has been superseded by historical sensibility, and the mission of history is to suppress the remaining vestiges of public memory (Nora 1989). All that contemporary society can do is to designate places of memory (*les lieux de mémoire*) as compensation for the memory-based culture that has disappeared.

Nora's interpretation has a brilliant clarity, but it is pursued with little reference to how historians actually relate to the public. He exaggerates the difference between 'memory' and 'history' and underplays the overlap between them. In the first place, many historians have signed up to projects that are closely aligned with identity politics. A notable feature of the past 50 years has been the enlargement of public memory among social groups previously 'hidden from history'. It is a process in which historians themselves have been heavily engaged, often sharing the liberationist politics of the groups they write about. Thus the first generation of women's historians in the 1970s regarded history as an instrument of liberation. By articulating a shared memory they intended to dispose of the collective amnesia that had condemned their sex to powerlessness (Davin 1972). A comparable politics can be found in the early exponents of black history and gay history.

Secondly, the total stand-off assumed by Lowenthal and Nora ignores the scope for cooperation between history and public memory. A striking instance was the bicentenary of the British abolition of the slave trade in 1807. This commemoration aroused an exceptional degree of public interest (as well as relatively lavish government funding). The bicentenary played to a public agenda of racial equality and a rising alarm about the incidence of human trafficking (Walvin 2009). But conflicting public memories were in play. The tradition of British paternalism was confronted by African-Caribbean voices that placed a different interpretation on both the slave experience and the drivers of emancipation (Beccles and Shepherd 2007; Reddie 2007). Public debate during 2007 was comparatively sophisticated because the ground had been prepared by a number of interventions during the previous two decades. Beginning in the 1970s James Walvin among others wrote scholarly books on slavery and the slave trade addressed to a lay audience (Walvin 1973, 1996, 2000). In the 1990s this work was adapted in a number of historical novels, while at the same time Bristol and Liverpool pioneered the development of museums that documented the local involvement in the trade (Wallace 2006). Historians and community activists were brought together in committees that advised museums on their plans for commemoration (Smith 2011). Public memory in 2007 therefore drew on museum exhibits, novels, film and TV, as well as formal works of academic history. Much of the public comment on the bicentenary was polarized between adulation of Wilberforce on the one hand and celebration of African agency on the other.

Historians were well placed to promote interpretations that recognized the complexity of the issue and addressed both perspectives. The abolition of the slave trade – and by extension the phenomenon of transatlantic slavery – is now lodged in the public memory as a result of the intense memorializing that took place in 2007. It is a reasonable assumption that popular understanding of the slave trade is more securely grounded in historical fact, not least because of the efforts of historians themselves.

Public memory and public life

It is evident from this discussion that historians have an important role in amplifying and correcting those renderings of the past that address cultural or political priorities in the present. But performing this role brings into public view a very narrow selection of historical scholarship. By a curious attenuation 'public' as a qualifier of 'memory' has come to be identified with a biased and blinkered approach to the past, as if that is the sum total of the public's historical sensibility. In order to explore history's full range of application we need to look more closely at the notion of 'the public'. The *Oxford English Dictionary*'s definition of the adjective *public* as 'of or pertaining to the people as a whole' reminds us that the ramifications of public concern are very wide. Social solidarity is only one aspect. The public interest is also expressed in debates about every conceivable collective concern – political, social, economic, and so on. In a classic exposition, Jürgen Habermas identified this political culture with the bourgeois public sphere in which citizens conducted 'critical-rational public debate' (Habermas 1989: 29). He was pessimistic about the survival of the public sphere in an era of mass politics and media manipulation. Open, informed and critical thinking is less evident in modern democratic societies than it was in the more restricted public arena of the eighteenth century. But no one who values democracy would willingly relinquish that aspiration. It remains the benchmark of civic maturity.

One way of understanding this aspect of public memory is to see history as a resource for policy-making. This is easier said than done. Most policy-makers do not have the time to work up the history which touches on their concerns. The most effective answer is to tailor the presentation of relevant history to the constraints of time and place. In Britain the History and Policy website has, since its foundation in 2002, posted over 150 short articles on specific policy issues, written in every case by specialist historians mindful of the topical relevance of their expertise (historyandpolicy.org). The model has been adapted in other countries, notably Australia (aph.org.au). This remarkable effort has been rightly welcomed as a contribution to evidence-based policy-making: a novel dimension of the knowledge economy (Cox 2013; Szreter 2011). But here too there is a tendency to confine the working definition of the public to too narrow proportions. 'Policy-makers' are defined as just that: ministers, civil servants and think tanks. The most successful practical work of History and Policy has been in conducting joint seminars with government; the evidence for public outreach is much less clear. Jo Guldi and David Armitage's *History Manifesto* (2014) makes an impressive case for the practical uses of 'deep history' and 'big data', but their target audience is the policy-making community rather than the enfranchised public.

The broadest and most demanding definition of public memory is to see it as the working memory of citizens: not a set of static images of the past, but an active resource for debate and action (Casey 2004). As Habermas emphasized, an effective democracy is to be judged not only by its procedures for electing a government, but by the quality of its public discourse. In such a polity citizens reason together, judging their policy options against the give and take of debate. This is what political theorists (in a tradition dating back to John Stuart Mill) call 'deliberative democracy' (Miller 2003). According to this perspective, contention about collective choices reflects the clash of political and moral values to be found in most political communities which must be resolved in public debate. Writers on deliberative democracy have less to say about the forms of supporting knowledge that might confirm or undermine those values. But clearly effective public debate also depends on the relevance and accuracy of such knowledge. Reference to the past is an almost unavoidable dimension of public debate. It may sustain a sense of progress or decline, or identify telling analogies in the past, or enlarge our sense of possible alternatives (as the case studies towards the end of this chapter will demonstrate). Politics is often characterized by implicit assumptions along these lines. The case for a civic engagement on the part of historians is that these assumptions need to be brought into the open, and replaced or supplemented by more reliable insights. According to this line of argument historians have a vital part to play in expanding the scope of public memory and enhancing its relevance to the political and social issues of the day.

Engagement with public memory is far from universally accepted in the historical profession. To many of the more recondite specialists it seems a distant irrelevance. A more weighty objection is that public memory takes history into a market-place governed by political expediency. 'Relevant' history has been a bugbear with the more conservative historians since G.R. Elton wrote *The Practice of History* in 1969. Elton was a refugee from Nazism, which made him acutely sensitive to the dangers of academic scholarship being exposed to political influence. To this day many historians advocate the total independence of historical scholarship from political concerns. But 'relevance' is a somewhat undifferentiated category. In this chapter I have used it in two senses. Public memory, in its usual definition of backward-projected cultural identity, is open to the charge of crude political manipulation: it makes the past relevant by assimilating it to modern perceptions and thereby leeching out its historicity. But in the wider definition that I am employing here, public memory is relevant in the sense of illuminating policy choices rather than shoring up social solidarities. Its fundamental role is to enhance a more critical understanding of the options available to us today.

Academic history and society since the late nineteenth century

Public memory has been named as a subject for analysis only in the past 30 years. But the phenomenon it describes has a much longer history. In Britain an active minority of historians has been concerned to enlarge the scope of public memory since the modern profession took shape in the mid-nineteenth century. The precursors were those Victorian historians who were alert to the implications of extending the franchise to the working class (a process that began in 1867 with the Second Reform Act). William Stubbs at Oxford and J.R. Seeley at Cambridge believed that effective citizenship required a sound historical knowledge. As Seeley put it, in a free country some instruction was needed to ensure that citizens 'may follow with some intelligence the march of contemporary history' (Seeley 1870: 296–7). Stubbs believed that if the recently expanded elementary school system featured the serious study of history, it would furnish 'the next generation of Englishmen with the means of exercising conscientiously, honestly and judicially, the great political power which is now in their hands' (Stubbs 1887: 113). Here was the germ of the idea that public memory should embrace not only a feel-good patriotism but the back stories that would illuminate the present.

The First World War was a major turning point, not only because it gave a big impetus to the study of international relations, but because history's explanatory claims became much more evident to lay people. The case for an enlarged public memory was most assiduously pushed by A.F. Pollard. He was an improbable champion. By training a Tudor historian, Pollard would later devote himself to founding the Institute of Historical Research as a standard bearer in rigorous historical method. But he reacted to the war by immersing himself in the minutiae of recent international history. He wrote a stream of articles for the press on German war aims, the freedom of the seas, the Russian Revolution and other current issues, all of them brought together in his book *The Commonwealth at War*, published in 1917.

The early twentieth century also saw a rising tide of engagement with the public on economic and social issues. Sidney and Beatrice Webb examined the origins of the Poor Law whose future was being reassessed by the Royal Commission in the Poor Laws between 1905 and 1909 (Webb 2010). Barbara and Lawrence Hammond probed the impact of the Industrial Revolution on the labouring classes in the light of universal male enfranchisement and the arrival on the parliamentary scene of the Labour Party. Such practical perspectives became the hallmark of the Workers Educational Association (WEA). Set up in 1908 it quickly became the largest provider of adult education in the country. Its direction owed a great deal to the historian and educational reformer R.H. Tawney, who believed passionately that history illuminated the true state of social relations in the present. As Lawrence Goldman has pointed out, economic history was central to Tawney's WEA classes because workers wanted to understand the social and economic forces that had made them what they were: this was not agitprop history, but citizenship in action (Goldman 2013: 6). Not all historians agreed with Tawney's distinctive angle of address, but there was widespread support for the role of the historian as public educator. The twentieth century thus gave practical shape to the proposition that the public could with profit draw on a more extended memory, in both international and domestic policies. Neither Tawney nor Pollard saw themselves as public historians, supplying 'public memory'.

That language did not yet exist, but it accurately denotes what they were attempting to do (Tosh 2014).

Case study: the British Poor Law

The proposition that history has practical application is hardly unfamiliar, but historians tend to proclaim it as an aspiration, rather than a fleshed-out programme. In the remainder of this chapter, I offer two case studies of the relationship between professional history and public memory; one concerned with Britain's domestic policy, and the other with Britain's relations overseas. The first concerns the state relief of poverty, while the second relates to one of Britain's former colonies.

In the field of welfare policy, by far the most prominent public memory is the Victorian workhouse, adapted from an earlier model by the Poor Law Amendment Act of 1834 (known then and now as the New Poor Law). The workhouse has long been a by-word for heartless and unimaginative provision: pointless labour, poor diet and virtual confinement within the four walls of the 'house'. Removal from ordinary society to a prison-like environment was profoundly stigmatizing. These conditions were endured by the victims of seasonal unemployment, and by more long-term inmates, especially the elderly. Notoriously, couples (both married and unmarried) were separated from each other, and from their children (Englander 1998; Longmate 2003). Not all of these conditions prevailed throughout the period, or in all parts of the country, but the workhouse undoubtedly fulfilled the declared intention of providing a deterrent. This shocking past has never passed out of popular recall. Oliver Twist, the workhouse boy who 'asked for more', is still the best-known character in Dickens's novels. Former workhouse buildings are not short of visitors (www.nationaltrust. org.uk/workhouses). A familiar trope in the BBC's *Who Do You Think You Are?* series is the revelation that a well-known personality is descended from a former workhouse inmate.

All this no doubt appeals to a popular fascination with people living *in extremis*, especially when children are involved. But memories of the workhouse also perform an important cultural role. The Victorian Poor Law serves as the morally charged antithesis of the more civilized values which were established by the welfare state after 1945. The workhouse – finally abolished in 1929 – symbolized the 'bad old days' from which the poor were now rescued. Following the Beveridge Report of 1942 the post-war Labour government channelled much greater resources into welfare provision 'from the cradle to the grave'. The key measures were a comprehensive scheme of national insurance providing unemployment and sickness benefits, and family allowances for all families with more than one child. Eligibility for the full range of benefits was a defining attribute of citizenship itself. The only remaining discretionary element was the supplementary benefit paid to the small minority who fell through the cracks of the main provision. In effect society shouldered collective responsibility to secure a minimum standard of living for everyone (Timmins 2001).

During Margaret Thatcher's time in power, and still more during the coalition government led by David Cameron, the universality of the welfare state came under attack. The growing cost of provision on the lines advocated by Beveridge is the justification usually given for making cutbacks. But there has also been a significant shift in social values. The growth of a consumer society has sapped the collectivist ethos that was in the ascendant during the post-war years. There is now more fertile soil for the argument that welfare promotes dependency. Both in government and in public opinion, compassion towards the needy has to contend with the moral virtue of self-reliance. The conditions attached to benefit in respect of unemployment, disability, housing and lone parenthood have been tightened with the intention of reducing demand, and many claimants have failed to receive relief on account of the bureaucratic hurdles placed before them. The level of some benefits is reduced below the point where they meet subsistence needs; and no opportunity is missed to brand the needy as 'skivers' or 'shirkers'. Ministers have even echoed Social Darwinist thought by identifying a category of 'hereditary' poor who transmit their moral failings from one generation to the next. Once again the poor are made to be responsible for their own condition. The rights of the citizen no longer extend to an assured and sufficient provision for those in need (Farrall and Hay 2014).

From the perspective of today's dominant welfare discourse, one might suppose that the laying out of the welfare state in the 1940s was a historical anomaly, attributable to the wartime ethos of social solidarity. But the principle of entitlement was not an innovation of the welfare state. In its current form public memory fails to recognize this because its reach is confined to the Victorian era. But the history of welfare extends back two centuries beyond the Victorians, and prior to the nineteenth century its guiding principle was one of inclusivity. It is true that poor relief was dispensed by the parish authorities rather than a centralized bureaucracy, but the claimant stood a good chance of assistance in a humane way. The Poor Law of 1601 confirmed a presumption of entitlement to relief. Historians disagree as to whether this right was upheld by the full force of statutory law, but it rested on more than a charitable impulse. The better off of the parish were legally obliged to pay a poor rate, out of which relief was paid. The services provided covered finance, health and housing – a 'welfare state in miniature' according to one historian (Digby 1989: 126). During the seventeenth and eighteenth centuries poor relief was a key function of government at the grass roots. The parish was an active moral community in which the rich discharged an obligation to assist the poor. As the reforming journalist William Cobbett famously put it, 'The poor man in England is as secure from beggary as the King upon his throne, because when he makes known his distress to the parish officers they bestow on him not alms, but his legal dues' (Slack 1990; Charlesworth 2011).

The Victorian Poor Law merits its dismal reputation not only because it consigned too many to the hated workhouse, but because it whittled away the principle of entitlement as of right. For poor people who recoiled from admission to the workhouse, deterrence was tantamount to denial of assistance. But in many ways the majority of applicants who applied for 'outdoor relief' (i.e. income supplement) were even worse off. Because they were the principal drain on the public purse their conditions of relief became increasingly stringent. In the case of the able-bodied poor, the amount of relief fell substantially below the cost of subsistence, and it had to be earned by submitting to the 'labour test': back-breaking and pointless manual work, comparable to what was imposed in prison. By these means the Poor Law administrators sought to make economies. But their ruthless economizing was supported by the conviction that the unemployed were to blame for their own condition: the able-bodied should not be rewarded for their indolence or improvidence (Englander 1998; Snell 2006).

Taking the long view, the anomaly in the history of welfare was not the welfare state set up in the 1940s but the machinery of repression administered by the Poor Law in Victorian England. This was the caesura in the long history of entitlement to relief extending back to the early modern period. But, as Lorie Charlesworth has pointed out, the new Poor Law has had a toxic effect on folk memory, its iniquities so vivid that they erased all pre-Victorian perspectives on the past (Charlesworth 2010: 203). Historians have not been backward in supplying a wider readership with a fuller context on the Victorian Poor Law (Longmate 2003; Fowler 2007). But the real challenge is to enlarge the scope of public memory in order to make available a broader sense of what might be possible or desirable in the present. Charlesworth's monograph on the legal basis of poor relief was accompanied by a paper for History and Policy (Charlesworth 2011) that did just that. In his book *Pauperland*, Jeremy Seabrook, a veteran writer on social issues, places poverty in that more extended time frame (Seabrook 2013). But these interventions are not enough to move popular memory beyond an exclusive focus on the workhouse. That remains a major project for historians.

Case study: Zimbabwe/Rhodesia

Although domestic issues occupy the foreground of public memory, it is important to recognize the part that public memory can play in our understanding of the world beyond our national borders. My earlier example of the historical antecedents of the Bosnian crisis in the 1990s suggests as much. Historical insight is also at a premium concerning other cases of distant and unfamiliar countries that suddenly come into the news because of a current crisis, for example Iraq in 2003 (Milton-Edwards 2003; Tosh 2008). But historical perspective is equally necessary in order to understand Britain's long-term neighbours and partners, like France and the United States with whom there is an ongoing relationship. Here an important category is those former colonies that were part of the British Empire and whose relations with Britain extended over many decades (centuries in the case of India). In Britain public memories of the Empire are superficial and often self-serving. But in the overseas territories the colonial experience has left a well of memories, some of them extremely painful, which exert a significant impact on the policies of these countries towards the metropole. Without a grasp of those memories in Britain, the antagonism periodically vented against Britain remains a mystery. Zimbabwe/Rhodesia provides a telling illustration of this theme.

Developed by a commercial company to promote the imperial ambitions of entrepreneur Cecil Rhodes, Rhodesia was a colony whose dispositions were more in keeping with speculative capitalism than long-term colonial exploitation. The country bears the scars of that early chapter to this day. Of all the grievances that fuelled African resistance during the guerrilla war in the 1970s, none was more resented than the grossly unequal distribution of land between African and white farmers. Since independence in 1980 this has been a running sore in British–Zimbabwean relations. The incoming ZANU government of Robert Mugabe was under intense pressure to address the land problem. At that stage they did not advocate expropriation (at least not in public); instead they demanded that Britain shoulder the cost of a programme of transfer by purchase from white farmers. In 1979 an independence deal was thrashed out at the Lancaster House conference which reached a compromise agreement on the constitution for the new country and on the terms of the ceasefire. On the nationalist side the key players were Robert Mugabe (later president) and his rival Joshua Nkomo. Their readiness to sign up to the deal was due in part to an off-the-record pledge by the British Foreign Secretary that Britain would bear *some* of the cost of land transfer (Davidow 1984; Bourne 2011). In subsequent years ZANU maintained that the British government had gone back on a binding commitment. Finally in 2000 ZANU unleashed the forcible occupation of white-owned land by so-called war veterans, holding Britain responsible for its actions. This programme was illegal, arbitrary and vindictive, and it was roundly condemned in these terms by the British press.

Yet with a more extended historical perspective it was evident that land seizures in the 2000s were the mirror image of land seizures in the 1890s. The colonization of Rhodesia had been initiated in 1890 by the British South Africa Company (BSAC), an agent of Cecil Rhodes's ambition to open up a 'second Rand' – northern gold fields to rival or outshine those of the Witwatersrand. The 200 incoming settlers – the so-called 'pioneer column' – expected to take their share of a gold bonanza; they were promised a comparatively modest land allocation of 3000 acres each. But when Rhodesia's mineral resources turned out to be relatively small, land became the principal attraction for the settlers. The scale of land grants by the Company was stepped up. By 1899 there were approximately 5000 Europeans in Rhodesia (by imperial standards a massive influx). Nearly 16 million acres – one sixth of the total – had been expropriated, including most of the land with the best potential for successful farming (Palmer 1977). White Rhodesians cited the Rudd Concession negotiated in 1888 with Lobengula, leader of the Ndebele, as the legal basis of the occupation. But the text of that agreement referred only to mineral discoveries, not the land (Keppel-Jones 1983: 78).

This was confiscation on a massive scale, and the responsibility of Britain was clear. It is true that Rhodesia in its early years was not governed by Colonial Office officials, but by appointees of the BSAC on behalf of its shareholders in London, and their interest was in short-term speculative gains. But Rhodesia was unequivocally part of the British Empire. Britain remained the sovereign power, but for reasons of *realpolitik* chose to show a blind eye to this buccaneering variant of colonial occupation.

It is this history that has been absent from public memory in Britain in recent years. The land occupation movement in Zimbabwe can be criticized on many grounds. It was a desperate expedient by a weak government, which terrorized citizens of the country and did terrible damage to its agricultural production. It is far from clear how much popular support there was in Zimbabwe for the seizure of land: white farming was, after all, a major provider of employment. But set against this was the memory of African land lost only three generations earlier. The seizure of white farms may have lacked legality, but it expressed a historical logic. Spokesmen for the regime maintained that the African people had been robbed by imperial asset-strippers, whose descendants should now pay the price for their misdeeds (Chigwedere 2001). Shona and Ndebele had risen against the settlers in 1896–7 in 'the first *Chimurenga*' or war of liberation. Now, said Mugabe, in taking on the white farmers they were engaged in 'the third *Chimurenga*' (the second one being the war of independence in the 1970s) (Raftopoulos and Mlambo 2009: 113). Britain bore responsibility for the land-grab in the 1890s; its failure to redeem the past left the Zimbabwe government with no choice but to take direct action.

To know something of this murky background was not to excuse the land occupations, but to recognize them as something more than the action of a tyrannical government, and above all to recognize Britain's own responsibility in a more profound and incriminating way than either the government or the media allowed. Clare Short, Tony Blair's Secretary of State for International Development, stated that Britain had no special responsibility to meet the costs of land purchase in Zimbabwe. Such a statement not only glossed over the pledge given in 1979; it airbrushed from history Britain's imperial past and its significance for the people of Zimbabwe (Bourne 2011).

Even at the time of the independence negotiations in 1979, there was little excuse for British ignorance of Zimbabwe's past. In the preceding 20 years a revolution had taken place in the understanding of African history – about the pre-colonial order in central Africa, the colonial takeover and, above all, the extent of African resistance and its rootedness in indigenous culture. The historical work that became a classic was Terence Ranger's *Revolt in Southern Rhodesia* (1967), an account of the initial African resistance to the Company's take-over. Well before the officially approved nationalist historiography of Zimbabwe took shape, Ranger documented not only the full extent of the first *chimurenga*, but also its survival in African memory. He concluded his book with a profoundly symbolic trans-generational encounter which occurred in 1962. Joshua Nkomo, leader of ZAPU, returning from exile was met at the airport by a 90-year old survivor of the risings who presented him with a spirit axe as a resistance symbol (Ranger 1967: 385). It was a perfect illustration of the continuity of African experience which Ranger aimed to convey to a public almost wholly ignorant of it. In the hope perhaps that British policy would take some account of this past, the book was reissued by a trade house in 1979, the year of the Lancaster House negotiations.

Public memory is sometimes taken to be an unchanging given, composed of enduring images of the national past. But the rationale of public memory is that it reflects and validates the preoccupations of the present, and by definition those preoccupations change. One of the ways in which historians can serve the public good is by assisting that process of adjustment. Britain's relations with the rest of the world present a challenging dimension of this agenda, because individual countries can suddenly demand attention and then recede from view. In the case of the British Empire, its long history and vast scale mean that public memory is inevitably selective. Rhodesia/Zimbabwe meant little to the British public before the 1960s, but since then it has been a major, if intermittent, preoccupation. Public memory was infused with assumptions that reflected a colonial mind-set. In exploring the history of expropriation and resistance historians have sought to enlarge and correct public memory in Britain. Yet fully to grasp the relationship between two countries requires more than an appeal to the documentary record. Zimbabweans have their own public memories of the colonial era, and these inform their reading of current politics and their evaluation of Britain's political objectives and moral standing. Irrespective of whether such memories are well founded, they furnish a crucial dimension to Britain's understanding of the attitudes of former colonial subjects. If historians do not supply this perspective, it is unlikely that anyone else will.

Conclusion

In Britain today 'memory culture' is thriving. Sustained by heritage sites, museums, television and community projects, it often appears more vigorous than anything that professional historians accomplish. It is easy to think of historians on a downward slide, condemned to play second fiddle to the memory specialists; there is talk of 'a crisis of authority' over the custodianship of the past (Hamilton 2003). At bottom such talk reveals a misinterpretation of the scope of memory and its place in human culture. The prevalent definition of public memory as the expression of identity politics is an unwarranted restriction on the quality of historical understanding that should prevail in a participating democracy. Historians should certainly be vigilant about the gross distortions that sometimes disfigure the public memory of emergent identities. But they have a larger responsibility. If they see public memory as nothing more than a travesty of the past, they will neglect a positive role of greater civic importance. Eric Hobsbawm observed that 'most young men and women . . . grow up in a sort of permanent present lacking any organic relation to the public past of the times they live in' (Hobsbawm 1994: 3). Though evidence is hard to come by, most observers are agreed that this generational amnesia has become more pronounced in recent decades. But public memory does not have to be so constrained. The narrowness of its definition in current discourse should not blind us to the potential scope of public memory and the immensely important role of historians in nourishing it. As the examples of welfare policy and the legacy of empire suggest, historians need to be proactive – not only deflating popular myth, but seeking to extend the scope of public memory to areas where important policy outcomes are at stake. As Jo Guldi and David Armitage declare, 'the power of memory can return us directly to the forgotten powers of history as a discipline to persuade, to re-imagine, and to inspire' (Guldi and Armitage 2014: 85).

Guide to further reading and online resources

The historical study of public memory is rich in suggestive case studies, but short on good systematic surveys of the field. The best one to date is Cubitt (2007). Burke (1989) offers a lucid introduction to the field. Hodgkin and Radstone (2003) provides an insightful introduction to a collection of case studies. Pierre Nora (1989) provides a helpful entrée into his immensely influential study of the material and symbolic expression of state memory. Ashplant et al. (2000) is a magisterial exploration of public memory in relation to wars in the twentieth century, with a wide range of national examples. The application of historical scholarship to the content of public memory has received less attention. But see Tosh (2008), Tosh (2014) and Stevens (2010).

An excellent way of teasing out the relation of historical scholarship to public memory is to compare different countries. For the USA see Philipps (2004) and John Bodnar (1994). For France, see Pierre Nora (1989), and his other edited works detailed in the Introduction to this book, *Realms of Memory: Rethinking the French Past*, 3 vols (New York: Columbia University press, 1996–98). For Australia, see Hamilton (2003).

An excellent online resource on the recent and current engagement of historians with the making of public policy are the websites of two organizations that seek to connect historians with policy-makers:

Britain: History & Policy: www.historyandpolicy.org
Australia: Australian Policy and History: www.aph.org.au

Note

1 Academic historians reached out to the public beyond their comfort zone in a variety of ways. 'Historians Take Issue with Mrs Thatcher', *New Statesman*, 27 May 1983; Michael Anderson, 'How Much has the Family Changed?' *New Society*, 27 October 1983; James Walvin, *Victorian Values* (London: André Deutsch, 1987).

References

Ashplant, T.G., Graham Dawson and Michael Roper (eds) (2000) *The Politics of War Memory and Commemoration*. London: Routledge.

Beccles, Hilary and Verene A. Shepherd (2007) *Saving Souls: The Struggle to End the Transatlantic Trade in Africans*. Kingston: Iain Randle.

Bentley, Michael (1999) *Modern Historiography: An Introduction*. London: Routledge.

Bodnar, John (1994) 'Public Memory in an American City: Commemoration in Cleveland', in John R. Gillis (ed.), *Commemoration: The Politics of National Identity*. Princeton, NJ: Princeton University Press.

Bourne, Richard (2011) *Catastrophe: What Went Wrong in Zimbabwe?* London: Zed.

Braunstein, Matthieu (2001) *François Mitterrand a Sarajevo: 28 juin 1992: le rendez-vous manqué.* Paris: L'Harmattan.

Burgoyne, Robert (2003) 'From Contested to Consensual Memory: The Rock and Roll Hall of Fame and Museum', in Katherine Hodgkin and Susannah Radstone (eds), *Contested Pasts: the Politics of Memory.* London: Routledge.

Burke, Peter (1989) 'History and Social Memory', in Thomas Butler (ed.), *Memory: History, Culture and the Mind.* Oxford: Oxford University Press.

Casey, Edward S. (2004) 'Public Memory in Place and Time', in Kendall R. Philipps (ed.), *Framing Public Memory.* Tuscaloosa, AL: University of Alabama Press.

Castle, Kathryn (1996) *Britannia's Children.* Manchester: Manchester University Press.

Charlesworth, Lorie (2010) 'England's Early "Big Society": Parish Welfare under the Old Poor Law', www.historyandpolicy.org/papers/policy-paper-108.html.

Charlesworth, Lorie (2011) *Welfare's Forgotten Past: A Socio-Legal History of the Poor Law.* Abingdon: Routledge.

Charmley, John (1993) *Churchill: the End of Glory: A Political Biography.* London: John Curtis.

Chigwedere, Aeneas (2001) *British Betrayal of the Africans: Land, Cattle, Human Rights: Case for Zimbabwe.* Marondera: Mutapa.

Clark, Christopher (2013) *The Sleepwalkers: How Europe Went to War in 1914.* London: Penguin.

Cox, Pamela (2013) 'The Future Uses of History', *History Workshop Journal* 75, 125–45.

Cressy, David (1994) 'National Memory in Early Modern England', in John R. Gillis (ed.), *Commemoration: The Politics of National Identity.* Princeton, NJ: Princeton University Press.

Cubitt, Geoffrey (2007) *History and Memory.* Manchester: Manchester University Press.

Davidow, Jeffrey (1984) *A Peace in Southern Africa: The Lancaster House Conference on Rhodesia, 1979.* Boulder, CO: Westview.

Davin, Anna (1972) 'Women and History', in Michelene Wandor (ed.), *The Body Politic: Women's Liberation in Britain.* London: Stage 1.

Digby, Anne (1989) *British Welfare Policy: Workhouse to Welfare.* London: Faber.

Elton, G.R. (1969) *The Practice of History.* London: Fontana.

Englander, David (1998) *Poverty and Poor Law Reform in 19th Century Britain, 1834–1914.* London: Longman.

Farrall, Stephen and Colin Hay (eds) (2014) *The Legacy of Thatcherism.* Oxford: Oxford University Press.

Fowler, Simon (2007) *Workhouse: The People, the Palaces, the Life Behind Doors.* London: National Archives.

Goldman, Lawrence (2013) *The Life of R.H. Tawney: Socialism and History.* London: Bloomsbury.

Guldi, Jo and David Armitage (2014) *The History Manifesto.* Cambridge: Cambridge University Press.

Habermas, Jürgen (1989) *The Structural Transformation of the Public Sphere.* London: Polity.

Hamilton, Paula (2003) 'Memory Studies and Cultural History', in Hsu-Ming Teo and Richard White (eds), *Cultural History in Australia.* Sydney: University of New South Wales Press.

Hobsbawm, E.J. (1994) *Age of Extremes: The Short Twentieth Century 1914–91.* London: Michael Joseph.

Hobsbawm, E.J. and T.O. Ranger (eds) (1983) *The Invention of Tradition.* Cambridge: Cambridge University Press.

Hodgkin, Katherine, and Susannah Radstone (eds) (2003) *Contested Pasts: the Politics of Memory.* London: Routledge.

Keppel-Jones, Arthur (1983) *Rhodes and Rhodesia: The White Conquest of Zimbabwe, 1884–1902.* Pietermaritzburg: University of Natal Press.

Longmate, Norman (2003) *The Workhouse: A Social History.* London: Pimlico.

Lowenthal, David (1985) *The Past is a Foreign Country.* Cambridge: Cambridge University Press.

Lowenthal, David (1996) *Possessed by the Past: The Heritage Crusade and the Spoils of History.* New York: The Free Press.

Mace, Rodney (1976) *Trafalgar Square: Emblem of Empire.* London: Lawrence & Wishart.

Mackenzie, John M. (1986) *Propaganda and Empire: The Manipulation of British Public Opinion, 1880–1960.* Manchester: Manchester University Press.

Miller, David (2003) 'Deliberative Democracy and Social Choice', in James S. Fishkin and Peter Laslett (eds), *Debating Deliberative Democracy.* Oxford: Blackwell.

Milton-Edwards, Beverley (2003) 'Iraq, Past, Present and Future: A Thoroughly Modern Mandate?', www.historyandpolkicy.org/papers/policy-paper-13.html.

Nora, Pierre (1989) 'Between Memory and History: *Les Lieux de mémoire*', *Representations* 26: 7–24.

Novick, Peter (1999) *The Holocaust in American Life.* London: Bloomsbury.

Palmer, Robin (1977) *Land and Racial Domination in Rhodesia.* London: Heinemann.

Philipps, Kendall R. (ed.) (2004) *Framing Public Memory.* Tuscaloosa, AL: University of Alabama Press.

Phillips, Robert (1998) *History Teaching, Nationhood and the State.* London: Cassell.

Pollard, A.F. (1917) *The Commonwealth at War.* London: Longmans.

Raftopoulos, Brian and A.S. Mlambo (eds) (2009) *Becoming Zimbabwe: A History from the Pre-Colonial Period to 2008.* Harare: Weaver Press.

Reddie, Richard S. (2007) *Abolition! The Struggle to Abolish Slavery in the British Colonies.* Oxford: Lion Hudson.

Ranger, T.O. (1967) *Revolt in Southern Rhodesia 1896–7: A Study in African Resistance.* London: Heinemann.

Samuel, Raphael (1994) *Theatres of Memory: Past and Present in Contemporary Culture.* London: Verso.

Schwarz, Bill (2005) '"Strolling spectators" and "practical Londoners" – Remembering the Imperial Past', in Jo Littler and Roshi Naidoo (eds), *The Politics of Heritage.* London: Routledge.

Seabrook, Jeremy (2013) *Pauperland: A Short History of Poverty in Britain.* London: Hurst.

Seeley, J.R. (1870) *Lectures and Essays.* London: Macmillan.

Slack, Paul (1990) *The English Poor Law, 1531–1782.* Cambridge: Cambridge University Press.

Smith, Laurajane, Geoff Cubitt, Ross Wilson and Kalliopi Fouseki (eds) (2011) *Representing Slavery and Abolition in Museums: Ambiguous Engagements.* Abingdon: Routledge.

Snell, Keith (2006) *Parish and Belonging: Community, Identity and Welfare in England and Wales, 1750–1950.* Cambridge: Cambridge University Press

Stevens, Mary (2010) 'Public Policy and the Public Historian: The Changing Place of Historians in Public Life in France and the UK', *The Public Historian* 32(3): 120–38.

Stubbs, William (1887) *Seventeen Lectures on the Study of Medieval and Modern History.* Oxford: Oxford University Press.

Szreter, Simon (2011) 'History and Public Policy', in Jonathan Bate (ed.), *The Public Value of the Humanities.* London: Bloomsbury.

Timmins, Nicholas (2001) *The Five Giants: A Biography of the Welfare State.* London: Collins.

Tosh, John (2008) *Why History Matters.* Basingstoke: Palgrave.

Tosh, John (2014) 'Public History, Civic Engagement and the Historical Profession in Britain', *History* 99(2): 191–212.

Wallace, Elizabeth Kowaleski (2006) *The British Slave Trade and Public Memory.* New York: Columbia University Press.

Walvin, James (2009) 'The Slave Trade, Abolition and Public Memory', *Transactions of the Royal Historical Society*, 6th series, 19, 139–49.

Walvin, James (1973) *Black and White in English Society.* London: Allen Lane.

Walvin, James (1993) *Black Ivory: A History of British Slavery.* Oxford: Fontana.

Walvin, James (1996) *Questioning Slavery.* London: Routledge.

Walvin, James (2000), *Making the Black Atlantic: Britain and the African Diaspora.* London: Cassell.

Webb, Sidney and Beatrice Webb (1910) *English Poor Law Policy.* London: Longmans.

Zeldin, Theodore (1981) 'After Braudel', *The Listener*, 5 November 1981.

2   Challenge or opportunity?

Postcolonialism and the historian

Toby Green

History as an academic discipline arose alongside modern nationalism. With the decline of traditional, religious origin myths in the West, it emerged as an intellectual framework within which to understand the emergence of the nation. Narrative was therefore a core aspect of the early historical method, as the names of key works in this ilk such as *Our Island Story* (Marshall 1905) make plain. From the late eighteenth century onwards, historians were the bards of the modern nation state, developing the national narrative within a genre that increasingly sought objective underpinnings.

Alongside these origins of the modern discipline of history, the centrality of the scientific method to intellectual activity provided an important benchmark. With science the epitome of objectivity, and historians keen to show that their analyses presented objective accounts of the succession of past events, concerns arose either side of the Second World War as to whether there could be such a thing as 'scientific history'. This was a question that preoccupied public intellectuals such as Isaiah Berlin, and that has remained under discussion among prominent public historians such as Richard J. Evans into more recent times (Evans 1997). It is important to grasp the significance of such discussions: if the discipline of history is to escape the charge of bias, it needs to present some sort of positivistic account of what sort of knowledge it offers, and such an account is often assumed to involve grasping the relationship between the historical mode of knowledge and the scientific.

After the end of the Second World War, moreover, new challenges were presented to the traditional historical mode of knowledge-production in the shape of postcolonialism and postmodernism. These emerged at a similar period, owing to related concerns, and often worked alongside one another as complementary critiques of 'knowledge' which challenged the very possibility of objective relations of the past and the priority of historical narratives. Classic postmodernist theorists include Jacques Derrida and Michel Foucault, both of whom sought to explore the inherent assumptions of the categories of Western thought. Postcolonialism is rather a means of challenging the hegemony *of* the Western worldview, than an exploration of it. Classic postcolonial theorists include Homi Bhabha, Stuart Hall, Edward Said, Gayatri Chakravorty Spivak and Ngugi Wa Thiong'o.

This new mode of criticism of objectivity posed fundamental challenges to the basis of the authority of the historical discipline. Postmodernism challenged the authority of historical sources, arguing that written sources could be reduced to texts which were always relational to present concerns, rendering void their ability to offer objective information the past. Postcolonialism challenged the authority of the historian, arguing that this was historically constituted on the basis of inequality and colonial violence, and thus offered an irreducibly partisan and Eurocentric view of historical change; moreover, archives used by these historians were themselves reproductions of the violence and inequality of colonial power relations, and thus all knowledge deriving from these sources was incomplete and partisan.

These critiques have had enormous influence on the way in which history as a discipline has been perceived since the 1960s. They have opened up not only a questioning of the validity of the historical method, but also new approaches to other forms of historical discourse. Thus in the case of African oral histories, scholars have also shown how present concerns influence the shaping of oral narratives (Wright 1991); moreover, as with the national narratives of Western histories, oral histories in Africa traditionally also recount the origin of a state or kingship lineage, making apparently distant historical discourses in actuality seem closer than they were previously thought to be.

This chapter assesses these challenges to the discipline of history. It assesses how and why both postmodernism and postcolonialism emerged, and examines what challenges these schools offer to the historian in the twenty-first century. It is divided into four sections: the first section examines the historical origins of postmodernism in the aftermath of the Second World War, and assesses its key claims; the second analyses frameworks of postcolonial thought that emerged at the same time, and how these related to imperatives of class, empire and postcolonial nation-building; the third scrutinizes the emergence of the idea of the 'subaltern' (a category defined below), and how this was used by postcolonial theorists to re-examine contexts for the production of sources; and the fourth and final section then uses the case study of the memorialization of Atlantic slavery as a window into examining the import of these challenges to the historical discipline for historians in the twenty-first century.

The rise of postcolonialism and postmodernism

Postmodernism emerged as an important theoretical school in the 1960s, when thinkers such as Roland Barthes, Jacques Derrida, Michel Foucault and Paul de Man acquired international notoriety. Barthes, Derrida and Foucault all worked in France, while de Man – although Belgian in origin – taught in the USA. Though their work was of enormous import to the discipline of the historian, these scholars were philosophers and literary critics, their work primarily concerned with textual analysis and the limitations inherent to any text's authority. This was soon seen to have urgent relevance to history, being a discipline that relies so heavily on the authority of textual sources: if such sources lacked authoritative objectivity, what hope was there for the ideal of scientific history?

The historical framework for the rise of postmodernism is important. With the 1960s a period for counter-culture and political agitation – epitomized by the civil rights movement in the United States, decolonization in Africa and the May 1968 riots in France – the emergence of this school of criticism fell on fertile terrain. As a cultural critique, postmodernism challenged accepted canons of analysis, and so naturally it found many supporters in an era like this, particularly in a country such as France which was at the heart of the anti-establishment political movements of the 1960s.

An equally important historical context was the aftermath of the Second World War. It is no accident that, as Perez Zagorin notes, the vast majority of postmodernist theorists in the 1960s emerged from France, and that their ideas had little traction among historians in the UK and the USA (Zagorin 1999: 5). These national relationships to postmodernism reflected the very different historical experiences of these countries during the Second World War. In France the conflict had been cataclysmic, almost destroying the country and leading to prolonged occupation (a trauma indirectly depicted in the highly popular *Asterix* comic-book series of the post-war years). By contrast, in the UK, the war had been a violent event riven with mortalities, but leading to a national triumph, while in the United States it was a global conflict from which that country emerged as the global superpower.

In this light, it is hardly surprising that while most Anglo-Saxon thinkers baulked at the challenges presented by postmodernism, French thinkers were prepared to accept the postmodern view, as described by Zagorin, of the end of the triumph of Western rationality and the ideology of progress (Zagorin 1999: 5). Similarly, as we shall see in this chapter, nor is it surprising that postcolonial theorists – weighed down by the murderous excesses of a century of imperial forced labour and land expropriations – joined in this philosophical programme with alacrity. There was a very particular historical context to the rise of the postcolonial and postmodern challenges to history, and it lay in the carnage of the Second World War and in the forced labour that was the norm in much of the colonial world. The challenge that this carnage and institutional violence represented to traditional liberal teleologies of History as Progress is what is most clearly captured in these alternative schools of history, and still today presents their most potent interrogation of history as a discipline.

Beyond the differing experiences of France, the UK and the USA, the aftermath of the Second World War also triggered the collapse of formal European empires, a historical moment which underpinned these philosophical movements. With the United States the unquestioned superpower in the West after 1945, the continued existence of European colonial empires became an anachronism; American power put increasing diplomatic pressure on European nations to decolonize, and with Europe in receipt of Marshall Fund donations for post-war reconstruction, and heavily dependent on American military power in the Cold War, decolonization moved swiftly. The partition and independence of India and Pakistan from the UK was achieved by 1947, and the independence of Indochina from France followed in the 1950s. The decolonizing 'winds of change' (Butler and Stockwell 2013) were soon rushing through Africa, with Ghana's independence under Nkrumah in 1957, and Guinea's independence from France under Sékou Touré in 1958. By the mid-1960s, most of Africa had achieved independence, with the major exceptions being in Rhodesia and the Portuguese African colonies, which saw violent independence wars continuing long into the 1970s. South Africa, meanwhile, was to represent a unique case of a colonial society continuing until the end of the twentieth century, where owing to the large white population minority rule continued until 1994.

This historical conjuncture is therefore very important in understanding both the rise of postcolonial theory and the relationship which this had to postmodernist ideas. The consequences of the Second World War triggered on the one hand the collapse of European empires and the emergence of the postcolonial political condition, and on the other the rise of postmodernism as a response to experiences of violent carnage, experiences which made the liberal model of historical 'progress' seem anodyne. At the same time, the rise of the United States as the Western superpower and the emergence of the Cold War with the Soviet Union also proved significant. The heavily armed rivalry between the two superpowers facilitated the success of the Cuban revolution in 1959, which proved very important in the development of postcolonial theories in the 1960s in the light of the support given by the revolutionary regime in Cuba to African independence struggles, in Angola, Congo and Guinea-Bissau in particular.

Before looking at postcolonial ideas in more detail, we need to explore postmodernist approaches to history, to which postcolonialism was so closely related. As mentioned already, these approaches to knowledge were based in a strong critique of existing frameworks of analysis. As Jacques Derrida put it in *Limited Inc.*, one of his most influential works, his theoretical model of deconstruction had an overtly political programme which it approached through language, seeking 'a *reversal* of the classical opposition *and* a general *displacement* of the system' (Derrida 1988 [1977]: 21). That is, instead of working with binary antithetical concepts, as was typical of Western rationality, postmodernists such as Derrida sought to overturn this mode of thought by deconstructing the rationality of *all* concepts. Through literary critics such as Barthes, postmodernism also sought to destroy the purported authority of the 'objective voice' of historians and others who sought to represent reality, or the history of reality. Thus the postmodern critique of language was actually a coded assault on Western rationality and on its purported universalism, as well as an attack on the coherence of Enlightenment concepts and ideals.

As a school of thought that was hostile towards the totalizing claims of Enlightenment rationality, postmodernism's relationship to the ideas of Michel Foucault are well worth exploring. Foucault's attack on the straitjacket of Western Enlightenment philosophy became especially fashionable in intellectual circles from the 1980s onwards. This followed his critique of repressive institutions such as prisons and mental asylums, the rise of which coincided with the Enlightenment, and his analyses of the impact that these institutions had on Western sexuality and the construction of ideas of aesthetics, morality and knowledge. Given that, as we have seen, the discipline of history itself arose in this Enlightenment era, Foucault was highly critical of the traditional practices of historians. He wrote in his essay *Nietzsche, Genealogy, History*: 'The final trait of effective history is its affirmation of knowledge as perspective. Historians take unusual pains to erase the elements in their work which reveal their grounding in a particular time and place, their preferences in a controversy' (Foucault 1977: 156).

Foucault's is, essentially, a direct postmodernist critique. What is in fact revealed is a critique of the particularism of Enlightenment rationality, based in its dependence on a specific time and place and on the institutions of that specific temporal locality. The relevance of this to history, and historians, is that the ideal of an objective historical account itself grew out of those institutions, and from that specific historical time and place. The 'linguistic turn' – the scholarly emphasis on the relationship between philosophy and language, as a key aspect of the analysis of thought (see Rorty 1967) – is so important to postmodernism because it represents the means by which postmodernism's true end, the coded assault on Western rationality, can be realized, through a direct critique of the purported authority of canonical texts and Enlightenment ideals.

This intellectual work began to have a direct bearing on the ways in which historians approached their work through the writings of the American theoretical historian Hayden White. Beginning in the 1970s, White authored a series of profound critiques of the historian as exercising an objective craft divorced from present concerns. White challenged the archival construction of historical analyses, arguing that archives were repository of texts, not facts, and could and should be read accordingly. He argued that narratives were imposed by historians on texts selected to fit these narratives; they therefore lacked the objective authority that was claimed for them. He here followed closely the critiques of the French anthropologist Claude Lévi-Strauss, who had argued in the 1960s that the impossibility of reproducing the totality of the past in the present made it impossible to construct an objective historical narrative (Lévi-Strauss 1966: 256–62).

Given that White is a professional historian, much writing on the relationship of postmodernism to history is grounded in his work. However, as this section has shown, White's ideas as developed in the 1970s depended very heavily on the postmodern school of thought that had gathered pace in the 1960s in France, and in turn derived from some of the post-war critiques of the Frankfurt School of philosophers as led by Adorno and Horkheimer, especially in their seminal work *Dialectic of the Enlightenment* (Adorno and Horkeimer 2002 [1944]). This critique of history related not only to its purported objectivity, but also to its presumption of Western universalism; and this was something that, at the same point in time, postcolonial theorists took up with a vengeance. As Hayden White put it in *Metahistory*:

> [Western historical consciousness] may be little more than a theoretical basis for the ideological position from which Western civilization views its relationship not only to cultures and civilizations preceding it but also to

those contemporary with it in time . . . in short, it is possible to view historical consciousness as a specifically Western prejudice by which the presumed superiority of modern, industrialized society can be retroactively substantiated.

(1975: 2)

Frameworks of postcolonial thought: culture, empire and nationalism

The wave of decolonization that occurred after 1945 had multiple effects on ideas and social movements around the world. This process signalled not only the end of European empires in Asia and Africa, but also the beginning of an intellectual quest for both the roots of the colonial worldview and the ways in which postcolonial nations could counteract this and so forge their own ideals of independent nationhood. These movements began very quickly to focus on the ways in which imperial historiographies constructed the world historical process 'from the centre out', counteracting this with ways of thinking historically that privileged what was at the time called the 'periphery' (that is, the formerly colonized nations). In so doing, postcolonial theorists challenged the presumed universality of the Western historical discipline that had gone before.

Postcolonial theory was influenced at first from multiple directions. The pan-African movement championed by leading black intellectuals such as Marcus Garvey was joined to the programme of reaffirmation of African historical and cultural frameworks known as *négritude*, driven by poets and philosophers from francophone Africa and the diaspora such as Léopold Sédar Senghor (later the first president of Senegal) and Aimé Césaire from Martinique. Joined to this was the significant programme sponsored by the UN and UNESCO in the aftermath of the Holocaust which produced various publications on the myth of 'races', undermining the supposed scientific nature of 'racial science' which had underpinned both the justifications of European empires and the Nazis' rise to power in pre-war Germany. The intellectual consensus as to the cataclysm which the false ideas of racial science had produced was thus allied to significant anticolonial movements of the intelligentsia in Africa and its diaspora, driving forward key phases in the school of postcolonial thought.

One of the most influential founders of postcolonialism was Frantz Fanon, a doctor from Martinique who served in French colonial Algeria during the independence war of the 1950s. Fanon wrote a series of works on the racial stereotypes and ideologies that underpinned French colonial power. In one of his most famous works, *Black Skins, White Masks* (Fanon 1967), he analysed for the first time the systematic inculcation of cultural inferiority among African subjects which lay at the heart of the colonial programme in francophone Africa, and the assimilation of 'superior' French cultural types which went with it. Fanon's emphasis on culture was significant. Whereas Marxist critiques of colonialism (so much in vogue in the 1940s and 1950s) grounded analysis solely in material forces such as economic conditions, Fanon's focus on culture showed the psychological aspect of colonialism at its rawest, and argued that it was this that postcolonial leaders would have to address most forcefully. Moreover, it argued strongly for the particular historical roots of every culture, against the universalism that subsequent postcolonial and postmodern writers criticized in the discipline of history.

This focus on culture was then taken up by one of the main champions of postcolonial ideas in the 1960s, Amílcar Cabral. Cabral was the leader of the independence movement of two tiny Portuguese colonies in Africa, Cape Verde and Guinea-Bissau. Though these countries were small in size and population, Cabral achieved global celebrity in the late 1960s and early 1970s as the independence struggle of some of the last European colonies in Africa became notorious; it was indeed Portugal's eventual defeat in Guinea-Bissau which triggered the 'Carnation Revolution' in Portugal and the end of the *Estado Novo* dictatorship in April 1974. Cabral was a darling of the left in these years, working closely with Fidel Castro, Che Guevara, Kwame Nkrumah and Sékou Touré, and though assassinated in January 1973 – before Guinea-Bissau had won independence – his influence ran deep.

Cabral developed crucial planks of postcolonial thought that challenged previous intellectual frameworks. Most fundamental of these was the nature of postcolonial nationalism. Like Fanon, Cabral emphasized the historical roots of a nation's culture as vital in shaping both understanding of current problems and potentials for their solution (see the essays in Manji and Fletcher Jr 2013). This emphasis on the interrelationship of culture and history was pitted against the ideology of the Portuguese colonial regime, which sought to justify colonialism through the 'objective history' of the longevity of Portugal's interrelationship with Africa: according to the Portuguese dictatorship's favourite ideologue, the Brazilian sociologist Gilberto Freyre, this gave Portuguese imperialism a milder and more humane face, and explained why it was not an anachronism in the postcolonial world of the post-war years. By emphasizing the particular historical roots of Bissau-Guinean culture, Cabral particularized the 'universality' of the Portuguese experience, offered a withering critique of Freyre, and showed up the limits and strategic intent of 'objective historical approaches' to the imperial past.

As we can see, the place of imperial narratives of history became very important in postcolonial ideas. The critique of perceptions of colonized peoples as 'outside history' or 'without history' was slowly moving to centre stage in the battle of ideas. One of the most important later theorists of this school was the Guyanese historian Walter Rodney, whose 1970 book on the history of the Upper Guinea Coast during the slave trade era was a pioneering study. Rodney's most important book, *How Europe Underdeveloped Africa*, was published in 1972, the year before Cabral's assassination. It shifted the focus not only onto the history of empire, but also fundamentally onto class relations. In this work, Rodney argued that African underdevelopment had been assured not only through the economic and political relations pushed through by European commercial interests, but also through alliances of African elites and European traders at the expense of the African poor. In the postcolonial era, Rodney implied, nationalists would have to work very hard to ensure that these relations were not reproduced, given the depth of their historic roots in African-European relations (or, as Cabral put it, class suicide by the African bourgeoisie would be required). Despite the fact that Rodney was assassinated in 1980, his ideas have remained very influential among black nationalists ever since (see Manji and Fletcher Jr 2013).

Of necessity, therefore, postcolonial theorists came to challenge Western historical narratives. The way in which both historical forces and historical narratives had constructed global inequalities, and their ideological superstructure, was among their prime concerns. History was not a footnote or a luxury to these thinkers: it was a fundamental battleground in the building of nationalisms that could move beyond the colonial paradigm. By foregrounding the importance of culture in building postcolonial nationalism, and the particularity of the historical roots of each culture, the teleology of liberal progress as the grand pattern of 'history' was deeply challenged. Ironically, postcolonialism was therefore given a deeply historical footing at the intersection of history and culture, even though it was itself suspicious of narratives of 'history'.

Though Cabral, Fanon and Rodney all died young, their ideas shaped the ways in which more recent generations of postcolonial theorists have approached their subject. The relationship between culture formation and imperial historical structures has been a key concern in both Anglophone and Francophone worlds. In Anglophone discourse, the cultural studies school led by Homi Bhabha (e.g. 1985) and Stuart Hall (e.g. 1980, 1997) emphasized the hybrid nature of the cultures created by imperialism in the British colonies of the Caribbean and the imperial Raj. Imperial ideologies had privileged the 'purity' of the imperial culture and its superiority over 'degenerate' mixtures which were seen as incapable of reproducing themselves (the word *mulatto* for someone of mixed racial origins in the Caribbean derived from *mula* – the mule – which cannot reproduce). Hall instead emphasized the 'creolization' of Caribbean cultures, which he argued offered mixed frameworks within an imperial structure; Bhabha meanwhile showed how these 'hybrid' cultures emerged in the space of resistance and contestation between empires and their subjects.

In the Francophone world, perhaps the leading current postcolonial theorist is Achille Mbembe. One of the most notable aspects of his critiques of the postcolonial condition is his emphasis on deep historical conjunctures (Mbembe 2001: 68–70, 2010: 24–7). Mbembe's analysis of the postcolonial condition is deeply connected to his approach to the historical conditions which have produced these relationships. Here he relates not only to the recent colonial past, but also to global structural relations that tied cycles of violence and economic underdevelopment to previous relations to empire through the slave trade. Here, Mbembe's approach is in many ways similar to Hall's, and Rodney's before them. What emerges is that the postcolonial framework forces a strong critique of history as a discipline, and yet is deeply concerned with the historical forces that have constituted current inequalities. It therefore forces us to recognize a key aspect of the craft of the historian, which is the difference between present historical narratives and the 'facts' on which they are based; for the postcolonialist, these 'facts' certainly have shaped present relationships, independently of the narratives which have been later constructed around them.

Moreover, in their emphasis on culture as a space for the critique of imperial narratives, these thinkers clearly followed in the tradition of Cabral, Fanon and Rodney. The imperial narrative of a superior culture absorbing other peoples into a dominant historical force was challenged. This in turn undermined the traditional liberal view of history as Progress, within which this imperial narrative had positioned itself by positively valorizing the assumed advancements offered by the dominant historical force of European empires. Postcolonial theorists thus challenge the ideal of an objective narrative voice of the historical record, through the interposition of many other voices which have also contributed fundamentally to the historical process.

Taken in the round, this is a critique that challenges both perceptions of empire and forces us to think very hard about what historians are doing when they construct narratives. On whose authority are historians in fact acting? What sort of narratives are they constructing, and how do these in fact relate to the past? For postcolonialists, history remains a highly contested space; for historians, postcolonialists force a great deal of thought as to what it is that the historian actually does, and on what basis their narratives are constructed.

Opportunities for the historian: subaltern voices and other sources of history

As we have seen, postcolonialism involved from its inception a critique of the discipline of history. Theoretically, however, the most prominent postcolonial activists and writers such as those mentioned in the preceding section did not always take the lead in delineating how the postcolonial conjuncture might impact the practice of historians. With their political and anticolonial concerns, the work of people like Cabral and Rodney was much more directed at the impact of history on colonized peoples than at the practice of the historian itself.

The main impact of postcolonialism on the craft of the historian therefore had to wait until the emergence of the 'subaltern studies' school in the 1980s. The subaltern studies school took as their explicit focus the narratives of the colonized, and the question of how it was possible to reconstruct indigenous voices when they were systematically excluded from the colonial archive. These thinkers emerged especially in the context of the Indian subcontinent, and from a post-Marxist desire to give voice to the socially marginalized 'subalterns' – the vast majority of individuals in colonial societies – whose voices do not appear in 'traditional' historical records. This school was something in which Homi Bhabha was himself heavily involved; one of his most famous pieces from the 1980s was precisely about the ways in which colonially produced sources from India could be used to read against the grain of the text to unpick the histories of subaltern challenges to both colonial power and colonial narratives (Bhabha 1985).

This deconstructionist approach to colonial archives clearly drew heavily on the debates surrounding the work of Jacques Derrida, the leading figure of deconstructionism in the 1970s and 1980s. Derrida's work excoriated traditional narratives, and it was also deeply hostile to Eurocentric approaches, which explains how postcolonial thinkers came to have much sympathy with it. Indeed, in his last interview before his death, in August 2004, Derrida described how 'deconstruction is in general an enterprise which many have rightly considered to be as a gesture of defiance towards all forms of eurocentrism' (*Le Monde* 2004). A close reading of Derrida's work reveals just how fertile it was for postcolonial historians: Derrida refused the definitive authority of the written work, and the hierarchical distinction between oral and written discourses and evidence. In criticizing the English philosopher John Searle's famous attack on his theories, Derrida noted that Searle 'continues to think within a traditional opposition of speaking and writing' (Derrida 1988 [1977]: 55). By opening up the question of why oral discourses should be approached differently from written archives, Derrida opened the way for historians and postcolonial critics to approach the question of historical evidence in a different manner entirely.

As Derrida's work became more influential, the approaches and critiques of the postcolonial school of historians gathered pace. After Bhabha, the most influential champion of the subaltern studies school was the philosopher Gayatri Chakravorty Spivak. Spivak took as her task the theorization of subaltern voices within the historical narrative, and in her critique of history as traditionally practised she explicitly acknowledged her debt to Hayden White, and his analysis of archives as texts, the use of which involved the interaction of a present reader with those texts (Spivak 1996, 1999: 202–3). Archives could never be mere repositories of facts, but required the interaction of the present reader and the past event in the recreation of those 'facts' within a narrative. 'The past for the past's sake' was a fraudulent idea, and could only exist, as White himself had put it, as the sort of errant fantasy of a cultural necrophile.

However, the field of subaltern studies offers the possibility of going beyond the classic postmodernist critique of texts. Spivak's philosophical programme can indeed be read on one level as a demolition of the authority of the colonial archive, and she certainly has a concern with the role of deconstructionist analysis of archives as enabling subaltern voices to speak (Spivak 1999: 271). Nevertheless, there is also a positive contribution to knowledge-claims inherent in the subaltern studies programme that goes beyond the critique of textual sources and the limits of the archive. For one of Spivak's explicit concerns is not only the power of the archive to structure historical reconstructions, but also the question of what constitutes the authority of any source, and how such authority could be given to the sorts of sources that might reproduce the subaltern voice in historical narratives. What might subaltern voices look like in a historical narrative, and how can they be retrieved?

This remains a key concern of subaltern studies, and should have an important impact on the ways in which historians construct their source bases. This reconstruction of subaltern voices therefore opened up in time the question of sources, and what constitutes legitimate sources for the construction of historical narratives. It is here that postcolonial theory can offer both opportunities as well as critiques for historians, in allowing them to think broadly about diversifying their source bases and thereby incorporating voices often occluded from the reconstruction of the past, as well as in reading archival sources against the grain of those who produced them.

The question of legitimate sources had in fact been a major concern for historians of 'subaltern peoples' for some time. Indeed, on one level, Spivak's programme could be said to have merely been catching up with the craft of some pioneering historians of Africa such as Jan Vansina and Joseph C. Miller, who since the 1960s had been stressing the significance of diversifying the sources used to reconstruct African history. As specialists on Congo and Angola, both Vansina and Miller (and after them, Paul Lovejoy in his work on the kola trade linking the Ashanti and Hausa empires) drew heavily on oral histories that related to the period between 1500 and 1800, and Vansina wrote several books in which he stressed the validity of oral sources and their importance in capturing narratives and perspectives otherwise inaccessible from the historical record. Nevertheless, although some historians of Africa had been using these techniques for some time, the subaltern studies school added important theoretical ballast to this programme, and has helped to diversify the sorts of sources used to reconstruct the past, beyond oral histories to historical anthropology and historical linguistic techniques such as glottochronology.

Here it is useful to offer some concrete examples of the types of work that have been done in the past couple of decades that open the door to a diversifying source base available to historians. In African history, historical linguistics has become an increasingly significant school in the reconstruction of the distant past. Using the techniques of glottochronology, historical linguists analyse related African languages to pinpoint the historical era in which they diverged, drawing on the associations of key root words. This data can then be used to develop ideas related to subjects as diverse as the changes in production techniques and the emergence of rice farming in the Republic of Guinea (Fields-Black 2009), and to the history of the family and gender relations in Uganda (Stephens 2013). This field is still growing, but it shows the possibilities for accessing aspects of African history previously thought to be inaccessible. The validity of these sources is questioned by some, but there is no question that the theoretical terrain opened by postcolonialism and subaltern studies has made this sort of work much more possible, facilitating the emergence of richer subaltern narratives.

Historical anthropology is also a growing discipline, and one that meshes the work of the anthropologist with that of the historian. This is something that has grown in the study of many geographical areas. In the Americas, it was pioneered especially by the late Neil Whitehead in his study of Native American resistance to colonialism, and also more recently by Fernando Santos Granero in his study of slavery in pre-Columbian America. Meanwhile, anthropologists such as Rosalind Shaw and Nicolas Argenti have used anthropological techniques of analysis of contemporary rituals and the historical record to reconstruct histories of African societies during the slave trade era. Here, what is key in opening up channels for voices often repressed by traditional historical methods is the meshing of traditional sources 'from the past' with anthropological analysis of contemporary rituals and memories; this reproduces these voices, and although also controversial, it is a school of approach which is increasingly finding many followers.

Subaltern studies has therefore theorized a space in which historians can offer a richer diversity of evidence and techniques than was previously thought possible. The power of this theoretical school came from the rise of postmodernist thought and associated schools of deconstruction, allied to the concerns of postcolonial thinkers about the uses to which historical narratives had so often been put. For historians in the twenty-first century, these movements present a challenge, but they also offer a tremendous opportunity in allowing them to consider types of sources and source collections that would have been unimaginable a generation ago. In time, therefore, postcolonial approaches to history have come to influence not just the ways in which histories are written of decolonized peoples, but also how all historians can approach their craft.

Postcolonialism and history in practice: memorializing the slave trade

When it comes to the impact of postcolonial theory on the practice of the historian in the twenty-first century, some concrete examples are helpful. This chapter now concludes by looking at one particular case study: the discourse surrounding the 2007 commemorations of the bicentenary of the abolition of the Atlantic slave trade by the British parliament. By thinking with the lenses of postcolonialism and/or postmodernism, this example shows clearly the variable significance of this major historical event, depending on viewpoint, historical legacy and political orientation: key pointers emerge surrounding the construction of historical narratives and the ways in which they are received, pointers to shape how we think about the costs and benefits of postcolonialism to historians.

In Britain the bicentenary events of 2007 were highly resonant and deeply contested. The bicentenary itself became important through government intervention and because of social changes in the UK. Following the 2005 Gleneagles G8 conference and the professed desire of the Labour government of the UK to develop an ethical foreign policy and lift billions out of poverty through aid programmes, the bicentenary developed a political importance through government ministries. Money was channelled into the development of major new institutions such as the National Museum of Slavery in Liverpool; important exhibitions were held around the country, such as the exhibition on Olaudah Equiano in Birmingham; and a key national institution, the National Trust, devoted a special issue of its magazine to the connections between their properties and the history of the slave trade.

The extent of the national focus on the 1807 Abolition Act was conveyed very eloquently by one of the main specialists on the history of slavery at work in the UK, James Walvin:

> Few major public institutions failed to offer their own, distinctive or local
> interpretation of the events leading up to the Act of 1807 . . . Government

departments (and the prime minister and his deputy) took an active interest, and there was even a debate in parliament about the abolition of the slave trade. TV and radio disgorged countless programmes on abolition: the BBC also created a string of excellent websites. Discussions about abolition, essays and commentaries filled the press (including some of the tabloids), and bookshop windows were crowded with new publications devoted to the end of the slave trade.

(Walvin 2009: 140)

In the main national narrative, the bicentenary came to symbolize both the complex history of Britain's relationship to its colonies, and the contemporary legacy in the country as expressed through its multicultural cities. By focussing on abolition, policymakers hoped to develop a historical narrative for multicultural Britain that expressed the positive elements of colonialism – abolition and its moral crusade – rather than the history of slavery and forced labour itself. It was therefore very much a Whiggish narrative of history as progress, which as this chapter has shown represented precisely the sort of narrative which postcolonial theorists have challenged so strongly in recent decades.

Naturally, therefore, this narrative did not go uncontested. It is worth first of all reflecting on the differences in memorialization between Britain and the rest of the world in 2007. In Jamaica, as Paul Annie (2009) shows, parish councillors in St Elizabeth decided not to join in the commemorations. This highlighted the ambivalence with which these memories were treated in many parts of the diaspora, and the desire that this commemoration should not become a celebration. In Barbados, meanwhile, Karl Watson shows that the activities were very muted. The meaning of 1807 was very different in Barbados from in the UK – slavery was not abolished in 1807, and this was the fundamental point underlying the difference in how this bicentennial was remembered (Watson 2009). Meanwhile, in Ghana, as Manu Herbstein showed, those commemorations that took place were in fact commissioned by the British Council, and perpetuated a somewhat benign view of the history of the slave trade and of British involvement in it (Herbstein 2009).

In Britain, official commemorations were carefully choreographed. There was a memorial event held at Westminster Abbey on the anniversary of the parliamentary act itself, attended by the Archbishop of Canterbury, the Prime Minister and the Queen. Media discourse meanwhile focussed very heavily on the activities of William Wilberforce, the MP for Hull who drove through the Act of Abolition in Parliament; Wilberforce was the subject of countless articles, a play and even a biography by the subsequent Foreign Secretary of the UK, William Hague. This focus led to a key critique of the commemorations, that it had constituted a 'Wilberfest' (Waterton and Wilson 2009).

This 'Wilberfest' promoted what many scholars deride as a 'great man' view of history, and many black British groups in particular were disappointed by this emphasis. The focus on British abolitionists overshadowed the vital work of black abolitionists such as Olaudah Equiano and Ottobah Cugoano, whose writings were very important in showing the irreconcilable contradictions within the proslavery worldview; moreover, there was little mention of the fundamental role of slave resistance, particularly through the enormity of the Haitian Revolution. The focus on British abolitionists also obscured the wider importance of the slave trading system in which Britain had played such an active role prior to the Abolition Act, of the profits that had accrued in British financial institutions, and of the debt that Britain owed both to African nations and Africans in the Diaspora for the economic surpluses that facilitated its birth as the imperial superpower of the nineteenth century (as outlined in detail in Inikori 2000).

Such critiques chimed too with what organizing committees found when they came to try to develop alternative bicentennial events surrounding 2007. It quickly became apparent to organizing committees working on the 2007 events that the historical narrative regarding abolition was, to put it mildly, murky. Why, after all, concentrate on abolition? What of the other relevant facts, such as that for the whole century preceding 1807 Britain dominated the Atlantic slave trade, so that by 1800 one in five slaves from Africa was carried on a ship based in Liverpool? Why celebrate the act of parliament through which the slave trade was abolished and not commemorate the many acts between 1670 and 1800 which promoted the trade (Walvin 2009)? Moreover, the Abolition Act did not promote the end of slavery itself: slavery continued in the UK colonies until 1838, when £20 million was paid in compensation not to slaves, but to their owners. It was then replaced by indentured labourers from India, largely Gujarat, brought over to work for starvation wages in the West Indies and, later, East Africa. When the matter was given careful thought, therefore, it appeared that the main reason to concentrate on abolition was to promote a view of British history as benevolent and morally upright.

When we compare memories of the history of slavery and of the abolition of the Atlantic slave trade as they played out in 2007, many issues emerging from the relationship of postcolonialism to history are foregrounded. In the first place, there is the continued presence of narratives of hegemony and empire from official institutions, buttressed by traditional sources (including parliamentary and national archives). However, as the controversies surrounding the memorialization of these events shows, such narrative strategies and their purported objectivity no longer have the historical field to themselves. Alternative responses, critiques, and narratives of history were developed to challenge the 'Wilberfest', the 'great man' view of history, and the Whiggish narrative that lay at the heart of the national focus on the 1807 Abolition Act.

Subaltern voices, as we might call them, made repeated intrusions into the official narrative, through both official and unofficial channels. Of the latter, the starkest example was the interruption of the Westminster Abbey commemorative service by a black activist protesting at the history of slavery and its true economic, political and social impact both in Africa and the Caribbean; determined that the official narrative should not go uncontested, the activist's shouts and protests were heard by TV viewers around the world. Equally significantly as the complexity of these issues became clear even to curators of national institutions, some of the exhibitions around the country came to illustrate the ambiguity of slavery in the history and relative economic power of the UK and its former colonies. Even the official narrative thus frayed at the edges when confronted by the multiplicity of voices and evidence pointing to alternative narratives.

The events of 2007 therefore exemplify the impact of postcolonialism on our historical thinking. Traditional historical narratives still exist, promoting their purported objectivity. However, these are constantly undercut by subaltern voices, and many historians now seek to find ways to incorporate these voices within their narratives, aiming to provide accounts of the past that are both more balanced and more complex. Moreover, critical though *postcolonialists* are of historical narratives, they do not take the extreme view of texts and facts of some *postmodernists*: historical facts exist, they shape inequalities, and it is the narratives of these inequalities that are to be contested rather than the historical past itself. To postcolonialists, the past is extremely important as explaining the present: it is not to be theorized out of existence, but rather presented anew, with multiple voices instead of a singular dominant and pseudo-objective master narrative.

Such a balance cuts to the heart of what the leading postcolonial theorist and writer Patrick Chabal called the challenge to postcolonial rationality (Chabal 2012). For historians, postcolonialism challenges not so much the reality of the past as the terms on which it is discussed and analysed. Incorporating multiple voices offers an opportunity to historians in diversifying source bases and increasing the complexity of how we analyse the past, and how we learn about its relevance to the present. The ways in which this interplay is embodied in the future will surely determine to a large part how the discipline of history evolves in the twenty-first century.

Guide to further reading and online resources

There are some excellent primers on the relationship of postmodernism and history. See in particular Jenkins (1997), and for a defence of the historian's craft Evans (1997). Several important essays on the idea of scientific history – including a seminal text by Isaiah Berlin – are to be found in Dray (1966), while LaCapra (1985) is an influential work. In the field of postcolonialism, Bhabha (1991) and Spivak (1999) are key resources. Among the key texts discussed in this essay, the most important works to read are Fanon (1967), Cabral (1979) and Rodney (1972). One of the most influential works pushing for the opening up of new sources is Gilroy (1996), while the entire oeuvre of Stuart Hall has been enormously influential.

On the international memorialization of the bicentenary of the abolition of the transatlantic slave trade, see the excellent essays in the special edition of *Slavery and Abolition*, 30(2) (2009). The question of how the British public institutions responded to the events of 2007 is well treated in a number of interesting articles, such as those by Kerr-Ritchie (2008), Tibbles (2008) and Walvin (2009).

A vital online resource is the Legacies of British Slave-ownership project at University College London. This database traces the financial beneficiaries of abolition in the UK, and the impact of slave ownership on the British economic structure: www.ucl.ac.uk/lbs.

References

Adorno, Theodor and Horkheimer, Max (2002 [1944]) *Dialectic of Enlightenment*. Stanford, CA: Stanford University Press.

Annie, Paul (2009) "'Do You Remember the Days of Slav'ry?" Connecting the Present and the Past in Contemporary Jamaica', *Slavery and Abolition*, 29(2): 169–78.

Bhabha, Homi K. (1985) 'Signs Taken for Wonders: Questions of Ambivalence and Authority under a Tree outside Delhi, May 1817', *Critical Inquiry*, 12(1): 144–65.

Bhabha, Homi K. (1991) *The Location of Culture*. London: Routledge.

Butler, L.J. and Sarah Stockwell (eds) (2013) *The Winds of Change: Harold Macmillan and British Decolonization*. London: Palgrave Macmillan.

Cabral, Amilcar (1979) *Unity and Struggle*. New York: Monthly Review Press.

Chabal, Patrick (2012) *The End of Conceit: Western Rationality After Postcolonialism*. London: Zed Books.

Derrida, Jacques (1988 [1977]) *Limited Inc*, trans. Samuel Weber. Evanston, IL: Northwestern University Press.

Dray, William H. (ed.) (1966) *Philosophical Analysis and History*. New York: Harper & Row.

Evans, Richard (1997) *In Defence of History*. London: Granta Books.

Fanon, Frantz (1967) *Black Skins, White Masks*. New York: Grove Press.

Fields-Black, Edda (2009) *Deep Roots: Rice Farmers in West Africa and the African Diaspora*. Bloomington, IN: Indiana University Press.

Foucault, Michel (1977) *Language, Counter-Memory, Practice: Selected Essays and Interviews*. Oxford: Basil Blackwell.

Gilroy, Paul (1996) *The Black Atlantic: Modernity and Double Consciousness*. London: Routledge.

Hall, Stuart (1980) "Cultural Studies: Two Paradigms", *Media, Culture and Society* 2(1): 57–72.

Hall, Stuart (1997) *Representation: Cultural Representations and Signifying Practices*. London: Sage, in association with the Open University.

Herbstein, Manu (2009) 'Reflections in a Shattered Glass: The British Council's Celebrations of the Bicentenary of the 1807 Act for the Abolition of the Slave Trade in Ghana', *Slavery and Abolition* 30(2): 197–207.

Inikori, Joseph E. (2000) 'Africa and the Trans-Atlantic Slave Trade', in *Africa, vol. I: African History Before 1885*, ed. Toyin Falola. Durham, NC: Carolina Academic Press.

Jenkins, Keith (ed.) (1997) *The Postmodern History Reader*. London: Routledge.

Kerr-Ritchie, J.R. (2008) 'Reflections on the Bicentennial of the Abolition of the British Slave Trade', *Journal of African-American History* 93(4): 532–43

LaCapra, Dominick (1985) *History and Criticism*. Ithaca, NY: Cornell University Press.

Le Monde (19 August 2004): Interview with Jacques Derrida, 12–13.

Lévi-Strauss, Claude (1966) *The Savage Mind*. London: Weidenfeld & Nicolson.

Manji, Firoze and Fletcher Jr, Bill (eds) (2013) *Claim No Easy Victories: The Legacy of Amilcar Cabral*. Dakar: Codesria.

Marshall, H.E. (1905) *Our Island Story: A Child's History of England*. London: T.C. and E.C. Jack.

Mbembe, Achille (2001) *On the Postcolony*. Berkeley, CA: University of California Press.

Mbembe, Achille (2010) *Sortir de la Grande Nuit: Essai sur l'Afrique Décolonisée*. Paris: Éditions la Découverte.

Rodney, Walter (1972) *How Europe Underdeveloped Africa*. London/Dar-es-Salaam: Bogle Louverture.

Rorty, Richard (ed.) (1967) *The Linguistic Turn: Recent Essays in Philosophical Method*. Chicago: University of Chicago Press.

Spivak, Gayatri Chakravorty (1996) 'Subaltern Studies: Deconstructing Historiography', in Donna Landry and Gerald MacLean (eds), *The Spivak Reader: Selected Works of Gayatri Chakravorty Spivak*. New York: Routledge, 203–34.

Spivak, Gayatri Chakravorty (1999) *A Critique of Postcolonial Reason: Towards a History of the Vanishing Present*. Cambridge, MA: Harvard University Press.

Stephens, Rhiannon (2013) *A History of African Motherhood: The Case of Uganda, 700–1900*. Cambridge: Cambridge University Press.

Tibbles, Anthony (2008) *Facing Slavery's Past: The Bicentenary of the Abolition of the British Slave Trade*, *Slavery and Abolition* 29(2): 293–303.

Walvin, James (2009) 'The Slave Trade, Abolition and Public Memory', *Transactions of the Royal Historical Society (Sixth Series)* 19: 139–49.

Waterton, Emma and Wilson, Ross (2009) 'Talking the Talk: Policy, Popular and Media Responses to the Bicentenary of the Abolition of the Slave Trade Using the "Abolition Discourse"', *Discourse and Society* 20(3): 381–99.

Watson, Karl (2009) 'Barbados and the Bicentenary of the Abolition of the Slave Trade', *Slavery and Abolition* 29(2): 179–95.

White, Hayden (1975) *Metahistory: The Historical Imagination in Nineteenth-Century Europe*. Baltimore, MD: Johns Hopkins University Press.

Wright, Donald (1991) 'Requiem for the Use of Oral Tradition to Reconstruct the Precolonial History of the Lower Gambia', *History in Africa* 18: 399–408.

Zagorin, Perez (1999): 'History, the Referent, and Narrative: Reflections on Postmodernism Now', *History and Theory* 38(1): 1–24.

3 Sites of memory

Keir Reeves

This chapter assesses contemporary presentations of key historical sites, often typified by their commemorative significance, with an emphasis on contested and 'difficult' heritage locations. Such sites are often referred to as *lieux de mémoire* ('memory places') – a phrase which came to prominence in the 1990s through the work led by the French historian Pierre Nora. These sites are defined, Nora argues, by their complexity: 'At once natural and artificial, simple and ambiguous, concrete and abstract, they are *lieux* – places, sites, causes – in three senses – material, symbolic and functional' (Nora 1996: 14). Such sites of memory are important to historians because they represent the enduring physical places where the past is remembered, commemorated and constructed in the present day. Nora's concept is useful because it brings to the fore the importance of particular places in the collective memory of nations and social groups. For field-based historians and those interested in the public presentation of heritage, a particularly appealing aspect of the concept of *lieux de mémoire* is that it calls for an evaluation of memory sites that blends first-hand experience and scholarly understandings: the history associated with the site, and its official presentation, must be interpreted alongside the reception of the site by the visiting public. Accordingly, sites of memory are touchstones for the community (and historians) to connect with the past through a connection with place. These *lieux de mémoire* are, in effect, heritage places of encounter between present-day public and scholarly agendas, where meaningful experience emerges (or perhaps fails to emerge) through that encounter.

For Nora '[*l*]*ieux de mémoire* are there because there are no longer any *milieux de mémoire*, settings in which memory is a real part of everyday experience' (Nora 1996: 1). Nora's work forms part of the *nouvelle histoire* (new history) approach in France, which emphasizes the significance of cultural history and is linked to the influential Annales School of historiography. Along with the medievalist Emmanuel Le Roy Ladurie, Nora is the best-known exponent of the *nouvelle histoire*. Nora was the director of *Les Lieux de Mémoire* project, a vast collaborative project, the outcomes of which were published in French in seven volumes between 1984 and 1992. In English, Nora's introductory essay on the concept first appeared in the journal *Representations* in 1989, followed by a broad selection of essays from the project in the three-volume *Realms of Memory: The Construction of the French Past* (1996–8), with further essays appearing in *Rethinking France:*

Les Lieux de Mémoire (2001–10). A massive undertaking comprising contributions from well over one hundred influential French scholars, these volumes focused on the memories of the French nation-state as well as on the national character of France itself. For Nora these memories were found in sites that were physical locations, in symbolic emblems such as national flags, as well as in cultural practices such as national holidays (Nora 1989: 19).

For the purposes of this chapter, the idea of sites of memory is used as a conceptual tool to discuss global history. In doing so it is important to emphasize that the *Realms of Memory* project was specifically written as major longitudinal study of *French* history and society and developed out of the particular context of historical writing in and about that country in the mid-1980s and early 1990s. Nora and his contributors examined how key sites and practices embodied the cultural memories of the French nation, were associated in the didactic transmission of those memories, and had the ability to provoke emotional affect among the French about their collective past. These memorial sites were regarded as increasingly important in late twentieth-century French society as they appeared to embody national memory at a time when environments of real memory – *milieux de mémoire* – had faded away or completely disappeared. Nora very specifically identifies the 1970s – shortly before the *lieux de mémoire* project was conceived – as the key period when authentic collective memory died out in France, to be replaced by the didactic 'patrimonial' memory associated with these sites (Nora 2001: xi–xii; Schwarz 2010: 48–58). His project has been widely critiqued as representing a nostalgic desire for a coherent sense of French nationhood, and failing to embrace a more social history-oriented and pluralistic reading of French history. However, the concept of *lieux de mémoire* remains a potent conceptual tool for historians considering global sites of memory. Perhaps the abiding paradox of Nora's work is that while it was not intended as a patriotic celebration, but rather sought to explain sites of memory as active forces in French society, when read from a twenty-first-century global perspective the project *itself* has become something of a *lieu de mémoire*: a monument to a particular approach at a particular time.

For cultural historians and human geographers Nora's concept of *lieux de mémoire* is now a key reference point when discussing memory and commemoration, ranging far beyond the parameters of his original project. Appraising Nora as a case in point, Søren Kolstrup argues that sites of memory 'are crossroads. They are the points where space and time meet memory' (Kolstrup 1999: 115). Nora's central argument can readily be applied more broadly: according to David Morley and Kevin Robins, it is a symptom of our globalized era that 'with our lack of memory, we have to be content with *lieux de mémoire*, places which remind us of the past, of a (broken) memory' (Morley and Robins 1996: 87). The legacy (embraced or contested) of Nora's historical concept of *lieux de mémoire* is extensive when thinking about the significance of places and the meanings ascribed to sites and landscapes of memory and commemoration. Accordingly, Nora's influential work remains an ideal departure point for a discussion of historical sites of memory across the globe.

The rise of the academic field of memory studies has prompted the widespread observation that 'since the last decades of the twentieth century, Western Europe and North America have been living through a "memory boom"' (Blacker et al. 2013: 1). This observation is reinforced by the parallel surge in new historical museums opening across the world during the past three decades. Historian Jay Winter has observed that this trend is 'also a reflection of another facet of the development of the "memory business"' (Winter 1997; see also Fedor 2015). Although Nora explicitly emphasized French national memory, much of the historical research about *lieux de mémoire* is intimately associated with war remembrance across the world, particularly in relation to the First and Second World Wars (Frank Bongiorno, for instance, provides a close reading of Gallipoli in Turkey, a key site of First World War memory and a contested touchstone for Australian identity, elsewhere in this book). However, in this chapter the emphasis is on recent major commemorations at site-specific places across the globe. Global comparison shows that many sites of memory share similar remembrance narratives that have regional, national and international significance. Often natural features at sites of memory accentuate visitor responses to the past and augment the impact on visitors of places that are inextricably linked to tragedy and horror. Sites such as the Sari Club in the resort of Kuta on the Indonesian island of Bali, where terrorist bombings killed over 200 people in October 2002, or the 'Killing Fields' at Choeung Ek in Cambodia, recalling the extermination of more than a million people by the Khmer Rouge regime in the late 1970s, are indicative examples of what Maria Tumarkin (2005) has termed 'traumascapes'. Often these are sites associated with war or terrorism, but sites of memory can also be associated with other events more broadly termed 'difficult heritage' (Logan and Reeves 2009: 1–7). Unsurprisingly, the increasing attention to commemoration during the 'memory boom' since the 1990s has occurred simultaneously with an increased scholarly interest in landscape, 'stressing its role as both material and discursive mediator of cultural values' (Wylie 2007: 191).

Part of the appeal of sites of memory is that they often take on a symbolic life of their own. This is a process whereby sites associated with key historical events become heritage constructions of the past in the present day, sometimes in unanticipated and even unruly ways. William Logan and Laurajane Smith have more broadly noted the dualistic way that heritage is 'used in positive ways to give a sense of community to disparate groups and individuals or to create jobs' and also harnessed by governments 'in less benign ways to reshape public attitudes' (Smith and Logan 2008). Accordingly, the politics of site management and community identity directly influence the cultural marking and commemoration that have occurred. Or to put it bluntly, *history* is the study of what occurred in the past whereas *heritage* (often the dominant determinant of significance at sites of memory) is the perception of the past as conveyed in the present day.

This has particularly been the case over the centenary of the First World War, during which the full array of resources by former combatant nations has been deployed to commemorate key historical themes of the conflict as determined by those states. If we accept the assertion that people and heritage are relationally constituted then it follows that communities where war has occurred are inextricably linked to conflict sites. This is the premise for examining key sites of memory in the context of history, memory and public life. Many such sites spring to mind in this regard, and invite comparison – for instance the Hiroshima Peace Memorial in Japan that includes the 1997 UNESCO listed Hiroshima Atomic Bomb Dome (Logan and Reeves 2009: 3), the Changi Museum on the grounds of the former Allied prisoner of war camp in Singapore (Twomey 2007), and the sombre National Memorial Arboretum near Birmingham in Staffordshire, opened in 2001 as a site of remembrance for the armed and civil service personnel of the United Kingdom. Far from being fixed, unified or predictable, war memory (so often associated with sites of memory and commemoration) has often been described as fluid. Many scholars of commemoration have also called for a more dynamic conceptualization of remembering and forgetting also noting that the memory of war is subjective and selective, revealing a commemorative vocabulary that often conceals as much as it remembers (Thomson 1994; Sturken 1997; Hoskins and O'Loughlin 2007; Connerton 1989).

Landscape in itself can be described as 'the last witness' of conflicts (Stichelbaut and Cowley 2016: 3–4). Indeed for younger generations in particular the initial confrontation with the past through site visitation can be an emotional experience. Martin Gegner and Bart Ziino suggest that such heritage sites are now central to how past wars are interpreted in the present (Gegner and Ziino 2012, 2). This observation is consistent with Winter's assertion that remembrance, history and memory are 'braided together in the public domain' (Winter 2006: 6), and with other recent discussions regarding how sites of memory and the contested of their meaning reinforce the interplay between history, heritage, remembrance and specific locations (Bird et al. 2016: 6–7). There is therefore a need to consider the

Figure 3.1 Western Front, World War One Hill Sixty situated near Ypres.
Photograph courtesy of the author, 2013.

experiential physical geography of war heritage pilgrimage sites in conjunction with their historical associations. The sense of place and the connectedness to the topography drives much of the motivation for visiting key sites of memory.

A number of such sites deserve mention here. At Gallipoli, for instance, the Chunuk Bair New Zealand Memorial is the key historical marker for the Wellington Brigade, standing at the highpoint reached by the New Zealander soldiers who occupied the summit on 8 May 1915 (Pugsley 2008). The memorial features a vertical slit through which the sun shines on 8 May each year as a commemorative reminder. Elsewhere, the sands of Juno Beach in France (associated with the D-Day Normandy landings during the Second World War) serve as a rallying destination for those with an interest in Canadians at war. Here the Canadian Army achieved a difficult, albeit highly successful, beach landing (in the process sustaining many casualties) on 6 June 1944. Similarly, the Vieng Xay cave complex situated near Xam Neua in Houphan Province of northeastern Laos was the heavily bombed redoubt of the Pathet Laos (the Laos Communist Party) during the Vietnam War, and is now a site of memory for locals and tourists alike. Vieng Xay also serves as symbolic reminder of the emergence of the modern communist state of Laos (Stuart-Fox 1997). Pearl Harbor in Hawai'i, meanwhile, remains a site of memory for Americans and serves as an historical reminder of this unprovoked surprise attack by Japan on the American homeland on 7 December 1941, and the nation's consequential loss of isolationist innocence. Similarly, the undulating ground of Gettysburg, Pennsylvania – the site of the bloodiest battle of the American Civil War, which was also the most crucial victory of the northern Union over the southern Confederate forces – remains a touchstone of the social divisions and immense loss of life associated with this four-year conflict (1861–5). There are many other global examples, including the Ground Zero site at the former World Trade Center in New York and the still fluid *lieux de mémoire* in Paris, Brussels and London associated with more recent terrorist attacks.

It is important to note that for many sites of memory there is an associated traumatic memory for some of those who visit them. This usually surrounds the loss of a relative in conflict and the family memories that run across generations. The most influential articulation of this idea is Marianne Hirsch's notion of 'postmemory', a form of remembrance whereby 'those family stories . . . have come to assume a life of their own' (Hirsch 2008, 103, 2012: 29–54). Understanding this involves historians employing non-conventional techniques such as the 'act of gathering bits and pieces of the past, and joining them together in public', in the process deliberately entering the public domain to capture the complexities of what Jay Winter and Edward Sivan have called 'collective remembrance' (Winter and Sivan 1999: 6). A key example is the use of cinema to frame narratives around historical memory of war. Collective remembrance can also be explored through the careful investigation of sites of memory, consideration of the role of museums, and attention to the increasingly digital memories associated both with sites and museums.

As historian John Gillis (1996: 41–60) has observed, memory is as central to modern politics as politics is central to modern memory. The idea of *contested*

memory provides one way of explaining interpretations of the past and management of these sites in the present. Academic historians' narratives can sometimes
compete with each other, and with interventions by politicians and others, to
reframe conflicts in the context of shared experience. There is often particular
sensitivity over the pace and manner in which sites of conflict over time become
increasingly associated with peace and reconciliation. In practical terms this means
that heritage management and interpretation strategies for former sites of imprisonment, for example, are often intricately linked with political concerns that
revolve around culturally sensitive matters. Examples include contested interpretations of the concentration camp at Auschwitz-Birkenau, or of the role of Pacific
Islanders in the Pacific theatre of war during the Second World War (White 1995).
Government policies are also often crucial in the decision-making processes that
determine the official significance of particularly sensitive sites, and how they are
historically interpreted for heritage tourists.

Processes of 'transcendence' can also attach to memory sites. Transcendence
occurs when a site, or a place, assumes a level of significance out of proportion
with actual events associated with it. This occurs when a place becomes experienced
as an emotional metaphor, exemplar or intensified quintessence of a broader
human emotion, experience or aspiration. A sense of unfamiliarity can be associated
with this process (which shares some interesting parallels with Hirsch's notion
of postmemory). Robben Island off the coast of Cape Town for instance – the site
where Nelson Mandela and other African National Congress activists were
imprisoned – is now almost universally understood as a reviled former bastion of
the oppressive apartheid regime. Its transformation into a site of resistance
memory mirrors the dramatic changes that have occurred in South African society
since 1990. One of his key roles of the site in its post-apartheid incarnation as a
site of memory has been to record the memories of former prisoners, and a key
objective of this oral history project has been to preserve the memory of the
freedom struggle. Former prisoners working at the site as guides for visitors
suggested the possibility that this activity might offer for them some form of
therapeutic benefit; this suggestion, though, was itself therapeutic for visitors
to the site seeking a positive story of forward progress, even if it was seldom the
reality for their guides (Colvin 2003). This was a trend Myra Shackley observed
as early as 1999, commenting that 'commodification of the island and its tragic
past threatens to "trivialise the experience"' (Shackley 1999: 361). A similar
process of contested remembering and memorialization takes place at many
other global sites of memory.

Reading sites of memory

Arguably there is a national, often government- and community-driven, need for
examples of transcendence. Wartime examples are manifold – to paraphrase
historian Ken Inglis's observation, there are thousands of such 'sacred places' in
Australia alone (Inglis 1999). Shrines; war memorials; battle sites; cemeteries:
the list is long. Indeed, all are inextricably associated with personal and collective

commitment, with sacrifice, and with death. So why is it that some monuments are more resonant than others, capturing an imagination – or longing – that spans generations, imbued not only with the efforts and sacrifice at a particular time or place, but also with the bitter knowledge and lost aspirations of entire conflicts? Paradoxically the act of remembrance and memorialization of major wartime conflicts at key sites is also a process of *forgetting* the events of other wartime conflicts and locations that are no longer observed, to some extent because they are displaced by these other, more compelling memories. How else do we explain and attribute varying degrees of significance to different conflicts, all of which are associated with death? A key example here is the increasing amount of Australian war heritage visitation to the remote regional city of Darwin, fuelled by the powerful lingering memories of the Japanese bombing of Australia's northern outpost during a mid-February morning in 1942 (Roberts and Young 2008). Heavy bombers escorted by Zero fighters left some 243 people dead and several hundred more were wounded as the Japanese sought to neutralize Darwin as part of their preparation to invade the nearby Southeast Asian island of Timor (in the process cutting Australia off from its allies as part of its wider strategy of war in the Pacific). While casualties were heavy, the massive attack also destroyed many civil and military buildings.

The legacy of the bombing remains powerful throughout Australia's Northern Territory. Each year on Anzac Day (25 April) in the early hours of the morning a convoy of cars travels to the Adelaide River war cemetery – an isolated community one hour's drive to the south of Darwin – where a crowd of approximately two thousand people gather. Equally large crowds gather on the Esplanade, and throughout Bicentennial Park, in Darwin, facing the direction from where the Japanese aircraft would have appeared over the horizon on the day of the attack. At Adelaide River, like Darwin, the key historical point of reference in war commemoration and pilgrimage remains the bombing. It serves as an enduring reminder that Australia was attacked and also that the city of Darwin was largely destroyed (*Age*, 20 February 1942). The potency of the bombing legacy at Adelaide River is particularly powerful as the memorialization is concentrated upon a war cemetery and on those who died.

The main significance of the bombing of Darwin to those visiting it as a Second World War destination is not only the universal theme of remembering the dead but also the isolated situation in which Australia found itself in during 1942. More subtly, other themes have emerged, highlighting how the passing of time tends to enable an increased emphasis on the message of peace and greater willingness to present alternative viewpoints. Today, Darwin is a site of memory for more than one community. It is a pilgrimage destination for American and Japanese war heritage pilgrims as well as a destination for Australians. The Japanese visitors follow their own war heritage trails and their presence reminds us that the process of commemoration is relevant for both aggressors and victims, and for both victors and losers.

This argument about sense of place in Darwin (and other war pilgrimage sites) can be understood on different levels. Inglis's pioneering discussion of place concentrated on the location of memorial sites within towns and designated precincts, and on how they reminded people not only of war but also shaped their perception of the place they were visiting. For Darwin the bombing not only serves as a historical marker for the war but also as a reminder in the present day of the enduring existence of the city itself – a city situated at such a geographical remove from the rest of the Australian population that its viability has not always been certain. When the bombing is invoked, thoughts turn not only to death and to the real or imagined invasion of Australia, but also to thoughts of Darwin as an enduring place that should be, and is, remembered by the rest of the Australian community in the present day as a place of destruction and resilience. In a sense, then, the bombing serves as a historical memory that reminds the wider Australian community of Darwin's continuing relevance as the remote northern outpost of the nation in the present day. Moreover the legacy of the bombing and its associated sites can also be viewed in the layout of the Cenotaph and other sites of commemoration situated on the Esplanade and other commemorative and memorial structures located throughout the park. Perhaps in part due to the organic nature of the process of memorialization and remembrance in Darwin there has not been criticism from the local community regarding potential disfranchisement from their history and the rewriting of that history as heritage.

Mathematics may be an exact science but when considering war memory and its commemoration the act of analysing and contextualizing numbers is inevitably to some extent subjective, as there are no straightforward comparative measures of suffering or loss. The classical granite and sandstone memorial erected in Melbourne by members of the Fifth Contingent, Victorian Mounted Rifles to their comrades who fell in the service of the British Empire in South Africa during the 1899–1902 conflict there displays 54 names of Victorian Mounted Rifles casualties. The memorial is a thing of elegance, designed by the Melbourne architect G. de Lacey Evans. But despite its prominent location it is a forlorn memorial, overlooked by passing commuters. By way of contrast, the Darwin Cenotaph, situated on the Esplanade in the designated government precinct, lists just 52 casualties of the First World War, two fewer than the Victorian Mounted Rifles memorial. On Anzac Day, Melbourne's marching thousands pass the 54 names on the Victorian Mounted Rifle's memorial with barely a glance. Yet in Darwin thousands regularly close on the Cenotaph, with its 52 names, at the dawn service and later as the prelude to the Anzac Day march, honouring their sacrifice.

Comparing the Boer War Cenotaph in Melbourne with Darwin's Second World War commemoration highlights the wider point that the manner in which these deaths are remembered is to a large extent determined by the place where they occurred. The experience of the Second World War, particularly the bombing, is lodged deeply in the public memory of the Darwin community. Over time, Australian memory practices have come to emphasize the role of Darwin in national myth and legend as the place where the Australian mainland was attacked and the Asia-Pacific theatre of the Second World War arrived on the nation's doorstep. In Darwin, various conflicts over time have been rolled into one homogenized Anzac memory. These are the powerful drivers of the significance

Figure 3.2 Anzac Day crowds surrounding the Cenotaph on the Esplanade, Darwin, 2011. Photograph courtesy of the author, 2011.

of Darwin as a pilgrimage destination and as a touchstone for Australians' understanding of that conflict in the present day.

Since the 1980s, memory work about war has been methodologically driven by a desire to better understand the traumatic conflicts of the twentieth century. This scholarship evaluates the ways in which the public presentation of key sites, and the emotional *raison d'être* for travelling to them, has shifted over time, in relation both to the perceived historical meaning and the political significance of these sites. In a sense this trend echoes Roland Barthes' observation that 'perhaps we have an invincible resistance to believing in the past, in History, except in the form of a myth' (Barthes 1981: 87–88). In understanding the impress of war during the twentieth century it is necessary for historians and others to engage with the recent historiographical commemoration of war. This process necessarily considers the intangible heritage associated with the process of remembering major conflicts such as the First and Second World Wars.

Examples of commemorative events such as the annual services at the British National Memorial Arboretum in Staffordshire provide one way of providing present day context for thinking about contested or contrasting interpretations of sites of memory. For some these events are poignant commemorations of war which bring the nation together, while for others they are seen at worst as militaristic and nationalistic ceremonies that implicitly revel in the tragedy and loss associated with war. Commemorative events at locations such as the Staffordshire Arboretum can be interpreted as aiming to establish a form of 'fictive kinship'

Figure 3.3 States of Jersey, Liberation Day, 2013. Photograph courtesy of the
author, 2013.

among those who attend them. This describes the bond between 'a collective of
individuals who have come together to memorialize and commemorate', among
whom a sense of kinship is formed, 'because they share a common experience,
either as next of kin or as veteran comrades of those who were killed', or because
they enter into strong identification with those people (Winter 2006; Bird et al.
2016: 5). The challenge for sustained remembrance of war is not so much
for those who were witnesses to events, such as comrades and next of kin, but
instead 'whether the commemorative ritual is adopted by the next generation' or
generations (Bird et al. 2016: 5).

Jersey Liberation Day in the British Channel Islands likewise serves as an
exemplar of the potency of enduring historical narratives – in this case the experience of the German occupation and subsequent liberation during the Second
World War – being reinforced in the present day at key sites of memory throughout the island. As I witnessed in 2013, the commemoration of liberation is a major
production, with Union Jack flags being flown and the States of Jersey Flag being
raised in the square now named Liberation Square, where the 1945 arrival of
British forces is re-enacted on a massive scale in front of thousands of people. To
an outsider such as myself the event had a Ruritanian flavour to it, with oranges
and sweets distributed to the crowd by local Sea Scouts. For some scholars the
obvious, and in many respects understandable, response would be to dismiss
the whole show as state-sanctioned nostalgia and constructed history. I would
suggest, however, that while this was indeed the case, there was also a heartfelt
popular support for the event as a cultural memory of the Second World War,
and that this sincere expression tells us a good deal that is valuable about
popular consciousness. This example of British identity as mobilized through war

commemoration (in this case the liberation of St Helier from Nazi occupation) is also consistent with historian Jenny Macleod's broader discussion of Britishness and commemoration which highlights the key role of war memorials for articulations of regional and national identities in Britain (Macleod 2013).

While Darwin in Australia provided a single site for the pilgrimages and memories of different communities, Jersey has developed parallel, and potentially competing, sites of memory. Elsewhere, on the same day as the Liberation Square celebrations, a more sombre event was held at the island's crematorium. The location was chosen as it 'commemorated the 101 forced and slave workers who died in the island and were buried in this location during the Occupation' (Carr 2014: 218). There is a contested history and heritage associated with Jersey that reveals much about the politics of remembering and indeed the forgetting of the occupation (Carr 2014: 193–238). Jersey was caught up in the complex politics that surrounded the fate of those interned as prisoners of war by the Nazis in the Channel Islands. Those who suffered included thousands of locals, most of whom had committed no crime, and some who were deported, including Eastern European forced and slave labourers, Spanish freedom fighters, North Africans and Jews (Carr 2014: 252). At the commemorative ceremony I witnessed the poignancy of the occasion was clear; indeed, the father of one of the organizers had fought against fascism during the Spanish Civil War. Against this backdrop in the second decade of the twenty-first century, some 75 years after those events, it nonetheless made sense to watch an elderly Spaniard laying a wreath draped in a Spanish flag and then impulsively shouting 'Viva la Republica!' to the crowd. The implications of this for understanding Jersey as a site of memory is that the visceral connection to place, along with the associations of those who were witnesses to events there, underscores the significance of the site, and the power of the memory of the occupation to resonate with the community in the present day.

The relationship between history and the public presentation of heritage is not always easy, particularly in relation to wars and conflicts in the recent past. An example of a site of memory from a later conflict is Anlong Veng in North Western Cambodia on the Dângrêk escarpment, a town that is the location of a redoubt of the former Khmer Rouge and also the site of a 'house museum' for Ta Mok, a senior figure in Pol Pot's notorious regime, known as 'the butcher' for his brutality, and the person who ultimately overthrew Pol Pot in April 1998. For visitors to the site a pressing question when considering the heritage of the region is the place of the house museum as a heritage site at a time when the when the genocide in Cambodia, and its pressing social, economical and political legacy, remain only very inadequately addressed (Long and Reeves 2009). One research field visit to Anlong Veng led to the troubling discovery that the guides at the house were former child soldiers of the Khmer Rouge. Another guide at the site told Holocaust studies researcher Mark Baker that he 'liked [Ta Mok] because he and Pol Pot were the ones who defended our nation and tried to liberate it' (*Age*, 3 September 2003). Indeed, as Brendan Luyt has highlighted in relation to Nora's concept of *lieux de mémoire*, this site undoubtedly helps its visitors to

Figure 3.4 Ta Mok's House Museum, Anlong Veng, Cambodia. Photograph
      courtesy of the author, 2005.

remember the past – but whom does it help, and to remember what (Luyt 2015: 1956–7)? Sometimes when trying to commemorate a site associated with difficult heritage, such as the Cambodian genocide, the impulse to conserve the past can be construed as an affront to the memory of the victims. A contentious conclusion might be that some historic places are better forgotten than interpreted as sites of memory.

Conclusion

Even when they are not read as nostalgic *lieux de mémoire*, physical sites remain central to popular and state-sanctioned memory. The processes of historical commemoration and remembrance (as well as forgetting or omission) are often best understood with regard to specific sites associated with conflict or otherwise 'difficult' heritage locations. In this chapter, a diverse range of historically significant places have been discussed, in order to suggest how sites of memory are meaningful both for historians and for the wider public. In closing it is worth re-emphasizing that the histories of sites of memory do not exist in a vacuum. The meanings attached to these places are constantly evolving, albeit not always in radically new ways, and the sites themselves sit within wider material and discursive landscapes that are also subject to change. These meanings are shaped by various forces and constituencies, including government officials, scholars, professional and volunteer site interpreters, families of historical actors and visitors themselves, from the victorious and the defeated sides in these conflicts. These sites are situated within diverse physical contexts, for instance sometimes surrounded by older monuments or by competing sites of memory. Scholars seeking to understand these settings traverse these landscapes and reflect on what they see. An especially productive way to get to grips with the presence of the past in the present is to follow suit, making one's own first-hand observations and testing existing scholarship against what one encounters. As the great English historian R. H. Tawney once opined, 'good historians need strong boots'.

Guide to further reading and online resources

Further reading on sites of memory should start with the work of Nora and his collaborators. Nora (1989) is the best place to start: this is based on his conceptual introduction to the *Lieux de mémoire* project. The essays in the two multi-volume translation series *Realms of Memory and Rethinking France* (both listed below) both cover a vast range of topics in French history, culture and topography, relating to all periods: readers should sample according to taste. For helpful discussions of Nora see Wood (1994), Carrier (2000) and Schwarz (2010).

On the memory and commemoration of sites of twentieth-century warfare, see Jager and Mitter (2007), Williams (2007), Winter (1995), and Sørensen and Dacia Viejo-Rose (2015). On trauma and 'difficult pasts' see Logan and Reeves (2009) and Tumarkin (2005). Laing and Frost (2017) provides an invaluable and wide range of recent essays on the relationship between travel, commemoration and sites of memory.

There are a number of online resources offering material relevant to the issues discussed in this chapter. A useful and wide-ranging comparative website on sites of memory is: www.sites-of-memory.de.

On the commemoration of the bombing of Darwin: www.defenceofdarwin. nt.gov.au.

The Cambodian Killing Fields Museum: www.killingfieldsmuseum.com.

Genocide Watch (for more information about the Cambodian genocide, as well as on other atrocities): www.genocidewatch.com.

The UK National Memorial Arboretum in Staffordshire: www.thenma.org.uk.

References

Barthes, Roland (1981) *Camera Lucida*. New York: Hill and Wang.

Bird, Geoff, Keir Reeves and Birger Stichelbaut (2016) 'Introduction: Landscape, Commemoration and Heritage' in Keir Reeves, Geoffrey R. Bird, Laura James, Birger Stichelbaut and Jean Bourgeois (eds), *Battlefield Events Landscape, Commemoration and Heritage*. London: Routledge.

Blacker, Uilleam Alexander Etkind and Julie Fedor (2013) *Memory and Theory in Eastern Europe*. New York: Palgrave Macmillan.

Carr, Gilly (2014) 'The Politics of Memory on Liberation Day', in *Legacies of Occupation: Heritage, Memory and Archaeology in the Channel Islands.* London: Springer.

Carrier, Peter (2000) 'Places, Politics and the Archiving of Contemporary Memory in Pierre Norra's *Les Lieux de Mémoire*', in Susannah Radstone (ed.), *Memory and Methodology.* New York: Berg.

Colvin, Christopher (2003) '"Brothers and Sisters, Do Not Be Afraid of Me": Trauma, History and the Therapeutic Imagination in the New South Africa', in Katherine Hodgkin and Susannah Radstone (eds), *Memory, History, Nation: Contested Pasts.* New York: Routledge.

Connerton, Paul (1989) *How Societies Remember.* Cambridge: Cambridge University Press.

Fedor, Julie (2015) 'War Museums and Memory Wars in Contemporary Poland', in *Blackwell Companion to Heritage.* London: Blackwell.

Gegner, Martin and Bart Ziino (2012) *Heritage and War.* London: Routledge.

Gillis, John R. (1996) *Commemorations: The Politics of National Identity.* Princeton, NJ: Princeton University Press.

Hirsch, Marianne (2008) 'The Generation of Postmemory', *Poetics Today* 29: 1.

Hirsch, Marianne (2012) *The Generation of Postmemory: Writing and Visual Culture After the Holocaust.* New York: Columbia University Press.

Hoskins, Andrew, and Ben O'Loughlin (2007) *Television and Terror: Conflicting Times and the Crisis of News Discourse.* Basingstoke: Palgrave Macmillan.

Inglis, Ken (1999) *Sacred Places: War Memorials in the Australian Landscape.* Carlton South: Miegunyah Press.

Jager, Sheila Miyoshi, and Rana Mitter (2007) *Ruptured Histories: War, Memory, and the Post-Cold War in Asia.* Cambridge, MA: Harvard University Press.

Kolstrup, Søren (1999) '*Wings of Desire*: Space, Memory and Identity', *O.V.A. Danish Journal of Film Studies* 8: 115–24.

Laing, Jennifer and Warwick Frost (2017) *Commemorative Events: Memory, Identities, Conflict.* London: Routledge.

Logan, William and Keir Reeves (eds) (2009) *Places of Pain and Shame: Dealing With 'Difficult' Heritage.* London: Routledge.

Long, Colin and Reeves, Keir (2009) 'Healing the Wounds: Heritage Practice at Toul Sleng and Choeung Ek, Cambodia', in *Places of Pain and Shame: Dealing With 'Difficult' Heritage.* London: Routledge.

Luyt, Brendan (2015) 'Wikipedia, Collective Memory, and the Vietnam War', *Journal of the Association for Information Science and Technology*, 67(8) 1956–61.

Macleod, Jenny (2013) 'Britishness and Commemoration: National Memorials to the First World War in Britain and Ireland', *Journal of Contemporary History*, 48(4) 647–5.

Morley, David and Kevin Robins (1996) *Spaces of Identity: Global Media, Electronic Landscapes and Cultural Boundaries.* London: Routledge.

Nora, Pierre (1989) 'Between Memory and History: Les Lieux de Memoire', *Representations* 26: 7–24.

Nora, Pierre (1996) *Realms of Memory: The Construction of the French Past. I: Conflicts and Divisions*, ed. Lawrence D. Kritzman, trans. Arthur Goldhammer. New York: Columbia University Press.

Nora, Pierre (1997) *Realms of Memory: The Construction of the French Past. II: Traditions*, ed. Lawrence D. Kritzman, trans. Arthur Goldhammer. New York: Columbia University Press.

Nora, Pierre (1998) *Realms of Memory: The Construction of the French Past. III: Symbols*, ed. Lawrence D. Kritzman, trans. Arthur Goldhammer. New York: Columbia University Press.

Nora, Pierre (2001) 'General Introduction', in *Rethinking France* I: vii–xxii.

Nora, Pierre (2001–10) *Rethinking France: Les lieux de mémoire*, 4 vols, trans. Mary Trouille and David P. Jordan. Chicago: University of Chicago Press.

Pugsley, Christopher (1998) *Gallipoli: The New Zealand Story*. Auckland: Reed Publishing.

Roberts, Julie and Martin Young (2008) 'Transience, Memory and Induced Amnesia: The Re-imagining of Darwin', *Journal of Australian Studies* 32(1) 51–62.

Schwarz, Bill (2010) 'Memory, Temporality and Modernity: Les *lieux de mémoire*', in Susannah Radstone and Bill Schwarz (eds), *Memory: Histories, Theories, Debates*. New York: Fordham University Press.

Shackley, Myra (2001) 'Potential Futures for Robben Island: Shrine, Museum or Theme Park?', *International Journal of Heritage Studies* 7(4) 355–63

Smith, Laurajane and William Logan (2008) 'Series Introduction', in Laurajane Smith and Natsuko Akagawa (eds), *Intangible Heritage*. London: Routledge, xii–xiii.

Sørensen, Marie-Louise, and Dacia Viejo-Rose (eds) (2015) *War and Cultural Heritage: Biographies of Place*. Cambridge: Cambridge University Press.

Stichelbaut, Birger and David Cowley (eds) (2016) *Conflict Landscapes and Archaeology from Above*. Farnham: Ashgate.

Stuart-Fox, Martin (1997) *A History of Laos*. Cambridge, Cambridge University Press.

Sturken, Marita (1997) *Tangled Memories: The Vietnam War, the AIDS Epidemic, and the Politics of Remembering*. Berkeley, CA: University of California Press.

Thomson, Alistair (1994) *Anzac Memories: Living with the Legend*. Oxford: Oxford University Press.

Tumarkin, Maria (2005) *Traumascapes*. Carlton, VIC: Melbourne University Press.

Twomey, Christina (2007) *Australia's Forgotten Prisoners: Civilians Interned by the Japanese in World War Two*. Melbourne: Cambridge University Press.

White, Geoffrey M. (1995) 'World War II, Fifty Years After: Remembering Guadalcanal: National Identity and Transnational Memory-Making', *Public Culture*, 7(3) 529–55.

Williams, Paul (2007) *Memorial Museums: The Global Rush to Commemorate Atrocities*. New York: Berg.

Winter, Jay (1995) *Sites of Memory, Sites of Mourning: The Great War in European Cultural History*. Cambridge: Cambridge University Press.

Winter, Jay (1997) Review of Pierre Nora (ed.), *Realms of Memory: Rethinking the French Past. I: Conflicts and Divisions*. H-France, H-Net Reviews, www.h-net.org/reviews/showrev.php?id=1354.

Winter, Jay (2006) *Remembering War: The Great War Between Memory and History in the Twentieth Century*. New Haven, CT: Yale University Press.

Winter, Jay, and Edward Sivan (eds) (1999) *War and Remembrance in the Twentieth Century*. Cambridge, Cambridge University Press.

Wood, Nancy (1994) 'Memory's Remains: Les Lieux de Mémoire', *History and Memory* 6: 123–49.

Wylie, John (2007) *Landscape*. London: Routledge.

4   Race, migration and national origins

Peter Heather

In the later nineteenth century, several strands of academic enquiry came together to make it possible, for the first time, to generate a coherent vision of the deep European past. The origins of this astonishing intellectual achievement lay in linguistics, but the rise of archaeology as a scientific discipline played an equally central role, and, from the start, the whole enterprise had intimate links to controversial political agendas. The consequences for twentieth-century European and even world history proved colossal, and the legacy of this simultaneously creative, yet toxic, moment in intellectual history continues to exercise profound influence upon both academic and political debate in the Europe of today.

Nationalism and knowledge

The later eighteenth and early nineteenth centuries were a pioneering era in the field of linguistics, when philology – the study of ancient texts and languages – developed a new, more comparative orientation. This enabled scholars to use phonological and morphological systems, syntax and the lexicon both to classify contemporary European languages into related groups, and to construct a history of their interrelationships. The interest was always diachronic: with a strong emphasis on working out the nature of the supposed 'original' language from which the related groupings descended, working backwards from its modern representatives. Much of the original work was undertaken by scholars interested in the family of Germanic languages (German, Dutch, the Scandinavian languages, English, etc.), with the Grimm brothers of fairy-tale fame, Jacob (1785–1863) and Wilhelm (1786–1859), playing a starring role. They successfully demonstrated that the operation of a sequence of systematic sound shifts explained both the initial separation of Germanic from other Indo-European languages, and much of the observable divergence between existing branches of the Germanic language family itself (Grimm's first and second sound shifts). The elder, Jacob, published a major work on German Grammar in 1822, and, together, the brothers began work on the first dictionary of the German language: the *Deutches Wörterbuch* (Hettinga 2001). Volume one (covering 'A' to the first part of 'F') was published in 1838, but the project took until 1960 to complete, with the full printed edition weighing in at an astonishing 84 kilogrammes. The brothers Grimm are only the

best-remembered of a whole group of intellectuals, however, working simultaneously on the origins and development of German, and others were quick to extend
the same methods to different language families. Worth particular notice (for
reasons we will come to a minute) is the Bohemian scholar Pavel Jozef Šafárik
who studied linguistic methods at Jena, before applying them to his native Slavic,
publishing a ground-breaking *Geschichte der slawischen Sprache und Literatur* in
1826 (Lehmann 1962; Anttila 1989; Janda and Joseph 2004).

For many scholars, this was not purely an academic enterprise. It was supposed
that each language grouping had begun with its own specific human community,
by whom it was spoken. But identifying putative historical human groupings on
the basis of language in the decades either side of 1800 was bound to have at least
potential political connotations within a general context where multi-national
Habsburg, Ottoman and Russian Empires still dominated Central and Eastern
Europe. Suggesting that humanity had once been alternatively ordered on the
basis of language groupings was potentially subversive of this existing order,
whose current frailties only added impetus to the enterprise. The enquiries of
the Grimm brothers were originally prompted by Napoleon's destruction of the
Holy Roman Empire, and developing senses of Slavic linguistic identity quickly
threatened to make the Turkish sick man of Europe feel a great deal worse. For
linguistics had managed to show that 'national', language-based communities
were much older than many existing political structures, and, for many, 'older'
carried a strong inherent sense of 'more fundamental' and hence 'more legitimate'.

Once the initial linguistic research had allowed an alternative, language-based,
political order to be envisaged, moreover, supportive research was undertaken in
a whole series of other fields to identify additional manifestations of the ancient
unities that had emerged from all the linguistic detective work. Again, the Grimm
brothers are representative. They are famous for their collection of folk tales,
but, in the brothers' opinion, these were unquestionably *German* folk tales. 'Folk'
translates the German word *Volk*, meaning 'people', and, for the Grimm brothers,
the oral culture of the people – as opposed to the artificial, learned culture of the
intellectual elite – preserved kernels of ancient, shared mythologies and beliefs
that had formed the bedrock of ancient German culture. Much of their activity
was devoted to collection, but the brothers always edited what they collected
to bring out what they considered to be 'ancient' and 'essentially German' (Tatar
1987, 2004; Zipes 2002).

Their methods never won universal academic consensus, but the fundamental
claim took a strong general hold. Linguistics had identified a European antiquity,
a world of independent political units based on shared languages and other cultural
elements, which was very different in its ordering from the present day, and
this sponsored a culture-rush to explore other dimensions of the same ancient
cultural strata, even if they had to be partly, or completely invented. Folk tales, folk
music, folk dances, folk costumes were all grist for the mill, with initial collection
being followed by more and less aggressive 'editing' processes to identify and bring
out what reflected that crucially important ancient unity. At its most blatant, the
great Norwegian composer, Edward Grieg (1843–1907), not only used folk tunes

in his compositions, but was encouraged to seek the quintessential spirit of Norwegian-ness in musical form (Grimley 2006). To the modern eye, all this can seem very strange: Grieg was a fabulously talented composer and pianist who happened to live in Norway. But he was composing in the era when Norway was working its way towards political independence from the union with Sweden (finally granted in 1905), and, in this context, 'rediscovering' a supposedly underlying and unifying national culture carried enormous significance. And Norway, of course, was not alone. Recovering supposedly ancient tradition to justify present political claims rapidly became a pan-European obsession.

What all this reflects, and what is sometimes hard now to grasp, is the quasi-religious fervour that the different nineteenth-century national projects managed to generate among significant elements of their target audiences. Possessing a distinct, and at least arguably 'ancient', culture was held to validate current, nationalist political claims. In a first flourishing of identity politics, the non-national political order of dynastically imperial Central and Eastern Europe could be portrayed as a later imposition that had bent the older, more legitimate and hence more 'correct' order of national communities – based on deep-rooted linguistic and cultural commonalities – out of shape. 'Collecting' and 'purifying' were the key scholarly activities, and the phenomenon spread right across Europe. In the 1830s, for instance, it was decided that it was necessary to codify – and hence distinguish as unique – the Croatian language, and, in the 1840s, despite his training at Jena and original work in German, Šafárik took the deliberate decision henceforth to publish only in his native Czech (Dolukhanov 1996). This was also the era in which many of the great, collective academic projects were initiated, which aimed to provide critical editions of all the historical texts – histories, chronicles, charters, law codes – relevant to a particular nation's early history. The great Monumenta Germaniae Historica project – initiated in 1819 under the motto *Sanctus amor patriae dat animum*: 'Holy love for the fatherland gives the spirit' – provided the model with separate series dealing with ancient histories and letters, laws, and charters. It was copied later in the century by intellectuals in Poland, Bohemia, and many other countries besides (Knowles 1960; Iggers 1983).[1]

It was also in this specific, highly charged cultural context, where the past was already being mobilised to support contemporary political agendas, that scientific archaeology first emerged as an academic discipline. An interest in antiquities, and the realisation that they could sometimes be unearthed by digging had, of course, much older roots. Already in the fifteenth and sixteenth centuries, humanist Popes and other patrons were commissioning enterprising excavators to hunt through the ruins of Nero's Domus Aurea and other known villa sites in the vicinity of Rome for classical statues. The landed gentry of eighteenth-century England, likewise, would occasionally go for picnics to watch their gardeners dig out Bronze Age burial mounds, and establish local museums to display the results (Bahn 2014; Renfrew and Bahn 2015). But on the back of a series of intellectual revolutions in geology, which demonstrated that rock strata had been formed sequentially, so that, generally speaking, the deeper you dug, the further back in time you were going (the same quantum leap of understanding that underlay Darwin's theory of evolution), archaeological investigation slowly transformed itself in the mid-to-late nineteenth century from treasure-hunting pastime of the rich into a sustained, analytical attempt to reconstruct the past.

As material began to be collected in much larger quantities, it rapidly became apparent that the items being recovered – at this point largely pottery – could sometimes be grouped together. Pottery of the same or closely related types was often demonstrably clustered both geographically and, thanks to developing understandings of the meaning of stratification, chronologically in particular European localities. Discovery of this patterning was largely an objective process, based on rigorous examination of what was actually found, although once the idea took hold that remains tended to come in clustered groupings, this generated a tendency to shoehorn materials that were only superficially similar into the same larger grouping or 'culture' as the clusters customarily came to be known (usually named after the site where a particular type of pottery had first been recovered). What quickly took a much less objective twist, however, was the process of giving human, historical meaning to this emerging patchwork of dateable archaeological cultures. Here the key interpretative leap is associated with two men: the Swedish archaeologist Oscar Montelius (1843–1921) and his younger German contemporary Gustaf Kossinna (1858–1931). Working in the hothouse, nationalist atmosphere of later nineteenth-century Europe, the obvious conclusion was that observable clusters of archaeological similarity must represent the material remains of the kinds of ancient language community that had already been identified by deduction via comparative linguistics. Just as the work of folklorists had dedicated itself to showing that the ancient language communities of Europe had specific non-material cultures (costumes, dances, oral tales, etc.), now archaeology was showing that these ancestors had had specific material cultures too. Very quickly, cultures came to be understood as the remains of 'peoples': proto-nations of culturally coherent, essentially endogamous human communities (Montelius 1888 [1873]; Kossinna 1911).

This conclusion, which won widespread (though again never complete) acceptance, had two important consequences. First, it naturally prompted attempts to date individual archaeological cultures and identify them with specific ancient language communities. German and Slavic scholars in particular wanted to find trace the ancestral descent (really ascent, as they were working backwards) of the Germanic and Slavonic communities of their own day. Written historical evidence for Europe's Germanic-speakers gave out more or less with Tacitus in the first century AD, and for Slavic-speakers in the early ninth century in the north, and in the sixth for the Balkans. The emerging discipline of archaeology now offered the intoxicating possibility of going back to incomparably more distant layers of the European past via the identification of particular archaeological cultures with particular ancient language communities. New (and often competing) narratives of the emergence of 'Slavs' and 'Germans' were quickly offered, which took the story back to at least the Bronze Age Europe of the second millennium BC (Kossinna 1928; Kostrzewski 1919).

Second, it put a huge emphasis on migration as the major cause of observable large-scale change in the deep European past. As analysis proceeded, it quickly became apparent that the archaeological record periodically threw up major caesuras, where one pattern of remains across a particular region was replaced – sometimes after a chronological gap, sometimes immediately – by another. If ancient 'peoples' all possessed their own, specific material cultures, then the natural interpretation of such disruptions was to suppose that one ancient language community, with its own specific material culture, had been replaced by another. What else could it mean? Such was the large-scale acceptance of culture/migration construct, that later nineteenth- and earlier twentieth-century visions of the pre-historic European past (and the history much of Central and particularly Eastern Europe had to be reconstructed using the methods of pre-history down to the end of the first millennium AD) were largely powered by migration of a very particular kind. This understood large-scale change as the direct result of the movement of 'closed' population groups with distinctive linguistic, non-material and material cultures. The development of European history, in effect, was driven by moments of mass migration accompanied by what we would now call ethnic cleansing (although the term had not yet been invented), which periodically saw one popula-tion group replace another in particular slots within the overall European landscape (Childe 1926, 1927 are classic statements; cf. Bahn 2014 and Renfrew and Bahn 2015 for more detailed commentary).

To give a specific illustration, the history of Britain was understood as having progressed, since the last glacial maximum receded in the third millennium BC, through the sequential domination of the landscape by a series of population groups who replaced each other in turn. The so-called 'Beaker' folk (named for the distinctive funnel shapes of their pottery) were succeeded by 'pre-Celts' at the end of the second millennium BC, and these in turn by Celtic-speakers, who were eventually succeeded – after a Roman interlude – by Anglo-Saxons. Each of these eras was marked by the appearance of new material cultural forms (Hawkes and Hawkes, 1943 is representative). In the case of the Anglo-Saxons, who arrived on the cusp of history, archaeological evidence – in the form of previously unknown weapons' burials and new types of jewellery as well as some very distinctive pottery – was reinforced by other types of evidence. There were some admittedly brief narrative sources that emphasised invasion, conquest and destruction. Equally, if not more important, enough linguistic research had been completed by the later nineteenth century for it to be apparent both that few Celtic loanwords had been adopted by the incoming Anglo-Saxons, and that virtually every place name of what is now England (except for the far southwest) was derived from the Germanic language of the Anglo-Saxon invaders. All older naming strata (Celtic, pre-Celtic, etc.) had been essentially wiped out, except for the names of major rivers (e.g. Reaney 1960). The natural conclusion from all this was that the Anglo-Saxons had swept the pre-existing Celtic population out of central and southern Britain into Wales, Cornwall and Brittany (Leeds 1913 is a classic early account; cf. Myres 1969 for a more developed version). Even more, this better-documented case, operating on the cusp between history and pre-history, was taken as further confirmation that it was right to understand the human history behind older, similar archaeological caesuras along the same kind of lines. The same broad interpretative approach to the past was adopted by intellectuals right across Europe by the turn of the twentieth century, with the result that many of the actual or potential national communities of contemporary Europe (Germans, Slavs of different kinds, Magyars, Croats, Bulgars, etc.) understood themselves as the direct descendants of a set of ancient migrants who occupied their particular corner of the European landscape after the last major archaeological 'break' in the region, inaugurating a pattern of continuous subsequent development that led directly to the modern day (Geary 2002).

One additional – coincidental – cultural development of enormous significance helped cement the dominance of this model in the public imagination. Not only was the later nineteenth century the first time that it had been possible to generate any remotely scientific overview of Europe's past, but its emergence coincided with the push for mass education that was a significant feature of the modern nation-state paradigm that was developing simultaneously (Cubberley 1920; Wardle 1970; Cook 1974; Ringer 1979; Heathorn 1994/5). For the first time, pretty much the entire population of large parts of Europe was receiving a significant quantity of education, and part of that education within each of the emerging nation states – naturally enough – was devoted to its own history. The higher-level textbooks used to explore these histories in secondary schools were written by the same historians and archaeologists who were busy refining their own territory's particular national saga from archaeological remains and the earliest historical records. Simpler versions of the same story filtered down to every level. My old *Ladybird Book of British History* told in pictures, in the 1960s, the same, now familiar story of Beaker folk, pre-Celts, Celts and triumphant Anglo-Saxons that had first emerged in the later nineteenth century. Not only was there a coherent unified story to tell – very much for the first time – but there was also a new captive audience to whom it could be rehearsed via mass education, and in whom it generated a shared understanding of past origins that was common to virtually the entirety of the population. As a result, the idea that modern Europe had essentially been created via a series of triumphant episodes of mass migration, accompanied by ethnic cleansing, inserted itself deeply into the European psyche via mass education, as the pioneering work of linguists, folklorists, historians and archaeologists was melded into a series of individual national sagas.

Deconstructing the paradigm

Like the nationalist paradigm that it has come to replace, the revisionist view of Europe's past, which has emerged since the 1960s, has diverse intellectual roots. On the face of it, there was nothing inherently toxic about understanding most modern European nations as the descendants of ancient immigrant communities. Except that the story of their settlement – *Landnahme* in the German – was usually (as with the Anglo-Saxons) told as a substantially violent one, and this kind of overall understanding generated a tendency to draw such clear lines between different modern communities, whose existence was understood to stretch back into the distant past, that it naturally engendered extremely powerful senses of 'them' and 'us'. This mattered particularly in Central Europe. There, the practical heritage of many centuries of dynastic imperial rule was a patchwork of culturally intermixed populations in many regions. This was bound to generate intense competition for control of particular geographical assets once aspirant regional leaders began to assert the overwhelming primacy of the national language community as the only legitimate mechanism for organising human communities. Who should control what?

Archaeology quickly contributed to some of these quarrels. If ancient language communities were Europe's founding fathers, the 'most legitimate' form of political community, then their original spread, as reflected in recovered archaeological cultures, could help legitimise modern boundary claims. At the Versailles peace conference, after the First World War, Kossinna and one of his erstwhile disciples, Kostrzewski, offered different identifications of the Iron Age Przeworsk Culture of north-central Europe – considering it the remains of respectively Germanic- and Slavic-speaking populations – because this was considered germane to the decision of where to place the new German/Polish border (Svennung 1972). This was inauspicious enough, but the mobilisation of an imaginary national past took a much nastier turn in the 1930s, when the Nazi regime massively increased the element of racial superiority that often accompanied nationalism's sense of 'them' and 'us', and the supposed spread of ancient Germanic-speakers was used to generate demands for *Lebensraum*. The history and archaeology of the Goths, whose domains had expanded from northern Poland into the Ukraine and the Crimea in the third and fourth centuries AD, was much cited in a political discourse of expansion and superiority whose ultimate trajectory lay in the death camps of Second World War (Wolfram 1988; Geary 2002). Not surprisingly, this generated an overarching revulsion after 1945 against introducing a supposed European past into discussions of the legitimacy of current European boundaries, which, combined with important intellectual developments in several separate fields of research, effectively undermined the entire pre-war nationalist paradigm.

One important challenge came from the social sciences. Up to the Second World War, most analyses had assumed that the 'normal' situation for most human beings was one basic group affiliation, inherited from their parents, which would not change. This affiliation expressed itself in a cocktail of measurable cultural traits, such as language and moral values, as well, perhaps, as clothing and the other kinds of material cultural items with which archaeologists were concerned. After 1945, however, a whole series of studies – starting with Edmund Leach's ground-breaking work in northern Burma – demonstrated, contrary to earlier assumptions, that there is no necessary correlation between claimed group identities and measurable check-lists of observable traits. Individuals who do not share any measurable traits sometimes consider themselves to belong to the same group, while individuals who appear similar in every measurable way can claim disparate group identities. What all this emphasised was that, most fundamentally, identity is not an objectively measurable category at all, but primarily a state of mind dictated by an individual's subjective perception and consciousness (Leach 1954).

Equally important, the quasi-nationalist assumption that individuals will 'normally' have one unchanging group affiliation was shown to be ill-founded. Group identity often comes in layers, composed of several overlapping affiliations to a whole series of imagined communities (e.g. village, town, county, regional, national, supra-national). Any or all of these can exercise stronger or weaker holds on individual loyalty, with the result that many individuals can and do change some or all of their larger-group identities in the course of their lifetimes. One particularly influential strand of work emphasised the extent to which individuals manipulate their available range of potential larger-group affiliations according to immediate (usually material) advantage, situating themselves in group A when that affords them advantage, but swapping easily to group B should that become more beneficial. The fundamental statement of this line of research remains *Ethnic Groups and Boundaries*: a set of essays edited in 1969 by the Norwegian anthropologist Frederik Barth. In its introduction, the editor formulated the collection's central finding in a much-quoted aphorism. Contrary to the essentialist, singular and objective assumptions of the nationalist paradigm, identity is, in Barth's words 'an evanescent situational construct, not a solid enduring fact' (Barth 1969: 9).

The basic conclusion that identity is fundamentally a subjective phenomenon, often subject to change, has found many applications, not least in studies of the whole phenomenon of nationalism itself, as the specific creation of a very particular cultural context. As a direct result, the idea that modern European nations can usefully be understood as the direct genealogical descendants of usually early medieval predecessor communities has been eroded. Nations – like all larger group identities – are a type of imagined community, but a type that is so large – requiring the mass participation of whole populations over wide geographical areas – that it requires modern technological apparatus to exist at all: at the very least mass circulation newspapers, but, better still, radio and television, not to mention mass education through broadly unified curricula. Without such structures and technologies, cultural commonality across such large areas as those occupied by modern nation states is inconceivable, and, on close inspection, the preceding pattern was much more one of intense localism for the vast majority of what was usually a peasant population (Anderson 1983; Gellner 1983; Connor 1990; note though the partial caveats of Smith 2000).

While nationalism's founding intellectuals (such as the Grimm brothers, or all the British place-name specialists) did much objectively sound research, subsequent work has also underlined the extent to which the supposed, ancient cultural bedrock of European nations was not so much recovered as invented. Not that there weren't folk tales and folk dances, but the national cultural structures – not least the national histories going back to ancestral, medieval communities – erected on the back of the collected materials were essentially a modern construct, which was in practice imposed to a considerable extent on the populations from whom it supposedly derived, as a whole school of enquiry into the concept of invented tradition has successfully demonstrated (Hobsbawm and Ranger 1983 among many possibilities). Peasants were effectively turned into Frenchmen, or Englishmen for that matter, by the potent cultural force of mass education that spread the unifying myths created by the selecting and editing work of the intellectuals to mass populations, often reinforced by the identity-creating experience of mass conscription. The details of the process varied from case to case, but there were always recognisable commonalities (Weber 1976; Colley 1992). In some parts of Central Europe, even childcare options, highly attractive to parents in industrialising contexts, were mobilised as part of the process, so that, in Bohemia, families who did not instinctively recognise a proffered choice between 'Czech' or 'German' identities were induced to make one in order to access desirable social services (Zahra 2006).

Such reinterpretations of group identity implicitly challenged existing understandings, after Montelius and Kossinna, of archaeological 'cultures' as the remains of ancient 'peoples': ancestral national communities, which were endogamous, closed groupings of humanity separated in very profound ways from any of their neighbours. If, as the post-1945 research seemed now to show, human group identities are not based on unchanging, inherited non-material cultural norms, why should their material counterparts have any greater claim to provide an accurate guide to political groupings of the past?

This certainly played some part in the profound revolution in archaeological interpretation that unfolded from the early 1960s, but even more important was an increasing dissatisfaction with the monolithic migration model of major archaeological change that the arguments of Montelius and Kossinna had brought in their wake. From the early 1960s, study after study demonstrated that even very large-scale material cultural transformation might have causes other than migration. So-called 'new' (or 'processual') archaeology, much in vogue in the Anglophone world in the 1960s and 1970s, particularly highlighted the role of human technological adaptation in the face of environmental changes as a profound, ever-present cause of material cultural transformation, and explicitly rejected older emphases on the importance of migration (Clark 1966 is a classic call to arms). Much work also pointed out simultaneously that, once you removed the overriding expectation that the material remains of the past *should* present themselves in neatly packaged 'cultures', and stopping ignoring inconvenient data, it was less much clear that they always did. Reality on the ground sometimes consisted of a patchwork of very small areas of distributional similarity, with the larger supposed culture existing mostly in the eye of the beholder, although attempts to dismiss the existence of 'cultures' outright never fully succeeded (Renfrew and Bahn 2015; Bahn 2014). Emphasis then broadened in the 1980s (in so-called 'post-processual' archaeology) to encompass a much wider range of potential causes of material cultural transformation, not least the importance of ideas, both in terms of stimulating invention and innovation, but also, perhaps still more fundamentally, in the construction of ideas-based worldviews, which manifest themselves in many of the ways that human beings order their lives and material possessions (Hodder 1982, 1991; Hodder and Hutson 2003).

Overall, numerous studies convincingly demonstrated that mass population replacement (now sometimes labelled the 'invasion hypothesis') was not the only major architect of material cultural transformation. So many, and so convincing, were these studies, and so complete had been the domination of the old migration-led model, that for many, particularly Anglophone archaeologists, adducing any element of migration into explanations of archaeological transformation rapidly became synonymous with 'simplicity', a harking back to an older (i.e. more primitive) era in the development of the discipline. For such archaeologists, and this was particularly true of processual archaeologists who led the original intellectual rebellion, any explanation other than migration became, by definition, preferable. As one scholar strongly influenced by this tradition has put it, to eliminate migration from your account of change in the past 'is simply to dispose of an always simplistic and usually groundless supposition in order to enable its replacement with a more subtle interpretation of the period' (Halsall, 1995 p. 61; cf. Bahn 2014; Renfrew and Bahn 2015). The loaded language in this quotation – 'simplistic' and 'groundless' versus 'more subtle' ('complex' is another favourite term of art) – is characteristic of a widespread conviction.

The overall effect of this intellectual reaction can be illustrated by the kind of revisionist account of the Anglo-Saxon takeover of southern Britain, which had become commonplace by the last decade of the twentieth century. This didn't eliminate Anglo-Saxon migrants entirely, but the numbers envisaged were much reduced, in part, at least, for extremely good reasons. In intellectual terms, the most important advance was the realisation that all those Anglo-Saxon place names which seemed to betoken a mass population replacement in fact belonged to a later phase in the history of the English landscape, when the pattern of nucleated villages still visible today emerged across it between the eighth and the eleventh centuries. At that point, as other sources confirmed, the landowning class was entirely Anglo-Saxon speaking, so that, as settlements formed, it was only natural that they, and every piece of landed resource attached to them, should be given an Anglo-Saxon name (Gelling 1997; cf. Hooke 1998 on the landscape history). But all this happened several centuries after the initial Anglo-Saxon takeover of the fifth and sixth centuries AD. Further research had also demonstrated that late Roman Britain, in the fourth century, had a much higher population than anyone had previously even begun to imagine – quite probably as high as the medieval maximum immediately prior to the onset of the Black Death in the fourteenth century (Todd 2004). Not only did the linguistic evidence no longer demand an immediate and total population replacement in the fifth century, but the broader, emerging picture of overall population history made it practically impossible. Southern Britain was just far too populous for it to be plausible any longer to assume that all these humans could either have been wiped out or driven west into Wales, Cornwall and Brittany.

When you added into the mix new understandings of identity as a highly malleable category and the determination particularly of processual archaeologists to find alternative explanations for material cultural change other than migration, the result was a very different picture of fifth- and sixth-century history. Instead of a great swathe of newcomers from across the Channel and North Sea, sweeping all before them, just small numbers of Anglo-Saxons were envisaged, all or mostly invited in by natives for their own purposes (whether to prop up their own position vis-à-vis other natives, or to throw off the last remnants of a declining Roman imperial system), whose presence then generated a new process of identity formation, which saw the native Romano-British adopt Anglo-Saxon language and material cultural attributes for their own purposes. This generated the new material cultural patterns visible in the weapons- and jewellery-rich burials of the fifth and sixth centuries, as natives became Anglo-Saxons in increasing numbers (Hills 2003; Halsall 2007).

By their very nature, such lines of thought could not generate such a magnificently straightforward and generalisable model of the past as the old nationalist paradigm of repeated bouts of migration and ethnic cleansing. But it did offer some big thematic ideas which were capable of more general application. Not the least important of these was the direct contradiction of the central anachronism of the era of rampant, quasi-religious nationalism. The European past had never been populated by linguistically defined, culturally monolithic, large-scale blocks of humanity acting as unified political entities. On the contrary, Europeans had been buying into different cultural and political identities throughout history according to advantage. By the same token, this implicitly removed – or at least dramatically downplayed – much of the conflict that had been envisaged under the old model. Because identity had always been essentially a flag of convenience rather than some essential, defining feature of an individual's life, it did not carry anything like the same supposition that the past is likely to have been shaped by fixed language groups periodically at war with one another for *Lebensraum* and access to the best resources. Entities such as the 'Beaker Folk', Celts, or 'Anglo-Saxons' – or Bulgars, or Magyars, or Slavs for the matter – could be eliminated from the mental map as formative forces engaged in epic, competitive struggles for control of Europe's landed assets.

Beyond revision

The revisionist approach to the European past encompasses major intellectual advances over its predecessor, both at macro and micro levels of analysis. The new understanding of the fundamental workings of human group identities, and hence of their capacity for change, so central to the new model, is based on a much more extensive and sophisticated body of research than the quasi-nationalist assumptions of singular identity that it replaced. Much superior, too, is the range of newer approaches that have emerged to understanding observable clusterings of archaeological similarity, and the reasons why these might break down over time. As a result, a monocausal narrative where major change had always to be explained in terms of sequential bouts of mass migration and ethnic cleansing has given way to one which puts much more emphasis on the importance of long-term socio-economic, technological and even ideological transformation in its account of the emergence of a historically more recognisable Europe from its dim and distant past. Typical, likewise, of the huge range of more specific gains in knowledge over the last few decades, which have also helped undermine the nationalist paradigm applied to other case studies, are the two that have played such a key role in undermining older accounts of the Anglo-Saxon invasion. We now have a much better idea how extraordinarily populous the late Romano-British countryside actually was, and appreciate, too, the relatively late date of most Anglo-Saxon place names.

But in the same way that the old nationalist paradigm was based not just on political prejudice but on some serious advances in knowledge (comparative linguistics and the objective observation of dateable archaeological patterning), so the alternative emphases of the revisionist understanding of Europe's past have their own relevant political and cultural context. The 1980s and especially the 1990s were the decades of maximum optimism (to date, at least!) for the European project. Europe's free trade area acquired greater political and legal teeth out of the Maastricht process, currency union was under way and membership was expanding following the collapse of the Soviet bloc (Berend 2016 among many possibilities). An optimistic internationalism was on the rise, and analysts were predicting the imminent emergence of a 'Europe of the Regions', where the nation state would fade into the background, as a new European centre dealt directly on a whole series of issues with regional authorities at a lower level, better placed than national governments to launch local initiatives for the good of all (Applegate 1999). In this context, an account of Europe's past that massively de-emphasised the importance of the nation state, making it the creature of a specific and recent moment in time, rather than the latest manifestation of very ancient senses of community, held obvious attractions. A continental past that had also not been shaped by entrenched conflict between deeply divided cultural communities, but where identities had often been happily and peacefully swapped according to advantage also very much fitted the developing political landscape of an emerging European Union, whose individual citizens were currently adding 'European' to the national identities into which they had been born.

In part, this was accidental chronological coincidence. The advances in archaeology and the social sciences that underlay the new paradigmatic vision of Europe's ancient past had their origins, as we have seen, in research completed twenty or more years earlier, in the 1950s and 1960s. As usual, this was followed by about a generation's worth of intellectual manoeuvring as the new thinking infiltrated the mainstream structures of academic life (not least with the retirement of senior academics strongly attached to older ways of thinking). In the meantime, the development of the European Union had been following its own, separate chronological pathway, which was heavily dependent on entirely unrelated processes, not least the semi-voluntary disbanding of the Soviet bloc between 1989 and 1991 (Walker 2003). But neither was the coincidence completely accidental.

To a significant extent, academic research, particularly when it comes to large-scale projects, is dependent on the awarding of grants, and the interest of grant-awarding bodies always increases when a project can be presented as tying in interesting ways into momentous current developments. In my own particular sub-field of the ancient European past, the mid-first millennium AD, the European Science Foundation funded a huge project on the Transformation of the Roman world in the early 1990s. This project was explicitly formulated to revise (= 'correct') older Gibbonian paradigms of the end of the ancient world. For the previous twenty years or so, momentum within the discipline had been building up behind a more optimistic view both of the late Roman world, which rejected old labels of imperial decline, and of the process of imperial dismemberment, which played down negative visions of collapse, conflict, and discontinuity. 'Transformation' was designed to move beyond the old preconceptions of Decline and Fall, and tied in neatly to 'Late Antiquity' – another recently coined term of art – whose significance was again to emphasise the importance of continuities particularly in cultural development between the third and eighth centuries AD which transcended the disappearance of less important political structures such as the Western Roman Empire in the fifth (Brown 1971 was the clarion call; cf. Bowersock et al. 1999). Intellectually, the five-year project that followed was hugely creative (not least for me; I was lucky enough to attend many meetings), generating many important contributions to knowledge, which go far beyond even the project's fourteen published volumes. Much of this will stand the test of time, but it is worth recognising that the ESF's willingness to fund such a project in the first place, with that specific rationale at that particular moment in time, was not an accident, notwithstanding its undoubted excellence. The ESF funds only a small minority of the proposals it receives, and does so by helping the project organisers to persuade individual national academies to contribute to the costs. By definition, therefore, it can only fund major projects that have a very wide appeal, and the appeal of this one, in that context, is self-evident.[2]

And since it was such a creature of its times, it is perhaps not too surprising, looking back on the 1990s after the passage of another twenty years, that some aspects of the revisionist paradigm for Europe's past, despite its undoubted superiority to what went before, have not won complete acceptance. Not least, research on group identity has continued apace since the 1960s. No serious scholars doubt any longer, I should emphasise, that group identities are fundamentally subjective in nature, or that individuals can change them. But whereas the really exciting idea for Barth, given the pervasive dominance of nationalist assumptions up to the 1960s, was the demonstrable fact of fluidity, research as a whole would now put just as much emphasis on structures that limit the capacity of individuals to swap allegiances freely. In some contexts, inherited norms can themselves generate such strong emotional attachments that they are difficult to cast off, even for more immediate material advantage. But there can also be strong institutional impediments to fluidity too, in contexts where groups want to police their own boundaries to exclude or limit would-be new members. As the recent refugee European crisis has demonstrated, groups will often seek to erect much tougher boundaries around themselves when current members perceive their existing economic or political advantages to be under threat, resisting a potential dilution of those advantages that might be supposed to follow from any major expansion in group membership. As a result, the literature as a whole now puts much less emphasis than Barth himself did on evanescent fluidity (Bentley 1987; Kivisto 1989; Laruelle 2016), and identity is being taken more seriously again as a force that sometimes (though not always) dictates human behaviour. To give one specific example, whereas it was normal in the 1980s to dismiss African 'tribal' group identities as the artificial creations of colonial administrators (Vail 1989), more recent treatments are much more cautious (Spear 2003).

The possibility that some groups might erect firmer boundaries was already inherent in the logic of Barth's characterisation of group identities as 'situational constructs'. In different situations, this suggests, groups might well erect harder or looser boundaries. Barth was overwhelmingly interested in fluidity, since this was what was so novel in the 1960s, but the fact that boundaries can and do harden is both equally important in overall intellectual terms, and has at least as many potential applications to the past. Much play has been made for instance of the fluidity in membership of the different so-called 'barbarian' groups who relocated onto Roman territory in the late fourth and fifth centuries (Goths, Vandals, Franks, etc.) to play a major role in the creation of the new successor kingdoms of the early middle ages. And certainly, there is a great deal of evidence that the intruding groups rearranged themselves on Roman soil to create new and much larger social units, making it clear that they were by not 'peoples' of the kind regularly envisaged under the old nationalist paradigm. But all the evidence for these groups indicates that, internally, they were hierarchically organised into three distinct social castes: freemen, semi-free and slaves. The freemen elite comprised maybe a quarter of all adult males, and all access to higher status positions within the groups (semi-free to free; slave to semi-free) was carefully controlled (Heather 2008). You could perhaps freely choose to join one of these groups, but clearly not as a member of its freeman elite. In the same way, the earliest tranche of reasonably plentiful evidence from Anglo-Saxon England, dating to the seventh century, shows that early English society was already marked by important differences in status – between free and unfree, and, in the case of the west Saxon kingdom between Anglo-Saxon and native sub-Romano Briton too – with huge implications for both opportunity and quality of life: higher status was a huge, practical advantage. Since it is a safe bet that no one would have really chosen to be slaves – and that the unfree were also a majority of the peasant population – this again suggests that there had been strong limits on the capacity of the inhabitants of southern Britain to exercise a free choice of identity over the preceding two centuries (Woolf 2007).

In my view, the determination to downplay conflict, too, smells more of wishful thinking than likely reality. The written sources for west Roman collapse in the fifth century, lacunose as they certainly are, are full of implicit and explicit references to substantial conflict, both for continental Europe and north of the Channel (Heather 2005; Ward Perkins 2005). This makes it even harder to envisage that the fierce status differences that characterise seventh-century Anglo-Saxon England as the product of a peaceful process of voluntary cultural assimilation. Much more likely, the Anglo-Saxon takeover was a messier version of the Norman Conquest, with a new, intrusive elite taking control of the landed assets of southern Britain by ejecting and demoting the existing owners. The indigenous population must have survived in large numbers, but probably found themselves largely turned into servile peasantry (Heather 2009, ch. 6). South of the Channel, too, the evidence for local Roman elites choosing a non-Roman future with apparent freedom all post-dates a violent process of land annexation which robbed the west Roman state of much of its tax base, and hence its capacity to maintain sufficient military forces to protect its provincial landowners. Rather than a freely chosen swapping of identity, what we're really seeing, therefore, is groups of Roman landowners making the best of a potentially disastrous situation. They had no real choice between coming to an accommodation with the new powers in their lands, and these accommodations certainly cost them some of their wealth (Porena 2012), or risk losing all their lands as happened to the Roman landowners of southern Britain (Heather 2005; Ward Perkins 2005).

All this is in the sources, and always was, and, given recent political developments in the Ukraine – very sadly – attempts to paint a broadly peaceful picture of ancient European history now look significantly less plausible than they perhaps did twenty years ago. History hasn't come to an end, and human conflict is sadly never too distant a prospect. Humankind, it is worth remembering, is straightforwardly the fiercest and most efficient predator that evolution has ever produced. And while other, especially larger, members of the animal kingdom have felt the effects of this efficiency most acutely, as convincingly argued by rewilding activists (e.g. Monbiot 2013), homo sapiens has generally shown equally little compunction about predating on other members of its own species.

If identity cannot always be easily swapped and evidence for violence needs to be taken with due seriousness, migration, too, is in the process of returning to the intellectual agenda. The last quarter-century has seen a massive flourishing in the relatively new discipline of comparative migration. This has re-emphasised that migration – in a wide variety of forms, and undertaken for an equally wide variety of reasons – is a normal feature of human life, often with massively transformative effects upon both migrants and hosts (Cohen 1995, 1996, 1997, 2008 for introduction). In my own work, the realisation, which much of this research underlines, that large-scale migration is a regular, structural accompaniment to broader processes of social and economic transformation has played a particularly significant role. Fundamentally, it undermines the binary choice that processual archaeologists – and historians influenced by them – had attempted to open up between migration and socio-economic transformation as competing lines of explanation for the transformations of the deep European past. In all documented modern contexts, the two are regular bedfellows because migration is one amongst a range of normal human responses to the kinds of social stress that major socio-economic change tends to generate. A worldview that responds to the evident oversimplification of the old invasion hypothesis by rejecting outright even the possibility that migration might have played an important role in past change, seems unlikely, therefore, to offer the most constructive way forward. A much better response, in my view, to the old oversimplifications is to draw on the insights offered by comparative migration studies to help generate more sophisticated migration models (Heather 2009, especially ch. 11).

Exciting recent advances in next-generation DNA sequencing have also reinforced the point, from an entirely different direction, that migration needs to be taken much more seriously again as an agent of change in the deep past. In the last few years it has emerged that the vast majority of indigenous modern Europeans have DNA from three main ancient sources: hunter-gatherers who originally colonised parts of the continent after the last glacial maximum, Middle Eastern farmers who arrived in the Neolithic (from c. 3000 BC) and a third population component from the Eurasian steppe which arrived maybe a millennium after that (Haak et al. 2015). The average proportions differ slightly between different regions, but it is now beyond doubt that three major waves of ancient migration created the basic demographic profile of modern Europeans. How exactly to imagine these waves and their interactions is still being vigorously discussed, although the fact that most Europeans possess DNA from all three indicates that the old ethnic cleansing model, in its simplest form, is not the answer, even if we might think that such large-scale intrusions are bound to have generated conflict on some level. When you add into this mix the current European refugee crisis, then the overall increase in recent academic interest in ancient migration is entirely predictable, with predictable effects, too, on the funding bodies. In 2015/16, three major projects on early medieval and ancient migration received significant awards from German funding bodies alone. All of these will produce significant written outputs in due course, and prompt, no doubt, a further range of scholarly responses. Whatever else may happen, however, migration is firmly back on the scholarly menu after a quarter-century or more of eclipse.

As I write, the overall situation is very much one of intellectual flux. Proponents of the revisionist paradigm hold many senior academic positions and its key points still receive regular airings (Brown 2014, xi ff. broadly reasserts, for instance, the transformation thesis first aired in Brown 1971, against some of the points raised by Ward Perkins 2005; Heather 2005). But if it's not clear at this point where any end point of consensus may eventually fall, what I would like to emphasise, by way of conclusion, is that the discipline is certainly not heading back full-circle, towards a migration-heavy view of the past with the same kind of emphasis on the importance of fixed and ancient group identities as the old nationalist paradigm. On the contrary, the intellectual history I've been charting in this essay is, in its own way, a modestly optimistic one.

On one level, while developing views of the past have consistently interacted with contemporary political agendas, the overall pattern in this developing relationship is, I think, broadly an encouraging one. The old paradigm was blatantly recruited to support political agendas in the heyday of European nationalism in the decades either side of 1900, and had indeed been partly created by intellectuals who were strongly invested in these agendas from the outset. But the broad interest shown in the alternative past of the revisionist paradigm during the first flourishing of the European Union operated in much more subtle ways. Over time, the relationship between past and present has become, I would argue, less programmatic (although specific examples of the older reflexes do still surface: some of Europe's neo-nationalists occasionally hark back to the old nationalist paradigm: Brown 2014, xv ff.). For the most part, however, rather than creating a past to serve present interests, which is what happened in the nineteenth century, it is now a much more random process, where heightened interest is shown at particular moments in elements of the past that seem relevant to present experience, and that possibly even offer some useful perspectives.

The other cause for optimism is that, while one might want to quarrel – sometimes considerably – with the different visions of the European past offered up at different points over the last two hundred years, each era has represented a significant advance over its predecessor in terms both of interpretative complexity and absolute knowledge. Without doubting for a moment that my own thoughts, as much as those of my peers, will be revised in due course, I am confident that the overall tale is one of sustained, long-term intellectual progress. Comparative linguistics, archaeology, the social sciences, comparative migration and DNA analysis: the list of academic fields whose major advances have helped illuminate different murky corners of the deep European past, and its relationship to the present, is already very long, and it would be foolish to suppose that there are no more intellectual revolutions to come. At this point, for instance, we are waiting to see if next-generation DNA sequencing can shed the same kind of light on European migration patterns of the mid-first millennium AD as it managed to do for the much deeper past when population levels were so much lower and the intermingling of the three basic sources of European DNA had only just begun. Whether it can or not, the existing track record gives cause for confidence that our understanding of the European past will become both stronger and less prone to being bent out of shape by the concerns of the present, with each scholarly generation.

Guide to further reading and online resources

The literature on human group identities, and its very particular relationship to the modern nation state, is enormous. Barth (1969) remains an essential and rewarding summation of the post-war revolution in understanding, even if, as argued here, its conclusions need to be modified in the light of subsequent literature. Anderson (1983) and Gellner (1983), likewise, both summed up a post-war response to the phenomenon of European nationalism, and kick-started vigorous and fruitful debate.

Each of the technical subject areas that have contributed at different (sometimes several different) moments to evolving understandings of the European past have their own extensive literatures. Any engagement with comparative linguistics should begin with the Grimm brothers, where Hettinga (2001) provides an excellent introduction. Otherwise, there is a multiplicity of excellent overviews and handbooks available, such as Janda and Joseph (2004). Archaeology, as a discipline, is particularly prone to intellectual navel-gazing, largely because of the vigorous methodological debates that have marked its progress over the last half century. But this means that there is a host of intelligent guides and overviews available, which never fail to situate present debates in the context of the past progression of interpretation within the discipline. Renfrew and Bahn (2015) is an excellent guide, if with slightly processual leanings, written with under-graduate teaching in mind. Hodder and Hutson (2003) does the same job with a more post-processual steer. Comparative migration research has so far generated fewer competitive schools of interpretation, but, again, there are excellent general introductions, among which I would particularly recommend Cohen (1995) and Cohen (2008).

There is a wealth of online material available at the websites of the leading university institutes concerned with some of the component subject areas that have been central to evolving reconstructions of the distant European past. Given modern concerns, it is not surprising to find that migration is particularly well served. Migration Oxford –www.migration.ox.ac.uk/resources.shtml – provides many useful further links, as does the more particularly focussed website of Forced Migration worldwide: www.forcedmigration.org/research-resources.

Much of online material concerned with DNA analysis, not surprisingly, is concerned with family history, but university departments with a specialism in applications, such as the Department of Genetics, Evolution, and Environment at UCL, are an excellent place to begin: www.ucl.ac.uk/biosciences/departments/gee.

Notes

1 The MGH website is a wonderful source for the origins and further development of the project: www.mgh.de/geschichte/geschichte-allgemeines/.
2 For more detail on the European Science Foundation, see its website: www.esf.org/. Full details of publications of the Transformation of the Roman world project can be found at www.brill.com/publications/transformation-roman-world.

References

Anderson, Benedict (1983) *Imagined Communities: Reflections on the Origin and Spread of Nationalism*. London: Verso.

Anttila, Raimo (1989) *Historical and Comparative Linguistics*. Amsterdam: Benjamins.

Applegate, Celia (1999) 'A Europe of Regions: Reflections on the Historiography of Sub-National Places in Modern Times'. *American Historical Review* 104: 1–29.

Bahn, Paul G. (2014) *The History of Archaeology: An Introduction*. London: Routledge.

Barth, Fredrik (ed.) (1969) *Ethnic Groups and Boundaries: The Social Organisation of Ethnic Difference*. Boston: Little, Brown.

Bentley, G.C. (1987) 'Ethnicity and Practice'. *Comparative Studies in Society and History* 29: 25–55.

Berend, Ivan T. (2016) *The History of European Integration: A New Perspective*. London: Routledge.

Bowersock, G.W., Peter Brown and Oleg Grabar (eds) (1999) *Late Antiquity: a Guide to the Postclassical World*. Cambridge MA: Harvard University Press.

Brown, Peter R.L. (1971) *The World of Late Antiquity*. London: Thames & Hudson.

Brown, Peter R.L. (2014) *The Rise of Western Christendom: Triumph and Diversity, A.D. 200–1000*. Hoboken, NJ: Wiley.

Childe, V. Gordon (1926) *The Aryans: A Study of Indo-European Origins*. London: Kegan Paul.

Childe, V. Gordon (1927) *The Dawn of European Civilization*. London: Kegan Paul.

Clark, Grahame (1966) 'The Invasion Hypothesis in British Archaeology'. *Antiquity* 40: 172–89.

Cohen, Robin (ed.) (1995) *The Cambridge Survey of World Migration*. Cambridge: Cambridge University Press.

Cohen, Robin (ed.) (1996) *Theories of Migration*. Cheltenham: Edward Elgar.

Cohen, Robin (ed.) (1997) *The Politics of Migration*. Cheltenham: Edward Elgar.

Cohen, Robin (2008) *Global Diasporas: An Introduction*, 2nd ed. London: Routledge.

Colley, Linda (1992) *Britons: Forging the Nation, 1707–1837*. New Haven, CT: Yale University Press.

Connor, Walker, (1990) 'When Is a Nation?'. *Ethnic and Racial Studies* 13: 92–103.

Cook, T.G. (1974) *The History of Education in Europe*. London: Methuen.

Cubberley, Ellwood P. (1920) *The History of Education: Educational Practice and Progress Considered as a Phase of the Development and Spread of Western Civilization*. London: Constable & Co.

Dolukhanov, P.M. (1996) *The Early Slavs: Eastern Europe from the Initial Settlement to the Kievan Rus*. London: Longman.

Geary, Patrick (2002) *The Myth of Nations: The Medieval Origins of Europe*. Princeton, NJ: Princeton University Press.

Gelling, Margaret (1997) *Signposts to the Past*, 3rd edn. Chichester: Phillimore.

Gellner, Ernest (1983) *Nations and Nationalism*. Oxford: Blackwell.

Grimley, Daniel M. (2006) *Grieg: Music, Landscape and Norwegian Identity*. Woodbridge: Boydell Press.

Haak, W. et al. (2015) 'Massive Migration from the Steppe was a source for Indo-European Languages in Europe', *Nature* 522: 207–11.

Halsall, G. (1995) *Early Medieval Cemeteries: An Introduction to Burial Archaeology in the Post–Roman West*. Skelmorlie: Cruithne Press.

Halsall, Guy (2007) *Barbarian Migrations and the Roman West, 376–568*. Cambridge: Cambridge University Press.

Hawkes, Jaquetta, and Christopher Hawkes (1943) *Prehistoric Britain*. Harmondsworth: Penguin.

Heather, Peter (2005) *The Fall of Rome: A New History*. London: Macmillan.

Heather, Peter (2008) 'Ethnicity, Group Identity, and Social Status in the Migration Period', in I. Garipzanov, P. J. Geary and P. Urbańczyk (eds), *Franks, Northmen, and Slavs: Identities and State Formation in Early Medieval Europe*. Turnhout: Brepols, 17–50.

Heather, Peter (2009) *Empires and Barbarians: Migration, Development, and the Creation of Europe*. London: Macmillan.

Heathorn, Stephen (1994–95) '"Let Us Remember that We, Too, are English": Constructions of Citizenship and National Identity in English Elementary School Reading Books, 1880–1914'. *Victorian Studies* 38: 27–49.

Hettinga, Donald (2001) *The Brothers Grimm*. New York: Clarion.

Hills, Catherine (2003) *The Origins of the English*. London: Duckworth.

Hobsbawm, Eric and Ranger, Terence (eds) (1983) *The Invention of Tradition*. Cambridge, Cambridge University Press.

Hodder, Ian (1982) *Symbols in Action: Ethnoarchaeological Studies of Material Culture*. Cambridge: Cambridge University Press.

Hodder, Ian (1991) *Reading the Past: Current Approaches to Interpretation in Archaeology*. Cambridge: Cambridge University.

Hodder, Ian, and Scott Hutson (eds) (2003) *Reading the Past: Current Approaches to Interpretation in Archaeology*. Cambridge: Cambridge University Press.

Hooke, Della (1998) *The Landscape of Anglo-Saxon England*. Leicester: Leicester University Press.

Iggers, Georg G. (1983) *The German Conception of History: The National Tradition of Historical Thought from Herder to the Present*. Middletown, CT: Wesleyan University Press.

Janda, Richard D., and Brian D. Joseph (eds) (2004) *The Handbook of Historical Linguistics*. Oxford: Blackwell.

Kivisto, Peter (1989) *The Ethnic Enigma: The Salience of Ethnicity for European-Origin Groups*. Philadelphia: University of Pennsylvania Press.

Knowles, D.M. (1960) 'Presidential Address: Great Historical Enterprises III. The Monumenta Germaniae Historica'. *Transactions of the Royal Historical Society*. 5th series. 10: 129–50.

Kossinna, Gustaf (1911) *Die Herkunft der Germanen: Zur Methode der Siedlungsarchäologie*. Würzburg: C. Kabitzsch.

Kossinna, Gustaf (1928) *Ursprung und Verbreitung der Germanen in vor- und frühgeschichtlicher Zeit*. Leipzig: C. Kabitzsch.

Kostrzewski, Józef (1919) *Die ostgermanische Kultur der Spätlatènezeit*. Leipzig und Würzburg: C. Kabitzsch.

Laruelle, François (2016) *Theory of Identities*, translated by Alyosha Edlebi. New York: Columbia University Press.

Leach, E.R. (1954) *Political Systems of Highland Burma: A Study of Kachin Social Structure*. London: G. Bell and Sons.

Leeds, Edward T. (1913). *The Archaeology of the Anglo-Saxon Settlements*. Oxford: Oxford University Press.

Lehmann, Winfred P. (1962). *Historical Linguistics: An Introduction*. New York: Rinehart & Winston.

Monbiot, George (2013) *Feral: Searching for Enchantment on the Frontiers of Rewilding*. London: Allen Lane.

Montelius, Oscar (1888 [1873]) *The Civilisation of Sweden in Heathen Times*. London: Macmillan and Co.

Myres, J.N.L. (1969) *Anglo-Saxon Pottery and the Settlement of England*. Oxford: Oxford University Press.

Porena, P. and Y. Rivière (eds) (2012) *Expropriations et confiscations dans les royaumes barbares: une approche régionale*. Rome: École française de Rome.

Reaney, P.H. (1960) *The Origin of English Place Names*. London: Routledge & Kegan Paul.

Renfrew, Colin, and Paul Bahn (2015) *Archaeology: Theories, Methods and Practice*. London: Thames & Hudson.

Ringer, Fritz (1979). *Education and Society in Modern Europe*. Bloomington, IN: Indiana University Press.

Smith, Anthony D. (2000) 'The Nation: Modern or Perennial?', in *The Nation in History: Historiographical Debates about Ethnicity and Nationalism*. Hanover, NH: University Press of New England, 27–51.

Spear, Thomas (2003) 'Neo-Traditionalism and the Limits of Invention in British Colonial Africa'. *The Journal of African History* 44: 3–27.

Svennung J. (1972) 'Jordanes und die gotische Stammsage', in U.E. Hagberg (ed.), *Studia Gotica*. Stockholm: Almqvist & Wiksell, 20–56.

Tatar, Maria (1987) *The Hard Facts of the Grimms' Fairy Tales*. Princeton, NJ: Princeton University Press.

Tatar, Maria (2004) *The Annotated Brothers Grimm*. New York: W.W. Norton & Co.

Todd, Malcolm (ed.) (2004) *A Companion to Roman Britain*. Oxford: Blackwell.

Vail, Leroy (1989) *The Creation of Tribalism in Southern Africa*. Berkeley, CA: University of California Press.

Walker, Edward W. (2003) *Dissolution: Sovereignty and the Breakup of the Soviet Union*. Oxford: Rowman & Littlefield.

Ward Perkins, B. *The Fall of Rome and the End of Civilisation*. Oxford: Oxford University Press.

Wardle, David (1970) *English Popular Education 1780–1970*. Cambridge: Cambridge University Press.

Weber, Eugen (1976) *Peasants into Frenchmen: The Modernisation of French Rural Society*. Stanford, CA: Stanford University Press.

Wolfram, H. (1988) *History of the Goths*, trans. T.J. Dunlap. Berkeley, CA: University of California Press.

Woolf, Alex (2007) 'Apartheid and Economics in Anglo-Saxon England', in N.J. Higham (ed.), *The Britons in Anglo-Saxon England*. Woodbridge: Boydell, 115–29.

Zahra, Tara (2006) '"Each Nation Only Cares for Its Own": Empire, Nation, and Child Welfare Activism in the Bohemian Lands, 1900–1918'. *American Historical Review* 111: 1378–402.

Zipes, Jack (2002) *The Brothers Grimm: From Enchanted Forests to the Modern World* (2nd edn). London: Routledge.

5 Mobility, migration and modern memory

Eureka Henrich

Commuters clad in business attire and tourists carting their holiday essentials swarm ceaselessly around a group of five children, standing together with their belongings: a violin, a teddy bear, a few suitcases and a rucksack. The children gaze curiously at their surroundings, against which they appear decidedly old fashioned – the girls wear blouses and braided hair, the boys sport blazers and caps, and attached to each is a tag with a number. Occasionally, a member of the crowd stops to inspect their presence, as it is not only their clothing that is strange. Made from bronze and placed on a knee-high pedestal at London's Liverpool Street Station, these children are part of a memorial called *Kindertransport – the arrival* (see Figure 5.1). The accompanying plaque reads:

> Children of the Kindertransport
> In gratitude to the people of Britain for saving the lives of 10,000 unaccompanied mainly Jewish children who fled from Nazi persecution in 1938 and 1939.
> *"Whosoever rescues a single soul is credited as though they had saved the whole world"* Talmud

A section of railway track beside the children conveys their mode of transport, and arranged around the track are markers detailing 16 points of origin, cities in Germany, Austria, Czechoslovakia and the then-Free City of Danzig (now part of Poland). The event commemorated emerges in this depiction as an epic journey from the jaws of danger to a place of refuge, and the sentiment captured in the dedication positions Britain and its people as central actors in the story. The poignancy of the sculpture is underpinned by its location, in 'Hope Square' at the very train station to which most *Kinder* arrived, ready to be taken to British foster homes and hostels.

While the events it refers to occurred almost 80 years ago, the Liverpool Street memorial itself reflects a story that is more contemporary. Tony Kushner has traced the lineage of this '*Kinder* narrative', pinpointing the 50th anniversaries and reunions of the late 1980s as the moment in which a collective identity as *Kinder* began to form among grown *Kindertransportees*, aided by the production of documentaries, the publication of memoirs and the organisation of memorials,

Figure 5.1 Kindertransport Memorial, Liverpool Street Station, London.
Photograph by Paul Dean, 2007. Licensed for use under Creative
Commons. See https://commons.wikimedia.org/wiki/
File%3AKindertransport-Meisler.jpg.

all of which were amplified by the attention of the media. In this context, the very different individual experiences of what was 'a scheme with many flaws' were ironed out, and an increasingly mythical and celebratory story of escape and redemption became dominant. As Kushner notes, the *Kindertransport* 'has been, if only recently, one of the most remembered journeys of any migrant group in the twentieth century' (2012: 155). The scheme's contentious features, including the strictly temporary nature of the children's protection in Britain, and the decision to bring *unaccompanied* children and not their parents or older siblings, are not so readily remembered. In a proud British story of welcoming refugees, the refashioned '*Kinder* narrative' is one of a privileged selection of migratory movements that are consciously remembered and celebrated – many more arrivals, attempted arrivals, and departures, are forgotten.

This chapter asks how human migration in the modern period has been remembered in different national contexts, and focuses particularly on the politics surrounding recent efforts to remember or forget aspects of various nations' migratory pasts in Europe, North America and Australasia. The representation of migration memories can involve confronting the most contested aspects of national histories, including racially discriminatory policies of immigration restriction, unfree labour and forced migration. Some modes of migration, such as settler colonialism, have provided settler societies like Australia and the United States with foundational 'pioneer' narratives. However, since the mid-twentieth century these proud nation-building stories have been unsettled by the claims and activism of those who their migrations displaced and dispossessed, as well as those determined to recognise migrants or refugees who have been recently excluded from the nation. Other claims for recognition have come from specific migrant communities whose memories have not been incorporated into dominant national narratives, such as post-colonial migrants in France. Whose pasts should be remembered? Which journeys, departures and arrivals should be celebrated, and which should be mourned? By exploring a range of museums and exhibitions, memorials and monuments, this chapter explains how these questions have shaped the construction of public and community memories of migration.[1]

History, memory and heritage

Monuments, memorials and museums all serve to perpetuate memory – to fix events and their meanings as a common or collective focal point for continual remembering (Lake 2006: 2). As we have seen with the *Kindertransport* memorial, this desire to preserve and promote collective memory can obscure the contested nature of past events. The interests of history, as an academic discipline that aims to reconstruct the past in all its complexity and contradiction through the interpretation of evidence, can easily come into conflict with those of memory, which have more to do with people's relationship to the past. Rather than purely providing an explanation of what took place and why, the representations of memory that we see in memorials or monuments tell us about the people who constructed them, how they wish to see themselves in relation to events or people in the past and what they wish to pass down to future generations.

In the contest between the interests of history and memory, museums and those who work in and with them occupy a complicated middle ground. Since their foundation in the nineteenth century in the context of growing nationalism, museums have been 'a potent force in forging self consciousness' (Kaplan 1996: 1). Museum exhibitions and collections presented the 'evidence' of a unified 'people', including their particular cultures, customs and conquests, and in doing so constructed a common heritage, national character and narrative of progress and success. The memories and experiences of those outside the nation – foreigners, immigrants, and other transient or travelling peoples – were not part of these national stories of becoming. However, by the late twentieth century, the selective concerns of national museums were under increasing pressure to become more responsive and representative. In post-colonial, often avowedly multicultural nations, histories of migration and the memories of migrant groups have played an important part in the process of democratizing the museum space, and challenging the previously accepted cultural and ethnic homogeneity of national narratives. We can detect the beginnings of this change in the rights movements of the 1960s and 1970s, and in the development and eventual flourishing of what is called 'the new social history' (Harrison 2004; Tosh 2010: 70–73). In both cases we see a demand for the inclusion of 'others', whether they be the working classes, women, Indigenous peoples, ethnic minorities or other marginalised social groups (Walkowitz and Knauer 2009: 3).

A useful way to think about the relationship between history-makers (historians, curators, and community members) and representations of the past is through the concept of heritage. Simply put, heritage is 'something that is inherited, either by individuals or collectively' (Davies 2004: 280) or, in David Lowenthal's words, 'things worth saving' (1979: 555). 'Things' can be tangible, like a physical setting, a building, or an object, or intangible, like a story, a folk song or even a language. In either case, it is the cultural, political or economic purpose that the thing can perform in the present that determines whether it is deemed worth saving, and these assessments change through time and in different contexts, depending on which state, organisation or individual is doing the deciding. So rather than a fixed entity, thinking about heritage as a 'process and a practice' can help us to better understand the contexts that ascribe meanings to 'things' from the past, and shape decisions about what is worth saving, and why (Ashworth et al. 2007: 2). The process by which migrant memories and belongings have been incorporated or excluded from the heritage of individuals, groups and nations is our concern in this chapter.

With the belated recognition and support of cultural pluralism in many Western nations in the late twentieth century, migrant heritage has become a feature of many local, state and national museum collections and exhibitions, and since the 1980s dozens of dedicated migration museums have been established across the Americas, Australia and a number of European nations. These museums are no less 'political' than their nineteenth- and twentieth-century predecessors.

While the first public museums aimed to educate the masses, in order to fashion them as useful and dedicated citizens, the underlying aims of contemporary migration museums and exhibitions may include the promotion of a particular group's achievements and contributions to the community or nation, the celebration of cultural diversity through migrant heritage, and the reinforcing of civic values, in order to encourage social cohesion. In this section we will consider three examples, all of which primarily focus on histories of *immigration*, or arrivals. Each case study considers the historical and political context in which the museum or exhibition was established, and asks what the curatorial approach can tell us about the place of migration history and memory within the heritage and identity of the nation in question.

Migrant heritage and the nation

Ellis Island Immigration Museum: commemorating the immigrant nation

Ellis Island in New York Harbor is the archetypal site of immigrant arrival. It began operation as America's first federal immigration processing station in 1892, and by the time it closed in 1954, 12 million people had been processed there and subsequently admitted to the country. Most of these immigrants were from southern and eastern Europe and travelled as steerage passengers.[2] Around 2 per cent of arrivals were refused entry, and others were detained there in quarantine, earning Ellis the dual reputation as an island of hope and an island of tears. But its iconic status has less to do with these events, and more to do with the concerted memory-making activities that have occurred at the site over the past three decades. In 1982 Chrysler Corporation chairman and son of Italian immigrants, Lee Iacocca, was appointed by President Ronald Reagan to head the new Statue of Liberty–Ellis Island Foundation, and tasked with raising funds to enable the restoration of both sites, including the main building on Ellis Island, where a museum of immigration history was to be established. The restoration and management of the site has since been shared between the Foundation and the National Parks Service, as part of the Statue of Liberty National Monument, and the entire monument was inscribed onto the UNESCO World Heritage List in 1984. To engage Americans in this national project, planners capitalised on the estimate that 100 million Americans have an ancestor who gained entry to the country through Ellis Island (Desforges and Maddern 2004: 447–448). Appealing to these genealogical links at a time when family history was booming and diverse ethnic identities were the subject of renewed academic and personal interest (Davison 2004: 208) was a highly effective strategy, not least as it fostered a potential audience of almost half of the population.[3] The main vehicle for individual donations was a new memorial, the American Immigrant Wall of Honor, where subscribers could, for a fee, have the name of their immigrant family member or ancestor transcribed permanently. The fundraising drive was a huge success, and the new museum and memorial opened with speeches and a citizenship

Figure 5.2 Ellis Island Immigration Museum as seen from the Circle Line Ferry
from Battery Park to Liberty Island in 2005. The American Immigrant
Wall of Honor is partially visible on the right. Photograph by Ken
Thomas, 2005. Licensed for use under Creative Commons. See
https://commons.wikimedia.org/wiki/File:Ellis_Island-27527.jpg.

ceremony for 50 immigrants on 10 September 1990. Media coverage of the
event focused on elderly Americans, who remembered arriving at Ellis Island as
children, and had been brought by their families to see their name unveiled
on the Wall of Honor (Henrich 2015: 330–331). Since then, Ellis Island (with
its main building restored to appear as it did in the immigration station's busiest
years, 1918–1924) has come to symbolise the story of America as an immigrant
nation writ large (see Figure 5.2). Historic arrivals at the island have been depicted
in feature films, documentaries and television series, and some 30 million visitors
have caught the ferry to the island to experience the site first-hand (History.com
website).

On arrival, visitors are invited to step back in time and walk in their immigrant
ancestor's footsteps: entering the Baggage Room with suitcases piled high,
climbing the stairs to pass through the corridors with adjacent rooms for medical
and physical examinations, and across the empty Great Hall, which would once
have echoed with the noise of hundreds of recent arrivals being interviewed by
immigration officials. Exhibitions on different themes relating to the 'immigrant
experience' and the history of the site occupy the three floors – these include *The
Peopling of America*, which tells the story of the nation through statistics and
demographic representations, *Through America's Gate* which draws on oral
histories to bring to life the experience of Ellis Island as an immigration station,

Treasures from Home which exhibits objects brought by prospective immigrants, and *Restoring a Landmark* which displays photographs tracing the restoration of the main building throughout the 1980s. With the exception of one display on the history of the island, and the longer historical context set by *The Peopling of America*, the permanent exhibitions focus on the immigration station's peak period of operation, and on the immigrant's experiences of becoming American. While this makes sense given the purpose of the museum, many historians and other scholars have pointed out the problematic implications of singling out one site, and cohort of arrivals, as emblematic of the American immigrant story (Green 2007: 240–241). And these are problems that museum workers are also aware of. As the head historian at the site, Barry Moreno, told historian David Walkowitz in 2004, 'complaints to guides and curators demonstrate that many people persist in thinking Ellis Island is the general and universal story of American immigration . . . some misinformed folks think their slave forebears passed through the island' (2009: 144).

Recent changes at Ellis Island can be seen as a response to these criticisms and misconceptions, but to what extent they address them remains a matter for debate. As part of the Peopling of America Center, which opened to the public in May 2015, new galleries addressing the pre- and post-Ellis eras have been added. *Journeys: The Peopling of America, 1550s–1890* explores the 'earliest arrivals', including Native Americans, Africans brought forcibly by slave traders and Europeans arriving on the eastern seaboard, while *The Journey: New Eras of Immigration* focuses on migration from the post-Second World War period to the present (Ellis Island website). Both galleries follow a similar structure, with sections on 'Leaving', 'Making the Trip', 'Arrival', 'Struggle and Survival' and 'Building a Nation' (Genzlinger 2015). At the heart of the revamped galleries is the 'World Migration Globe' illustrating global migration patterns throughout human history; however, this nod to the universal values the site is ascribed by its world heritage status is the only deviation from the national story. The exhibitions now tell a more representative story of immigration to America, including migrations by foot over the southern borders, but the extent to which comparisons can or even should be drawn productively between very different forms of free and unfree movement is an unresolved tension. Sites of arrival elsewhere – such as Angel Island off the coast of San Francisco, where thousands of Asian immigrants were detained, or Sullivan's Island in Charleston, South Carolina, which was North America's main port of entry for enslaved Africans who survived the Middle Passage – have in the past decade been transformed into heritage sites. Is it desirable, or even appropriate, to represent these histories and memories on an island in New York Harbor? From the perspective of the State of Liberty–Ellis Island Foundation, it was a strategy of survival. As President Steve Briganti told reporters, if the museum were to remain in its previous guise, 'we would lose visitors because we had become out of date' (Dunlap 2015). The 2015 renaming of the museum as the 'Ellis Island *National* Museum of Immigration' expresses the ambition to become as inclusive as possible.

Australian multiculturalism and the first migration museum

Unlike the United States, Australia has no single site of migrant arrival that acts as a commemorative anchor for memories of migration – the island continent's entire coastline has instead been imagined as a barrier to (or opportunity for) arrivals from elsewhere. With its modern origins as a British penal colony in the late eighteenth century, colonial Australia was often portrayed as a natural prison, an isolated outpost at the bottom of the earth. A much earlier history of arrivals connects the continent to the original epic human migration out of Africa, some 75,000 years ago, from which today's Indigenous Australians can claim the world's oldest continuous cultures. Despite these ancient and contemporary migration histories, it was not until the late 1970s that a narrative connecting migration and national identity began to be woven into political rhetoric, public discourse and public representations of the past. The increasingly untenable notion of Anglo cultural homogeneity and loyalty to the 'mother country' – Britain – gradually gave way to an acceptance and embrace of cultural pluralism, or 'multiculturalism', which is both a descriptive term denoting cultural and ethnic diversity, and a public policy designed to respond to that diversity. In 1978, Prime Minister Malcolm Fraser stated that his government wished to 'give significant further encouragement to develop a multicultural attitude in Australian society' and 'foster the retention of the cultural heritage of different ethnic groups and promote intercultural understanding' (Koleth 2010: Part 1a). Alongside new research centres and education programmes in schools, museums became venues though which 'multicultural attitudes' could be encouraged.

The earliest example of a state-funded museum established with these ideas in mind is the Migration and Settlement Museum, which opened in Adelaide, South Australia in 1986. Its name was later shortened to the Migration Museum, and unbeknownst to the curators it was the first of its kind in the world. Three main historical 'actors' were involved in the museum's establishment, each with different agendas to pursue: government bodies willing to lend financial support to multicultural initiatives that could also drive cultural tourism; a small team of curators, who were all interested in the 'new social history' and saw an chance to challenge Anglo-centric national narratives; and, importantly, migrants themselves, who saw an opportunity to have their heritage officially recognised and displayed. Many of these so called 'ethnic' communities (government terminology at the time for non-English speaking groups) had already established their own community organisations and historical societies, and were actively preserving their cultures, politics and histories long before government bodies were willing to support them. They were a diverse group: descendants of German Lutheran immigrants from the nineteenth century, various Italian and Greek groups whose chain migrations over generations had solidified communities with close ties to particular villages, islands or regions back 'home', and other European migrants and former-displaced persons who were part of Australia's large post-Second World War immigration scheme.

The opening galleries of the museum reflected all these ambitions. Rather than displaying only the 'attractive cultural heritage' of ethnic groups (as one early proposal suggested), curators developed a chronological approach to the history of South Australia. The beginning of the narrative portrayed the departure of the first British colonists from England – rather than pioneers or settlers, they were presented as migrants, carrying their own 'cultural baggage' (beliefs, attitudes, cultures) and ethnicities (not only British, but Irish, Welsh and Scottish). A gallery called *Colonisation or Invasion?* reflected the engagement of the curators in current historiography and public debates about the dispossession of Indigenous peoples; however, they stopped short of involving Indigenous South Australians in the process (later adaptations to the galleries would remedy this oversight). The twentieth-century galleries incorporated the personal stories of British, European and Asian migrants, and their keepsakes, within a focus on changing immigration policies. The racially discriminatory 'White Australia Policy' was conveyed using an interactive game, where visitors could press a button to see whether their chosen character would have been able to enter Australia between 1901 and 1958. The chronological narrative of the galleries concluded in the 1980s with panels addressing ongoing problems faced by migrants, including language difficulties, homesickness, cultural isolation and racism. This wasn't a dark, shameful past ending in positive, diverse present, but an ongoing history conveying the challenges of migration and settlement in a strange place and the impacts of that change on Indigenous Australians.

Museums and exhibitions about migration history have been a part of Australia's public history now for three decades, yet tensions surrounding how immigrant identities should be represented remain. At the centre of these is the question of 'who is a migrant?' When a second museum devoted to migration opened in Melbourne, Victoria in 1998, curators adopted the communication objective: 'there is an immigration experience in the life or family history of all non-Indigenous Victorians' (Henrich 2012: 213). But even a clear dichotomy between immigrant and Indigenous experiences provokes further questions. What about Indigenous Australians who identify with the migrant heritages of one or more of their family members? And, after six or more generations of non-Indigenous arrivals, how can museums represent migration experiences that have not survived in family memory, and relate to people who do not identify as descendants of migrants? In recent years exhibitions like *Identity: Yours, Mine, Ours* at Melbourne's Immigration Museum have begun to explore these issues, moving away from the 'migrant journeys' narrative of many previous displays (Henrich 2011). We will see other examples of exhibitions that address migration through the prism of identity later in the chapter. Relationships between migration history, memory and identity are even more fraught in countries with longer histories of migrant settlement, where the origins of ancestors have been long forgotten and recent 'immigrants' are often thought of as 'foreigners'. A national immigration museum in Paris, France, is an example of a project that attempted to 'reassert the power of history over memory', foregrounding the role of migration in the making of the French nation (Green 2007: 251).

History versus memory? The Cité nationale de l'histoire de l'immigration, Paris

The Cité nationale de l'histoire de l'immigration (National Museum of the History of Immigration, or CNHI) was the result of planning and lobbying by advocates, chief among them immigrants and French historians of immigration (Stevens 2008: 59–60). After the concept found government support in 2004, and an available building had been found and restored to accommodate the exhibitions, it opened to the public in 2007. The Palais de la Porte Dorée in the suburbs of Paris was a controversial choice for a museum about immigration. Originally constructed for the International Colonial Exhibition in 1931, the building is decorated both inside and out with stereotypical images of colonial subjects labouring in Africa, Asia, the Americas and the Pacific Islands (see Figure 5.3). France's imperial history (as with all imperial histories) is closely linked to migration. Following decolonisation in the 1950s and 1960s many people who had formerly lived under French colonial rule moved to France. Their presence and apparent cultural difference became highly politicised, fuelling a

Figure 5.3 Façade of the Cité nationale de l'histoire de l'immigration, Paris. Photograph by Jean-Pierre Dalbéra, 2013. Licensed for use under Creative Commons www.flickr.com/photos/dalbera/9071014930.

right-wing anti-immigration movement that has continued to be a major force in French politics. Riots in the poor mainly immigrant suburbs of Paris and other French cities in 2005 were a flashpoint in an ongoing debate about the 'failure' of integration, and added fuel to the anti-immigrant fire. The CNHI was thus an opportunity to challenge and defuse the characterisation of immigration as a 'problem' in modern France, 'to strengthen social cohesion and give immigrants some markers of identity' (Labadi 2013: 313). But as Nancy Green has pointed out, the CNHI 'has had to construct itself *against* the building in which it is housed, rather than *thanks to* it, as Ellis Island' (Green 2007: 244). The legacies of French colonialism, largely unacknowledged in French society, add an additional layer of complexity to the representation of migration history.

While Australia's first migration exhibitions and museums emerged from the introduction of multiculturalism as a public policy, multiculturalism in France has widely been seen to be at odds with republicanism, the bedrock of the French state since the late eighteenth century. Any religious, cultural or ethnic identity runs second to an individual's identity as a French citizen – the former is seen as a private matter, the latter public (the prohibition of religious dress in public schools and government workplaces is one example of this ideology in practice). This separation between public civic life and private religious life has resulted in the invisibility of migration in public memory, and what historian Gérard Noiriel has called 'a genuine phenomenon of collective amnesia' concerning the role of migration in French history (1996: xii). The team of historians who devised the permanent exhibitions of the CNHI chose to confront this amnesia with an 'all-inclusive history of immigration', representing the old, forgotten waves of European arrivals alongside 'new' migration flows from North Africa, Sub-Saharan Africa, Turkey, China and other locations (Green 2007: 248). Maps and census data on large cards in the introductory area demonstrate global migratory flows since the nineteenth century and how they impacted upon the population and economy of France; for instance, the 1891 card maps the journeys of Belgian, Italian, German and Swiss migrant workers, noting their important role in the industrial revolution (CNHI website 2015). The permanent exhibition is organised thematically rather than chronologically, and divided into three parts. The first showcases personal experiences of immigration through migrants' belongings and oral histories, and addresses why people left, why they chose France, how they travelled, and how they negotiated the French authorities and people on arrival. The second section focuses on settled migrant communities and their experiences of living and working in France. Objects on display include posters and cartoons that document the racism, anti-Semitism and stereotyping to which many groups were subject (Dixon 2012: 81). The third includes a positive narrative of immigrant 'contributions' – for example, to sport, literature and music, politics and science. The museum also includes a temporary exhibitions gallery that features changing displays on different immigrant communities, and a 'Contemporary Issues' space where computer workstations and filmed interviews explore recent debates relating to migration.

Displaying common experiences of people from a variety of countries of origin across two centuries was intended to show that 'irrespective of the differences between them, those who have settled in France since the 19th century have faced the same challenges, lived through the same formative experiences and developed the same aspirations' (CNHI website 2015). In other words, recent arrivals, like those before them, have contributed to the nation and become citizens. However, some critics maintain that the emphasis on success and integration has been achieved at the cost of more accurate and complex portrayals of the contemporary immigrant experience in France. Sophia Labadi argues that the museum has missed an important opportunity to explore 'hybrid identities' and as a result has failed to attract immigrants and their children, or to construct any meaningful relationship with them (2013: 320). The notion that a 'people' have to share a common past and aspire towards a common future in order to belong to the nation has in this case has remained embedded within the museum's permanent exhibitions, and migrant cultures remain peripheral to the culture of France.

In all three immigration museums we have seen collections and exhibition themes shaped by museums workers' and stakeholders desires to revise culturally homogeneous national narratives, or to 'correct memory with history'. Government policies of migrant settlement, ranging from the French model of integration to Australian multiculturalism, have to different degrees made these new representations possible in mainstream institutions. In recent years, however, the limits of the archetypal immigration narrative have become more obvious. What about those who come, stay and work for a time, and then move on? Or people who move within their own countries – while they cross no international borders, are their journeys not also migrations? And how might migrant communities articulate their own hybrid identities and heritages? To answer these questions we need to look at alternative spaces to museums of immigration.

Place, identity and belonging: temporary exhibitions and community museums

Aside from dedicated immigration museums, there are a variety of spaces where histories and memories of migration have been displayed. Permanent exhibitions such as *Passports* at the Museum of New Zealand Te Papa Tongarewa, and *Journeys: Australia's Connections with the World* at the National Museum of Australia reflect the centrality of migration to the history and heritage of settler nations. By contrast, Cobh Heritage Centre and the Ulster American Folk Park reveal the importance of emigration, primarily to North America, in Irish history. Emigration has also been a major theme in Italian museums, including entire institutions like the Museo Nazionale del l'Emigrazione Italiana in Rome. Individual permanent exhibitions have also begun to address immigration, such as *Memoria e Migrazioni* at the Galata-Museo del Mare e delle Migrazioni in Genoa (Cimoli 2015: 285). And like Cobh and Genoa, other maritime port cities around the world include museums that represent migration journeys by sea, often as part of wider narratives about trade, technology and travel. Exhibitions relating to migration can also be found in city museums, local museums and community museums, all of which focus on the history and heritage of a particular place or people. In this section we will consider two recent European exhibitions about migration – one from a museum of emigration, the other from a city museum – as well as one Canadian community museum. In all three cases, place and identity are key themes, but varying aims, authors and audiences have shaped presentations that interact in different ways with dominant national narratives.

Germans in Australia, 1788–Today *at the German Emigration Centre*

At the Deutsches Auswandererhaus (German Emigration Centre) in Bremerhaven, Germany, the permanent exhibitions tell the story of the 1.2 million emigrants who travelled to the 'New World' from the maritime port in the nineteenth century. The narrative reflects the dominance of America as a destination, including a recreation of a waiting room at Ellis Island. Additions to the original exhibitions in 2012 added the story of Germany as a country of immigration. But curators were aware that audiences were also interested in the relationship between Germans and Australia – small numbers, as we have seen, were part of nineteenth-century migrations, a larger influx occurred after the Second World War, as a result of refugee resettlement and assisted immigration, and since 2000 a new wave of young Germans have come to the country temporarily under the Australian Government's Working Holiday Scheme. The temporary exhibition *Germans in Australia, 1788–Today*, which was on display during 2013 and 2014 (see Figure 5.4), aimed to represent these layered histories. For immigration

Figure 5.4 The exhibition room (with a reproduction of the Uluru monolith on the left-hand side). Photograph courtesy © German Emigration Center/Foto: Kay Riechers.

museums, it can be difficult to represent people who leave, because they take their stories and objects with them, and the result can be a misleadingly linear narrative of arrivals and nation-building. By contrast, emigration museums, established in the country of origin, can capture both the story of departures, and returns. By exploring how different cohorts of Germans experienced Australia, and how they maintained connections to their homeland, the exhibition was able to present the complex web of expectations, experiences and personal relationships that shape the lives and identities of those who leave, those who are left behind and those who return years later. A photo album on display documented the journey of one family, who lived in Australia for 15 years before returning 'home' in 1974. A team of curators also travelled to Australia to interview Germans and descendants of Germans, and to ask them why they stayed. The exhibition text noted that many return migrants 'maintain a lifelong emotional connection with Australia', just as many of those who chose to stay remain connected to their Germany identity or heritage (Henrich 2014). In countries where an 'insider–citizen' and 'outsider–migrant' dichotomy is embedded in debates about immigration, exhibitions like *Germans in Australia* can provide a productive and even provocative inversion. The memories of migration evoked in this exhibition belong not to 'migrants' or to an ethnic minority, but to Germans – fellow citizens who have embarked on personal migratory journeys, arriving elsewhere as outsiders.

Becoming a Copenhagener *at the Museum of Copenhagen*

Personal migration journeys change lives, and generations of immigration can underpin national narratives, but the routine coming and going of people, ideas and goods is also a constant source of transformation for streets, suburbs and cities across the world. When staff at the Museum of Copenhagen decided to develop an exhibition that could offer an alternative to the dominant Danish discourse on migration, they adopted this wider definition – including migration from rural to urban areas within national borders, cross-border migration and temporary migration (Parby 2015: 124). The exhibition *Becoming a Copenhagener* ran from 2010 until 2015, and, as the title suggests, the central theme was the character of the capital city, and how it shapes and is shaped by the people who choose to live there. In the words of Helen Clara Hemsley, an artist from South Africa who lived in the US, England and Scotland before moving to Denmark: 'I like the fact that I don't feel particularly Danish – partly because Danish is difficult. But I feel like a Copenhagener. I AM a Copenhagener' (Museum of Copenhagen website, 2015).

The exhibition was divided into four themes: 'Arrivals' presented various first impressions of Copenhagen over time; 'Wanted–Unwanted' provided a history of different immigrant groups and asked who had been welcomed/excluded and in what contexts; 'Cosmopolitan Copenhagen' revealed how people from around the world have shaped the city, including connections wrought through colonialism; while 'Urban Communities' deconstructed the idea of the monolithic city to explore communities 'based on music, culture, home, language, civic virtue and resistance' which 'create and remodel the city's many different cultures and help newcomers find their feet' (Museum of Copenhagen website, 2015). In putting together these themes, museum workers came across some unexpected discoveries. As curator Jakob Parby explains, 'looking at migration from the perspective of Copenhagen, research confirmed that immigration from near and far, as well as the exchange of ideas, goods, fashions and blood generated partly by this human mobility, was as old as the city itself'. Comparing demographic information revealed that 'the share of foreign-born citizens in eighteenth-century Copenhagen was actually higher than in Contemporary Copenhagen' (2015: 125). This kind of information proved useful in combatting assumptions about the homogeneity of Danish society – assumptions that were also reflected in the museum's collections. Although the museum had extensive collections documenting the city's urban planning history, social history and municipal history, curators found little in the way of individual migrants' experiences. They instead had to '[reinscribe] new meaning into the collections' by reinterpreting objects that were collected to document the progress of the city, but which could also tell audiences something about the movement of ideas and people (Parby 2015: 127). Arranging loans and donations of extra material from personal contacts helped to tell other stories – including international adoption, which is not often represented in migration exhibitions and was not otherwise part of the museum's collections (131). In the curatorial team's aims and method the idea of identity being tied primarily to the nation state was destabilised, enabling a blurring of the term 'migrant' and all its negative associations, rather than, as many migration exhibitions have done, attempting to show how migrants have integrated or assimilated into the nation as productive citizens.

Immigrant self-representation: the Sikh Heritage Museum, Canada

Thus far we have considered how mainstream museums represent migration heritage in their exhibitions and collections. But how might these representations differ if an immigrant community establishes a museum of their own? As we saw in the case of Adelaide's Migration Museum, community or 'ethno-specific' museums often precede state efforts to commemorate immigrant heritage, after which they become valuable collaborators for professional museum curators in state-sponsored institutions. The official recognition of immigrant heritage can bring new funding sources and audiences to small museums, sometimes elevating their heritage to a national status. So as well as recognising the circumstances in which these museums are established, it is important to ask how, and why, they change.

An example of immigrant community self-representation analysed by Susan Ashley (2014) is the Sikh Heritage Museum at the Gur Sikh Temple in Abbotsford on the west coast of Canada. The museum is located within North America's oldest Gurdwara, completed in 1911 by a small group of Sikh settlers, who had emigrated from the Punjab in north-west India to work on farms and in the lumber industry. These male workers faced unexpected hardships, including labour exploitation, prejudice and discriminatory laws that restricted their wives and children from joining them (Ashley 2014: 157). Despite these obstacles, the Punjabi Sikh community survived and thrived, amounting today to some half a million across Canada. The Abbotsfod Gudwara, since extended and renovated, symbolises this wider success. In 2002 it was designated as a National Historic Site, reflecting the Canadian government's moves to recognise the heritage of ethnic minorities (Ashley 2005: 9) and in 2011, to coincide with the 100th anniversary of the arrival of the first Sikh settlers, a small museum was created in the building's basement, supported by the Department of Canadian Heritage. The museum's organisers, all Sikh-Canadians descended from the early settlers, wanted to 'dispel myths about their heritage, present a story not told in mainstream museums, and assert [their] legitimacy as part of the national Canadian historical narrative' (2014: 157). The result was an exhibition that told the classic migrant success story, from hardship and sacrifice through to success, integration and prosperity. The public face that many immigrant communities seek to present is one of cohesiveness and positive contributions, which Ashley noted 'tends to mythologize, rather than to dwell on, continuing difficulties in the present' (157). In this particular example, racial tensions exist only in the past, whereas inter-community divisions and politics (namely those who support Indian Sikh movements towards an independent Sikh state) are entirely absent. To understand these decisions we must return to the present-focused nature of heritage-making: what political, cultural or economic role is this museum intended to play for those who constructed it? Ashley sees the Sikh Heritage Museum as an 'indicator of nation-state citizenship' (160), a positive, public show of a past that is located within the Canadian national story. In other words, the commemorative activities surrounding the restoration of the site and the opening of the museum strengthen the community's 'hyphen of identity' as Sikh-Canadians (Winter 2001: 55). But the museum is also an effort to fix selected memories in place as a foundation story, so they act as a perpetual anchor for community identity. As one of those involved in the project told the media on opening day: 'future generations will cherish the museum' (Toth 2011).

Memorializing migration: witnessing loss

Memorials and museums of migration, particularly when they are located at places of migrant arrival or departure, often form what Pierre Nora dubbed *lieux de mémoire* (sites of memory). They become a place that holds particular memories, strengthening a group's identity by connecting them to a common heritage (Nora 1989: 7). As we've seen, the *Kindertransport* memorial at London's Liverpool Street Station commemorates a series of arrivals and receptions, honouring the host society and creating a marker of identity for globally scattered survivors, family members and descendants, while Ellis Island's American Immigrant Wall of Honor symbolically writes immigrants' names into the story of the American nation, creating a shared locus for a national immigrant legend. Participatory migrant memorial walls have also been established at museum sites in Canada and Australia, where they have proven a popular device for incorporating diverse family stories and individual memories of migration into a multicultural, egalitarian vision of the nation (Henrich 2015). The recent proliferation of these kinds of migrant memorials mean it is important to ask what kinds of migrant memories may not find expression within their stylistic, institutional and ideological parameters. In this final section we will consider a selection of other memorials to migration, all of which, in different ways, complicate the celebratory migrant success story and undermine or unsettle cohesive nation-building narratives.

The Memorial Wall, Migration Museum, Adelaide, South Australia

At Australia's first Migration Museum curators spent much of the early years establishing working relationships with different community groups through artistic, oral history and exhibition projects. This process was a practical response to the museum's need for migrant objects and stories, and to gain the confidence of communities who had not previously found interest or support from government cultural institutions. It also laid the foundation for relationships of trust and mutual respect. One unanticipated outcome of this work was that six years after opening, in 1992, representatives of the Baltic Communities Council of South Australia approached curators with a request to erect a permanent memorial to honour the memories of thousands killed in their homelands under Soviet rule. The placing of the plaque on an external and publicly visible wall marked the beginning of a new role for the museum – not only a venue for the exhibition of migration history and migrant heritage, it became a site imbued with the memories of migrant communities, dozens of whom have added their own plaques to the wall in the years since and continue to gather at the site to hold annual commemoration ceremonies. Not all the plaques represent particular 'ethnic communities' – one is dedicated to those who were brought to Australia from Britain as unaccompanied child migrants by charitable and religious organisations, with government support, between the mid-nineteenth and mid-twentieth centuries. Many of these children were separated from their families without consent, and suffered childhoods of institutionalisation and abuse (Gill 1998). Formal government apologies to former child migrants in Australia in 2009 and Britain in 2010 brought individuals and groups into contact with museums and libraries to record their memories, develop exhibitions and also to plan memorials. These memories are only now being recognised as a traumatic and shameful chapter in Australia's history of immigration, and memorial projects funded by government bodies are in part a gesture of atonement.

The organic growth of the Memorial Wall demonstrates the importance of public commemorative sites to remember and communicate the grief, trauma and loss felt in many migrant or 'diasporic' communities, who remain connected intimately with their homelands and involved in changing political regimes, and desire justice and recognition for past wrongs. Where 'official' memorials capable of representing these wishes are unavailable, migrant communities have sought out recognition on their own terms. As the then-senior curator of the Migration Museum, Christine Finnimore, wrote: 'The overwhelming need for a community that carries a burden of grief is to discharge that grief by making their history known. They are the living representatives of that history. They need to bear witness to what they have experienced' (1998: 3).

The SIEVX Memorial Project, Canberra

On the south-western shores of Lake Burley Griffin in Australia's national capital, Canberra, are 353 decorated poles, winding through the grassy landscape to form the outline of a boat. Each pole represents a life lost on 19 October 2001, when an overcrowded fishing boat sank on its way from Indonesia to Christmas Island, north of Australia, carrying men, women and children from Iraq and Afghanistan hoping to seek asylum on Australian soil. Despite the shocking scale of this tragedy, Australian media coverage was brief. SIEVX – a naval acronym for Suspected Illegal Entry Vessel – was a blip on the national consciousness in the midst of a national election campaign that was shaped by concerns about security and borders, soon after the events of 11 September that same year in the United States (Ashton et al. 2012: 96).

The SIEVX memorial was the result of a grassroots community project determined to remedy this national forgetting, to educate future generations about Australia's responsibility for the wellbeing of those seeking refuge, and 'to assist and share in the grief of the victims' (Ware 2008: 62). It involved an initial design competition, which sourced and exhibited ideas from Australian high school students, and a community arts project to decorate the poles proposed in the winning design, undertaken across Australian schools, universities, churches and other community groups, and by survivors and relatives of the victims. Since the initial launch in 2006, the memorial has remained in place through seven temporary permits and a three-year licence, and is now approved to stay until at least 2033 (*Canberra Times* 2012). The continuing debate between state and federal heritage bodies over whether the memorial belongs in Canberra reflects the volatile place of asylum seekers, and political responses to them, in Australia's recent history, and the difficulty in incorporating these attempted 'irregular' arrivals into the safer, more celebratory 'nation of immigrants' narrative. Historical echoes of 'irregular' arrivals going back to the British invasion of 1788 contribute to the unease. But as designer Sue-Anne Ware points out, the SIEVX Memorial Project also questions the very nature of contemporary memorialisation practices, provoking the question 'who is worthy of memorials?' (2008: 62). Those who never arrived, in this case, are brought firmly into the national consciousness as potential-Australians, as people with whom Australians hold something in common, and therefore as people whose deaths should be remembered: 'They could so easily have been safely living among us now, their kids at school with ours' (SIEVX Project website).

Figure 5.5 'Porta di Lampedusa – Porta d'Europa' (Gateway to Lampedusa – Gateway to Europe). Photograph by Carlo Alfredo Clerici, 2010. Licensed for use under Creative Commons. See www.flickr.com/photos/psicologiaclinica/4881935828.

Porta di Lampedusa – Porta d'Europa, Lampedusa

On a cliff of the small Mediterranean island of Lampedusa stands a gateway, five metres high and three metres wide, which appears from a distance silhouetted against sky and sea (see Figure 5.5). Up close it reveals itself as a public artwork made from refractory ceramic, augmented by three-dimensional ceramic objects including hands, feet, shoes and bowls – a jumble of human pieces and belongings stuck fast to the structure. 'Porta di Lampedusa – Porta d'Europe' (Gateway to Lampedusa – Gateway to Europe) is the work of Italian artist Mimmo Paladino and was first unveiled in 2008 as a memorial to the tens of thousands who have died trying to reach the island's shores. As the southern-most point of Europe, located closer to Tunisia than Sicily, Lampedusa has since the 1990s become a gateway to Europe for hundreds of thousands of African and Middle Eastern migrants and refugees who, at the hands of smugglers and traffickers, risk everything for the chance of a better life. The non-government organisation behind the memorial, Amani, explained its intended purpose in a press release:

> The fundamental significance of this work is to consign to memory this last two-decade period in which we have seen thousands of migrants perish at sea

in an inhumane way in an attempt to reach Europe . . . often without burial and therefore without pity.

(*Spiegel Online* 2008)

In the absence of traditional rituals of mourning and burial, the Gateway stands as a reminder of the human loss witnessed on Lampedusa. It demands that locals, visitors and international observers bear witness to what has and continues to happen here, events that cannot be easily incorporated into any national narrative. In the future the site may be augmented – plans for a migration museum on the island gained final municipal approval in 2013, and the Gateway has been proposed as a branch of the institution. The museum looks to the past, by safeguarding migrant heritage, but also to the future, as it aims to build on links between migrants and the local community already established through outreach projects including arts and music festivals. Activities which began as anti-authority interventions are now being recognised by the local municipality as valuable cultural projects (Cimoli 2014: 117). It is an ongoing process, in which memories of recent migratory movements are slowly being incorporated into the heritage landscape of Lampedusa.

Conclusions

In the past three decades, conscious efforts to remember migration have characterized memorials, exhibitions and even whole museums. While the migratory movements they represent occurred tens or hundreds of years ago, the focus of state bodies, museum workers and other history-makers has been on what these pasts can 'do' for present relations between people within a community, city or nation. Pluralistic or more inclusive pasts have been constructed by a variety of actors in an effort to right past wrongs, extend full membership of the nation to minorities though the representation of cultural heritage, or patch up tears in the social fabric wrought through inequality, discrimination or prejudice. But some pasts have proven easier to incorporate than others – the celebration of success remains a simpler task than the mourning of loss, especially when such loss reflects badly on the authorities who define local or national heritage. It is often individuals, communities and activists who intervene and draw attention to migratory pasts others might prefer to forget. Rather than seeing this apparent conflict between forms of commemoration and representations of the past as divisive, it is important to recognise the very process of contesting heritage as one which 'drives cultural change' – once acknowledged, tensions can be used to 'produce more complex understandings of citizenship and belonging' (Elder and Whelan 2011: 243, 268). Developments on Lampedusa, and the other sites of memory canvassed here, show this process at work.

The process of contesting migrant heritage does not occur in isolation, but extends beyond the museum or memorial site to reflect and interact with broader concerns. Human mobility, and state efforts to regulate it, currently polarize political debates on topics ranging from border security to human rights, welfare provision and national values, and key voices in these debates frequently reference the past to bolster their proposed policies (Reinisch 2015). Noticing, examining and contextualizing the migratory pasts represented in public spaces and institutions enables us to engage on a deeper level with these debates, to identify inclusive or homogenizing narratives and to question their historical accuracy and contemporary function. Like memorials, these narratives often tell us more about the attitudes and values of those who construct them than they do about the historical events to which they refer. And just as efforts to retain migrant memories as permanent markers in the landscape and in museum collections reflect a process of cultural change, they also have the power to influence personal views and identities. Many more people will encounter migration history through museums exhibitions and memorials, as well as other 'informal' ways such as family history and film, than would ever read an academic book on the topic. For these reasons, representations of migratory pasts, whether in a museum or memorial site, a school classroom or a public debate, demand our critical attention as students of history.

Guide to further reading and online resources

A good starting point for research into museums and memorials of migration is the comprehensive and detailed websites that many museums maintain. Information on past and present exhibitions, educational resources and even virtual museums and memorials can be accessed online, and some museums have digitised catalogues of their collections. Some excellent museum websites include the National Museum of Australia, Museum Victoria (including the Immigration Museum, Melbourne), the Australian National Maritime Museum (especially the Virtual Welcome Wall), the Canadian Museum of Immigration at Pier 21, the Deutsches Auswandererhaus (German Emigration Centre) in Bremerhaven and the archived version of the NSW Migration Heritage Centre, which includes multiple online exhibitions produced in collaboration with migrant communities. For more detail on individual museums and exhibitions from the perspective of museum and heritage professionals and historians, there are a number of recently published collections: see Goodnow et al. (2008); Kleist and Glynn (2012); Gourievidis (2014); Whitehead et al. (2015). Academic journals that feature articles on the connected themes of history, heritage, memory and migration are spread widely across a number of disciplines, including history, sociology, geography, archaeology, heritage management, museum studies and cultural studies.

Notes

1 While examples are drawn from Europe, North America and Australia, similar debates will be found in New Zealand, Asia, Africa and South America.
2 First- and second-class passengers were not subject to screening on the island.
3 The population of the United States in 1980 was 226.5 million. See www.census. gov/history/www/through_the_decades/fast_facts/1980_new.html (accessed 16 December 2015).

References

Ashley, Susan (2005) 'State Authority and the Public Sphere: Ideas on the Changing Role of Museums as a Canadian Social Institution', *Museum and Society*, 3(1): 5–17.

Ashley, Susan (2014) 'A Museum of Our Own' in L. Gouriévidis (ed.), *Museums and Migration: History, Memory and Politics*. Abingdon: Routledge.

Ashton, Paul (2009) 'The Birthplace of Australian Multiculturalism? Retrospective Commemoration, Participatory Memorialisation and Official Heritage', *International Journal of Heritage Studies*, 15 (5): 381–98.

Ashton, Paul, Paula Hamilton and Rose Searby (2012) *Places of the Heart: Memorials in Australia*. Kew, VIC: Australian Scholarly Publishing.

Ashworth, G.J., Brian Graham and J.E. Tunbridge (2007) *Pluralising Pasts: Heritage, Identity and Place in Multicultural Societies*. London: Pluto Press.

Canberra Times (2012) 'Government Backs the SIEV X Memorial', 2 February. Online: www.canberratimes.com.au/act-news/govt-backs-the-siev-x-memorial-20120202-1t8f7.html (accessed 8 January 2016).

Cimoli, Anna Chiara (2015) 'Identity, Complexity, Immigration: Staging the Present in Italian Migration Museums' in Christopher Whitehead, Katherine Lloyd, Susannah Eckersley and Rhiannon Mason (eds), *Museums, Migration and Identity in Europe: People, Places and Identities*. Farnham: Ashgate.

Davidson, John (2004) 'History, Identity and Ethnicity', in Peter Lambert and Phillip Schofield (eds), *Making History: An Introduction to the History and Practices of a Discipline*. London: Routledge.

Davies, Susan (2004) 'History and Heritage', in Peter Lambert and Phillip Schofield (eds), *Making History: An Introduction to the History and Practices of a Discipline*. London: Routledge.

Desforges, Luke and Joanne Maddern (2004) 'Front Doors to Freedom, Portal to the Past: History at the Ellis Island Immigration Museum, New York', *Social & Cultural Geography*, 5 (4): 437–57.

Dixon, Carol Ann (2012) 'Decolonising the Museum: Cité Nationale de l'Histoire de l'Immigration', *Race & Class*, 53 (4): 78–86.

Dunlap, David W. (2015) 'Ellis Island Museum to Update the Story of Immigration in America', *New York Times*, 26 April. Online: www.nytimes.com/2015/04/27/nyregion/ellis-island-museum-to-update-the-story-of-immigration-in-america.html (accessed 20 December 2015).

Elder, Catriona and Yvonne Whelan (2011) 'Tracing the Past in Dublin and Canberra: Memory, History and Nation' in Katie Holmes and Stuart Ward (eds), *Exhuming Passions: The Pressure of the Past in Ireland and Australia*. Dublin: Irish Academic Press.

Finnimore, Christine (1998) 'Grief, Protest and Public History: the Memorial Wall in the Migration Museum, Adelaide', paper presented at Museums Australia National Conference, Exploring Dynamics: Cities, Cultural Spaces, Communities, Brisbane, May. Online: http://pandora.nla.gov.au/pan/30569/20070213-0000/www.museumsaustralia.org.au/whatwedof161.html (accessed 12 January 2016).

Genzlinger, Neil (2015) 'Your Tired, Your Poor and Your Xenophobes at a Rebuilt and Re-envisioned Ellis Island', *New York Times*, 19 May. Online: www.nytimes.com/2015/05/20/arts/design/your-tired-your-poor-and-your-xenophobes-at-a-rebuilt-and-re-envisioned-ellis-island.html (accessed 20 December 2015).

Gill, Alan (1998) *Orphans of the Empire: The Shocking Story of Child Migration to Australia*. Milsons Point, NSW: Vintage.

Goodnow, Katherine, Jack Lohman and Philip Marfleet (2008) *Museums, the Media and Refugees: Stories of Crisis, Control and Compassion*. New York: Berghahn.

Gouriévidis, Laurence (ed.) (2014) *Museums and Migration: History, Memory and Politics*. Abingdon: Routledge.

Green, Nancy L. (2007) 'A French Ellis Island? Museums, Memory and History in France and the United States', *History Workshop Journal*, 63 (1): 239–53.

Harrison, Robert (2004) 'The "New Social History" in America', in Peter Lambert and Phillip Schofield (eds), *Making History: An Introduction to the History and Practices of a Discipline*. London: Routledge.

Henrich, Eureka (2011) 'Identity: Yours, Mine, Ours at the Immigration Museum, Melbourne', *reCollections*. 6 (2). Online: http://recollections.nma.gov.au/issues/vol_6_no_2/exhibition_reviews/identity (accessed 5 December 2015).

Henrich, Eureka (2012) 'Whose Stories Are We Telling? Exhibitions of Migration History in Australian Museums, 1984–2001', PhD thesis, University of New South Wales.

Henrich, Eureka (2013) 'Museums, History and Migration in Australia', *History Compass*, 11 (10): 783–800.

Henrich, Eureka (2014) 'Germans in Australia: 225 years of German Immigration (1788–2013) at the German Emigration Center, Bremerhaven', *reCollections*, 9 (2). Online: http://recollections.nma.gov.au/issues/volume_9_number_2/exhibition_reviews/germans_in_australia (accessed 5 December 2015).

Henrich, Eureka (2015) '"Paying Tribute": Migrant Memorial Walls and the Nation of Immigrants', in S.P. Mosland, A.R. Petersen and M. Schramm (eds), *The Culture of Migration: Politics, Aesthetics and Histories*. London: I.B. Tauris.

Kaplan, Flora E.S. (ed.) (1996) *Museums and the Making of "Ourselves": The Role of Objects in National Identity*. London: Leicester University Press.

Kleist, J. Olaf (2013) 'Remembering for Refugees in Australia: Political Memories and Concepts of Democracy in Refugee Advocacy Post-Tampa', *Journal of Intercultural Studies*, 34 (6): 665–83.

Kleist, J. Olaf and Irial Glynn (eds) (2012) *History, Memory and Migration: Perceptions of the Past and the Politics of Incorporation*. Basingstoke: Palgrave Macmillan.

Koleth, Elsa (2010) *Multiculturalism: A Review of Australian Policy Statements and Recent Debates in Australia And Overseas*. Canberra: Australian Parliamentary Library. Online: www.aph.gov.au/About_Parliament/Parliamentary_Departments/Parliamentary_Library/pubs/rp/rp1011/11rp06#_Toc275248118 (accessed 4 December 2015).

Kushner, Tony (2012) *The Battle of Britishness: Migrant Journeys, 1685 to the Present*. Manchester: Manchester University Press.

Labadi, Sophia (2013) 'The National Museum of Immigration History (Paris, France), Neo-colonialist Representations, Silencing and Re-appropriation', *Journal of Social Archaeology*, 13 (3): 310–30.

Lake, Marilyn (ed.) (2006) *Memory, Monuments and Museums: The Past in the Present*. Carlton, VIC: Melbourne University Press in association with the Australian Academy of the Humanities.

Lowenthal, David (1979) 'Environmental Perception: Preserving the Past', *Progress in Human Geography*, 3 (4): 550–59.

Noiriel, Gérard (1996) *The French Melting Pot: Immigration, Citizenship, and National Identity*, trans. G. de Laforcade. Minneapolis, MN: University of Minnesota Press.

Nora, Pierre (1989) 'Between Memory and History: Les Lieux de Mémoire', *Representations*, 26: 7–24.

Parby, Jakob Ingemann (2015) 'The Theme of Migration as a Tool for Deconstructing and Reconstructing Identities in Museums: Experiences from the Exhibition *Becoming a Copenhagener* at the Museum of Copenhagen' in Christopher Whitehead, Katherine Lloyd, Susannah Eckersley and Rhiannon Mason (eds), *Museums, Migration and Identity in Europe: People, Places and Identities*. Farnham: Ashgate.

Reinisch, Jessica (2015) 'History Matters . . . But Which One? Every Refugee Crisis Has a Context', *History & Policy* paper. Online: www.historyandpolicy.org/policy-papers/papers/history-matters-but-which-one-every-refugee-crisis-has-a-context (accessed 25 April 2016).

Stevens, Mary (2008) 'Immigrants into Citizens: Ideology and Nation-building in the Cité nationale de l'histoire de l'immigration', *Museological Review*, 13: 57–73.

Szekeres, Viv (2011) 'Museums and Multiculturalism: Too Vague to Understand, Too Important to Ignore', in Des Griffin and Leon Paroissien (eds), *Understanding Museums: Australian Museums and Museology, Canberra: National Museum of Australia*. Online: http://nma.gov.au/research/understanding-museums/VSzekeres_2011.html (accessed 6 December 2015).

Tosh, John (2010) *The Pursuit of History: Aims, Methods and New Directions in the Study of Modern History*, 5th edn. Harlow: Longman.

Toth, Christina (2011) 'First Sikh Museum Opened Saturday with Lt.-Gov. Point', *The Abbotsford Times*, 16 December. Online: www.sikhnet.com/news/first-sikh-museum-opened-saturday-lt-gov-point (accessed 14 December 2015).

Walkowitz, Daniel J. (2009) 'Ellis Island Redux: the Imperial Turn and the Race of Ethnicity', in Daniel J. Walkowitz and Lisa Maya Knauer (eds), *Contested Histories in Public Space: Memory, Race and Nation*. Durham, NC: Duke University Press.

Walkowitz, Daniel J. and Lisa Maya Knauer (eds) (2009) *Contested Histories in Public Space: Memory, Race and Nation*. Durham, NC: Duke University Press.

Ware, Sue-Anne (2008) 'Anti-memorials and the Art of Forgetting: Critical Reflections on a Memorial Design Practice', *Public History Review*, 15: 61–76.

Whitehead, Christopher, Katherine Lloyd, Susannah Eckersley and Rhiannon Mason (eds) (2015) *Museums, Migration and Identity in Europe: People, Places and Identities*. Farnham: Ashgate.

Winter, Jay (2001) 'The Memory Boom in Contemporary Historical Studies', *Raritan*, 21 (1): 52–66.

Electronic resources

CNHI Website, 'Industrialisation – 1891' and 'Exhibition Guide'. Online: www.histoire-immigration.fr/musee/collections/industrialisation-1891; www.histoire-immigration.fr/musee/guide-de-l-exposition (accessed 27 November 2015).

History.com (2009) 'Ellis Island'. Online: www.history.com/topics/ellis-island (accessed 10 December 2015).

Museum of Copenhagen website. Online www.copenhagen.dk/en/whats_on/previous_special_exhibitions/the_population_of_copenhagen/theme_arrivals and www.copenhagen.dk/en/whats_on/previous_special_exhibitions/the_population_of_copenhagen/theme_urban_communities (accessed 15 December 2015).

SIEVX National Memorial Project Website. Online: www.sievxmemorial.com/about-sievx.html (accessed 8 January 2016).

Spiegel Online 'Africans remembered: a memorial for Europe's lost migrants'. Online: www.spiegel.de/international/europe/africans-remembered-a-memorial-for-europe-s-lost-migrants-a-560218.html (accessed 10 January 2016).

6 Memory and the city

Simon Sleight

Introduction: memory lane

Memory is spatial. 'Let us close our eyes', proposes Maurice Halbwachs, the sociologist and philosopher, 'and, turning within ourselves, go back along the course of time to the furthest point at which our thought still holds clear remembrances of scenes and people. Never do we go outside space' (Halbwachs 1980 [1950]: 157). Fellow French thinker Paul Ricoeur agrees: '"things" remembered are intrinsically associated with places', he notes. 'And it is not by chance that we say of what has occurred that it *took place*' (Ricoeur 2004: 41; my emphasis). Such indeed is the accepted symbiosis between reminiscence and space that in English the phrase 'memory lane' is a commonplace for thinking about the past. 'I am with you, wandering through Memory Lane', croons the American singer Irving Kaufman on a 1924 recording; 'Living the years, laughter and tears, over again.'[1] As this chapter will elaborate, Kaufman's twin expressions of joy and sorrow are often equally apt in assessing the topic of memory and the city.

If memory and space are closely associated, might it also be said that the patterns and pathways of an individual's memory resemble those of a city? Psychoanalyst Sigmund Freud certainly thought so, at least for a time. Pondering the persistence of 'memory traces' in his patients, he settled on Rome – the 'Eternal City' – as an appropriate simile. Freud saw in the Italian capital the 'vestiges' of earlier phases of development, the older remnants juxtaposed with (or obscured by) subsequent additions. In a similar way to gaining an understanding of Rome's streetscape through personal exploration, Freud determined that acquiring first-hand knowledge of the architecture of the mind would help explain the lingering presence of the past, and the powerful hold on his patients of the recollected fragment. Later, Freud left aside the city comparison, deciding that urban space could not support so many coexistences in the same location as the mind allows (Pile 2002: 111–13). Nonetheless, the much older (and still popular) 'memory palace' and 'memory theatre' mnemonic techniques for associating things worth remembering with a sequence of locations attest to the endurance of the city analogy. Author Italo Calvino's fictional metropolis of Zora is described in just such terms: 'The city . . . is like an armature, a honeycomb in whose cells each of us can place the things he wants to remember' (Calvino 1997: 13). Selectivity as well as storage emerge here as key features. Urban memory, it will be shown, is always partial.

This chapter examines the processes by which some aspects of the past are physically and emotionally inscribed into the urban landscape while others are overlooked, or forgotten. In offering pathways, methodologies and case studies for understanding memory and the modern city, the discussion ranges across city settings on five continents. More 'transurban' than transnational in approach (Roger 2015), the analysis is premised on the utility of a comparative method as described in recent writing on cities. Through comparison, it is held, what is particular and what is shared can be more sharply appreciated. Picking up on older accounts by the likes of Fernand Braudel (1981) and Asa Briggs (1963), historians including Andrew Brown-May (2008), Nicolas Kenny and Rebecca Madgin (2015) have enhanced an intellectual rationale for comparing city settings, be they 'precincts' within cities considered similar or whole cities markedly different in scale or function. For our purposes here, it is to cities – and most often to the longstanding centres of cities – that we can look to perceive the work of memory in space particularly clearly. This chapter turns to such localized settings to take in urban memories both built and intangible, memories shared and memories contested, memories performed and memories lost.

The urban palimpsest

In order to evaluate how memory functions in urban settings, we first need to think about how we perceive the city as an entity. Here I want to introduce the notion of the city as a *palimpsest*. A palimpsest is a multilayered written record, an object of accretion that still bears traces of its earlier form. One of the first scholars to propose reading urban space in this way was Geoffrey Martin, an archivist and historian. Martin argued that:

> Successive generations leave their mark upon [the town], and some of the marks have proved surprisingly durable; they stay there to be read if anyone cares to read them. The visual evidence which is our concern here is the evidence that presents itself when we look at the town: the patterns of its streets and buildings, the blemishes upon the uniformity of the present that remind us of the past. If we think of what we see as a text, we recognise very soon that it is not a simple one: beneath the characters that we first trace, there are other words and phrases to be read: the town is a palimpsest.
>
> (Martin 1968: 155)

Martin's references to 'blemishes' and words beneath words are important – the evidence of the past in cities is always over-written, smudged and partly erased (May 2016). The layout of streets and lanes can provide an enduring framework, sometimes lasting centuries even as the buildings around them are replaced, but such configurations are also vulnerable to alterations or complete erasure. Reading memory at the surface of the city is hence only a first stage, albeit an important one.

Metaphors of peeling and excavating are useful in this context. One might, for example, imagine the city as akin to an onion, its surface layers amenable to removal through analytical incisions. Reflecting on his turn-of-the-century upbringing in Berlin during a period of exile to 1930s Paris, German-Jewish intellectual Walter Benjamin conjured the analogy of the archaeologist. 'He who seeks to approach his own buried past must conduct himself like a man digging', Benjamin declared (Benjamin 1999: 611). Those investigating individual or collective memory can follow Benjamin's advice, figuratively removing and sifting city strata through close observation and careful research. Investigating words as well as objects is central to this activity. As interdisciplinary scholar Andreas Huyssen argues, although the notion of the palimpsest is tied to writing, the 'texts' with which those researching urban memory are concerned are both literary and built (Huyssen 2003: 7). Or put another way – in the phrasing again of Italo Calvino – 'the city must never be confused with the words that describe it. And yet between the one and the other there is a connection' (Calvino 1997: 53).

It is sometimes said that the past lies buried in the present, or else that the past is not really the past at all. Unexpected finds can lay this point bare. After a large-scale demolition of buildings in the Rocks district of Sydney, an archaeo-logical dig in 1994 revealed the former dwellings and possessions of convict labourers brought to the infant colony from the late 1780s (Karskens 1999). The youth hostel that now sits atop this site rather wonderfully makes an attrac-tion out of this once-buried history by presenting arriving backpackers with displayed finds and information panels on 'Fragments of a lost neighbourhood' (see Figure 6.1). More recently, tunnelling beneath London to create the Crossrail

Figure 6.1 Layers of living history at the Rocks youth hostel in Sydney. Photograph courtesy of the author, 2013.

train link has uncovered a number of mass graves, some associated with the Black Death of the fourteenth century, others with the later Bethlem or 'Bedlam' asylum. Up to seven metres of soil rests between the surface of present-day London and the Roman city of Londinium (Museum of London Archaeology 2011). How many more artefacts, one wonders, must lie below the city's streets and buildings?

The analogy of the palimpsest, however, entails something more than the isolated recovery of old bones and quotidian treasures lurking beneath or behind. If urban memories resemble layered scripts those scripts also reference each other, meaning that wider contexts must be evaluated. Individual and collective memory hence draws on and is constantly re-shaped by memories circulating elsewhere, in public discussions, for example, or among peers. Urban palimpsests of memory, then, run beneath ground as well as behind facades; they are subject to alterations through time and operate in often crowded settings of competing recollections. Thick with history, cities also play host to dense, interconnected and shifting layers of memory.

Prism cities

Three cities figure especially prominently in recent scholarly understandings of memory and the city, and it is worth assessing the interleaving histories of each before opening out the discussion into a more thematic analysis. Hiroshima, Berlin and New York have all witnessed shattering upheavals in the twentieth and twenty-first centuries, with each city serving subsequently as a prism through which debates about history and memory are refracted.

On the morning of 6 August 1945, the first atomic bomb used as a weapon of war fell on the Japanese city of Hiroshima. Cataclysmic damage resulted; at least 80,000 people were killed instantly and some 62,000 of the 90,000 buildings in the city were destroyed. As the dust cleared, up to five square miles of the city centre lay in ruins (Atomic Heritage Foundation 2016). Such bald figures are mere approximations of an event that continued to unfold years later as city-dwellers succumbed to radiation sickness, as damaged buildings collapsed or were torn down, and as debate raged regarding how to rebuild.

In the aftermath of the attack on their city, Hiroshima's survivors harboured what historian Lisa Yoneyama calls 'dark' memories (Yoneyama 1999: 44). In this context, decisions regarding what to do with the skeletal frames of ruined buildings and the harrowing sites of medical treatment became contested matters. While some of the *Hibakusha* – the Japanese collective noun for survivors of the atomic bombing – welcomed the preservation of key locations, others wished not to confront sites of horror as they continued their lives (Yoneyama 1999: 72–5). As a case in point, the remains of the former exhibition hall now dubbed the 'A-Bomb Dome' elicited painful flashbacks for many city-dwellers during the period of post-war reconstruction (Utaka 2009: 37–8). Saved from demolition through the fostering of consensus, and reinforced by added steel, this edifice now stands amidst a Peace Memorial Park. According to Yoneyama, the preservation of the building and the creation of the park around it served to 'tame' memories of the bombing. By hiving off just a small portion of the city for intense reflection, surrounding neighbourhoods – many left equally desolate by the bomb – could hence regenerate without such permanent reminders (Yoneyama 1999: 43–65). 'People built this city to forget', observed a journalist, visiting in 1962 (Zwigenberg 2014: 228).

The park itself continues to be an extraordinary place of memorial culture. Over 50 sites of commemoration dot the landscape, including a memorial cenotaph (unveiled in 1952) that houses in a coffin-like object the names of all of those who perished, a circular memorial mound containing the ashes of up to 70,000 unidentified dead, and a Children's Peace Monument (unveiled in 1958), festooned with folded paper cranes in memory of origami practitioner 12-year-old Sadako Sasaki, killed by radiation poisoning in October 1955 (see Figure 6.2). The significance of this site for what historian Ran Zwigenberg calls 'global memory culture' is attested by the granting of 'World Heritage' status to this location in 1996 (Zwigenberg 2014), as well as, one might add, by the necessity for offsite storage of the countless thousands of paper cranes sent to Hiroshima from around the world for intended display. The presence of the past is keenly felt in other ways, too; volunteers (some of them *Hibakusha* and their descendants) offer readings of oral history survivor accounts to visitors and teach overseas tourists the art of folding paper cranes. Zwigenberg finds the Peace Park and associated museum to be constrained, 'perhaps even too calm' given the destruction visited upon the city and the continued threat of nuclear war (Zwigenberg 2014: 1–2). Arguably, though, it is the contrast between contemporary tranquillity and abiding trauma that makes visiting Hiroshima's Peace Park all the more memorable. Attesting to the enduring complexities of changing attitudes regarding the nuclear attack, only recently, in 2008 and 2016, have high-ranking American politicians (including President Barack Obama) been invited into this memorial space for organized commemorations.

While central Hiroshima is now internationally significant as a site for reflecting on the horrors of war, another city ravaged by conflict harbours its own ghosts. Berlin has been termed a 'paradigmatic public memory space' and 'a city text frantically being written and re-written' (Huyssen 2003: 9, 49). Subject in the twentieth century alone to the rise and fall of dictatorship, expulsions, warfare, physical partition and reunification, Berlin has hosted the vigorous playing out of remembering and forgetting for decades.

As with Hiroshima, what we might term the 'burden of absences' is an enduring concern in Berlin, nowhere more so than at architect Daniel Libeskind's Jewish Museum Berlin, opened in 2001. The central axis for the building is a blank space bereft of collected objects, a cavernous void suggesting the rupture and loss occasioned by the Holocaust. Although other areas of the museum address the longstanding and substantial contributions of Jewish citizens to Berlin's history, the void must be crossed and re-crossed by visitors – in the words of Libeskind it

Figure 6.2 The Children's Peace Monument in Hiroshima. Designed by Kazuo Kikuchi, the memorial depicts a young girl holding aloft a golden crane in a prayer for peace. Note the display cases containing garlands of donated paper cranes in the background. Photograph courtesy of the author, 2014.

is 'an absence that will never go away, no matter how much is built there; an absence which is always going to be part of the city' (Libeskind 2009: 71). Further historical cleavages associated with Nazi persecution can be encountered across Berlin. At a train station in suburban Grunewald, for example, an empty platform has since 1991 hosted an iron walkway with raised letters detailing the number of Jews deported, the dates of departure and their destinations. No trains ever leave this particular platform, notes Svetlana Boym; instead 'the past is stored here in its unredeemable emptiness' (Boym 2001: 194). Nearby, a concrete wall featuring hollow human forms frozen in the act of walking underscores the point, these seven exemplars representing some 50,000 individuals who trod the same path to oblivion at this single railway station (see Figure 6.3). Back in central Berlin, gazing downwards at the Bebelplatz next to Humboldt University reveals yet another absence. An empty room beneath a transparent viewing panel bears shelves that hold no books, a commemoration of the festival of book burning orchestrated by the Nazis in May 1933. Loss of culture is again the overriding motif, with such absences designed to force connections with the past in the minds of those looking on.

'Library', as the Bebelplatz memorial is called, was unveiled in 1995. That decade proved especially important in Berliners' responses to their past. Not only did these years see the city address publicly its role in the Holocaust (the decision

Figure 6.3 Karol Broniatowski's 1991 'Memorial to the Jews Deported from Berlin' at Grunewald Station. The sign to the right points towards the Track 17 memorial. Photograph courtesy of Philipp Ruff, 2017.

to build Berlin's stark Holocaust Memorial was also taken at this time), but following the reunification of East and West Germany in 1990 city-dwellers also faced a complex series of decisions regarding what to retain from the more recent past, and how – or even whether – to commemorate division. Renewed capital city status and a desire to acknowledge difficult histories in formerly Soviet East Berlin (the chosen location of the Holocaust Memorial) amplified the tone of public discussion. Attention focused strongly on the one hundred miles of the Berlin Wall, officially known as 'the antifascist protective rampart' and later as simply 'the border' in the Socialist East (Ladd 1998: 18). Erected from August 1961 onwards by the East German authorities, the security zone had sliced through the heart of Berlin for nearly 30 years by the time of its breach in November 1989. Official demolition began the following summer, concluding in 1992, with various sections and fragments donated to public institutions around the world, souvenired by locals and sold to tourists. During this time, many choices had to be made: what to do with the crosses commemorating those killed while trying to flee across the Wall to the West; whether to keep the stone monuments marking the deaths of East German border guards; whether to preserve the political graffiti adorning sections of the Wall; how (or if) to mark the former route of the boundary; and whether to leave any sections in place as permanent reminders (Ladd 1997: 24–31). The public debates around these issues – debates coterminous with the rise of Wall tourism and concerns regarding authenticity – provide particularly rich pickings for scholars of history and memory.

East Berlin's buildings, statues and plaques also focussed attention following the collapse of the German Democratic Republic (GDR). Obvious targets included the former headquarters of the Stasi (the state secret police; now a museum) and busts of hated figures displayed in public. From March 1992 an independent commission considered the case of East Berlin's monuments (Ladd: 196–9, 201). Not at risk were the Soviet memorials commemorating the battle for Berlin; under the terms of an international treaty in 1990, Germany's leaders had pledged protection in part-exchange for securing unification (Ladd: 194). A different fate eventually befell the Palace of the Republic, home at the height of the GDR to the East German parliament as well as eateries, an art gallery, bowling alley, concert hall and ballrooms. For many East Berliners, the building inspired ambivalence – it embodied state power, but it had also offered welcome attractions and a taste of modernity. Furthermore, in 1990 free elections had taken place in the Palace, and it was there that plans for reunification were announced (Boym 2001: 187–8). Amidst public protests, politicians decided in 2003 to demolish the Palace before agreeing to construct in its place something hardly less controversial in nature: a part re-creation of the Prussian *Stadtschloss*, or Berlin Palace, a building originally dynamited by the Socialists in 1950 for its imperialistic overtones. The site's history might be especially convoluted, but in this city such is the norm. Fanning out across Berlin, past and present collide at locations ranging from iconic buildings to domestic residences with stories to tell, or to forget.

Our final 'prism city' takes us to a third continent. New York has long show-cased a particularly rich 'memory infrastructure' (Mason 2009: xxv–xxviii). Waves of immigrants have left their mark and been remembered; buildings and memorial representations flag local concerns as well as national milestones. Since at least the 1890s, argues historian Randall Mason, progressives and preservationists have sought to add or protect memorial fixtures amidst the flux of a heightened modernity of change, redevelopment and property speculation (Mason 2009: xx–xiv), entailing that by the close of the twentieth century the 22.7 square miles of Manhattan Island ranked among the world's most thickly populated areas for formal memorialization. On all of this there is rich and insightful scholarship (see, for instance, discussion of Ellis Island elsewhere in this volume). But a survey of such writing is not my purpose here. Instead I turn my attention to the effects of a dual intrusion into the fabric of New York, and Manhattan in particular.

The deliberate collision of two passenger airliners with the twin towers of the city's World Trade Center on 11 September 2001 is an event of such significance that it generated its own shorthand name, '9/11', as well as a military conflict and a period of agonized debate about how best to remember the victims. Unlike the examples of Hiroshima and wartime Berlin, this was a defining episode that could be watched live on television and later replayed to infinity via documentaries and by video-sharing websites such as YouTube. As with the case of the Berlin Wall, discussions about potential means of public memorialization were held while recollections were still very raw. The challenge, as outlined by Huyssen, was how to reconcile the desire to re-use a prized piece of real estate in lower Manhattan with the need to commemorate the dead and to memorialize a portentous historical event (Huyssen 2003: 158).

Such large-scale concerns mattered little in the immediate aftermath of the attacks. Even as underground fires continued to send plumes of smoke across the New York skyline, city-dwellers created their own 'vernacular' memorials, partly in the hope of eliciting information about missing loved ones, and partly as commemorative acts in the absence of recovered bodies. Urban anthropologist Elizabeth Greenspan and historian Kay Ferres have assessed these ephemeral memorial sites, recording their own personal reflections as well as the reactions of those around them (Greenspan 2005; Ferres 2013). Visiting the cordoned-off perimeter around the collapsed buildings to take field notes in the weeks after the destruction, Greenspan observed clusters of homemade memorial objects such as posters, poems, photographs and drawings. Boundary fencing also carried thousands of inked messages, turning what was intended as a barrier into a 'col-lective project of remembrance and grieving', and simultaneously initiating a heritage site (Greenspan 2005: 374–8). Some memorials recorded individual lives, Greenspan observed; others expressed ideals transcending national concerns and suggested that 'Ground Zero', as it became known, was a global memory place (Greenspan 2005: 379–80). Writing more than a decade on from the events of September 2001, Ferres locates the people's tributes (commemorations long since removed and in some cases retained by museums) as a preliminary stage in an unfolding process of memorialization. To this end, the first anniversary of the attacks initiated a change, with greater official oversight of commemorative impulses hereon in – bells tolling to mark the times of collision, for instance, and politicians and surviving family members invited down into cleared land at Ground Zero to bear witness to a solemn roll call of the dead (Ferres 2013: 48).

The question of what to do with the site itself remained. Architect Daniel Libeskind, by now famous for his work in Berlin, assumed responsibility as master planner amidst considerable public rancour. His original designs referenced memory in multiple ways: a new 'Freedom Tower' was to top out at 1776 feet (the number matching the date of the American Declaration of Independence); the original footprints of the Twin Towers were to remain visible; surrounding buildings would echo the upward sweep of the Statue of Liberty, casting no shadows over the area (Libeskind 2009: 80–81). Little remains of Libeskind's detailed vision on site today, though two significant aspects of his 'Memory Foundations' plan persisted through multiple revisions and the hiring and firing of new architects. A new skyscraper, One World Trade Center, retains the height originally envisaged, and the footprints of the Twin Towers survive as memorial spaces. Some 5,201 submissions were received from 63 nations for the design of these spaces, another treasure trove of contemporary (and global) responses to memorialization.[2] Michael Arad's winning entry, opened to the public in September 2011, features cascading waterfalls and the names of the deceased cut into metal sheets flanking square pools (see Figure 6.4). As in Berlin, the presence of absence is again prevalent. An attempt 'to express the inexpressible', notes Ferres, the trope of the void 'stands for unintelligibility as much as for loss' (Ferres 2013: 50). Deciduous trees planted nearby – including a surviving pear tree from the original World Trade Center site – soften the memorial precinct, and are intended to signify rebirth (Arad and Walker 2003: 526). Visitors can also tour the 9/11 Memorial Museum, descending beneath ground to take in artefacts including twisted steel girders and the possessions of the deceased. There are striking similarities here with Hiroshima's Peace Memorial Park, with the site as a whole offering a bounded yet nonetheless global space for affective connection with the past.

Voids; absences; suffering; renewal: it would seem that Hiroshima, Berlin and New York each foreground the idea of memory-as-trauma, trauma to which contemplative spaces aim to confer a form of therapy. With post-9/11 books on memory and the city bearing such titles as *Wounded Cities, Traumascapes, Among the Dead Cities* and *Heritage That Hurts* (Schneider and Susser 2003; Tumarkin 2005; Grayling 2006; Sather-Wagstaff 2011), it can be tempting to conflate urban memory with an inventory of horrors. This would be short-sighted. As Huyssen argues, to collapse memory into trauma alone is excessively narrow because it unduly limits the role of human agency. 'Memory', Huyssen implores, 'whether individual or generational, political or public, is always more than only the prison house of the past' (Huyssen 2003: 8). A particular definition of urban memory is useful here in extending our scope and suggesting further avenues of inquiry. In an edited collection on the topic, architectural historian Mark Crinson suggests that urban memory commonly 'indicates the city as a physical landscape and

Figure 6.4 'Reflecting Absence': memorialization at the site of one of the Twin Towers in New York. Each year flowers are placed into the metal sheeting on the birthdays of those remembered here. Beyond the trees the new One World Trade Center building climbs skywards. Photograph courtesy of the author, 2014.

collection of objects and practices that enable recollections of the past and that embody the past through traces of the city's sequential building and rebuilding' (Crinson 2005: xii). In suggesting *things* as well as *activities*, Crinson's delineation promises a more thematic approach, an approach pursued in the remainder of this chapter.

Monumental memory

Mention monuments as a category of analysis, and thoughts might turn towards ruins like the A-Bomb Dome in Hiroshima. But most likely one will think first of statues – these are ossified or frozen history, representing (in the words of jurist Sanford Levinson) deliberate efforts 'to stop time' (Levinson 1998: 7). As discussed by Keir Reeves in Chapter 3 of this volume, French historian Pierre Nora conceived such objects as '*lieux de mémoire*', sites of memory that aimed to trigger recollections. Importantly, Nora argued that such encouragements to remember blossomed in France at a time when the collective context of memory in modern society – the *milieu de mémoire* – was declining (Nora 1989). One could buttress Nora's grand theory by considering a veritable boom in the erection of statues in many world cities from the late 1800s. Producing a detailed catalogue of Queen Victorias across the former British Empire, for example, would be revealing in this regard, allowing the dates of construction to be compared and explained alongside such aspects as local context, scale and the inclusion of representational regalia.

Statues and monuments, of course, are mere stand-ins for broader understandings of the individuals and causes they represent, though their existence and the intentions behind them – intentions often helpfully elaborated at moments of unveiling – can provide insights into historical preoccupations. Power dynamics surround the construction of statuary and these forces warrant examination, too. 'Public monuments do not arise as if by natural law to celebrate the deserving', argues Kirk Savage; 'they are built by people with sufficient power to marshal (or impose) public consent for their erection' (Levinson 1998: 63). When regimes change and relations of power alter, statues can often serve as awkward reminders of a past many people would rather forget. Note here Coronation Park in Delhi, for instance, which houses a diminishing gallery of notables associated with the British Raj, relocated there in the 1960s and recently largely broken up (McGarr 2015), or the treatment accorded to statues of Lenin in cities like Vilnius since the sweeping political changes of the early 1990s. 'Written in stone' these figures may have been, but initial prominence does not necessarily entail permanent survival.

Discerning public reactions to contemporary or historical statues is far from straightforward. Historians can sometimes locate tantalizing suggestions, like evidence of the 'hundreds' of personal messages left at the base of London's Cenotaph war memorial in the 1920s and 1930s (Michalski 1998: 80), but following urban historian Graeme Davison we are entitled to ask plainly: 'do statues (still) speak?' (Davison 2000). 'If cities are characterised by any one mood,' argues Steve Pile, 'then maybe it is indifference' (Pile 2002: 122). Feelings of exhaustion – or at least very delayed journeys – would surely result, so the argument goes, if citizens engaged meaningfully with all the triggers for reflection that cities yield. Author Iain Sinclair goes further still, contending that 'Memorials are a way of forgetting' (Sinclair 2003: 9). Perhaps there is some truth in this claim. One could point as evidence towards a 1960s survey of Liverpool's residents that found only patchy knowledge of the existence of statuary outside the city's central St George's Hall and general confusion about which figures were remembered there. Half of those interviewed also failed to recall the presence of statues flanking the entrance to the Queensway Tunnel, opened only around 30 years earlier amidst huge crowds and royal fanfare (Lynch 1998 [1972]: 63). Certainly there is something to be said, then, for researching the changing pulling power of statuary through time.

Yet public indifference cannot explain the contests that periodically flare around existing statues. For the American city of Cleveland, historian John Bodnar demonstrates that such tussles are not confined to the contemporary era. It was here, in the early 1890s, that proposals to replace a memorial erected in 1860 to commemorate the Anglo-American War of 1812–15 with a monument honouring Union fighters in the subsequent American Civil War met with stiff resistance. After increasingly militant proponents of the new monument (including Civil War veterans) staked out their claim with fencing, defenders of the existing statue gathered to tear down the fence and display their hostility to change. Public speeches and the letters pages of local newspapers became arenas for the dispute to simmer, with nothing less than an Ohio Supreme Court intervention required to force the removal of one memorial and its replacement with another (Bodnar 2004: 78–9). In this city at least, the representational value of public statuary was hardly disregarded. I shall return to this theme in a later section of this chapter, updating the story and explaining why the presence, absence or design of public statuary continues to spark lively debates.

Signified memory

Aside from cohering around prominent statues and monuments, memory operates in the city in more subtle ways. Scholars who pursue 'semiology' – the study of signs and symbols, most famously as advocated by French theorist Roland Barthes (1967) – have helped initiate alternative ways of reading city spaces. Such signs can say much about the relationship of memory and history for those who care to notice. Street names, for instance, often signify people considered notable, or else record for intended posterity events, activities or places. To this end, Shoe Lane and Petticoat Lane in London recall commercial activities while the grand and sweeping Boulevard Haussmann in Paris is named after the influential urban planner of the mid-nineteenth century, 'Baron' Georges-Eugène Haussmann. In Australia, by contrast, the suburb of St Kilda in the city of Melbourne (appellations bearing Scottish and English origins respectively) plays host to raft of Ukrainian-inspired street names referencing the Crimean War of

1853–6. The aftermath of battle coincided with suburban expansion, and colonial loyalists looked to recent history for inspiration. Indeed, in settler societies such as Australia, Canada and New Zealand one can find an abundance of names taken from elsewhere and intended to offer a sense of rootedness in a European past. Indigenous placenames were also commonly adopted for smaller districts and towns, albeit in frequently altered or misspelled formulations (for instance the suburbs of Cardup and Yangebup in Perth, each word a mishearing of local Aboriginal names for particular flora and fauna). The ultimate indication of the power of urban naming is revealed when shifting historical contexts prompt whole cities to be retitled – hence Salisbury's renaming as Harare, capital of Zimbabwe (formerly Rhodesia) in 1982, the transformation of French colonial Saigon into Communist Ho Chi Minh City (in 1976), or Saint Petersburg's evolution from its earlier titles of Leningrad and Petrograd. India alone contains dozens of examples for the post-independence period, perhaps most famously the alterations of Calcutta to Kolkata (2001), Bombay to Mumbai and Madras to Chennai (both 1996). Earlier examples in the immediate aftermath of British withdrawal include Cawnpore's new designation as Kanpur (1948) and the switch from Ellore to Eluru (1949). Over 80 streets in Mumbai also bear new titles.

Within the carefully named streets of deliberately named suburbs of purpose-fully named cities, one can sometimes find heritage walking routes, another form of signified history. Boston in America has its Revolutionary 'Freedom Trail', while Shanghai promotes the Bund, a 1.5 kilometre walk stitching together many important colonial buildings from the later 1800s. Each route features plaques to aid navigation and to indicate waypoints. In London and other British towns and cities, blue plaques mounted on walls are a common sight, scattered across city centres and suburbs to indicate the dwelling places of people considered 'eminent' or the location of events regarded as foundational. Periodic walking tours take in collections of the plaques, with the attribution scheme – currently overseen by English Heritage – stretching back to 1866. Websites and apps offer further aids to peripatetic connoisseurs of history and memory in Britain and beyond, part of a broader digitization of public and personal reminiscences.[3]

Urban epitaphs can also be less prominent. Park benches denote often touching personal memories of lives lead and absences felt; by June 2016, some 4,223 such memorial plates, each 'with stories to tell' and benefactors to pay for them, could be found affixed to benches in New York's Central Park alone (*New York Times*, 17 June 2016). As with gravestones in cemeteries, the inscriptions operate at different levels; their affective power is clearly heightened for acquaintances and loved ones, and not necessarily noticed by others. Weathering or neglect can take their toll, too – be they personal or public, memorials need tending to remain legible. So-called 'vernacular' memorials might be more ephemeral still, encompassing flowers and cards taped to a lamppost to commemorate a tragic road death, white spray-painted 'ghost bicycles' at the scenes of fatal collisions, or 'love locks' attached to fencing or railings to signify relationships (Ashton et al. 2012). Signified urban memory can be accidental, too, constituting 'unintentional monuments' in Boym's helpful categorization (Boym 2001: 78). Examples of the

Figure 6.5 Attempts to 'fix' memory: 'love locks' attached to the Passerelle Léopold-Sédar-Senghor in Paris. Photograph courtesy of the author, 2017.

latter include faded shop signs recording former trades, abandoned or repurposed industrial buildings (sometimes retaining in name a former activity), outdated graffiti bearing political messages, or old bill posters for events now passed. One select group of intrepid urban explorers, psychogeographers, take special delight in recording such traces, sometimes relating them to their own recollections of the same neighbourhoods (Self 2007; Micallef 2010; Sinclair 2003). Following their lead, rather than studying memorials in isolation, it can be especially effective to study *landscapes* of different types of commemoration across city spaces, though the balance between breadth and depth of analysis has to be weighed. And, as ever, it is also important to ponder the memorial signs *not* permitted or seen – in the Belleville quarter of Paris, for instance, no street names recall the radical weeks and bloody end of the Paris Commune of 1871, nor is the important role of the neighbourhood's municipal building marked at the site (Zederman 2014: 114–16). Absences and erasures can be accidental or deliberate – city texts of history and memory do not write themselves.

Performances of memory

Intended fixity characterizes the forms of urban memory assessed so far. Civic performances showcase a different aspect: memory-on-the-move via processions or parades through the streets, pageants and theme parks conveying versions of the past, or personal provocations for reflection amidst the bustle of city life. Scholars agree that grand-scale public commemorations reached a high point in Europe, the United States and Australasia in the late nineteenth and early twentieth centuries, during an era of heightened nationalism (Hobsbawm and Ranger 1983; Davison 1987; Glassberg 2001; Brown-May and Graham 2006). Memory specialist Paul Connerton, among others, references as an emblematic example the fanfare associated with Bastille Day in Paris (commencing in 1880, and recalling a key episode in the French Revolution) (Connerton 1989: 63). Whether prompted by the convenience of the anniversary calendar or the desire to 'invent' something new based on something purportedly older, a classic itinerary for such events consisted of mustering, processing with props through streets regarded as significant, and listening to lessons of the day from speechmakers (usually politicians, clerics or both). Social cohesion around a shared view of history – often combined with a reminder about 'traditional' hierarchies of authority, rooted in the past – was a common aim, likely amplified by city fathers' anxieties concerning accelerated social changes. One cannot assume, however, that the intended message was received; studies show that group spectatorship and even collective participation did not necessarily equate with shared sentiment (Glassberg 2001: 62; Sleight 2013: 197; Griffiths 2014: 153–82).

The processional message was as much local as national by the early 1900s, sponsored by suburban ideals and city boosterism. In Ilford, a district then located at London's eastern periphery, a carnival in 1910 featured representations of rural life including blacksmiths and milkmaids alongside floral motifs. This pastoral emphasis was significant, argues urban historian Dion Georgiou, because it came just as Ilford was being encroached upon by metropolitan sprawl. Amidst the laying out of new streets, the procession can hence be read as at least in part an effort to assert continuity with a slowly vanishing past, an emphasis also evoked in selected press commentary at the time (Georgiou 2014: 228–39). A romantic vision also characterized Philadelphia's 1908 festivities marking the city's 225th birthday. One float, titled 'City Beautiful', presented to crowds a colossal Quaker woman unifying through prayer the 28 pre-existing localities. Pointedly, descendants of early settlers were invited to dress and parade as their forebears, while representatives of later arrivals including the Irish, Italians and Poles were overlooked (Glassberg 2001: 68). Addressing the selectivity of collective memory is always critical in understanding such events. Belfast in Northern Ireland – discussed in Ian McBride's chapter elsewhere in this book – is a case in point in this regard, its summer 'marching season' a tinderbox of competing claims to history and territory (Gorby 2004).

Performances of memory can also take us to re-created streets bounded by ticket booths and gift shops. Albeit often located outside cities (given the constraints of available space), so-called 'living history' museums are commonly focused on urban themes. On the outskirts of Nikkō in Japan, for instance, sightseers can 'step back in time' at Edo Wonderland, taking in a re-created market, sword-smith's and courtesan procession, while at Sovereign Hill in the city of

Figure 6.6 Historical 'activators' at Ballarat's Sovereign Hill. Re-created nineteenth-century buildings line the street. Photograph courtesy of the author, 2016.

Ballarat the Australian gold rush of the 1850s is brought to life by costumed 'activators' venturing up and down a re-presented Main Street (see Figure 6.6) or guiding visitors through recreations of underground mine workings.[4] Offering depictions of eighteenth-century Virginian life, Colonial Williamsburg is the largest visitor attraction of this type, and one among dozens in the United States alone. Such experiences help fulfil what historian Raphael Samuel calls 'the quest for immediacy, the search for a past which is palpably and visibly present' (Samuel 2012: 175). Like 'open world' video games offering participant exploration of historical settings rendered digitally, this is immersive history, available for the price of an entry ticket.

That many more people engage with the past in this way than through studiously footnoted library books can be a cause for consternation – and indeed annoyance – among some professional historians, who worry about the authenticity of living history attractions. 'Real' period buildings (or else sometimes very carefully researched approximations of them) can lend a sense of verisimilitude, it is argued, but the complexities and inequities of urban living are usually overlooked. Academic historians can hence be sniffy about what many perceive as a sanitized version of an unchanging past (Evans 1991). As summarized by Samuel:

'Living history' . . . shows no respect for the integrity of either the historical record or the historical event. It plays snakes and ladders with the evidence, assembling its artefacts as though they were counters in a board game. It treats the past as though it was an immediately accessible present, a series of exhibits which can be seen and felt and touched. It blurs the distinction between fact and fiction . . .

(Samuel 2012: 197)

And yet, Samuel continues, the practice and ambition of living history actually corresponds with several traditional scholarly aims, not least the desire to give voice to the dead, to make 'flesh-and-blood figures out of fragments'. Historians similarly dramatize evidence, he observes, offering choreographed versions of the past using a cast of characters that they themselves select (Samuel 2012: 197). The academic art of 'thick description', one might add – namely the technique of taking the reader direct to the unfolding historical moment through an informed portrayal of the past – is perhaps also not so far removed from the re-created Main Street, or the delights of Edo Wonderland. Certainly there is scope for rich comparative analysis of the multitude of living history museums opened across the world since the mid-twentieth century, and room to further evaluate what they imply about the relationship between past and present.

The performances of the past showcased in processions, pageants and historical theme parks are ephemeral: parades pass by and entry to historical theme parks is time bound (pun intended). More fleeting still is a final category of performed memories: pop-up enactments. Coinciding with the centenary of the First World War, for instance, the British 'we're here because we're here' project garnered very substantial public attention in 2016. On 1 July, a hundred years on from the first day of the Battle of the Somme, some 1,400 volunteers dressed in reproduced military uniforms appeared unannounced across the United Kingdom, clustering together in shopping centres, car parks and train stations. Periodically breaking out into song – 'we're here because we're here' was a caustic refrain in the trenches – the volunteers marched or stood in silence, boarded trains (including the London Underground) and when approached handed out small cards detailing the particulars of one of the 19,240 soldiers from British regiments killed in France on a single day in 1916. 'Most memorials you have to go to', explained Jeremy Deller, the artist behind the performance piece; 'This is a memorial that will actually come to you just when you're not expecting it.'[5] Photographs of the event capture a ghostly atmosphere of past and present comingling, lost legions made flesh and blood in the form of mostly mute volunteers.

While town and city centres provided the most prominent settings for Deller's pop-up commemorations, 'we're here because we're here' was not solely concerned with urban memory. Other artists tackle this theme directly, however. As cases in point, a number of photographers have been prompted to produce documentary interventions by the relentless demolition and construction within Chinese cities since the 1990s. In Chen Shaoxiong's 1997 *Street* series, for example, three-dimensional photo-collages of Guangzhou are held by the artist in front of matching locations around the city, and photographed again for posterity. The task is hopeless, admits the artist: 'I feel that the speed at which I photograph the streets of Guangzhou will never catch up with the speed at which the streets of Guangzhou are changing . . . For this reason I don't dare to leave Guangzhou for long' (Jiang 2015: 46). To the north, in Beijing, Wang Jinsong's *One Hundred Chai* series (1999) also performs the work of memory within a rapidly changing urban environment. The series features photographs of the Chinese character *chai* (meaning 'to demolish') daubed by the authorities on domestic exterior walls, doors and windows across the city as a prelude to destruction (Jiang 2015: 103–5). Wang's images of these modest homes, homes condemned to make space for high-rise accommodation, are an elegy to a disappearing age and documentary evidence of humble living arrangements. For the keen student of urban memory, displays of such artworks, as well as chance encounters with historically themed performances or visits to living history sites, provide important resources. Cities are alive to possibilities for perceiving refracted versions of the past in the present and a kaleidoscope of shifting scenes awaits those who stop to look, and inquire.

Intangible urban memory

My penultimate category of urban memory brings to the foreground our very personal engagements with city spaces. Something intangible is something without physical presence; it might be sincerely felt yet not seen, sensed by some, but missed by others. As I define it, intangible urban memory is often individualistic – reminiscences of an absent friend in a particular location, for instance, or recollections of personal triumphs and misfortunes triggered by return in thought or in person to the site of a former school, workplace or lodging. Although not necessarily shared, these reflections are nonetheless democratic. As historian and geographer David Lowenthal observes, preserved buildings (and indeed monuments) offer distorting views of the past; they are most often the creations of the most prosperous social classes in the most prosperous times (Lowenthal 1975: 29). Personal connections, on the other hand, can apply anywhere and to anyone; they are also likely to be deeper (Lynch 1998: 60–1). The notion of intangible urban memory opens the city to everyone as an intimate memorial space, or perhaps more accurately to the city as a jumbled mosaic of overlapping memories attached to particular places that harbour meaning.

How can historians seek to understand this endlessly rich assortment? A number of research strategies have been deployed to bring to light what is usually discreet or hidden. Autobiographical accounts of urban living in times past have been scrutinized, for example, their findings regarding remembered sites of significance read alongside diaries, semi-autobiographical novels and other so-called 'ego texts' like surviving letters (Chauncey 1994; Sleight 2013). For contemporary history, scholars have also interviewed city-dwellers, sometimes asking them to sketch out on paper places of personal attachment. Kevin Lynch's *The Image of the City* (1960) was pioneering in this regard, hosting within its pages composite drawings of Boston, Jersey City and Los Angeles as remembered by residents. He later extended the exercise, this time publishing the drawings of individual interviewees, many of them adolescents, for five global cities (Lynch 1977). Carla Pascoe's *Spaces Imagined, Places Remembered* (2011) extends Lynch's chronological scope, marrying analysis of twenty-first-century drawings of recollected 1950s Melbourne with insights from detailed oral history interviews.

Most recently, based on discussions with one hundred Australians, public historian Anna Clark has assessed both rural and metropolitan attachments to place. One interviewee, Sarah, spoke of the role of Sydney's waterside landmarks in prompting potent memories:

> My dad was very closely connected with Sydney Harbour, and when he died I had this, and my family, we just spent a lot of time around the harbour . . . it was part of a sort of coming to terms with his life and the loss of him. And now, Sydney Harbour and the Harbour Bridge *powerfully* remind me of my dad. It's a really, you know, strong connection.
>
> (Clark 2016: 123–4)

Significantly, Clark discerned especially deep and multi-generational urban memories among Australia's Indigenous communities, for whom the concept of spiritual attachment to the 'country' of one's ancestors is foundational. Douglas, for instance, felt particularly connected to the past in Marickville, an inner-western suburb of Sydney. 'There are so many different layers that have happened here, including the Aboriginal population – there's still a sense of their presence', he observed. 'So . . . even though I'm not from Marickville, Marickville's my home and my place of connection' (Clark 2016: 132). We shall return to this felt sense of an Indigenous past in the last section of this chapter.

Acts of accidental or deliberate forgetting in city spaces coexist with moments of concerted or coincidental remembering. Once the keepers of intangible urban memories pass away, those memories are liable to fade without the presence of an ongoing group to sustain them, or the efforts of amateur or professional historians to recover them. Other factors of influence are also at play. Popular representations of cities past and present supplement and mould conceptions, for example. 'Envisaged London is a composite of personal experience, contemporary media, and historical images ranging from Hogarth and Turner to Pepys and Dickens', argues Lowenthal. Hence 'we conceive of places not only as we ourselves see them but also as we have heard and read about them' (Lowenthal 1975: 6). Over time, and sometimes supported by such depictions, memories can also shade into nostalgia, with difficult aspects subconsciously edited out, or outlying details quietly left aside when those memories are reactivated. Even eyewitness accounts of very recent events – so beloved of broadcast news organizations in the immediate aftermath of urban calamity – are necessarily partial. These complexities offer challenges as well as opportunities for scholars of urban memory. If, as Clark observes, 'the significance of place in our historical consciousness is relative, to say the least' (Clark 2016: 131), we need to seek to better understand why this is so. We also need to consider appeals in public to reflect on the pluralities of people's backgrounds and orientations as well as on so-called 'counter-memories' – aspects of memorial culture running against the grain of dominant (often state-sponsored) viewpoints (Boyer 1994: 28). I move next to addressing these matters among others; I do so through tuning in to a number of recent and often controversial discussions about memory in cities around the world.

Intersections of memory

In her celebrated 1995 book *The Power of Place: Urban Landscapes as Public History*, historian of the United States Dolores Hayden asked a direct question: 'where are the Native American, African American, Latino, and Asian American landmarks?' (Hayden 1997 [1995]: 7) For over two decades now, those concerned with urban memory across the world have been grappling with the implications of this urgent query. A diversity of strategies has resulted: lobby groups have sought to raise new memorials, students have led demands for icons of earlier eras to be torn down, and historians have helped compose fresh information panels for monuments regarded (albeit rarely universally) as problematic. Pioneering research has also yielded new accounts of historically disenfranchised groups. These efforts build on older campaigns to sponsor annual cycles of remembrance and celebration such as National Hispanic Heritage Month (in the United States) and Black History Month (also in the United States, as well as in Britain and Canada). Competing in already crowded calendars, bookshops and city squares, such activities are *intersectional* because they overlap with and cut across other forms of memory-making, often acknowledging the multiplicity of historical identities attached to places and people. A focus in what follows on Indigeneity and then on sexuality bears out the possibilities and potential pitfalls of these initiatives for a more rounded culture of urban memory.

The public recognition of Indigenous histories that have both pre-dated and endured the establishment of settler colonial cities has been regarded as particularly pressing since the turn of the century. As postcolonial Latin Americanist Gustavo Verdesio comments, the histories of Indigenous pasts are often 'invisible at a glance', disguised by dominant Western regimes of seeing landscapes (2010: 347–50). For the Native American and First Nations territories of North America, historian Coll Thrush is among a growing cadre of scholars helping to bring to light the suppressed and the hidden through painstaking research including partnerships with local Indigenous communities. In *Native Seattle: Histories from the Crossing-Over Place* (2007), Thrush assesses a city that would seem on first encounter to buck a trend. Seattle, Thrush observes, has long emphasized its Native American history – via totem poles, festivals, naming practices and the motifs of urban infrastructure – but such recognition has commonly served only to marginalize Native Americans as passive, metaphorical, anti-urban and lost to the march of time (Thrush 2007: 3–16). In an effort to help counter practices of widespread cultural appropriation, ignorance, misnaming and much more, Thrush and linguist Nile Thompson consulted to create 'An Atlas of Indigenous Seattle'. This extraordinary document fully employs the concept of the palimpsest, 'peeling back' decades of overlaying structures and memories to reconstruct complex geographies of everyday life on the eve of white settlement. Intended as a prelude to further mappings of subsequent Native American urban occupation, the atlas flags the locations of former towns, fisheries, trails where canoes were carried, and places with especially strong spiritual meaning (Thrush and Thompson 2007: 209–55).

As in North America, so in Australia and South Africa: among cities thick with memorials to settler colonial endeavour, few sites of formal public memory connect in meaningful ways to pre- or post-contact Indigenous histories. Occlusions are manifold – Canberra's national War Memorial, for instance, acknowledges Indigenous soldiers who served Australia and the British Empire in global conflicts, but overlooks those Indigenous warriors who fought the white invaders during Australia's frontier wars. In post-apartheid South Africa, the gargantuan Voortrekker Monument on the outskirts of Pretoria presents similar paradoxes. Built between 1937 and 1949, the monument honours the memory of the 'Great Trek' in which (white) Afrikaners colonized interior lands in the early nineteenth century. Given its celebratory Afrikaner symbolism, and fearing its potential demolition under the imminent rule of Nelson Mandela, Afrikaner cultural organizations privatized the structure in the early 1990s to protect it. This turned an object announcing national significance into something more parochial, argues historian Albert Grundlingh, effectively 'shrinking' its representational power (Grundlingh 2009: 164). While many black South Africans still find the monument highly insensitive and historically flawed, the declaration of black singer Abigail Kubeka, performing at the site in the year 2000, that 'the last inch of the country is now part of the nation' served to alter perceptions (Grundlingh 2009: 168–9). A new Freedom Park, telling an alternative history of the South African nation, now stands directly across the road from the Voortrekker Monument, further reducing that monument's 'political voltage' in the telling phrase of the site's historical interpreter (Grundlingh 2009: 173). To the southwest in Cape Town, the Langa Pass Office – a place where government passbooks allowing limited movement were issued to black South Africans under apartheid – is now a museum following a process of consultation among a multiracial group of heritage professionals and local residents (Nieves 2009: 198–205), while on campus at the city's main university a statue of British colonialist Cecil Rhodes was removed in April 2015 following prolonged student protests that have since spread to Britain. Legacies linger, however, and across cities connected to fallen regimes history in public remains especially hotly contested.

Artistic interventions constitute an alternative form of speaking back to the absence of bricks-and-mortar memorials honouring non-white individuals and groups, or else to monuments portraying only Indigenous loss instead of agency. Spray-can slogans or sanctioned projections (like the nightly illumination with Indigenous art of Sydney Opera House in 2017) represent one type of response, personal performances another. Tahltan Nation artist Peter Morin's 'Cultural

Graffiti' project, for instance, witnessed Morin transport First Nation songs from present-day Canada to London's monuments in 2013, singing Indigenous spiritual meaning into the surfaces of stones regarded as living embodiments of colonial power.[6] Sound also accompanies visual acknowledgement at William Barak Bridge in Melbourne. This pedestrian walkway, which carries the Anglicized name of Beruk Barak (1824–1903), a Wurundjeri leader and emissary, is most frequently used by spectators passing to and from the nearby Melbourne Cricket Ground on match days. Since 2006 it has hosted 'Proximities: local histories/global entanglements', a multi-channel sound installation that projects the voices of some 53 nationalities – one for each Commonwealth nation then represented in the Australian census – interweaved with an Indigenous soundscape of clapsticks, speech and song.[7] The simultaneous sounds produced by 'Proximities' exemplify my points about intersectional urban memories, introducing thousands of Melburnians, as well as interstate and overseas visitors, to a diversity of voices in a single location every week, and perhaps in turn stimulating urban memories anew.

Without similar care, however, memorial artwork can prove short-sighted. Across town in Melbourne, for example, an apartment block that bears across the balconies of its 32 storeys the face of William Barak has been criticized for its location (on the site of a former brewery), its associations (luxury dwelling for sale in the context of the Indigenous land rights struggles), and its superficiality (see Figure 6.7). For art historian David Hansen, the 'Portrait' building uses the patina of Aboriginality to mask motives of profit, glossing over 'the painful truth of Indigenous and settler history' (Hansen 2012). Despite some similar reservations, historian Christine Hansen is more generous, deeming the building 'a poetic and welcome intervention in the cityscape', reminding Melburnians of meanings that underpin the contemporary fabric of metropolitan sprawl (Hansen 2015). Whether loved or loathed, the building has certainly inspired dialogue, and perhaps such debate is another step towards a fuller appreciation of the city's deep history.

Switching attention from race to sexuality – though the focus could equally be on gender, age, social class, disability status, religion or other social demarcations – let us now revisit one final time some of the cities already introduced in this chapter. This act of returning is important for my arguments about entanglement; as I hope is by now clear, urban memory is complex, and only through repeated engagement can sustained understanding of the many coexisting layers of urban memory arise. In Chapter 13 of this book, Laura Gowing's essay on queer histories constitutes an essential companion piece to what follows; readers should turn to that discussion for analysis of important terminology and assessments of supporting case studies.

On 18 November 2016, pink filing cabinets and protestors appeared at carefully chosen sites across London. From Vere Street in Camden (location in 1810 of the White Swan molly house) to Piccadilly Circus (a historic gay cruising area) and 239 Kings Road in Chelsea (home between 1931 and 1985 to Gateways, a famous lesbian nightclub), a coalition of LGBTQI+ campaigners had gathered – with

Figure 6.7 The Portrait building on Melbourne's Swanston Street. Designed by
ARM Architecture for Grocon and unveiled in 2015. Photograph
by Chris Samuel, 2015. Licensed for use under Creative Commons.
See www.flickr.com/photos/chrissamuel/19810111189.

their handmade cabinets – to call for a new 'Queer Museum' in the capital. Of the 13 locations selected, none was at that time publicly memorialized for its queer significance, hence the comment of activist Nadia Asri that 'Even though homosexuality is legal now our history is still being locked away in cabinets and it feels very, very temporary . . . and I think it's really important to make our histories and collective memories accessible' (*Evening Standard*, 18 November 2016). Inspired by the existence of such institutions as the Gay Museum in Berlin (opened in 1985), and mourning the loss through gentrification of iconic lesbian and gay venues like The Glass Bar outside Euston Station (in 2008) and The Black Cap in Camden (2015), the pink filing cabinet campaigners desired a permanent place to showcase the achievements and setbacks of a technicolour history.

Colour – or more precisely its absence – has also been central to recent discussions about memorialization in New York.[8] It is there that the hands and faces of two white male figures depicted in the Gay Liberation Monument, installed after protracted debate in 1992 to commemorate the 1969 Stonewall Riots, were painted brown and adorned with wigs in August 2015. An accompanying sign declared that 'BLACK LATINA TRANS WOMEN LED THE RIOTS STOP THE WHITEWASHING'. Highlighting the complexities of intersecting identities, and the shifting memorial culture within which all statues are located, one of the anonymous painters alluded to the purported shortcomings of a new feature film, *Stonewall*, in getting its history right (*Pink News*, 19 August 2015). 'What we did was rectification, not vandalism', the activists argued – a proposition partly supported by the fact that two other all-white figures depicted in the monument were left untouched, as well as by scholarship on the mythologization of the Stonewall episode (Armstrong and Crage 2006). Two months later and the Gay Liberation Monument was again in the news, this time for the appearance of a 'Just Married' sign at the feet of two of the seated women in the sculpture. Cast in 1980 from the contours of Leslie Cohen and Beth Suskind, the two real-life women had wed, prompting the tribute (*The Villager*, 5 November 2015).

Adopting and re-working approaches from black history, scholars of the queer past have also moved beyond the focus on the individual statue or sculpture as a locus of memorial reflection. LGBT History Month is now ensconced on the calendar in the United States and United Kingdom, as well as in Berlin. In London, the British Museum and Croydon Museum have launched onsite LGBT history trails to encourage fresh interpretations of their collections, while in Birmingham the National Trust supported queer readings of, and performances at, its nineteenth-century back-to-back working-class properties between 2010 and 2012 (Vincent 2014: 113–14). Outdoor history walks including coastal Brighton's 'Piers and Queers' tour also aim to connect sites of significance, a central purpose shared by the ongoing digital mapping project 'Pride of Place' (assessed by Gowing in Chapter 13). That buildings including playwright Oscar Wilde's former home in Kensington and the Royal Vauxhall Tavern have been re-listed by Historic England in recognition of their queer heritage is further testament to a growing willingness to protect and celebrate sites of simultaneous, ever-evolving meaning.[9]

In *The Power of Place*, the book with which I began this section, Dolores Hayden called for a more 'socially inclusive' urban history (Hayden 1997 [1995]: 11–12). Recognizing that cities host many coexisting sites – indeed landscapes – of significance, and that addressing shared meanings through understanding multiple intersections of the past offered a fruitful strategy, Hayden's first concerns were for broader appreciations of race and space, as well as the gendered and classed patterns of urban memory (Hayden, 1997 [1995]: 11, 136, 235). Scholars and campaigners have amplified and extended this remit in recent years to encompass an expanding range of social demarcations. There is still much to discover and to learn. What makes an intersectional approach so alluring for scholars of memory and the city is that it promises radical new perspectives tied to the distant past as well as to the always-changing present moment. Such an approach, moreover, tethers research unashamedly to activism, recognizing that subjectivities cannot be ignored. By embracing specific urban settings, neighbourhoods and even whole cities as the objects of study, more socially encompassing – and hence ultimately more honest – histories continue to emerge.

Figure 6.8 Flagstone installation by Slobodan 'Braco' Dimitrijević in Bern, Switzerland (installed in 1984). Photograph courtesy of the author, 2016.

Conclusions

Densely populated, cities are also thickly inhabited by memories. As this chapter has demonstrated, cities across the world are much more than mere mausoleums, graveyards for lives once led. Memory in the city can be fleet of foot as well as cast in stone, celebratory as well as sorrowful, contested as well as consensual. Once one knows how to look and what types of sources to examine, cities become ever more fascinating places for perceiving memorial culture. Here the personal jostles with the communal, and the national inflects the global. Across diverse metropolitan landscapes nothing is ever fully settled and the process of inscription is open to all. 'Human memory is both heightened and endangered in the urban landscape', surmises public historian Eric Sandweiss. 'Etched into their hardened fabrics of brick and stone, records of human interaction mark cities as sites of endurance as well as of change' (Sandweiss 2004: 25). As historians of urban memory, our task is part recovery and preservation, and part decoding and analysis. Through these activities we can seek to know how life was – and is – understood, and approach both the present and the past on their own terms, ever aware that between these temporalities runs a bustling two-way street.

Guide to further reading and online resources

The scope for investigating urban memory is vast, and an extensive body of scholarship awaits the keen researcher. In addition to the works cited above, recommended texts on individual cities include: Catriona Kelly, *St Petersburg: Shadows of the Past* (2014); Mark Peel, *Good Times, Hard Times: The Past and the Future in Elizabeth* (1995); Allan Pred, *Lost Words and Lost Worlds: Modernity and the Language of Everyday Life in Late Nineteenth-Century Stockholm* (2005); and Dirk Verheyen, *United City, Divided Memories? Cold War Legacies in Contemporary Berlin* (2008). Especially insightful personal accounts include Orhan Pamuk, *Istanbul: Memories of a City* (2006) and Walter Benjamin, *Berlin Childhood Around 1900* (2006). Significant treatments of Indigenous perspectives – a vital and growing field of research in recent years – include Victoria Jane Freeman, '"Toronto Has No History!" Indigeneity, Settler Colonialism, and Historical Memory in Canada's Largest City' (2010), Coll Thrush, *Indigenous London: Native Travelers at the Heart of Empire* (2016) and Maria Nugent, *Captain Cook Was Here* (2009). Among works addressing multiple cities are Indra Sengupta, *Memory, History and Colonialism: Engaging with Pierre Nora in Colonial and Postcolonial Contexts* (2009), Jörg Arnold, *The Allied Air War and Urban Memory: The Legacy of Strategic Bombing in Germany* (2011), Jane M. Jacobs, *Edge of Empire: Postcolonialism and the City* (1996), Marita Sturken, *Tourists of History: Memory, Kitsch, and Consumerism from Oklahoma City to Ground Zero* (2007), Quentin Stevens and Karen A. Frank (eds), *Memorials as Spaces of Engagement: Design, Use and Meaning* (2016) and Abidin Kusno, *The Appearances of Memory: Mnemonic Practices of Architecture and Urban Form in Indonesia* (2010). Important interventions with general applicability are made by Michael Hebbert, 'The Street as a Locus of Collective Memory' (2005) and Umberto Eco, 'Architecture and Memory' (1986).

As this chapter has elaborated, urban memory is subject to rapid evolution. Published book-length accounts should hence be treated as inherently time-bound, and the same holds true for academic articles published in leading journals like *History & Memory* and *Urban History*. For more immediate responses, local and national newspapers are a vital resource, while websites and personal blogs also showcase an abundance of useful information. Recommended examples of websites addressing formal memorialization include London Remembers, Open Plaques and Monument Australia. The website of the UNESCO recommendation on the Historic Urban Landscape hosts updates on world cities on its website, following an international agreement in 2011. On vernacular and unintentional memorials in city settings, see for instance the Ghost Signs blog, and Pavement Graffiti. Urbanists on social media also share resources daily. Melding digital and real world encounters, podcasted walking tours can further supplement personal observations of city spaces.

Notes

I wish to acknowledge my dual affiliations – to King's College London (as Senior Lecturer) and to Monash University (as Adjunct Research Associate) in the writing of this chapter. I am grateful to my co-editors, as well as to James Lesh, Mathilde Zederman, Dion Georgiou and Anna Maguire, for their comments on drafts of this work. Thanks also to Philipp Ruff and Raj Patel for their assistance with the Berlin photograph.

1 For usages of the phrase 'memory lane', including by Kaufman, see www.oed.com and https://english.stackexchange.com/questions/223590/whats-the-origin-of-the-memory-lane (accessed 3 July 2017).
2 All of the submissions can be viewed on the World Trade Center website: www.wtcsitememorial.org/ent/entI=683388.html (accessed 3 July 2017).
3 See, for instance, the Open Plaques website: http://openplaques.org/ (accessed 3 July 2017).
4 See http://edowonderland.net/en/ and www.sovereignhill.com.au/ (accessed 3 July 2017).
5 For information regarding the performance, as well as the quotation (taken from a video interview), see the project website https://becausewearehere.co.uk/ and a news report concerning its impact www.theguardian.com/stage/2016/jul/01/wearehere-battle-somme-tribute-acted-out-across-britain (accessed 3 July 2017).
6 Edited film of the performances, alongside Morin's explanations of his 'Cultural Graffiti' project, can be found in a short video: https://vimeo.com/119944337 (accessed 3 July 2017)
7 Further information, as well as sound clips from the installation, can be found online. See for example www.sounddesign.unimelb.edu.au/web/biogs/P000587b.htm (accessed 3 July 2017).
8 My thanks to Agnes Arnold-Forster for sharing her insights on modes of commemoration in the city.
9 For further information, see https://historicengland.org.uk/whats-new/news/england-queer-history-recognised-recorded-celebrated (accessed 3 July 2017).

References

Arad, Michael and Peter Walker (2003) 'Reflecting Absence', in Steven H. Corey and Lisa Krissoff Boehm (eds), *The American Urban Reader: History and Theory*. New York: Routledge.

Armstrong, Elizabeth A. and Suzanna M. Crage (2006) 'Movements and Memory: The Making of the Stonewall Myth', *American Sociological Review*, 71: 724–51.

Arnold, Jörg (2011) *The Allied Air War and Urban Memory: The Legacy of Strategic Bombing in Germany*. Cambridge: Cambridge University Press.

Ashton, Paul, Paula Hamilton and Rose Searby (2012) *Places of the Heart: Memorials in Australia*. Melbourne: Australian Scholarly Publishing.

Barthes, Roland (1967) *Elements of Semiology*, trans. Annette Lavers and Colin Smith. London: Jonathan Cape.

Benjamin, Walter (1999 [1932]) 'A Berlin Chronicle', in *Selected Writings*, Vol. 2, 1927–1934, ed. Michael W. Jennings, Howard Eiland and Gary Smith, trans. Rodney Livingstone et al. Cambridge, MA: Harvard University Press.

Benjamin, Walter (2006) *Berlin Childhood Around 1900*, trans. Howard Eiland. Cambridge, MA: Harvard University Press.

Bodnar, John (1994) 'Public Memory in an American City: Commemoration in Cleveland', in John R. Gillis (ed.), *Commemorations: The Politics of National Identity*. Princeton, NJ: Princeton University Press.

Boyer, M. Christine (1994) *The City of Collective Memory: Its Historical Imagery and Architectural Entertainments*. Cambridge, MA: MIT Press.

Boym, Svetlana (2001) *The Future of Nostalgia*. New York: Basic Books.

Braudel, Fernand (1981) *Civilization and Capitalism 15th–18th Century: Volume I: The Structures of Everyday Life*. London: Fontana.

Briggs, Asa (1963) *Victorian Cities*. Watford: Odhams.

Brown-May, Andrew (2008) 'In the Precincts of the Global City: The Transnational Network of Municipal Affairs in Melbourne, Australia, at the End of the Nineteenth Century', in Pierre-Yves Saunier and Shane Ewen (eds), *Another Global City: Historical Explorations into the Transnational Municipal Moment, 1850–2000*. New York: Palgrave Macmillan.

Brown-May, Andrew and Maja Graham (2006) '"Better than a Play": Street Processions, Civic Order and the Rhetoric of Landscape', *Journal of Australian Studies*, 89: 3–13 & 163–64.

Calvino, Italo (1997) *Invisible Cities*, trans. William Weaver. London: Vintage.

Chauncey, George (1994) *Gay New York: Gender, Urban Culture and the Making of the Gay May World, 1890–1940*. New York, Basic.

Clark, Anna (2016) *Private Lives, Public History*. Melbourne: Melbourne University Press.

Connerton, Paul (1989) *How Societies Remember*, Cambridge: Cambridge University Press.

Davison, Graeme (1987) 'Centennial Celebrations', in Graeme Davison, J. W. McCarty and Ailsa McLeary (eds), *Australians 1888*. Broadway, NSW: Fairfax, Syme & Weldon.

Davison, Graeme (2000) 'Monumental History: Do Statues (Still) Speak?', in *The Use and Abuse of Australian History*. St Leonards: Allen & Unwin.

Eco, Umberto (1986) 'Architecture and Memory', *Via: The Journal of the Graduate School of Fine Arts: University of Pennsylvania*, 8: 88–95.

Evans, Michael (1991) 'Historical Interpretation at Sovereign Hill', *Australian Historical Studies*, 24: 142–52.

Ferres, Kay (2013) 'The Wounded City: Memory and Commemoration in Lower Manhattan', *Communication, Politics & Culture*, 46: 41–54.

Freeman, Victoria Jane (2010) '"Toronto Has No History!" Indigeneity, Settler Colonialism, and Historical Memory in Canada's Largest City', PhD thesis, University of Toronto.

Georgiou, Dion (2014) '"The Drab Suburban Streets were Metamorphosed into a Veritable Fairyland": Spectacle and Festivity in The Ilford Hospital Carnival, 1905–1914', *The London Journal*, 39: 227–48.

Glassberg, David (2001) *Sense of History: The Place of the Past in American Life*. Amherst, MA: University of Massachusetts Press.

Gorby, Christine (2004) 'Diffused Spaces: A Sacred Study of West Belfast, Northern Ireland', in Eleni Bastéa (ed.), *Memory and Architecture*. Albuquerque, NM: University of New Mexico Press.

Grayling, A. C. (2006) *Among the Dead Cities: Is the Targeting of Civilians in War Ever Justified?* London: Bloomsbury.

Greenspan, Elizabeth (2005) 'A Global Site of Heritage? Constructing Spaces of Memory at the World Trade Centre Site', *International Journal of Heritage Studies*, 11: 371–84.

Griffiths, John (2014) *Imperial Culture in Antipodean Cities, 1880–1939*. Basingstoke: Palgrave Macmillan.

Grundlingh, Albert (2009) 'A Cultural Conundrum? Old Monuments and New Regimes: The Voortrekker Monument as Symbol of Afrikaner Power in a Postapartheid South Africa', in Daniel J. Walkowitz and Lisa Maya Knauer (eds) *Contested Histories in Public Spaces: Memory, Race, and Nation*. Durham, NC and London: Duke University Press.

Halbwachs, Maurice (1980 [1950]) *The Collective Memory*, trans. Francis J. Ditter, Jr. and Vida Yazdi Ditter. New York: Harper & Row.

Hayden, Dolores (1997 [1995) *The Power of Place: Urban Landscapes as Public Memory*. Cambridge, MA: MIT Press.

Hebbert, Michael (2005) 'The Street as a Locus of Collective Memory', *Environment and Planning D: Society and Space*, 23: 581–96.

Hobsbawm, Eric, and Terence Ranger (1983) *The Invention of Tradition*. Cambridge: Cambridge University Press.

Huyssen, Andreas (2003) *Present Pasts: Urban Palimpsests and the Politics of Memory*. Stanford, CA: Stanford University Press.

Jacobs, Jane M. (1996) *Edge of Empire: Postcolonialism and the City*. London: Routledge.

Jiang, Jiehong (2015) *An Era Without Memories: Chinese Contemporary Photography on Urban Transformation*. London: Thames & Hudson.

Karskens, Grace (1999) *Inside the Rocks: The Archaeology of a Neighbourhood*. Alexandria, NSW: Hale & Iremonger.

Kelly, Catriona (2014) *St Petersburg: Shadows of the Past*. New Haven, CT: Yale University Press.

Kenny, Nicholas, and Rebecca Madgin (2015) 'Introduction: "Every time I describe a city": Urban History as Comparative and Transnational Practice', in Nicholas Kenny and Rebecca Madgin (eds), *Cities Beyond Borders: Comparative and Transnational Approaches to Urban History*. Farnham: Ashgate.

Kusno, Abidin (2010) *The Appearances of Memory: Mnemonic Practices of Architecture and Urban Form in Indonesia*. Durham, NC: Duke University Press.

Ladd, Brian (1998) *The Ghosts of Berlin: Confronting German History in the Urban Landscape*. Chicago: University of Chicago Press.

Levinson, Sanford (1998) *Written in Stone: Public Monuments in Changing Societies*. Durham, NC: Duke University Press.

Libeskind, Daniel (2009) 'Global Building Sites – Between Past and Future', in Uta Staiger, Henriette Steiner and Andrew Webber (eds), *Memory Culture and the Contemporary City*. New York: Palgrave Macmillan.

Lowenthal, David (1975) 'Past Time, Present Place: Landscape and Memory', *Geographical Review*, 65: 1–36.

Lynch, Kevin (1960) *The Image of the City*. Cambridge, MA: M.I.T. Press.

Lynch, Kevin (1998 [1972]) *What Time Is This Place?* Cambridge, MA and London: M.I.T. Press.

Lynch, Kevin (ed.) (1977) *Growing Up in Cities: Studies of the Spatial Environment of Adolescence in Cracow, Melbourne, Mexico City, Salta and Warszawa*. Cambridge, MA: M.I.T. Press.

McGarr, Paul (2015) '"The Viceroys are Disappearing from the Roundabouts in Delhi": British Symbols of Power in Post-Colonial India', *Modern Asian Studies*, 49: 787–831.

Martin, G. H. (1968) 'The Town as Palimpsest', in H. J. Dyos (ed.), *The Study of Urban History*. London: Edward Arnold.

Mason, Randall (2009) *The Once and Future New York: Historic Preservation and the Modern City*. Minneapolis, MN: University of Minnesota Press.

May, Andrew (2016) 'Centering the City: Spaces of Practice in Australian Urban and Regional History', opening comments at Australian Historical Association conference panel, Ballarat.

Micallef, Shawn (2010) *Stroll: Psychogeographic Walking Tours of Toronto*. Toronto: Coach House Books.

Michalski, Sergiusz (1998) *Public Monuments: Art in Political Bondage*. London: Reaktion.

Museum of London Archaeology (2011) *Londinium: A New Map and Guide to Roman London*. London: MOLA.

Nieves, Angel David (2009) 'Places of Pain as Tools for Social Justice in the "New" South Africa: Black Heritage Preservation in the "Rainbow" Nation's Townships', in William Logan and Keir Reeves (eds), *Places of Pain and Shame: Dealing with 'Difficult Heritage'*. London: Routledge.

Nora, Pierre (1989) 'Between History and Memory: Les Lieux de Mémoire', *Representations*, 26: 7–24.

Nugent, Maria (2009) *Captain Cook Was Here*. Cambridge: Cambridge University Press.

Pamuk, Orhan (2006) *Istanbul: Memories of a City*, trans. Maureen Freely, New York: Vintage.

Pascoe, Carla (2011) *Spaces Imagined, Places Remembered: Childhood in 1950s Australia*. Newcastle upon Tyne: Cambridge Scholars.

Peel, Mark (1995) *Good Times, Hard Times: The Past and the Future in Elizabeth*. Carlton, VIC: Melbourne University Press.

Pile, Steve (2002) 'Memory and the City', in Jan Campbell and Janet Harbord (eds), *Temporalities: Autobiography and Everyday Life*. Manchester: Manchester University Press.

Pred, Allan (2005) *Lost Words and Lost Worlds: Modernity and the Language of Everyday Life in Late Nineteenth-Century Stockholm*. Cambridge: Cambridge University Press.

Ricoeur, Paul (2004) *History, Memory, Forgetting*, trans. Kathleen Blamey and David Pellauer. Chicago: University of Chicago Press.

Roger, Richard (2015) 'Reflections: Putting the "Trans" into Transnational Urban History', in Nicolas Kenny and Rebecca Madgin (eds), *Cities Beyond Borders: Comparative and Transnational Approaches to Urban History*. Farnham: Ashgate.

Samuel, Raphael (2012 [1994]) *Theatres of Memory: Past and Present in Contemporary Culture*: London: Verso.

Sandweiss, Eric (2004) 'Framing Urban Memory: The Changing Role of Museums in the American City', in Eleni Bastéa (ed.), *Memory and Architecture*. Albuquerque, NM: University of New Mexico Press.

Sather-Wagstaff, Joy (2011) *Heritage That Hurts: Tourists in the Memoryscapes of September 11*. Walnut Creek, CA: Left Coast Press.

Schneider, Jane and Ida Susser (eds) (2003) *Wounded Cities: Destruction and Reconstruction in a Globalized World*. Oxford: Berg.

Self, Will (2007) *Psychogeography*. London: Bloomsbury.

Sengupta, Indra (ed.) (2009) *Memory, History and Colonialism: Engaging with Pierre Nora in Colonial and Postcolonial Contexts*. London: German Historical Institute London.

Sinclair, Iain (2003) *Lights Out for the Territory: 9 Excursions in the Secret History of London*. London: Penguin.

Sleight, Simon (2013) *Young People and the Shaping of Public Space in Melbourne, 1870–1914*. London: Routledge.

Stangl, Paul (2008) 'The Vernacular and the Monumental: Memory and Landscape in Post-war Berlin', *Geojournal*, 73: 245–53.

Stevens, Quentin and Karen A. Frank (eds) (2016) *Memorials as Spaces of Engagement: Design, Use and Meaning*. New York: Routledge.

Sturken, Marita (2007) *Tourists of History: Memory, Kitsch, and Consumerism from Oklahoma City to Ground Zero*: Durham, NC: Duke University Press.

Thrush, Coll (2016) *Indigenous London: Native Travelers at the Heart of Empire*. New Haven, CT: Yale University Press.

Thrush, Coll (2007) *Native Seattle: Histories from the Crossing-Over Place*. Seattle, WA: University of Washington Press.

Thrush, Coll and Nile Thompson (2007) 'An Atlas of Indigenous Seattle', in Coll Thrush, *Native Seattle: Histories from the Crossing-Over Place*. Seattle, WA: University of Washington Press.

Tumarkin, Maria (2005) *Traumascapes: The Power and Fate of Places Transformed by Tragedy*. Carlton, VIC: Melbourne University Press.

Utaka, Yushi (2009) 'The Hiroshima "Peace Memorial": Transforming Legacy, Memories and Landscapes', in William Logan and Keir Reeves (eds), *Places of Pain and Shame: Dealing with 'Difficult Heritage'*. London: Routledge.

Verdesio, Gustavo (2010) 'Invisible at a Glance: Indigenous Cultures of the Past, Ruins, Archaeological Sites, and Our Regimes of Visibility', in Julia Hell and Andreas Schönle (eds), *Ruins of Modernity*. Durham, NC: Duke University Press.

Verheyen, Dirk (2008) *United City, Divided Memories? Cold War Legacies in Contemporary Berlin*. Lanham, MD: Lexington.

Vincent, John (2014) *LGBT People and the UK Cultural Sector: The Response of Libraries, Museums, Archives and Heritage Since 1950.* Farnham: Ashgate.

Yoneyama, Lisa (1999) *Hiroshima Traces: Time, Space, and the Dialectics of Memory.* Oakland, CA: University of California Press.

Zederman, Mathilde (2014) 'Memories of the Paris Commune in Belleville since the 1980s', *History & Memory*, 26: 109–35.

Zwigenberg, Ran (2014) *Hiroshima: The Origins of Global Memory Culture.* Cambridge: Cambridge University Press.

Newspapers and online sources

Atomic Heritage Foundation, 'Bombings of Hiroshima and Nagasaki': www. atomicheritage.org/history-page-type/bombings-hiroshima-and-nagasaki (accessed 3 July 2017).

Ghost Signs blog: www.ghostsigns.co.uk/blog.

Hansen, Christine (2015) 'Melbourne's New William Barak Building is a Cruel Juxtaposition', *The Conversation*, online edition: https://theconversation.com/ melbournes-new-william-barak-building-is-a-cruel-juxtaposition-38983?sa=google &sq=barak&sr=1 (accessed 3 July 2017).

Hansen, David (2012) 'Headstone', *Griffith Review*, 36, online edition: https:// griffithreview.com/articles/headstone/ (accessed 3 July 2017).

Historic Urban Landscape: www.historicurbanlandscape.com.

London Remembers: www.londonremembers.com/.

Monument Australia: http://monumentaustralia.org.au/.

New York Times: www.nytimes.com/.

Open Plaques: http://openplaques.org/.

Pavement Graffiti: www.meganix.net/pavement/.

Pink News (UK): www.pinknews.co.uk/home.

The Villager (New York): http://thevillager.com/.

7 Hagiography and biography
Narratives of 'great men of science'

Anna Maerker

Entering the Great Hall of the Natural History Museum in London, visitors are greeted by a statue of Charles Darwin, seated in a pose that indicates deep contemplation. The sculpture is in an elevated position and larger than life, forcing visitors to look up to this giant of modern science. The history of science has often been told as the story of a succession of 'great men' whose ideas and inventions created the modern world. In such accounts, Copernicus gave rise to Kepler, who gave rise to Galileo, who gave rise to Newton. Indeed, scientists themselves have contributed to this image of scientific progress; Newton famously stated that he was 'standing on the shoulders of giants'. Today, however, historians are critical of this type of narrative. It no longer represents the state of the art in historical scholarship as the focus on outstanding individuals does not reflect the collaborative nature of scientific practice, or the subtlety of historical explanation. It also sits uneasily with the ideals and goals of much public history, such as the mission of museums to appeal to diverse audiences. While a focus on exceptional individuals provides familiar entry points for general audiences accustomed to stories of 'great men' as sources of collective pride and individual inspiration, their potential for identification is limited, and their exceptionalism potentially alienating.

This essay investigates the emergence of 'great men' narratives in the history of science in public life, and the functions they performed for scientists themselves, for philosophers interested in improving scientific method, for nation-states celebrating their achievements and for educators who wished to inspire future generations. It highlights how this narrative has been criticized by historians, and the influence of political activism for developing new perspectives on the history of science beyond the contribution of famous individuals. Finally, the essay uses examples from biography and museums to investigate how academic and public historians have responded to these challenges, and how they tell the history of science today.

Histories of science and biographies of scientists before 1900

To this day, histories of science are often told by scientists themselves. Scientists create accounts of the emergence of their disciplines for a number of purposes such as placing themselves and their achievements within a lineage of illustrious

Figure 7.1 Sculpture of Charles Darwin at the Natural History Museum, London. Photograph courtesy of the Trustees of the Natural History Museum, 2017.

scientific ancestors, and encouraging students to emulate role models from the past. Science did not always enjoy the high level of public approval and trust that it has received for much of the twentieth century. In the early modern period, celebratory stories of scientific achievement became an important way to bolster science's claims to authority and public utility. Leading figures were central to these narratives, which were often modelled on medieval accounts of the lives of saints, hagiographies, which presented models for pious emulation, or even went back to forms of biography from classical antiquity. In ancient Greece and Rome, accounts of 'heroic teachers' had served as moral exemplars (Taub 2007: 20), and this function of biography was transferred to the lives of exceptional scientists in the early modern period. The elevation of seventeenth-century natural philosopher René Descartes, for instance, began immediately after his death. His biographer Adrien Baillet claimed that Descartes 'among philosophers is almost like the saints of the church of God', and argued that this comparison was justified because Descartes had 'suffered [his enemies' reproaches] with the patience of a saint' (Beretta 2016: 19). In the same period, Galileo's students worked hard to shape the memory of their master in the wake of his conflicts with the Catholic Church, and to turn him from a controversial figure into a 'martyr of science' (Gattei 2016). In the eighteenth century, 'modelling the self on some figure of 'representative virtue' was a commonplace psychological exercise' (Outram 1996: 90). The newly founded scientific academies of the period used eulogies of deceased members to celebrate their achievements, but also to act as exemplars for young scholars to emulate, and to strengthen science's claims to authority (Weisz 1988; Söderqvist 2007b). In this period, philosophers debated how science could or should contribute to the creation of an enlightened society, and how eulogies of important figures could help establish this new role of science for the public good. According to philosopher and academician d'Alembert, eulogies had to be 'interesting, so that the public can hear and read them with pleasure, and understand the deeds of those great men who have died for them and for the good of the nation' (Adkins 2014: 98). While academicians supported the inspiring potential of such narratives, they did not necessarily agree that the deceased colleague should be turned into a saint-like figure. Thus when philosopher Condorcet was in charge of eulogies for members of the French Academy of Sciences he argued that 'one owes the dead only that which can be useful to the living – truth and justice' (Hankins 1979: 1), and his accounts of fellow academicians' lives revealed their flaws as well as their achievements (see, e.g., Adkins 2014: 99). For Condorcet, only a truthful account of the past could be truly useful.

In the nineteenth century, histories of science and medicine written by practitioners themselves continued to celebrate the achievements of their heroes and their contributions to the improvement of mankind, as well as the nation (Waddington 2011: 2). They helped create a 'cultural niche' for science (Laudan 1993: 1). However, other uses of historical investigation emerged in the period. In the early nineteenth century, the British philosopher and scientist William Whewell wrote the history of science as a way to understand how science worked – how to develop a better understanding of nature, and how best to apply it for the benefit of mankind. Like the enlightened academicians of the eighteenth century, Whewell's goal was to turn science from a fairly esoteric pastime of natural philosophers into a systematic and key endeavour of society. However, for Whewell history was not just a way to celebrate the achievements of past scientists in order to increase the appreciation of science in society. Whewell also attempted to use historical case studies in order to 'extract from the actual past progress of science, the elements of a more effectual and substantial Method of Discovery' (Whewell 1847: v–vi). Thus, the science of the past could provide insights for constructing the science of the future by improving the scientific method.

Just as saints were revered through objects such as relics, scientists were commemorated through physical fragments from their past. Early museums used items associated with individual scientists to tell stories to convince the public of the utility and benevolence of scientific research. An early example was the Museum of Physics and Natural History in Florence which was founded by the Tuscan grand duke in 1775. Much like the French academicians, the grand duke considered science a powerful force to contribute to the public good. The museum was to provide science education for his subjects in order to generate a basic understanding of science, and to instil enlightened values in the population. The museum displayed specimens and instruments that served mainly to communicate the current state of scientific knowledge. However, it also exhibited some items of historical significance, such as the lenses that Galileo had used in his experiments over 100 years earlier. This display helped celebrate the tradition of Tuscan science, and placed the new Habsburg dynasty in line with the glorious past of the formerly reigning Medici family, who had been important patrons of scientists such as Galileo (Maerker 2011: 37). In the early nineteenth century, the museum even created an entire 'Tribune of Galileo' where Galilean memorabilia were put on display (Gattei 2016: 86). Thus, celebratory images of 'great men of science' were constructed not only through text, but also through objects.

The rise of academic history and the uses of biography in the nineteenth century

When history emerged as an academic discipline in the nineteenth century, influential historians considered exceptional individuals the key agents of historical change, and adopted the use of biography both as a way to explain historical events and to inspire their readers. In his book *On Heroes, Hero-Worship and the Heroic in History* (1841), Thomas Carlyle programmatically declared that

> Universal History, the history of what man has accomplished in this world, is at bottom the History of the Great Men who have worked here. They were the leaders of men, these great ones; . . . all things that we see standing accomplished in the world are properly the outer material result, the practical realization and embodiment, of Thoughts that dwelt in the Great Men sent into the world: the soul of the whole world's history, it may justly be considered, were the history of these.

To study the accomplishments of these great individuals, then, was crucial for accounting for historical change, but also useful as a means of inspiration, 'a flowing light-fountain . . . of native original insight, of manhood and heroic nobleness' (Carlyle 1841: 1–2).

Such biographies of outstanding individuals were popular in the nineteenth century across the Western world, and Carlyle in particular influenced the works of thinkers as diverse as the French historian Victor Cousin, the American poet Ralph Waldo Emerson and the German philosopher Friedrich Nietzsche. However, even in the nineteenth century this vision of individuals' role in history was not without critics. The American philosopher William James, for instance, drew on the new evolutionary theory of Charles Darwin to suggest that great men were the product of their environment (James 1880), while in his 1869 novel *War and Peace* Tolstoy contrasted the heroic military commander Prince Bagration with the haphazard actions of common soldiers in the battlefield, suggesting that individual leadership was an illusion (Berlin 1953).

Questions about the role of the individual for historical change and innovation were especially important for nineteenth-century attempts at writing the history of science. Biographies of 'great men' raised issues which went to the very core of questions about the nature of science, as well as the nature of historical explanation. Were new ideas the product of an inspired genius, or the result of the careful and patient application of the 'scientific method'? Did the scientist's own morality matter for the truth or utility of their ideas? At the core of this debate was the emergence of the new concept of the 'genius', a concept that was crucially shaped by eighteenth- and nineteenth-century accounts of the life and work of Isaac Newton. While in the early modern period 'genius' was used largely to refer to a person's skill, both mental and manual, in the Romantic era it came to denote a person himself, one possessed not only of singular intellectual abilities, but also one who was 'driven by an inner creative force' (Fara 2002: 167; see also Chaplin and McMahon 2015). Newton's celebration as a unique genius posed a conundrum to biographers: if indeed his insights were the product of flashes of inspiration then there was little to be learned from accounts of his life. Biographers and historians of science then had to consider carefully how much weight they should give to individual imagination on the one hand and methodical observation on the other (Higgitt 2007: 7–8). Some contemporaries feared that the concept of genius might discourage those who did not consider themselves exceptionally gifted, to prompt them to shrink 'back from their ingenuous labour, as if to cherish hope was madness; since disappointment only could reward toil' (Grisenthwaite 1830: 8f.; see also Higgitt 2007: 8). But the notion of the genius also posed a paradoxical problem for historical explanation: 'The concept of genius obviously favours a biographical approach to the history of science, because it assigned discoveries to single individuals. But it also limits what biography can do, because a creation of genius, by definition, cannot be explained' (Hankins 2007: 96).

Despite these issues, stories of individual genius remained popular in the nineteenth century for a number of reasons. Contemporaries suggested that biographical accounts were an appropriate appreciation of those who helped bring about the 'material grandness' of the time (Söderqvist 2007a: 6), as Victorians celebrated scientific progress as a motor of technological advancement. Biographies were also still considered useful for explicitly didactic purposes, as they had been for centuries. In *Heroes of Science: Botanists, Zoologists, and Geologists* (1882), Peter Martin Duncan, vice-president of the Geological Society in Great Britain, presented the outstanding achievements of 'heroes of science' to young readers as evidence of the reward of application and labour, rather than as the inspiration of genius. While he acknowledged that some men had 'special gifts', he stressed that these gifts had to be 'properly fostered and cultivated' through hard work (Duncan 1882: viii–ix).

Biographical accounts of great men could serve not only to inspire young would-be scientists, but could also be appropriated to support the author's political position. The Nobel Prize winner Philipp Lenard, an early supporter of National Socialism in Germany who opposed Einstein's theory of relativity, used his collection of short biographies *Great Men of Science* (1929) to suggest that 'great men of science . . . were much more above the common run of humanity than the most widely read biographies suggested' (Lenard 1938 [1929]: ix). Contrasting past glories with the present state of science, Lenard frequently diverged from his biographical accounts to lament what he considered the degeneration of science – its loss of simplicity and almost-mystical contact to nature. For Lenard, true scientists should help mankind to return to 'the greatness of nature itself' (Lenard 1938 [1929]: 246), but such a communion with nature was prevented by modern science's use of advanced mathematics and its insistence on technical utility. 'The mastery of motors and wireless waves . . . does not ennoble humanity; it coarsens and degrades them, and even makes them obviously more stupid. On the other hand, the joy at newly found insights lifts them up, when understanding for it has been cultivated' (Lenard 1938 [1929]: 246). Not least, as Lenard fought a losing battle against the acceptance of Einstein's theories in the scientific community, stories of 'misunderstood and insulted' scientists of the past offered obvious identificatory potential for the author himself and his followers (Lenard 1938 [1929]: 286).

Another Nobel Prize winner, the German chemist Wilhelm Ostwald, also published a collection of brief accounts of 'great men' in the early twentieth century, albeit for a very different purpose. Like Whewell 100 years earlier, in *Große Männer: Studien zur Biologie des Genies* (*Great Men: Studies on the Biology of Genius*, 1909–1932) Ostwald used historical investigations into the past of science in his quest to improve the science of the future. He collected biographical accounts of individuals such as chemist Justus Liebig and physicist James Clerk Maxwell to study 'the biology of genius'. He was especially interested in the question how age mattered for the productivity of great scientists. Like eighteenth-century academician Condorcet, Ostwald criticized the 'mythologizing' tendencies of biographies which tended to ignore the deficiencies of their subjects. For his purposes this approach was not sufficiently objective, and thus could not serve to establish a true understanding of genius and what professional environment would serve it best. Ostwald derided biographies written by former students and disciples, whose respect for the deceased prevented them from offering an honest image of their former teacher and mentor. He concluded that

objective biographies of great men provided evidence for scientists' declining productivity in advanced age. Ostwald used this observation to suggest reforms for
the German university system – in particular, to suggest that academic scientists
should be forced to retire in old age in order to make room for younger, more
innovative colleagues (Ostwald 1909–32: 13). Biography could be used to challenge the status quo in different ways. In the nineteenth and twentieth centuries,
women's rights campaigners and African-American activists used biographical narratives as evidence for the intellectual, physical and moral capabilities of women
and African-Americans – and, by implication, their right to political, legal and
social equality. In the 1850s the American campaigner Caroline H. Dall published
a series of brief, accessible biographies of female leaders, artists and scholars
through the ages in *The Una*, the influential journal of the women's rights movement (republished in book form in Dall 1860). 'To inquire what [women] had
already done', Dall argued, 'might decide the question, "What have they a right
to do?"' Her biographies documented women's capacity for extraordinary achievements as rulers, scientists and artists, and thus, she concluded, 'Women . . . should
be encouraged to the full use of whatever strength their Maker has given them'
(Dall 1860: 165, 168). Similarly, in *Black Pioneers of Science and Invention*, a collection of short biographies written for children and teenagers, Louis Haber
documented the 'significant contributions made by black scientists and inventors'
to inspire his young readers (Haber 1992 [1970]: vii). Indeed, even half a century
after its original publication the book continues to attract large numbers of readers
who appreciate its inspirational potential. As one reader put it, 'This book has
inspired me (African in America) to know I am of a long line a great men who
have overcome great odds and I have no excuse either not to follow.'[1]

Practices of commemoration since the nineteenth century

In addition to the rise of history as an academic discipline, two other nineteenth-
century developments crucially shaped the development of biographical narratives:
the rise of the nation-state, and the emergence of science as a profession. Sciences
such as physics and chemistry became established as academic disciplines with
their own degree programmes, rather than being subsumed under the study of
'natural philosophy' as they had been before. Universities began to create pur-
pose-built experimental laboratories, and in 1833 the British philosopher William
Whewell coined the term 'scientist' which was soon adopted as an umbrella term
for those who made a living from the study of the laws of nature and their application. The growing professionalization of science was demonstrated at national and
international professional meetings and congresses, starting with the inaugural
gathering of the Society of German Naturalists and Physicians (Versammlung
der Deutschen Naturforscher und Ärzte) in 1822, which provided an opportunity
for those new professions to articulate shared values and a shared identity.

A key activity for this articulation of a common identity was the practice of
commemoration. Professional meetings celebrated the anniversaries of heroes
of science and their inventions. Thus, for instance, for the 1927 International

Congress of Physicists (Congresso internazionale dei Fisici) a local industrialist sponsored the construction of a 'temple' dedicated to the Italian scientist Alessandro Volta to commemorate the centenary of Volta's death. Such occasions enhanced scientists' identification with the new professional community through the creation of a shared tradition (Anderson 1991; Hobsbawm and Ranger 1983), and signalled to lay audiences that science was important for society as a key contributor to progress. Such commemorations also served to articulate who counted as a professional scientist, to 'legitimize succession, to delineate the inheritors of authority, and to demonstrate whose claims can be set aside' (Maier 1999: ix). However, such celebrations also provided opportunities for political actors to instrumentalize the increasing cultural authority of science for its own purposes. Mussolini's Fascist regime, for instance, appropriated the Volta commemorations of 1927 (Gamba and Schiera 2005), while the eighteenth-century polymath Mikhail Lomonosov was celebrated as a Russian hero both by Russian nationalists in the nineteenth century, and by the Soviet regime in the twentieth (Usitalo 2013).

The rise of the nation state was accompanied and supported by the emergence of practices of commemoration of national events and heroes. This has been particularly well documented for the case of France. Here, commemorative events often centred around individuals such as successful artists and scientists who were to serve as a 'republican substitute for royals and saints' after the (temporary) abolition of the monarchy (Abir-Am 1999: 29; Sinding 1999: 62–64). In 1791, during the French Revolution, the Paris church Sainte-Geneviève was converted into the Panthéon, a temple dedicated 'To Great Men' by the 'Grateful Motherland' (Sinding 1999: 62). The influential French historian Pierre Nora has explained the French predilection for commemorative events with its particular political developments, beginning with the French Revolution, but also the subsequent decline of its international influence in the twentieth century (Nora 1986; see also Ozouf 1986). However, other nations developed similar commemorative traditions in this period (see, e.g., Gillis 1994; Hoock 2007).

With the rise of the nation-state the nineteenth and twentieth centuries also saw the rise of national rivalries, which were often articulated through commemorative activities (Gillis 1994). Despite scientists' claim to the creation of universal knowledge which transcended national boundaries, they frequently understood their activities in terms of national competition. In this context, the staging of commemorative events raised key questions for the identity of science, and its relationship to the state and the public: Who should be remembered, and how? By whom: by scientists themselves, or political representatives? Who should be the audience? As in biographical accounts, in practices of commemoration there was a tension between instrumentalizing the past and creating a truthful account of the past: was it legitimate to create a celebratory narrative that was not historically accurate?

Commemoration was instrumentalized by scientists themselves to strengthen their authority and sense of community, but also by political regimes. Thus, for instance, both Germany and Poland used commemorative events to claim ownership of the astronomer Copernicus who introduced the modern heliocentric view of the universe and who had been born in the predominantly German-speaking town of Toruń (Thorn) which was part of the Kingdom of Poland at the time. Both Germans and Poles carefully cleansed the national affiliations of Copernicus in commemorative celebrations to their advantage. Such commemorations could even have a subversive potential: efforts to publish Polish translations of Copernican texts in Latin were confiscated at the 1873 anniversary of Copernicus' ground-breaking text *De revolutionibus* when Copernicus' home region was under German, not Polish rule (Gingrich 1999: 41). In 1943, on the occasion of the text's 500th anniversary, Copernicus was co-opted by Nazi Germany (which occupied Poland at the time) as a 'great German astronomer' (Gingrich 1999: 45). Meanwhile, exiled Poles were instrumental in commemorative events in the United States which proudly proclaimed that Copernicus 'fixed the sun, he moved the earth, he was a Pole' (Gingrich 1999: 48). Similarly, at the height of the Cold War the centenary of the birth of Nobel Prize winner Max Planck was celebrated (and exploited) both in the capitalist West and the communist East Germany (Hoffmann 1999). The key role of political agendas and contexts for practices of commemoration is thus highlighted especially clearly by comparative studies of commemorative events in different countries or eras. As such examples show, investigations of commemorative practices in the past and present can provide us with insights into the politics of science – into science as a collective enterprise shaped by factions and allegiances, as a central element of modern culture, but also as an enterprise that has consciously adopted the role of a key driver of social and technological progress, and thus claimed for itself a key role in society, with all the political and social entanglements this brings.

Twentieth-century histories and biographies: critiques and new approaches

In the twentieth century, stories of scientific progress propelled by the insights and heroic deeds of great men increasingly came under scrutiny. Scientists themselves looked critically at the way in which science contributed to society in the past and present, and was shaped by social forces in turn. Most provocative in the first half of the twentieth century was the Russian physicist Boris Hessen's influential essay 'The Social and Economic Roots of Newton's *Principia*' of 1931. Like William James 50 years earlier, Hessen suggested that 'great men' were the product of their environment. Unlike James, he developed his argument on the basis of the Marxist theory of history which postulated that 'the mode of production of material life conditions the social, political and intellectual life process of society' (Hessen 2009 [1931]: 42). Even Newton's unique contributions, Hessen argued, were shaped crucially by the historical context in which they emerged. Newton had not only 'stood on the shoulders of giants', but his work on theoretical mechanics was motivated by the 'technical demands presented by communications, industry and war' for the early English bourgeoisie (Hessen 2009 [1931]: 53).

The twentieth century also saw the emergence of the history of science as an academic discipline in its own right. In 1912, the Belgian chemist and historian George Sarton founded *Isis*, the first international academic journal dedicated to the history of science. In the second half of the century a number of universities created academic departments. The new professional historians of science who emerged from these programmes rejected the kinds of celebratory accounts which historian Herbert Butterfield called 'Whiggish' (Butterfield 1931): 'the writing of history as the story of an ascent to a splendid and virtuous climax' (A.R. Hall, quoted in Hankins 1979: 5). However, historians of science split into what became known as 'internalist' versus 'externalist' approaches. Influential historians such as Alexandre Koyré and Charles Gillespie advocated a history of science 'from within' which would enable scholars to understand the inner logic of how science works (much as William Whewell had done in the early nineteenth century). Others took up the approach of historians such as Boris Hessen in foregrounding the explanatory power of historical context – the social, political and cultural factors that shaped the emergence of new ideas. Whether historians inclined to internalist or externalist explanations, biography seemed to have no place in the new professional history of science. At the time, historian Thomas Hankins suggested that the internalist historian was 'positively anti-biographical, immersing himself entirely in the subject matter of the science without reference to anything outside of it', while the externalist 'seeks the origin of scientific ideas in a context much broader than the individual scientist's mind' (Hankins 1979: 3).

Beyond new historiographical impulses within the history of science itself, the discipline was also shaped by developments in the field of history more generally, and in society. In the 1960s and 1970s historians increasingly turned to the social sciences in search of large-scale social mechanisms to explain historical change – explanations that were incompatible with the assumption that outstanding individuals were the prime movers of history. In the same period, science itself came under increasing scrutiny from political activists who challenged the idea of science as an unproblematic force for the public good. Examples such as the use of the atomic bomb in the Second World War and the severe effects of chemical warfare in Vietnam, as well as the collaboration of scientists in totalitarian regimes such as Nazi Germany and the Soviet Union, highlighted that science was not 'innocent'. At the same time, feminist calls for recognizing women's contributions to history went hand in hand with calls to write 'history from below', to acknowledge and understand the agency of underrepresented actors beyond kings, generals and statesmen.

These methodological and political challenges have had far-reaching consequences for the historiography of science. Academic historians responded to the problematic nature of 'great men' narratives in different ways. Some explicitly engaged with the question of the agency of individual historical actors to construct more nuanced accounts of the role of 'context' beyond the debates between 'internalists' and 'externalists', an approach which became known as 'social constructivism' (for an overview see Golinski 2005 [1998]). Scholars who followed this approach wrote biographies of scientists in new ways that highlighted, for instance, the crucial impact that Galileo's position as a court philosopher had on the creation and distribution of his scientific work (see Biagioli 1993). Other historians turned their efforts to making visible the contributions of groups and individuals that had frequently been overlooked, such as the 'go-betweens' who enabled knowledge exchange across different cultures (especially in colonial contexts), 'invisible technicians' such as artisans and servants whose low social status excluded them from published accounts of experiments, and members of scientists' families and households (see, e.g., Abir-Am and Outram 1987; Harkness 1997; Shapin 1989; Kohlstedt 1999; Raj 2007). Some scholars aimed to balance the historical record by recovering the contributions of female scientists and African-American inventors (Rossiter 1982; Haber 1970; Christie 1990). Others even replaced the agency of the human individual with that of animals or objects, creating 'object biographies' to ask what the history of science would look like from the perspective of a guinea pig, or a glass model of a flower (Daston 2004; Endersby 2007). Others still have turned their attention to the question how an individual's reputation and status as a 'great man' was created in the first place, either during the person's lifetime or posthumously (see, e.g., Geison 1995; Jordanova 2000; Fara 2002; Higgitt 2007; MacLeod 2007; Golinski 2016).

Biographies have thus experienced something of a revival in academic history of science in recent decades, paralleling a 'biographical turn' in historical scholarship more generally (Caine 2010; Renders et al. 2017). Beyond academia, accounts of celebrated figures of science never stopped being big business: popular books on Galileo, Newton and Darwin are still a sizeable industry. At the time of writing this essay, biographies of 'great men' such as Albert Einstein and Alexander Graham Bell are high on the Amazon bestseller list. However, even among popular biographies there are increasingly attempts to broaden the scope, to write about female and minority scientists, and innovative combinations of individual biography with biographies of scientific objects such as Rebecca Skloot's *The Immortal Life of Henrietta Lacks* (2010), which traced not only the history of the cancer patient herself, but also the subsequent 'life' of the cell cultures obtained from her, which played a key role in modern biomedical experimentation. Historians themselves, while in the business of deconstructing simplified narratives of heroic invention, acknowledge that such narratives may still serve causes beyond historical scholarship, and continue to inspire students and lay audiences. According to Princeton historian of science Gerald Geison, for instance, the 'standard legend of Pasteur' provides 'a sense of human drama and excitement as opposed to the impersonal, collective sense of science about which so many complain today'; a case where 'rarely has science been made so wonderfully simple, or so wonderfully grand and useful at once' (Geison 1995: 277).

Museums and 'great men' narratives

Today, 'great men' (and less frequently women) of science still are often at the core of attempts to engage general audiences with science and its history. In museums, celebrated individuals frequently take centre stage. As a pensive Darwin

Figure 7.2 Galileo's finger bones at Museo Galileo, Florence. Museo Galileo, Florence. Photograph by Franca Principe.

greets visitors at the Natural History Museum in London, the Museum of the History of Science in Florence was recently renamed the Museo Galileo in honour of Tuscany's most revered scientist. Much as the Tuscan grand duke had chosen to exhibit Galileo's lenses in the late eighteenth century, today it is Galileo's (middle) finger which is prominently displayed, mounted in a decorated shrine like the reliquaries used to house the remains of Christian saints.

However, today critiques of 'great men' narratives from academic historians of science and political activists question such celebrations and challenge museums to engage critically with their own purpose and missions. The International Committee on Museums (ICOM) defined education in the museum context as 'the mobilisation of knowledge stemming from the museum and aimed at the development and the fulfilment of individuals, through the assimilation of this knowledge, the development of new sensitivities and the realisation of new experiences' (ICOM 2010: 31). But what sort of knowledge are science museums supposed to mobilize in their visitors? Are museums primarily 'cathedrals of science' (Sheets-Pyenson 1988) intended to celebrate its achievements, and to convince lay audiences to accept the authority of science? Are visitors expected to emerge from a museum visit with a better knowledge of scientific laws and methods, or a better understanding of its potential impact on society? Should museums try to motivate visitors to become scientists themselves? Should they focus on presenting the science of the past, or the present? As curator and historian of science Jim Bennett pointed out, 'Taking seriously the simple fact that science is formed in history implies a different meaning to "the public understanding of science", but one that might engender a more realistic attitude to the vagaries of the scientific enterprise' (Bennett 1998: 182).

Some science museums today respond to this challenge by leaving their mission statements deliberately open-ended. The Science Museum in London, for instance, presents itself as 'the home of human ingenuity' and states that it aims to 'inspire visitors' and to strive 'to be the best place in the world for people to enjoy science'. It proposes to achieve these goals by using 'iconic objects and stories of incredible scientific achievement', and highlights its responsibility for preserving 'an enduring record of scientific, technological and medical achievements from across the globe'.[2] The Deutsches Museum in Munich, an institution that since its opening in 1925 has been dedicated to the representation of 'Masterpieces of Science and Technology', today posits in its mission statement that its aim is to represent both the current state of science and its history, to provide 'an overview of historical developments while offering insights into the latest research'. This communication is supposed to 'foster innovation in our society', and also to enable 'museum visitors to reach informed decisions and act as informed citizens in political decision-making processes'.[3]

Can stories of great individuals support these missions? Visitors to science museums are accustomed to such narratives, and they expect to encounter their scientific heroes in museum exhibitions (Jordanova 2014). However, the same problems that plagued popular science biographers are also salient for exhibition makers and museum curators: Do stories of individual genius discourage those who consider their own talents to be more modest from engaging with science? Are images of great (white, male) individuals alienating for female or non-white visitors? Today, museums create a range of historical narratives to respond to these issues, and to take account of historiographical developments in the history of science. Thus, for instance, in its section on the Industrial Revolution the Science

Figure 7.3 Panels illustrating the heroization of James Watt, Science Museum, London. Photograph courtesy of the author, 2017.

Museum presents the workshop of engineer James Watt, transferred from Watt's Birmingham home to the museum in 1924. It shows the tools and materials as they were left in disarray by the pioneer of the steam engine upon his death in 1819, and suggests that for Watt the process of innovation was an ongoing work of tinkering and engaging with materials, rather than a disembodied, miraculous inspiration of genius. A diagram next to the workshop further explains how Watt was embedded in several social, professional and cultural networks. Finally, a series of panels and images illustrate how Watt was posthumously turned into a heroic figure through commemorative statues and popular images.

Such relationships, the display suggests, were crucial to the development of Watt's technology and to its success. Similarly, at the temporary 'Collider' exhibition the Science Museum highlighted science as a practice that could be awe-inspiring and mundane at the same time, showcasing the charismatic mega-technology of a modern particle accelerator while also reproducing the sensation of being in an ordinary workplace characterized by a high degree of collaboration and everyday routine. Other museums embrace their role as places to highlight great achievements while simultaneously providing more general narratives. The Florence Nightingale Museum in London, for instance, is a place where nurses come to celebrate the life of Florence Nightingale, the founder of professional nursing who is an important identificatory figure for nurses today. However, the museum simultaneously represents the history of nursing as a profession. Most recently, and against the resistance of some Nightingale enthusiasts, the museum has become a space to celebrate not only Nightingale herself, but also the Jamaican British nurse Mary Seacole whose achievements as an outsider of the Victorian establishment may inspire future generations of nurses. However, museums' attempts to develop alternative storylines may conflict with audience expectations. At the British National Maritime Museum's 2014 exhibition *Ships, Clocks, and Stars: The Quest for Longitude*, for instance, curators carefully developed a deliberately anti-heroic account that used sophisticated historical scholarship to demonstrate that the problem of determining longitude at sea was a collaborative effort involving a wide range of individuals, institutions and technologies. Visitors, however, frequently informed by Dava Sobel's bestselling book *Longitude* (1995), largely expected a story of the achievements of clockmaker John Harrison, who was presented by Sobel as an isolated genius labouring in obscurity to solve the problem single-handedly with the development of his 'charismatic' timekeeper (Higgitt 2017: 378). Stories of 'great men' are thus deeply embedded in narratives of invention and innovation.

Conclusion

Accounts of the 'great men of science' have served a wide range of purposes in public life since their emergence in the early modern period. Eulogies of recently deceased scientists were an opportunity for former students and disciples to celebrate the achievements of their mentors, and to place themselves in an exalted lineage. Such hagiographic accounts of saint-like scientists also served to establish science's claims to authority and utility, and to instil public trust. Biographies were also used to motivate children and students to emulate great scholars and inventors. Commemorative practices could be used to create a shared identity for scientists in the process of professionalization, but could also be instrumentalized to celebrate national achievements, to articulate national rivalries and to support particular political ideologies. Finally, biographical accounts were used to investigate how science works, either in terms of method (Whewell) or in terms of the scientist's own biology (Ostwald). However, biographical accounts always posed conceptual challenges: historians had to interrogate the role of individual agency for historical change, an issue that went to the heart of historical explanation. Other biographers questioned whether accounts of genius might discourage readers who did not feel they possessed similarly outstanding qualities.

In the twentieth century, 'great men' narratives came under scrutiny from many different sides. The emerging academic discipline of the history of science found biography irrelevant for its ways of explaining historical change: 'internalists' were keen to uncover the internal, universal logic of science, while 'externalists' saw scientific knowledge as the product of its social, political and cultural context. For both camps, the lives of individual scientists were ultimately irrelevant. Further critiques came from political movements – from activists who engaged critically with science's potential for destruction and for its appropriation by totalitarian regimes, but also from feminists and minority activists who drew attention to the contributions of hitherto ignored individuals to the making of scientific knowledge. These pressures contributed to the emergence of the approach of 'social constructivism' which attempted to find a third way beyond 'internalist' versus 'externalist' approaches, and which paid attention to scientific contributors beyond those celebrated as 'great men'. Biographies took different turns under this influence: some historians and popular biographers directed their attention to women and minority scientists, to the role of technicians, translators, families and the social networks that made scientific work possible. Others explored the agency of animals and objects such as scientific instruments in 'object biographies'. Others still turned their attention to the question how the image of the 'great man of science' was created in the first place. Museums continue to exploit the appeal of popular figures who provide name recognition among general audiences. However, they increasingly supplement the traditional celebratory narratives of 'heroes of science' with alternative accounts, making visible underrepresented contributors, scientists' social networks and the routine of everyday research. Overall, the development of stories of 'great men' of science in academic and popular history shows that, historically, science had to establish its authoritative position in European culture and its claims to public utility. In an age of 'fake news' where the rejection of expert authority is politically instrumentalized, science has come under attack from groups such as anti-vaccination activists and climate change deniers. In this moment it is ever more urgent to develop opportunities for meaningful public engagement with science. We must find new approaches to tell the story of science in ways that illuminate its character as a shared human activity, and that enable citizens to evaluate its claims to authority and utility. This entails a re-framing of concepts of authority in ways that are collective rather than individual, and that are neither gendered nor racialized. The work of historians in public life is central to these efforts.

Guide to further reading and online resources

The textbooks by Peter J. Bowler and Iwan Rhys Morus, *Modern Science: A Historical Survey* (2005) and Keir Waddington, *An Introduction to the Social History of Medicine: Europe since 1500* (2011), and the *Companion to the History of Science* edited by Bernard Lightman (2016) provide useful introductions to the field, and include brief overviews of the development of its historiography. More detailed analyses of the historiography of science and medicine are Golinski (2005 [1998]), Huisman and Warner (2004), and most recently Wilson (2017).

Underrepresented historical actors in the history of science and medicine have been foregrounded in much academic scholarship of the past 30 years. For influential examples see, for instance, Steven Shapin on the contributions of 'invisible technicians' in experimental practice (Shapin 1989), Deborah Harkness on the role of households and families (Harkness 1997), Kapil Raj on the interactions between Indian and British knowledge traditions (Raj 2007), and Roy Porter on the patient in medical history (Porter 1985). Important scholarship on individuals that challenged hagiographic accounts include Biagioli (1993); Browne (1995 and 2002); Latour (1988).

For reflections on the opportunities and challenges of biography for the history of science see the journal *Isis* 97(2), Focus: Biography in the History of Science (2006); Shortland and Yeo (1996); Söderqvist (2007). Insightful case studies include Fara (2002); Higgitt (2007); MacLeod (2007). For critical reflections on the public uses of scientific biography and hero narratives see Jordanova (2014). For a current perspective on the uses of biography in history more generally see, for instance, Renders et al. (2017). On commemoration see the contributions in Abir-Am (1999); Beretta et al. (2016). Some museums of science, technology and medicine have documented their own histories and changing goals and narratives: see, for instance, Morris (2010). On the question of how to include the insights of academic history in museum contexts see Bennett (1998).

Much relevant material can now be found online. Key texts from the nineteenth and early twentieth centuries that are out of copyright have been reproduced online on sites such as archive.org and Google Books; for instance Carlyle's *On Heroes, Hero-Worship, and the Heroic in History* (1840), Whewell's *Philosophy of the Inductive Sciences* (1840) and Dall's *Historical Pictures Retouched* (1860).

Some critical commentaries on narratives of scientific genius are available online such as Jordanova (2014) and Peter Dizikes (2006).

Museum websites frequently provide mission statements, descriptions and maps of exhibitions. See, for example, www.deutsches-museum.de/en/information/about-us/mission-statement and www.sciencemuseum.org.uk/about-us.

For scholarship on different aspects of museum theory and practice see especially the open-access journals *Science Museum Group Journal* and *Museum and Society*.

Notes

1 Customer review by Bizzy773 (14 April 2015): www.amazon.com/Black-Pioneers-Science-Invention-Louis/product-reviews/0152085661/ref=cm_cr_getr_d_paging_btm_7?ie=UTF8&reviewerType=avp_only_reviews&sortBy=re.cent&pageNumber=7 (accessed 2 August 2017).
2 Science Museum (n.d.): 'About Us', www.sciencemuseum.org.uk/about-us (accessed 2 August 2017).
3 Deutsches Museum (n.d.): 'Mission', www.deutsches-museum.de/en/about-us/mission-statement/ (accessed 2 August 2017).

References

Abir-Am, Pnina G. and Clark A. Elliott (eds) (1999) *Osiris*, second series, volume 14: *Commemorative Practices in Science: Historical Perspectives on the Politics of Collective Memory*.

Abir-Am, Pnina G. and Dorinda Outram (eds) (1987) *Uneasy Careers and Intimate Lives: Women in Science, 1789–1979*. New Brunswick, NJ: Rutgers University Press.

Adkins, G. Matthew (2014) *The Idea of the Sciences in the French Enlightenment*. Newark, NJ: University of Delaware Press.

Anderson, Benedict (1991) *Imagined Communities: Reflections on the Origin and Spread of Nationalism*. London: Verso.

Bennett, Jim (1998) 'Can Science Museums Take History Seriously?', in Sharon Macdonald (ed.), *The Politics of Display: Museums, Science, Culture*. London: Routledge, 45–54.

Beretta, Marco, Maria Conforti and Paolo Mazzarello (eds) (2016) *Savant Relics: Brains and Remains of Scientists*. Sagamore Beach, MA: Science History Publishing.

Berlin, Isaiah (1953) *The Hedgehog and the Fox: An Essay on Tolstoy's View of History*. London: Weidenfeld & Nicolson.

Biagioli, Mario (1993) *Galileo, Courtier: The Practice of Science in the Culture of Absolutism*. Chicago: University of Chicago Press.

Bowler, Peter J. and Iwan Rhys Morus (2005) *Making Modern Science: A Historical Survey*. Chicago: University of Chicago Press.

Browne, Janet (1995) *Charles Darwin: Voyaging*. Volume 1. New York: Alfred Knopf.

Browne, Janet (2002) *Charles Darwin: The Power of Place*. Volume 2. New York: Alfred Knopf.

Browne, Janet (2010) 'Making Darwin: Biography and Changing Representations of Charles Darwin'. *Journal of Interdisciplinary History* 40, 347–73.

Butterfield, Herbert (1931) *The Whig Interpretation of History*. London: G. Bell.

Caine, Barbara (2010) *Biography and History*. Basingstoke: Palgrave Macmillan.

Carlyle, Thomas (1841 [1840]) *On Heroes, Hero-Worship, and the Heroic in History*. London: James Fraser.

Chaplin, Joyce E. and Darrin McMahon (eds) (2015) *Genealogies of Genius*. New York: Palgrave Macmillan.

Christie, John (1990) 'Feminism in the History of Science', in R. Olby, G. Cantor, J.R.R. Christie and M.J. Hodge (eds), *Companion to the History of Modern Science*. London: Routledge, 100–9.

Dall, Caroline H. (1860) *Historical Pictures Retouched*. Boston: Walker, Wise, and Company.

Daston, Lorraine (ed.) (2000) *Biographies of Scientific Objects.* Chicago: University of Chicago Press.

Daston, Lorraine (2004) 'The Glass Flowers', in L. Daston (ed.), *Things that Talk: Object Lessons from Art and Science.* New York: Zone Books, 223–55.

Deutsches Museum (n.d.) 'Mission', www.deutsches-museum.de/en/about-us/mission-statement/ (accessed 2 August 2017).

Dizikes, Peter (2006) 'Twilight of the Idols', *The New York Times* (5 November), www.nytimes.com/2006/11/05/books/review/Dizikes.t.html?_r=0.

Duncan, Peter Martin (1882) *Heroes of Science: Botanists, Zoologists, and Geologists.* London: Society for Promoting Christian Knowledge.

Endersby, Jim (2007) *A Guinea Pig's History of Biology: The Plants and Animals Who Taught us the Facts of Life.* London: William Heinemann.

Fara, Patricia (2002) *Newton: The Making of Genius.* New York: Columbia University Press.

Gamba, Aldo and Pierangelo Schiera (eds) (2005) *Fascismo e scienza: Le celebrazioni voltiane e il Congresso internazionale dei Fisici del 1927.* Bologna: Il Mulino.

Gattei, Stefano (2016) 'From Banned Mortal Remains to the Worshipped Relics of a Martyr of Science', in Marco Beretta, Maria Conforti and Paolo Mazzarello (eds), *Savant Relics: Brains and Remains of Scientists.* Sagamore Beach, MA: Science History Publishing, 67–92.

Geison, Gerald (1995) *The Private Science of Louis Pasteur.* Princeton, NJ: Princeton University Press.

Gillis, John (ed.) (1994) *Commemorations: The Politics of National Identity.* Princeton, NJ: Princeton University Press.

Gingrich, Owen (1999) 'The Copernican Quinquecentennial and its Predecessors', *Osiris*, second series, volume 14: *Commemorative Practices in Science: Historical Perspectives on the Politics of Collective Memory*, edited by Pnina G. Abir-Am and Clark A. Elliott, 3–60.

Golinski, Jan (2005 [1998]) *Making Natural Knowledge*, revised second edition. Chicago: Chicago University Press.

Golinski, Jan (2016) *The Experimental Self: Humphry Davy and the Making of a Man of Science.* Chicago: University of Chicago Press.

Govoni, Paola and Zelda Alice Franceschi (eds) (2014) *Writing About Lives in Science: (Auto)biography, Gender, and Genre.* Göttingen: Vandenhoeck & Ruprecht.

Grisenthwaite, William (1830) *On Genius, in Which it is Attempted to be Proved That There is no Mental Distinction Among Mankind.* London: Hamilton and Adams.

Haber, Louis (1992 [1970]) *Black Pioneers of Science and Invention.* New York: Harcourt.

Hankins, Thomas (1979) 'In Defense of Biography: The Use of Biography in the History of Science', *History of Science* 17, 1–16.

Hankins, Thomas (2007) 'Biography and the Reward System in Science', in Thomas Söderqvist (ed.), *The History and Poetics of Scientific Biography.* Burlington, VT: Ashgate, 93–104.

Harkness, Deborah E. (1997) 'Managing an Experimental Household: The Dees of Mortlake and the Practice of Natural Philosophy', *Isis* 88(2), 247–62.

Hessen, Boris (2009 [1931]) 'The Social and Economic Roots of Newton's *Principia*', in Gideon Freudenthal and Peter Mc Laughlin (eds), *The Social and Economic Roots of the Scientific Revolution: Texte von Boris Hessen und Henryk Grossmann.* Heidelberg, New York: Springer, 41–101.

Higgitt, Rebekah (2007) *Recreating Newton: Newtonian Biography and the Making of Nineteenth-Century History of Science*. London: Pickering & Chatto.

Higgitt, Rebekah (2017) 'Challenging Tropes: Genius, Heroic Invention, and the Longitude Problem in the Museum', *Isis* 108(2), 371–80.

Hobsbawm, Eric and Terence Ranger (eds) (1983) *The Invention of Tradition*. Cambridge: Cambridge University Press.

Hoffmann, Dieter (1999) 'The Divided Centennial: The 1958 Max Planck Celebration(s) in Berlin', in Pnina G. Abir-Am and Clark A. Elliott (eds), *Osiris*, second series, volume 14: *Commemorative Practices in Science: Historical Perspectives on the Politics of Collective Memory*, 138–49.

Hoock, Holger (ed.) (2007) *History, Commemoration, and National Preoccupation: Trafalgar 1805–2005*. Oxford: Oxford University Press.

Huisman, Frank and John Harley Warner (eds) (2004) *Locating Medical History: The Stories and their Meanings*. Baltimore, MD: Johns Hopkins University Press.

ICOM International Committee for Museology (2010) *Key Concepts of Museology*, edited by André Desvallées and François Mairesse. Paris: Armand Colin.

James, William (1880) 'Great Men, Great Thoughts, and the Environment', *Atlantic Monthly*, October.

Jordanova, Ludmilla (2000) *Defining Features: Scientific and Medical Portraits, 1660–2000*. London: Reaktion Books in association with the National Portrait Gallery.

Jordanova, Ludmilla (2014) 'On Heroism', *Science Museum Group Journal* 1, n.p.

Kohlstedt, Sally Gregory (ed.) (1999) *Women in Science: Readings from Isis*. Chicago: University of Chicago Press.

Latour, Bruno (1988) *The Pasteurization of France*. Cambridge, MA: Harvard University Press.

Laudan, Rachel (1993) 'Histories of Science and Their Uses: A Review to 1913', *History of Science* 31, 1–34.

Lenard, Philipp (1938 [1929]) *Great Men of Science*, trans. from the 2nd German edn. New York: Macmillan.

Lightman, Bernard (ed.) (2016) *A Companion to the History of Science*. Malden, MA: Wiley-Blackwell.

MacLeod, Christine (2007) *Heroes of Invention: Technology, Liberalism and British Identity, 1750–1914*. Cambridge: Cambridge University Press.

MacLeod, Christine and Jennifer Tann (2007) 'From Engineer to Scientist: Reinventing Invention in the Watt and Faraday Centenaries, 1919–31', *British Journal for the History of Science* 40(3), 389–411.

Maerker, Anna (2011) *Model Experts: Wax Anatomies and Enlightenment in Florence and Vienna, 1775–1815*. Manchester: Manchester University Press.

Maier, Charles S. (1999) 'Preface', *Osiris*, second series, volume 14: *Commemorative Practices in Science: Historical Perspectives on the Politics of Collective Memory*, edited by Pnina G. Abir-Am and Clark A. Elliott, ix–xii.

Morris, Peter J.T. (ed.) (2010) *Science for the Nation: Perspectives on the History of the Science Museum*. Basingstoke: Palgrave Macmillan.

Nora, Pierre (1986) 'L'ere de la commémoration', in *Les lieux de mémoire*, edited by Pierre Nora, vol. 3, *Les France*. Paris: Gallimard, 977–1012.

Ostwald, Wilhelm (1909–1932) *Große Männer: Studien zur Biologie des Genies*. Leipzig: Akademische Verlagsgesellschaft.

Outram, Dorinda (1996) 'Life-paths: Autobiography, Science and the French Revolution', in Michael Shortland and Richard Yeo (eds), *Telling Lives in Science: Essays on Scientific Biography*. Cambridge: Cambridge University Press, 85–102.

Ozouf, Mona (1986) 'Le Panthéon: L'École Normale des morts', in *Les lieux de mémoire*, edited by Pierre Nora, vol. 1, *La République*. Paris: Gallimard, 139–66.

Porter, Roy (1985) 'The Patient's View: Doing Medical History from Below', *Theory and Society* 14(2), 175–98.

Raj, Kapil (2007) *Relocating Modern Science: Circulation and the Construction of Knowledge in South Asia and Europe, 1650–1900*. Basingstoke: Palgrave Macmillan.

Renders, Hans, Binne de Haan and Jonne Harmsma (eds) (2017) *The Biographical Turn: Lives in History*. London: Routledge.

Rossiter, Margaret (1982) *Women Scientists in America: Struggles and Strategies to 1940*. Baltimore, MD: Johns Hopkins University Press.

Science Museum (n.d.) 'About Us', www.sciencemuseum.org.uk/about-us (accessed 2 August 2017).

Shapin, Steven (1989) 'The Invisible Technician', *American Scientist* 77: 554–63.

Sheets-Pyenson, Susan (1988) *Cathedrals of Science: The Development of Colonial Natural History Museums during the Late Nineteenth Century*. Kingston: McGill-Queen's University Press.

Shortland, Michael and Richard Yeo (eds) (1996) *Telling Lives in Science: Essays on Scientific Biography*. Cambridge: Cambridge University Press.

Sinding, Christiane (1999) 'Claude Bernard and Louis Pasteur: Contrasting Images through Public Commemorations', in Pnina G. Abir-Am and Clark A. Elliott (eds), *Osiris*, second series, volume 14: *Commemorative Practices in Science: Historical Perspectives on the Politics of Collective Memory*, 61–85.

Söderqvist, Thomas (2007a) 'Introduction: A New Look at the Genre of Scientific Biography', in Thomas Söderqvist (ed.), *The History and Poetics of Scientific Biography*. Burlington, VT: Ashgate, 1–15.

Söderqvist, Thomas (2007b) 'No Genre of History Fell under More Odium than that of Biography: the Delicate Relations between Scientific Biography and the Historiography of Science', in Thomas Söderqvist (ed.), *The History and Poetics of Scientific Biography*. Burlington, VT: Ashgate, 241–62.

Taub, Liba (2007) 'Presenting a "Life" as a Guide to Living: Ancient Accounts of the Life of Pythagoras', in Thomas Söderqvist (ed.), *The History and Poetics of Scientific Biography*. Burlington, VT: Ashgate, 17–36.

Usitalo, Steven (2013) *The Invention of Mikhail Lomonosov: A Russian National Myth*. Boston: Academic Studies Press.

Waddington, Keir (2011) *An Introduction to the Social History of Medicine: Europe since 1500*. Basingstoke: Palgrave Macmillan.

Weisz, George (1988) 'The Self-Made Mandarin: The Eloges of the French Academy of Medicine', *History of Science* 26, 13–40.

Whewell, William (1847 [1840]) *The Philosophy of the Inductive Sciences, Founded Upon their History*, second edition. London: John W. Parker.

Wilson, Adrian (2017) 'Science's Imagined Pasts', *Isis* 108(4), 814–26.

Part II
Difficult pasts

8 Remembering Anzac
Australia and World War I

Frank Bongiorno

National sentiment is largely the product of memories. And the Australian, as an Australian, has no memories worthy of the name.

(Buchanan 1907: 308)

Gallipoli

In the early hours of 25 April 1915 three dozen row-boats, each carrying its share of Australian soldiers and pulled by steam pinnaces, moved quietly across the smooth Aegean. Soon after four o'clock, the light of the approaching dawn made the land ahead faintly visible. Rifle and machine-gun fire rang out from the hills above the beach, and the steamers began casting off their row-boats. The men waded ashore at a narrow beach called Ari Burnu. It would become part of the Gallipoli myth that these men were on the wrong stretch of coast, but the plans for the landing were vague; in truth, the force ended up roughly where it was

Figure 8.1 The Gallipoli landing, 25 April 1915. Photograph courtesy Wikimedia Commons/Archives New Zealand. https://commons.wikimedia.org/wiki/File:The_Landing_at_Anzac,_25_April_1915_(17510339796).jpg.

supposed to land. Those who made it to the beach threw off their packs and pushed up towards their objective, the third ridge in the broken country above them. The men began picking their way through a maze of gullies, ravines and bushes that led to the high ground.

On this part of the peninsula, the Ottoman soldiers were few in number, probably about 200. Still, there was fierce fighting, as outnumbered Turkish troops were reinforced, and thousands more Australians and New Zealanders arrived. The allied commanders considered evacuating the men at the end of the first day, but orders came through from Sir Ian Hamilton, the campaign commander, that they should remain. The troops dug trenches rather like those that already disfigured the landscape of Belgium and northern France and 'a sort of miniature Flanders' ensued, just as one British military doomsayer had predicted (Prior 2015: 79). It was much the same kind of stalemate elsewhere on the peninsula, wherever the troops from Britain, Australia, New Zealand, Newfoundland, India, France and its African colonies confronted the enemy.

Most historians agree that the campaign against an enemy controlling high ground with modern weaponry was doomed from the beginning. The brainchild of First Lord of the Admiralty, Winston Churchill, its ambitious goals included the capture of Constantinople, the destruction of the Ottoman regime and the entry into the war on the Allied side of a coalition of Balkan states. It was designed, overall, to break the deadlock between the Allies and Germany on the Western Front, as well as to assist the Russians in the east. But there was no clear plan for securing the Dardanelles if the naval campaign that preceded the landings failed, as it had. Gallipoli would eventually be evacuated by early 1916, but only after months of costly fighting. The Australians alone, who were 'fighting for a secondary objective in a secondary theatre' (Crawley 2015: 71), lost 8,000 men, with more than three times that number figuring as causalities. Allied casualties were more than 132,000, with 46,000 killed (Prior 2015: 242). Nobody knows how many Ottoman troops lost their lives, but the numbers were probably considerably higher than those of the Allies.

Long before that evacuation, however, the day of the landing had been recognized as the most significant moment in Australian history; when the nation was 'born', or had a 'baptism of fire', or had 'come of age' – no one seems to have ever been quite sure which metaphor best suited. Today, 'Anzac' – the acronym for the Australian and New Zealand Army Corps that quickly passed into common usage – is central to Australian national identity. Anzac Day – 25 April – is observed every year as a public holiday and widely accepted as Australia's 'national day'. There is precious little recognition that the second and third letters in the acronym signal a shared history with New Zealand; Anzac has rather been translated, for most Australians, into a narrowly national tradition.

It might also seem peculiar that a military defeat should assume such status; or that an invasion of a foreign country on the other side of the world, on behalf of an empire that has long since passed into history, could still be marked by a society changed beyond recognition since. But this would be to overlook one strain in settler Australian culture that has been prepared to celebrate noble failure, and another that has emphasized 'the odyssey' – the overseas expedition or adventure – as a suitable context for the performance of national identity (Davison 2010: 41–8). Possibly, too, many Australians were willing to overlook that the campaign had been a strategic disaster because for them it had been redeemed by the conviction that Gallipoli brought them nationhood. It was, redeemed, too, by the allied victory of 1918, and the Australian part therein, which has been predictably inflated by nationalists ever since.

Nonetheless, reverence for Gallipoli as the national founding moment, for Anzac as the centrepiece of national culture, and for 25 April as 'the one day of the year' (Seymour 1962), has ebbed and flowed across the last century. In 1915 most Australians saw themselves as British as well as Australian; a century later, not only is the empire is gone, but so is the collective memory that Anzac began as an imperial as well as a national legend. Indeed, Anzac can sometimes today take on a rather anti-British complexion, one in which Australians are presented as innocent victims. As Australia moved towards greater independence and away from the mother country, the meaning of Anzac changed to accommodate this shift.

The idea of blood sacrifice is integral to modern nationalism, as evident in the myth-making that accompanied the Great War as it had been in the earlier revolutionary histories of America, France and Ireland (McLachlan 1989: 29). Alfred Buchanan, a journalist, explained what was lacking in Australian nationhood in 1907 when he declared: 'The altar has not been stained with crimson as every rallying centre of a nation should be' (Buchanan 1907: 308). Other countries also made nationalist myths of blood sacrifice out of the war, and a few out of Gallipoli itself. Like Australia, New Zealand drew on Gallipoli as a founding myth and 25 April quickly emerged as an occasion for commemorative ritual. It was not the landing itself, however, but an episode in the August offensive – New Zealand troops' heroic if short-lived occupation of the high ground at Chunuk Bair – that became that dominion's defining Gallipoli moment and the site of its memorial. More than Australia, 'bicultural' New Zealand has had an alternative founding legend that has competed for attention with Anzac: the Treaty of Waitangi of 1840. All the same, in New Zealand Anzac Day now overshadows Waitangi Day, 6 February. While the insistence on Anzac as the repository of almost any national virtue worth considering is far weaker in New Zealand than Australia, governments have increasingly elevated the significance of Anzac as a marker of a distinctive identity (Macleod 2015: 103–25; Gentry 2015: 49–55).

The other country, of course, that made of Gallipoli a foundation myth was Turkey, which emerged as a secular republic out of the collapse of the Ottoman Empire. Mustafa Kemal (Atatürk), a senior officer at Gallipoli, is regarded as the father of the modern Turkish state and would serve as its president until his death in 1938. The place of Gallipoli in Turkish collective memory was intimately connected with Atatürk's significance as a nationalist leader, but the War of Independence that followed the Ottoman defeat in 1918 provided a more powerful founding story. Turkish celebration of the Gallipoli campaign focuses on the day of the naval victory of 18 March. The growing intensity of Turkish commemorative activity in recent decades has been, in part, a response to Anzac memory work, while a new political leadership, less enamoured of the Kemalist legacy than its predecessors, has seen in Gallipoli the source of a selective version of Ottoman history that could be used to assert Islamic identity as the basis of Turkish national belonging (Ilhan 2015: 25–35; Macleod 2015: 154–87).

For the other participants, Gallipoli would not figure largely in their collective memory of the war. Understandably for the British, the largest component of the Mediterannean Expeditionary Force, as well as for the French, Gallipoli quickly came to be overshadowed by the Somme and Verdun. These campaigns – each on a scale that left Gallipoli well behind – came to be seen as symbolic of the futility of the war and as such, they did a very different kind of memory work than Gallipoli did for the Australians and New Zealanders. The large proportion of African colonial troops among the French forces at Gallipoli has helped generate some revival of interest at both the popular and official levels, but the campaign has remained a very poor relation in France's collective war memory of the twentieth century (Graves 2015: 56–63). Unsurprisingly, Gallipoli has not figured at all in Indian nationalist imaginings. 16,000 troops fighting for the British Empire provided most unpromising materials for an Indian national legend in the age of decolonisation (Stanley 2015: 283–302). The Irish presence in the British Army at Gallipoli was also largely forgotten for similar reasons of anti-colonial nationalist politics, at least until recent efforts by political leaders in the republic to promote collective memory of Irish soldiers' sacrifices in a friendlier era of Anglo-Irish relations; one changed especially by the Good Friday Agreement of 1998 (Macleod 2015: 141–53). For the Protestants of Northern Ireland, it was the devastation of the first day of the Battle of the Somme that loomed large as symbolic of their sacrifice and loyalty to the United Kingdom. Canada, meanwhile, has looked to the Battle of Vimy Ridge in April 1917 as its nationally defining war moment. The only 'Canadians' at Gallipoli were Newfoundlanders, who were then not part of the Canadian Confederation (Lemelin 2015: 183–91).

Such diversity is a reminder that the process by which history is turned into what has been called 'collective memory', 'collective remembrance' or 'social memory' is a complex one (Halbwachs 1992; Connerton 1989; Winter and Sivan 1999). Paul Connerton, the social anthropologist, in his book *How Societies Remember*, recounts the tale of an Italian doctor, artist and author, Carlo Levi, sent into exile in southern Italy by the Fascist government in 1935. Prompted by seeing the names of the dead on a local memorial, he asked villagers about the Great War. The subject was not taboo; it is just that the locals were uninterested in it. On the other hand, the wars between the brigands and the Italian army that had ended in 1865 were recalled as if they had just happened, even though few in the village were old enough to remember them. The point about collective or social memory here is to consider which past is put to work in expressing the shared memory and identity of a group. For Australians, Gallipoli and the Great War have indeed served this function, and the Anzac legend has been the country's most persistently fruitful source of 'commemorative ceremonies' and 'collective biography' (Connerton 1989: 20–1, 70–1).

Making the Anzac legend

The only account of the Gallipoli landing that Australian readers were able to read at first was that of Ellis Ashmead-Bartlett, an English war reporter. Watching the landing at what would become known as Anzac Cove from a warship, Ashmead-Bartlett still claimed confidently that 'There has been no finer feat in this war', as 'this race of athletes proceeded to scale the cliffs without responding to the enemy's fire. They lost some men, but did not worry.' Of the wounded, he declared: 'They were happy because they knew that they had been used for the first time and had not been found wanting' (Ashmead-Bartlett 1915). Here was an account that owed much to the Victorian imperial military tradition of daring charges and flashing bayonets, 'the heroic-romantic myth' (Macleod 2004: 135). Ashmead-Bartlett's stirring account appeared in the Australian press on 8 May 1915, and was soon being reproduced for use in schools.

Yet, for all of the gilding of the lily indulged in by imperial propagandists, there was widespread agreement that Australians had a more impressive physical stature than the English soldiers. Charles Bean, the Australian war correspondent and later official historian, presented the Australians as having 'developed more fully the large frames which seem normal to Anglo-Saxons living under generous conditions', by which he meant particularly 'the open-air life in the new climate' and the 'greater abundance of food' (Bean 1938: 5). Bean was here drawing on the Australian bush legend, which pictured the man of the rural interior as 'the typical Australian' (Ward 1958: 1–2). And it was more than just a matter of physical virility. For Bean, the social and political conditions of life in Australia had produced a particular kind of man: one who was independent, resourceful and egalitarian, eschewing 'tradition and authority', refusing 'to take for granted . . . prescribed opinions' (Bean 1938: 5). The Australian – and especially the Australian male – was supposedly a superior specimen of Britishness, one made better by favourable environmental, social and political conditions. While the avowedly racial and explicitly 'British' or 'Anglo-Saxon' dimensions of this thinking have been worn away in the century since, the core ideas have been resilient. In the minds of many Australians, anti-authoritarianism, egalitarianism, endurance, mateship and the amalgam of mischief-making and humour they call larrikinism remain the essence of 'the Anzac spirit'.

Waiting for war

The manner in which white Australians embraced Gallipoli as a founding moment can only be grasped once a longer settler history is taken into account, for Australians had been waiting for war for much of their history before 1914. On 1 January 1901, the day that the Commonwealth of Australia came into existence with the federation of the six colonies, Australians were fighting in contingents from their respective colonies in the South African war. Australians emphasized, exaggerated and often regretted the peacefulness of their past. Some had discussed the violent clashes between Australian Aboriginal people and British settlers in terms that suggested they thought it was a form of warfare. The killing of settlers by Indigenous people and, in far greater numbers, of Indigenous people by settlers, had occurred from the earliest years of British colonization through to the end of the 1920s. Yet especially by the time of the federation, there was a growing disinclination to dignify what had happened on the frontiers of settlement as war (Reynolds 2013: 15–17). This reluctance is echoed today by the Australian War Memorial (AWM) in Canberra which, although now comfortable in honouring Indigenous people in the armed forces, has resisted allowing frontier warfare to be commemorated in its precinct (Ashenden 2013). Nonetheless, professional military historians have long accepted that what happened between Indigenous people and white settlers on Australian soil amounted to warfare (Grey 1990: 29–40; Connor 2002).

Much as they might have dreamed about the British redcoats fighting in defence of the glorious Empire (Wilcox 2009), settler Australians have tended to regard their own local history as distinctly peaceful. 'A proper war', it has been suggested, 'would have dignified the settlers' violence, brought it out in the open and allowed them the romance of heroes and campaigns' (Griffiths 2003: 27–8). Australians' heroes before 1915 were men whose military exploits had been those of the Empire, such as Admiral Nelson and the Duke of Wellington (Inglis 1993: 283). Sacrificial death was understood by Victorians and Edwardians as the foundation of nationhood and, as far as most Australians were concerned, nobody had yet shed blood for the freedom and independence of their country.

Rise

The Australian Imperial Force (AIF) occupied a status in the society to which its soldiers returned that was probably higher than returned men in any other country. Australian voters had, on two occasions during the war, rejected in a referendum a proposal to reinforce the AIF with conscripts. As a result, Australia's army remained, almost uniquely, a volunteer force. It was probably for this reason that Australian war memorials were unusual in so commonly honouring those who had served and not only the 60,000 who had lost their lives (Inglis and Phillips 1991: 186). But the voluntary nature of war service affected the whole manner in which the Anzacs viewed themselves, and were treated by the society to which they returned. The Anzacs were regarded as a special caste: men who had been so patriotic, so selfless, that they had answered their empire's call in its hour of need, stormed the cliffs of Gallipoli, endured the mud of the Western Front and the dust of Palestine. Such attitudes stimulated a sense of entitlement that was divisive in a society that had experienced bitter antagonism over conscription and wartime industrial disputes (McLachlan 1968: 306–8).

Anzac Day developed in large part as a recognition of the heroism and sacrifice of such men. The first celebration of an occasion called 'Anzac Day' occurred in Adelaide as early as 13 October 1915. It was also Eight Hours Day (celebrating the achievement of the eight-hour working day), rebadged as a fundraiser for wounded soldiers, but it was no solemn occasion – among the attractions were people dressed as cavemen and dinosaurs (Knapman: 2012). Anzac Day, as it developed from 25 April 1916, emerged out of a panoply of often festive wartime fundraising events of this kind. It also drew to some extent on existing rituals and scripts for national commemoration such as Eight Hours Day, Anniversary Day (26 January), Empire Day (24 May), and the colonial/state foundation days. But among those most concerned about how 25 April should be marked, there was recognition that Anzac Day could not simply be allowed to develop as yet another secular celebration. Canon David Garland, an Anglican clergyman in Brisbane, believed the day needed solemnity if it were to perform its roles as a day of mourning, a ritual of thanksgiving to God for the benefits conferred by empire, and a means of promoting recruitment (Moses and Davis: 2013). Above all, Anzac Day needed to be sacred; not for nothing were 'relics' of the Gallipoli conflict (some gathered by a returning Charles Bean) later displayed at the AWM. It has now become customary to think of Anzac as a 'civil religion' whose history is interwoven with the decline of traditional religious observance (Inglis 1999: 8, 467, 470).

Anzac Day was marked all over the country in April 1916. The politicians seem to have been of secondary importance in its early development in Australia although some, like New South Wales Labor premier William Holman, recognized the opportunity to exploit it, his government hiring a well-known theatrical producer to organize the parade and associated events (Andrews 1993b: 13). But the federal minister for defence, George Pearce, believed 25 April, as the prelude to a defeat, was unworthy of national commemoration and he expected that a more suitable day would later emerge. There was accordingly no national ceremony in 1916 (Connor 2011: 62). Melbourne, then the federal capital, held several low-key events. In Brisbane, the influential Anzac Day Commemoration Committee worked hard in 1916 and beyond to enact Garland's vision of a day of solemn and ecumenical Christian observance (Moses and Davis, 2013).

The first Anzac Day commemoration in London was, according to one historian, 'an astute and cynical propaganda exercise', with marching Anzacs acclaimed by an enthusiastic crowd (Andrews 2013a: 88–91) as they proceeded to a Westminster Abbey service. It was surely easy, amid all the excitement, to overlook that the campaign had failed. While subsequent wartime Anzac Days in London were much quieter, that on 25 April 1919, the first after the armistice, was like that of 1916 a carefully stage-managed affair, a public reminder of what Australians had contributed to victory. Five thousand Australian troops marched with fixed bayonets, a spectacular display of virile white Australian manhood at a time when Prime Minister William Hughes was resisting Japanese efforts in Paris to have the principle of racial equality recognized by the new League of Nations.

Marches were not, however, an inevitable feature of early Anzac commemoration in either Australia or London. Melbourne had one in 1921, but then did not introduce the march as a regular feature until 1925 (Wilson 1974: 200). In some cities, the widows and children of relatives were permitted to march, in others they were not. (Today, the practice of family members' marching – and wearing the medals of one's Anzac relative – has become ubiquitous.) Holding a march

Figure 8.2 Anzacs marching to Westminster Abbey, London, 25 April 1916.
Photograph courtesy Wikimedia Commons/National Library of
Australia. https://commons.wikimedia.org/wiki/File:Australian_
and_New_Zealand_soldiers_marching_to_Westminster_Abbey_to_
commemorate_the_first_Anzac_Day,_London,_25_April_1916_
(16798510390).jpg.

on 25 April itself essentially depended on Anzac Day being marked as an official
holiday, and this only occurred gradually in the various Australian states during
the 1920s. The Returned Sailors' and Soldiers' Imperial League (RSSILA) pushed
for a public holiday on Anzac Day that banned commercial activities while
providing for solemn observance in the morning, and sporting and other sociable
activities in the afternoon. It did not accept that Anzac Day should be primarily
one of 'mourning'. Rather, it should be a national day in which the country
celebrated the nation-making achievements of its soldiers (Moses 2002: 63).

In its origins, Anzac Day also retained a critical place for small scale, semi-
private commemoration such as graveside pilgrimage. The dawn service gradually
emerged as a significant Anzac Day ritual (Macleod 2015: 83). Based on a military
'stand to', it was sometimes regarded as men's business, as an opportunity for
returned soldiers to remember mates lost to the war. Women were increasingly
marginalized in Anzac commemoration between the wars (Luckins 2004:
81–106, 189–208). Meanwhile, members of the radical left used Anzac Day to
express sympathy for 'the brave men . . . who were slaughtered during the
armed world war of 1914–1918', while promising to do their 'utmost to prevent
the world imperialist war which now threatens, and which at any moment may be
forced upon the over-burdened masses of the world', and 'oppose . . . the present

struggle of the imperialist Powers for a redistribution of the world's markets' (Cassells 2010: 103; 'Police Remove Wreath: Inscription Deemed Offensive', *Age*, 1934).

Decline?

By the time Anzac's national 'temple', the Australian War Memorial, was opened in Canberra in 1941, the world was again at war. In terms of the number of lives lost by Australians, World War II would be less costly, but this time Australia itself was threatened, conscription was introduced for service in the Pacific, and thousands of Australians would end up in Japanese captivity. Victory provided the early post-war Anzac Day marches with a celebratory tone. In 1946 in Sydney, there were 50,000 marchers and 200,000 spectators:

> Big contingents of men who served in the Second World War swelled the marching columns to twice their normal strength, and gave a new character to the day's commemoration. . . . The veterans of Gallipoli seemed reborn in their sons, and the youthful gaiety which the years had stolen lived again.
>
> ('50,000 in Record Anzac Day March',
> *Sydney Morning Herald*, 1946)

Inevitably, perhaps, numbers seemed to have dropped in the following decade; 1954 saw 21,000 marchers in Melbourne and that city's 'smallest Anzac Day crowd for years – 90,000 – [who] gave yesterday's marching veterans the poorest acclaim on record' ('Smallest crowd for years sees Anzac Day march', *Argus*, 1954). In Sydney, the numbers marching and looking on remained large into the mid-1960s but by 1971 there were 23,000 marchers, and the press reported a small crowd comprising mainly family groups, no cheering and minimal applause that was 'more affectionate than wildly enthusiastic' (Nicklin 1971: 1).

Such evidence, while meaningful, needs to be treated cautiously. Media reporting becomes clichéd, especially when it is faced with a ritual that seems to vary little from one year to the next. Many probably watched the ceremonies and march on television (Grey 2016). The supposed decline of Anzac Day was frequently associated with generational change, and social and political transformation. Among the most significant developments was the end of British Australia. Britain's application to join the European Economic Community in 1961, and the wave of decolonization in the same era, meant that Britishness as an identity was less available. A debate ensued from the early 1960s about how a modern Australian identity might be forged. There was talk of a 'new nationalism', but Anzac did not much figure as a possible focus for a renovated sense of nationhood. There were obvious reasons for such reticence; Anzac was so identified with Australia's British imperial history that it seemed an unlikely place to look for a post-imperial identity (Curran and Ward 2010: 197–9).

A further issue was Anzac's identification with what was now often called 'militarism'; it was of obvious symbolic interest for those who wished to protest

Figure 8.3 A soldier's son wearing his father's medals, Anzac Day, Brisbane, 1954. Photograph courtesy Wikimedia Commons/State Library of Queensland. https://commons.wikimedia.org/wiki/File:Soldier%27s_son_wearing_his_father%27s_medals_on_Anzac_Day,_Brisbane,_1954_(4536575731).jpg.

the Vietnam War, not least because of the Returned and Services League (RSL)'s staunch anti-communism. In 1966, for instance, women from the anti-war Save Our Sons movement were prevented from laying a wreath at Melbourne's Shrine of Remembrance (Scates 2009: 240–4). On Anzac Day in 1968, there were protests, as well as arrests, at the cenotaph in London involving a group that called itself Australians and New Zealanders Against the Vietnam War ('London Anzac Day clash – nine charged', *Canberra Times*, 1968; McKenna: 2010, 130). On Anzac Eve in Melbourne in 1971, protestors painted on the Shrine of Remembrance the word 'PEACE!' as well as the symbol designed for the British Campaign for Nuclear Disarmament (Scates 2009: 242). It was at this time that Eric Bogle, a recently arrived Scottish migrant and singer, composed 'And the Band Played Waltzing Matilda', which told the story of a bushman going to Gallipoli, having his legs blown off and watching an Anzac Day parade from his porch, reflecting that 'someday no one will march there at all' (Bogle 1971).

Revival and reinvention

Bogle was wrong in his prediction, but he could have been forgiven for missing the first modest shoots of revival. These appeared in 1965, the fiftieth anniversary of Gallipoli. The RSL that year organized a pilgrimage to Gallipoli by a group of World War I Anzacs, and they were accompanied by the historian Ken Inglis, who reported on the visit for the press. Also in 1965, an article by Inglis, 'The Anzac Tradition', appeared in the cultural journal *Meanjin*, sparking debate about the origins, development and meaning of Anzac, and reviving interest in Bean's legacy (Inglis 1965). Meanwhile, a young postgraduate student, Bill Gammage, began working at the Australian National University in Canberra on soldiers' letters and diaries as research towards a doctoral thesis. Published as *The Broken Years* (1974), Gammage's social history was ground-breaking in its emphasis on the experiences of the ordinary soldier, as well as for the post-imperial sensibility it brought to the story of Anzac. And this would have implications far beyond the immediate audience for his book, since Gammage worked as a consultant on Peter Weir's 1981 film *Gallipoli*. Weir treated Gallipoli not as the prelude to later triumphs, but as a loss of innocence, with Britain cast more as villain or bungler than loving mother. The explicitly racial overtones of national distinctiveness and virtue were gone, but not the egalitarianism, mateship, independence and resourcefulness that Bean had seen as quintessentially Australian. Importantly, the climax of the film was not the landing in April, but the costly attacks at the Nek in August, which underlined Australians' status as victims and the campaign as wasteful and futile. The ill-judged order to go over the top was actually given by an Australian officer, but in the film he was made to sound English. Viewers of the film saw wave after wave of Australian lighthorsemen shot down soon after leaving their trench.

The 1980s now appear as the critical decade in the reinvention and rejuvenation of Anzac memory. The Anzac revival developed against a background of fear of atomic warfare, but the decline of Cold War tensions later in the decade eased concerns about the prospect of a nuclear holocaust. This eclipse might in fact have been a precondition for Anzac revival; it would have been harder to uphold a military legend as the basis of national identity while fear of nuclear war remained intense and the peace movement strong. Yet paradoxically, another way that Anzac was renewed and reimagined was through the growing attention it received from social movement activists. From the 1970s, feminists had the Anzac legend in their sights as one of the buttresses of patriarchy and women protesting against rape in war staged Anzac Day demonstrations in Australian cities in the first half of the 1980s (Shute 1975; Lake 1992; Twomey 2013b). Others, such as gay ex-servicemen, also sought inclusion, yet they met with resistance from ageing Anzac keepers in the RSL.

The Anzac legend was undergoing a subtle change. One was a partial eclipse of the warrior tradition. Apart from the Australian general Sir John Monash, the most famous Australian soldier at the end of World War I was Albert Jacka, Australia's first Victoria Cross winner in the war, a highly accomplished killer. But there was a rather gentler figure who also emerged from the war. John Simpson Kirkpatrick was the 'man with the donkey', celebrated for his rescue of wounded soldiers from the Gallipoli battlefield. Peter Cochrane (1992) has revealed the manner in which Simpson was mythologized during the war to promote recruitment and conscription, and later to uphold a conservative imperial politics. In reality, Simpson was a working-class radical as well as a recent migrant from Britain, not the Australian larrikin of legend. The Simpson of legend had long been a staple of primary school teaching on Anzac as an example to children of initiative, humility and sacrifice. From the 1970s, however, he emerged as the Anzac par excellence. A large statue of Simpson and his donkey was commissioned by the Australian War Memorial in Canberra and unveiled in 1988. In 2005 the federal government sent posters depicting Simpson and his donkey into all of the nation's state schools; a list of approved 'Values for Australian Schooling' was superimposed over the image. There have been calls for Simpson to be awarded a posthumous Victoria Cross, while an annual history essay competition on Anzac is called the Simpson Prize.

The emergence of Dr Edward 'Weary' Dunlop, the World War II surgeon and prisoner of war (POW), as a national icon in the 1980s, has similar roots in this transition to a collective memory of the carer and healer, at the expense of the fighter and killer. The World War II POW experience became more prominent in Australian collective memory during the 1980s and 1990s. It found expression in pilgrimage by ageing POWs to places of their former suffering, a new round of memorial construction at home and abroad, and numerous newspaper articles, books, films and a multi-part radio programme. Dunlop's own wartime diaries were published (Ebury 2009: 378–82). Previously, the ravaged bodies and troubled minds associated with captivity had placed POWs on the fringes of an Anzac tradition more comfortable with the virile fighting man. Now, the qualities with which commentators credited the original Anzacs were translated to POWs. But there was an ingredient in these newly manufactured public memories that had never had such explicit recognition in the past. War trauma, as conveyed through personal testimony, was becoming central to the way their experience figured in public discourse. The cultural elevation of the POW was probably stimulated in part by anti-Japanese sentiment at a time when there were growing fears of that country's financial power, but the language of trauma was cosmopolitan, emerging as an aspect of a global 'memory boom' (Twomey 2013a: 326).

Another group was also angling for inclusion: Vietnam veterans. 'The Gallipoli men came home heroes', one man explained, after burning his medals in Brisbane's eternal flame. 'The Vietnam blokes came home losers who nobody wants to know' (Bongiorno 2015: 259). A Welcome Home parade staged in Sydney in 1987 was a landmark in the reimagining of their relationship to the Anzac Legend, and subsequent reporting of Anzac Day marches suggested either that Vietnam veterans were more numerous, or that journalists were now more inclined to notice them (Bongiorno 2015: 259; Bromfield 2017). Indigenous people and migrants, too, recognized in Anzac a path to greater acceptance and recognition. The RSL refused to allow Aboriginal servicemen and women in Melbourne to march as a separate group in the 1980s, so they organized their own effort (Bongiorno 2015: 261). Memorials to Indigenous service began to appear, as did books on 'black diggers' (Inglis 1999: 444–51; Hall 1989). There have also been efforts to recover a multicultural history of Anzac. In 2012 Tim Soutphommasane, later Australia's Race Discrimination Commissioner, called on Australians to view the Anzac tradition not primarily in the context of 'an ethnic or genealogical understanding of the nation' but as a 'civic touchstone . . . that reflects – if only in fragments – Australia's pluralism' (Soutphommasane 2012: 105–6). Here, Anzac is seen to provide a usable set of historical memories, the building blocks of a cohesive and diverse society.

During the 1980s, the media reported ever larger crowds of spectators and so contributed to an impression of a revived ritual. Mark McKenna has plausibly suggested that a reinvented Anzac Day emerged in the 1990s out of the failure of the 1988 Bicentenary of British settlement as an exercise in enacting national unity. Anzac Day offered itself 'as a less complicated and less divisive alternative' to Australia Day (26 January), McKenna argues, one that did not need to grapple so directly with the problem of white invasion (McKenna 2010: 116). Scholars have long debated the role played by the state in promoting shifts in collective memory, and Anzac is a revealing case study of this process. Historians such as Marilyn Lake have emphasized 'the militarization of Australian history' as a top-down process in which governments have played an active role in promoting an authorized (Anzac) narrative at the expense of other stories about the Australian past. She draws particular attention to the increasing involvement of the Department of Veterans' Affairs in this process through its resources for schools (Lake 2010). Yet the initial impulses towards Anzac reinvention and revival were only indirectly dependent on state policy or action. Bob Hawke, Labor prime minister from 1983 until 1991, seems only to have gradually recognized Anzac's potential as a source of national symbolism. In 1984 he responded to a proposal from the Gallipoli Legion of Anzacs by announcing that his government would ask its Turkish counterpart to rename Ari Burnu as Anzac Cove. This change occurred in 1985, with an Atatürk Peace Park being established in Canberra as one aspect of the Australian end of this memorial diplomacy. But it was the 1990 seventy-fifth anniversary pilgrimage that truly gave Hawke his opportunity to put his mark on the legend. Fifty-eight Gallipoli veterans were accompanied by Hawke and about 10,000 Australian 'pilgrims', many of them young backpackers. The government provided lavish funding. Anzac Day 1990 was a moment when the state moved decisively to gain more substantial sway over Anzac memory, effectively assuming the role previously performed by the RSL as keeper of the legend. But it was now painting on a canvas that was increasingly both popular and global (Bongiorno 2015: 261–2).

Paul Keating, Hawke's successor, sought to shift the focus of Anzac memory from the World War I to World War II, from Gallipoli to Kokoda – the successful campaign to stop the overland advance of Japanese in New Guinea during 1942 – as part of his effort to reconfigure Australia as an independent republic attuned to Asia. In a dramatic gesture, he kissed the ground at Kokoda on Anzac Day 1992. But it was his speech of 11 November 1993 at the AWM, on the occasion of the reburial of the unknown soldier, that is best remembered. The decision to locate the body of an unidentified Anzac from the Western Front and bury him in Canberra was itself a mark of the nation's more independent status. Delivering a speech crafted by his speechwriter, the historian Don Watson, Keating declared the soldier being reinterred as 'all of them' and 'one of us' – words now set on his tomb in the Hall of Memory. Keating's message was egalitarian, democratic, nationalist, even subtly republican; he would also drama-tize his push for a republic as the quest for a head of state who was 'one of us'. But for all its utility as an intervention in present politics, Keating's speech owed much to the ethos of Gammage's *The Broken Years*, elevating ordinary men and women to the status of war heroes, and delivering 'the lesson . . . that they were not ordinary' at all (Keating 1993; Holbrook 2014: 181–2, 186–7).

'A Century of Service'

Anzac is now at the centre of Australian collective memory, national identity and commemorative culture. The centenary of World War I – or, in Australia, 'The Centenary of Anzac' – provides a remarkable opportunity for understanding the dynamics of the legend's role in contemporary culture. Years of planning and preparation by a variety of state, commercial, educational and community organizations have preceded the anniversaries, which adopted the slogan 'A Century of Service'; that is, the commemoration would honour not only the original Anzacs but 'the generations of Australian servicemen and women who have defended our values and freedoms, in wars, conflicts and peace operations' (Australian Government 2015). The spending of state and federal government on commemoration, alongside contributions by the business sector, is around $AUD 600 million. Australia has a population about one-third the size of each of Britain and France, and it suffered only a fraction of their casualties, but it will spend twice as much money as all other countries combined in commemorative activities. One English historian concluded, only with some exaggeration: 'The

Australian Government is going to erect a monument everywhere a Digger took a piss during the war' (Honest History, 'Anzac Commemoration Spending around $500 Million – and Rising: Factsheet', 2015).

These differences tell us a great deal about Australia's heavy level of symbolic investment in the war. For both Britain and France, while it is easy enough to accept that World War I was a great tragedy, and that those who lost their lives in it should be honoured, the war does not for these nations provide a foundation story. In truth, any attempt to commemorate the war in Western Europe is inevitably shadowed by an understanding that what was supposed to be the war to end war did nothing of the kind. The French government has sought to put the centenary to work for European unity and cooperation at a time when Euroscepticism has been on the rise, if not as intense as in Britain (Fathi 2015: 550). For Germany, the war has an uncertain and contested place, seen by some as a precursor to Hitler's later aggressions, by others as the outcome of European diplomatic failure rather than of German aggression – an interpretation recently propounded by the Cambridge-based Australian historian Christopher Clark in a bestselling work that was a hit with the German reading public (Clark 2012). The rise of the Nazis, World War II and the Holocaust have provided democratic post-war Germany with its (negative) foundation myth (Bayer 2015: 555). For Russia, it is World War II that retains its cachet as a patriotic unifying experience, with the Great War being rather the cradle of national disintegration and communist revolution. For the United States, which only entered the war in 1917, the Civil War and World War II consume most of the commemorative oxygen available. The Great War has never there had a prominent place in collective memory, being treated as President Wilson's folly almost as soon as the guns went silent (Craig 2015: 568–75).

Commercial interests have also been active in Australia in a manner that does not seem as salient elsewhere. The word 'Anzac' has been protected by the federal government since 1916 (Hawkins, 2015), but the centenary has seen a proliferation of Anzac kitsch. One company advertises a limited edition 'Lest We Forget Cuckoo Clock': 'At the start of every hour, a trio of diggers emerge from the top of the clock as a faithful rendition of The Last Post fills the air. Each man represents a hero – your hero – never to be forgotten by their families or their country' (Bradford Exchange, 2015). The Australian Football League has since 1995 promoted a game between Essendon and Collingwood on 25 April as an Anzac Day clash, complete with ample helpings of war rhetoric and ritual. This is a highly successful promotion for Australian rules football, and one that greatly strengthens the traditional connection between war, sport and masculinity, not least through the awarding each year of the 'Anzac Medal' to the player judged to have best exhibited 'the Anzac spirit – skill, courage in adversity, self-sacrifice, teamwork and fairplay'.

Yet, while large crowds attended the major official ceremonies in Australia on 25 April 2015, and there were many more applications to attend the Gallipoli dawn ceremony than there were places in the government-run ballot, Anzac-themed television programming sometimes rated poorly. The term 'Anzackery', although apparently coined in 1967, came into such frequent use as a perjorative term from 2014 that it acquired an entry in the latest edition of the *Australian National Dictionary*, defined as: 'The promotion of the Anzac legend in ways that are perceived to be excessive or misguided' (Moore 2016: 33). There was also talk of 'commemoration fatigue' (Beaumont 2015: 540). The suspicion that some businesses were trying to turn Anzac into a racket reached its climax over the effort of one of the country's two major supermarket chains, Woolworths, to adapt its usual slogan, 'The Fresh Food People', to 'Fresh in Our Memories' (complete with the image of a soldier, with the online publicity encouraging people to upload an image of their own Anzac). The campaign was quickly withdrawn amid a not entirely unpredictable public outcry. Yet, without much controversy, Carlton United Breweries has for several years promoted its Victoria Bitter brand of beer with a campaign that encourages Australians to 'Raise a Glass' to the Anzacs. The cooperation of the RSL and Legacy, a war charity, as well as the handing over of a portion of the profits for good works, provides this exercise in product promotion with a cloak of legitimacy (Brown 2014: 117–24).

Tourism is an especially notable aspect of Anzac commercialization. While 'pilgrimages' to former battlefields have occurred since the 1920s, the relative cheapness of modern air travel means that many thousands of Australians, in every section of the travel market from backpacker to luxury, head to battlefield sites of note from each of the world wars (Scates 2006). The adventure tourism experience of walking the Kokoda track has received much publicity and thousands of patrons in recent years, being popular among sporting teams (who see it as an opportunity for maintaining their fitness and male bonding in the Anzac spirit) and politicians seeking publicity (Hawkins 2013). Whereas only a handful of young travellers turned up to meet the pilgrims of 1965, thousands of Australians have been present every year for the Gallipoli dawn service, although the threat of terrorism has recently reduced numbers drastically. A visit to Gallipoli has become nearly obligatory for Australian backpackers, but the assembly of large numbers of young people on 24–25 April, in a rock concert atmosphere, has led to rowdy behaviour and condemnation at home. Family history, now much easier to research via the web, often plays a role in such travel; backpackers look for the graves of their relatives and often claim to find the encounter moving, but some academic commentators have pointed to the role played by 'a sentimental and conservative nationalism' in evoking highly emotional responses (McKenna and Ward 2007; McKenna 2014: 156). In 2015 it became possible to go backpacking closer to home. Camp Gallipoli, an initiative for the Anzac Centenary, was 'an opportunity for . . . school kids, families, teachers and their school communities to come together to share a night under the stars as the original ANZACs did over 100 years ago' (Camp Gallipoli, 2015).

The concept of 'postmemory' is potentially helpful in understanding such activities. Marianne Hirsch has explained that postmemory refers to the process by which experiences – often of a traumatic nature – are transmitted from one generation to another 'so deeply and affectively as to *seem* to constitute memories in their own right' (Hirsch 2008: 107). Hirsch suggests that family

Figure 8.4 Australian backpacker wrapped in flag at Gallipoli dawn service, Anzac
     Day, 2000. Photograph courtesy Mike Bowers/Fairfax Syndication.

plays a critical role in postmemory work, although it is also shaped by the images
and narratives that circulate publicly. Yet whereas she is concerned primarily
with second-generation inheritance, the 'memories' of Australian Gallipoli
pilgrims today are sometimes several generations removed from those of the
original Anzacs of World War I. Here, Jan Assmann's distinction between two
types of 'collective memory' – 'communicative' and 'cultural' – appears relevant.
Communicative memory is everyday communication leading to 'numerous
collective self-images and memories', and it is distinguished by 'its limited
temporal horizon'. This variety of memory has a shelf-life of three or four generations: 80–100 years. 'Cultural memory', by way of contrast, is characterized by
its 'distance from the everyday', as well as its role in constituting a social group's
identity. The modern Australian collective memory of World War I appears to
match Assmann's definition of 'cultural memory' very precisely (Assmann 1995:
127, 129–30).

State actors, through the public narratives they articulate and those they
'forget', continue to play a critical role in mediating memory (or postmemory).
Australia and Turkey use Gallipoli as an opportunity to promote their bilateral
relations. The Armenian genocide, which occurred at the same time as the
Gallipoli campaign, is never mentioned on such diplomatic occasions, just as it
barely figures in Australian collective memory today – despite Antipodean
knowledge of Turkish atrocities in 1915–16 and humanitarian efforts by
Australians at home and abroad to help the victims (Manne 2007; Babkenian and

Stanley 2016). Rather, probably the most quoted words about Gallipoli are those attributed to the military officer, and later first president of the Turkish republic, Mustafa Kemal (Atatürk), in 1934:

> You are now lying in the soil of a friendly country. Therefore rest in peace. There is no difference between the Johnnies and Mehmets to us where they lie side by side here in this country of ours . . . You, the mothers, who sent their sons from faraway countries, wipe away your tears; your sons are now lying in our bosom and are in peace. After having lost their lives on this land they have become our sons as well.

There has recently been considerable research on these words, which appear on memorials in both Australia and Turkey. They are not, in anything much like this form, the words of Atatürk, but were rather assembled later and then popularized to serve the purpose of 'friendship' between the two countries. The crucial line about 'Johnnies' and 'Mehmets' was the invention of a Brisbane Gallipoli veteran, seeking some lines to place on a new memorial in that city in 1978 (Daley 2015; McKenna and Ward 2015–16: 42). The passage nonetheless speaks to how Australians and Turks now wish to recall their respective parts in the Gallipoli campaign. Whereas for Australians Britain has virtually disappeared from popular memory – if she is not recalled as the oppressor of innocent and unworldly Australians – Turkey, as the unlikely friend, looms larger than ever.

Meanwhile, the status of the prime minister as Anzac high-priest or mourner-in-chief has strengthened in recent years. John Howard (prime minister, 1996–2007) worked hard to elevate the Anzac legend. At a time when Australians were fighting in Afghanistan and Iraq, the existence of a continuity between the sacrifice of the original Anzacs and that of present-day service personnel became a cliché of prime ministerial speech-making. But in his address for the centenary dawn service at Gallipoli, another conservative prime minister, Tony Abbott – unlike Howard, a Catholic – took Anzac rhetoric much further:

> The official historian, Charles Bean, said of the original Anzacs: 'their story rises as it will always rise, above the mists of ages, a monument to great hearted men; and, for their nation a possession forever'.
>
> Yes, they are us; and when we strive enough for the right things, we can be more like them.
>
> So much has changed in one hundred years but not the things that really matter.
>
> Duty, selflessness, moral courage: always these remain the mark of a decent human being.
>
> They did their duty; now, let us do ours.
>
> They gave us an example; now, let us be worthy of it.
>
> They were as good as they could be in their time; now, let us be as good as we can be in ours.
>
> (Abbott 2015)

In this passage, the Anzacs are no longer mere mortals, having been elevated to a far more significant role than the taking of the Dardanelles. Once human but also saintly, they are exemplars of holiness. The Anzacs have ceased to be merely democratic everymen; Abbott has taken both 'them' and 'us' out of 'history' understood in any secular sense. In a most peculiar turn of phrase, he also symbolically erases any distinction between the original Anzacs and his audience ('Yes, they are us'). Australians, dead and living, belong to a single, community of believers, the nation as an Anzac Communion of Saints.

The theological theme here takes us somewhat away from the 'heroic-romantic' tradition of Ashmead-Bartlett while at the same time still gesturing towards its continuing – and perhaps renewed – power. But Abbott's Anzacs are not heroic male warriors in a secular history so much as suffering saints in a sacred one. In this respect his speech is utterly modern in its post-imperial and post-secular sensibility. The actual strategic goals at stake in the Gallipoli campaign are long forgotten. Britain and the Empire do not figure at all. Gallipoli has become a shared Australian and Turkish experience – with New Zealand added for the sake of politeness. What remains is a myth of an Australian nationhood forged by its soldiers in 1915, made real once again by 'flashes of imagery' and 'broken refrains', embedded in a foreign yet familiar landscape far from home (Hirsch 2008: 109).

Guide to further reading and online resources

The Australian publishing industry has a major stake in Anzac memory. The military history section of most shops is full of books about Anzac and Australian war history, with Gallipoli among the most popular topics, competing valiantly for space with Hitler and the Nazis. Popular histories are necessarily of uneven quality; Les Carlyon's *Gallipoli* (2001) is the best of those written for the general reader. Readers seeking a general history of Australia in World War I can do no better than Joan Beaumont's *Broken Nation: Australians in the Great War* (2013), the first book to bring together home front, battlefront and memory. Bruce Scates, Rebecca Wheatley and Laura James, *World War One: A History in 100 Stories* (2015) approaches the war through stories of Australian men and women whose lives were touched by it. The title of Peter Stanley's *Bad Characters: Sex, Crime, Mutiny, Murder and the Australian Imperial Force* (2010) provides a fair indication of its subject matter and issues a welcome reminder that the AIF, except with respect to age, represented a cross-section of Australian male society with its rogues, its heroes, and some with a foot in both camps.

D.A. Kent's ground-breaking '*The Anzac Book* and the Anzac Legend: C.E.W. Bean as Editor and Image-Maker' (1985) inaugurated a body of literature on the Anzac legend and digger culture influenced by folklore studies and labour history, to which more recent contributions include Graham Seal, *Inventing ANZAC: The Digger and National Mythology* (2004), Nathan Wise, *Anzac Labour: Workplace Cultures in the Australian Imperial Force during the First World War* (2014) and Frank Bongiorno, Raelene Frances and Bruce Scates (eds),

Labour and the Great War: the Australian Working Class and the Making of Anzac,
a special issue of *Labour History* (2014).

The growing interest in memory, mourning, museums, heritage and tourism
has greatly stimulated Anzac studies since the 1990s. The key foundational text
was Alistair Thomson, *Anzac Memories: Living with the Legend* (1994) which
especially through oral interviews with old diggers, explored the relationship
between collective and individual war memory. Scholars such as Joy Damousi,
Liz Reed, Tanja Luckins, Bart Ziino, Bruce Scates, Joan Beaumont and Marina
Larsson have developed the field of World War I memory history with a series
of important studies, while the British historian Jenny Macleod has injected a
much-needed transnational note into studies of Gallipoli memory. The three-
volume *Cambridge History of the First World War* (2013–16), edited by Jay Winter
(himself a major influence on World War I studies everywhere, including Australia)
and the Editorial Committee of the International Research Centre of the Historial
de la Grande Guerre, provides an indication of the globalisation of the field
amid the persistence of nationally based historical research and memory. Joy
Damousi and Marilyn Lake (eds), *Gender and War: Australians at War in the
Twentieth Century* (1995), brings together an important collection of essays on
the social and cultural history of war in Australia. However, Michael McKernan,
The Australian People and the Great War (1980), remains unsurpassed as a history
of the home front.

Students of Anzac and World War I are increasingly well served by internet
resources. The Australian War Memorial (https://www.awm.gov.au/) brings
together much material, including all of the *Official History of Australia in the
War of 1914–18*. But content generated by the AWM needs to be seen in light of
that institution's role as Anzac guardian. The National Archives of Australia's
Discovering Anzacs (http://discoveringanzacs.naa.gov.au/) is a portal to a large
number of official records with material contributed by members of the public.
It has also been digitizing repatriation records, accessible in some instances via
Discovering Anzacs, which give a unique insight into the war's legacy for returned
servicemen and their families. The State Library of New South Wales, which has
a large collection of diaries and letters, has been digitizing and transcribing parts
of its collection (http://ww1.sl.nsw.gov.au/resources/research) The Australian
Newspapers Online section of the National Library of Australia's Trove database
(http://trove.nla.gov.au/) contains a large and growing number of digitized
newspapers, but note that most digitization does not extend beyond 1954, the
Canberra Times (ending at 1995) being an exception. Some key Australian
newspapers, such as the *Sydney Morning Herald* and the Melbourne *Age*, appear
in incomplete runs for more recent times on Google News Archive (https://
news.google.com/newspapers/). The remarkable AIF Project, hosted by the
University of New South Wales, www.aif.adfa.edu.au/index.html, allows
individuals to search for details of particular individuals gleaned from a range
of sources. A group of citizens and historians concerned about the impact of
Anzac remembrance on historical understanding initiated the Canberra-based
Honest History (http://honesthistory.net.au/), now a major repository of

resources. David Stephens and Alison Broinowski (eds), *The Honest History Book* (2017), is a product of their endeavours.

References

Abbott, Tony (2015) Speech at the 2015 Dawn Service, Anzac Cove, Gallipoli, http://parlinfo.aph.gov.au/parlInfo/search/display/display.w3p;query=Id%3A %22media/pressrel/3798640%22.

Andrews, E.M. (1993a) *The Anzac Illusion: Anglo-Australian Relations During World War I*. Cambridge: Cambridge University Press.

Andrews, Eric (1993b) '25 April 1916: First Anzac Day in Australia and Britain', *Journal of the Australian War Memorial*, No. 23: 13–20.

Ashenden, Dean (2013) 'The Australian Wars That Anzac Day Neglects', *Eureka Street*, Vol. 23, No. 8, 21 April, www.eurekastreet.com.au/article.aspx?aeid=35629#. Vptwhdhf2M8.

Ashmead-Bartlett (1915) 'Story of the Landing: Australians Face Death: "They Rose to the Occasion"', *Argus* (Melbourne), 8 May, 19.

Assmann, Jan (1995) 'Collective Memory and Cultural Identity', *New German Critique*, No. 65: 125–33.

Australian Government, 'The Anzac Centenary National Program' (2015) www. anzaccentenary.gov.au/anzac-centenary-national-program.

Babkenian, Vicken and Peter Stanley (2016) *Armenia, Australia & the Great War*. Sydney: NewSouth Books.

Bayer, Martin (2015) 'Commemoration in Germany: Rediscovering History', *Australian Journal of Political Science*, Vol. 50, No. 3: 553–61.

Bean, C.E.W (1938 [1921]) *The Story of Anzac: From the Outbreak of War to the End of the First Phase of the Gallipoli Campaign, May 4, 1915*, Eighth Edition, *Official History of Australia in the War of 1914–18*. Sydney: Angus and Robertson.

Beaumont, Joan (2013) *Broken Nation: Australians in the Great War*. Sydney: Allen & Unwin.

Beaumont, Joan (2015) 'Commemoration in Australia: A Memory Orgy?', *Australian Journal of Political Science*, Vol. 50, No. 3: 536–44.

Bogle, Eric (1971) 'And the Band Played Waltzing Matilda', http://ericbogle.net/ lyrics/lyricspdf/andbandplayedwaltzingm.pdf.

Bongiorno, Frank (2015) *The Eighties: The Decade That Transformed Australia*. Collingwood: Black Inc.

Bongiorno, Frank, Raelene Frances and Bruce Scates (eds) (2014) *Labour and the Great War: The Australian Working Class and the Making of Anzac*, a special issue of *Labour History*, No. 106: 205–28.

Bradford Exchange (2015) 'Lest We Forget Cuckoo Clock with Rendition of The Last Post', www.bradford.com.au/products/403KEN0701_lest-we-forget-tribute-clock.html.

Bromfield, Nicholas (2017) 'Welcome Home: Reconciliation, Vietnam Veterans, and Anzac During the Hawke Government', *Australian Journal of Political Science*, Vol. 52, No. 2: 288–302.

Brown, James (2014) *Anzac's Long Shadow: The Cost of Our National Obsession*. Collingwood: Redback.

Buchanan, Alfred (1907) *The Real Australia*. London: T. Fisher Unwin.

Camp Gallipoli (2015) 'Camp Gallipoli Melbourne', www.campgallipoli.com.au/melbourne/.

Carlyon, Les (2001) *Gallipoli*. Sydney: Macmillan.

Cassells, Kyla (2010) 'Politics and Meaning: Melbourne's Eight Hours Day and Anzac Day, 1928–1935', *Marxist Interventions*, No. 2: 79–108, www.anu.edu.au/polsci/mi/2/mi2cassells.pdf.

Clark, Christopher (2012) *The Sleepwalkers: How Europe Went to War in 1914*. London: Allen Lane.

Cochrane, Peter (1992) *Simpson and the Donkey: The Making of a Legend*. Carlton, VIC: Melbourne University Press.

Connerton, Paul (1989) *How Societies Remember*. Cambridge: Cambridge University Press.

Connor, John (2002) *The Australian Frontier Wars, 1788–1838*. Sydney: University of New South Wales Press.

Connor, John (2011) *Anzac and Empire: George Foster Pearce and the Foundations of Australian Defence*. Cambridge: Cambridge University Press.

Craig, Douglas (2015) 'Commemoration in the United States: "The reason for fighting I never got straight"', *Australian Journal of Political Science*, Vol. 50, No. 3: 568–75.

Crawley, Rhys (2015) 'Marching to the Beat of an Imperial Drum: Contextualising Australia's Military Effort During the First World War', *Australian Historical Studies*, Vol. 46, No. 1, March: 64–80.

Curran, James and Stuart Ward (2010) *The Unknown Nation: Australia After Empire*. Carlton, VIC: Melbourne University Press.

Daley, Paul (2015) 'Ataturk's "Johnnies and Mehmets" words about the Anzacs are shrouded in doubt', *Guardian*, 20 April, www.theguardian.com/news/2015/apr/20/ataturks-johnnies-and-mehmets-words-about-the-anzacs-are-shrouded-in-doubt.

Damousi, Joy and Marilyn Lake (eds) (1995) *Gender and War: Australians at War in the Twentieth Century*. Cambridge: Cambridge University Press.

Davison, Graeme (2010) *Narrating the Nation in Australia*. London: Menzies Centre for Australian Studies, King's College London.

Ebury, Sue (2009) *Weary: King of the River*. Carlton, VIC: The Miegunyah Press.

Fathi, Romain (2015) 'French Commemoration: The Centenary Effect and the (Re)discovery of 14–18', *Australian Journal of Political Science*, Vol. 50, No. 3: 544–52.

'50,000 in Record Anzac Day March', *Sydney Morning Herald*, 26 April 1946, 1.

Gammage, Bill (1974) *The Broken Years: Australian Soldiers in the Great War*. Canberra: Australian National University Press.

Gentry, Kynan (2015) 'New Zealand', in 'Remembering Gallipoli in a Global Context', *History Australia*, Vol. 12, No. 1: 49–55.

Graves, Matthew (2015) 'France and Senegal', in 'Remembering Gallipoli in a Global Context', *History Australia*, Vol. 12, No. 1: 56–63.

Grey, Jeffrey (1990) *A Military History of Australia*. Cambridge: Cambridge University Press.

Grey, Jeffrey (2016) 'The Fall and Rise of Anzac Day? 1965–1990', in Tom Frame (ed.), *Anzac Day Then & Now*. Sydney: NewSouth Books, 156–67.

Griffiths, Tom (2003) 'The Frontier Fallen, *Eureka Street*, Vol. 13, No. 2, March: 24–30, www.eurekastreet.com.au/article.aspx?aeid=1297#.VptxSthf2M8.

Halbwachs, Maurice (1992) *On Collective Memory*, ed. and trans. Lewis A. Coser. Chicago: University of Chicago Press.

Hall, Robert A. (1989) *The Black Diggers: Aborigines and Torres Strait Islanders in the Second World War*. Sydney: Allen & Unwin.

Hawkins, Jo (2015) 'Anzac for Sale: Consumer Culture, Regulation and the Shaping of a Legend, 1915–21', *Australian Historical Studies*, Vol. 46, No. 1: 7–26.

Hawkins, Jo (2013) '"What better excuse for a real adventure": History, Memory and Tourism on the Kokoda Trail', *Public History Review*, Vol. 20: 1–23.

Hirsch, Marianne (2008) 'The Generation of Postmemory', *Poetics Today*, Vol. 29, No. 1: 103–28.

Holbrook, Carolyn (2014) *Anzac: An Unauthorised Biography*. Sydney: NewSouth Books.

Honest History (2015) 'Anzac commemoration spending around $500 million – and rising: Factsheet', http://honesthistory.net.au/wp/anzac-commemoration-spending-around-400-million-and-rising-factsheet/.

Ilhan, M. Mehdi (2015) 'Turkey', in 'Remembering Gallipoli in a Global Context', *History Australia*, Vol. 12, No. 1: 25–35.

Inglis, K.S. (1965) 'The Anzac Tradition', *Meanjin Quarterly*, Vol. 24, No. 1: 25–44.

Inglis, Ken (1993 [1974]) *Australian Colonists: An Exploration of Social History 1788–1870*. Carlton, VIC: Melbourne University Press.

Inglis, K.S., assisted by Jan Brazier (1999 [1998]) *Sacred Places: War Memorials in the Australian Landscape*. Carlton, VIC: The Miegunyah Press.

Inglis, K.S. and Jock Phillips (1991) 'War Memorials in Australia and New Zealand: A Comparative Survey', *Australian Historical Studies*, Vol. 24, No. 96: 179–91.

Keating, Paul (1993) 'Eulogy delivered by the Prime Minister, The Hon. P.J. Keating MP, at the funeral service of the Unknown Australian Soldier, 11 November 1993', www.awm.gov.au/commemoration/keating.asp.

Kent, D. A. (1985) '*The Anzac Book* and the Anzac Legend: C.E.W. Bean as Editor and Image-Maker', *Historical Studies*, Vol. 21, No. 84: 376–90.

Knapman, Gareth (2012) 'Adelaide and the Birth of Anzac Day', in Nigel Starke (ed.), *Legacies of War*. North Melbourne: Australian Scholarly Publishing.

Lake, Marilyn (1992) 'Mission Impossible: How Men Gave Birth to the Australian Nation – Nationalism, Gender and Other Seminal Acts', *Gender and History*, Vol. 4, No. 3: 305–22.

Lake, Marilyn (2010) 'How Do Schoolchildren Learn about the Spirit of Anzac?', in Marilyn Lake and Henry Reynolds with Mark McKenna and Joy Damousi, *What's Wrong with Anzac? The Militarisation of Australian History*. Sydney: NewSouth Books.

Lemelin, Raynald Harvey (2015) 'Newfoundland', in 'Remembering Gallipoli in a Global Context', *History Australia*, Vol. 12, No. 3: 183–91.

'London Anzac Day Clash – Nine Charged', *Canberra Times*, 27 April 1968, 7.

Luckins, Tanja (2004) *The Gates of Memory: Australian People's Experiences and Memories of Loss and the Great War*. Fremantle, WA: Curtin University Books.

McKenna, Mark (2010) 'Anzac Day: How Did It Become Australia's National Day?', in Marilyn Lake and Henry Reynolds with Mark McKenna and Joy Damousi (eds), *What's Wrong with Anzac? The Militarisation of Australian History*. Sydney: NewSouth.

McKenna, Mark (2014) 'Keeping in Step: The Anzac "Resurgence" and "Military Heritage" in Australia and New Zealand', in Shanti Sumartojo and Ben Wellings (eds), *Remembering the Great War: Nation, Memory, Commemoration*. Bern: Peter Lang.

McKenna, Mark, and Stuart Ward (2015–16) 'An Anzac Myth: The Creative Memorialisation of Gallipoli', *Monthly*, Issue 118: 40–7.

McKenna, Mark, and Stuart Ward (2007) '"It was Really Moving, Mate": The Gallipoli Pilgrimage and Sentimental Nationalism in Australia', *Australian Historical Studies*, Vol. 38, No. 129: 141–51.

McKernan, Michael (1980) *The Australian People and the Great War*. West Melbourne: Nelson.

McLachlan, N.D. (1968) 'Nationalism and the Divisive Digger: Three Comments', *Meanjin*, Vol. 27, No. 3: 302–8.

McLachlan, Noel (1989) *Waiting for the Revolution: A History of Australian Nationalism*. Ringwood: Penguin.

Macleod, Jenny (2004) *Reconsidering Gallipoli*. Manchester: Manchester University Press.

Macleod, Jenny (2015) *Gallipoli*. Oxford: Oxford University Press.

Manne, Robert (2007) 'A Turkish Tale: Gallipoli and the Armenian Genocide', *Monthly*, February, 20–28, www.themonthly.com.au/monthly-essays-robert-manne-turkish-tale-gallipoli-and-armenian-genocide-459.

Moore, Bruce (ed.) (2016) *The Australian National Dictionary: Australian Words and Their Origins A-L*, second edition. South Melbourne: Oxford University Press.

Moses, John (2002) 'The Struggle for Anzac Day 1916–1930 and the Role of the Brisbane Anzac Day Commemoration Committee', *Journal of the Royal Australian Historical Society*, Vol. 88, Part 1: 54–74.

Moses, John A. and George F. Davis (2013) *Anzac Day Origins: Canon D.J. Garland and Trans-Tasman Commemoration*. Barton, Australian Capital Territory: Barton Books.

Nicklin, Lenore (1971) 'Their March was a Truly Solemn Affair', *Sydney Morning Herald*, 26 April, 1.

'Police Remove Wreath: Inscription Deemed Offensive, *Age*, 26 April 1934, 7.

Prior, Robin (2015 [2009]) *Gallipoli: The End of the Myth*. Sydney: NewSouth Books.

Reynolds, Henry (2013) *Forgotten War*. Sydney: NewSouth Books.

Scates, Bruce (2006) *Return to Gallipoli: Walking the Battlefields of the Great War*. Cambridge: Cambridge University Press.

Scates, Bruce (2009) *A Place to Remember: A History of the Shrine of Remembrance*. Cambridge: Cambridge University Press.

Scates, Bruce, Rebecca Wheatley and Laura James (2015) *World War One: A History in 100 Stories*. Melbourne: Viking.

Seal, Graham (2004) *Inventing ANZAC: The Digger and National Mythology*. St Lucia: University of Queensland Press.

Seymour, Alan (1962) *The One Day of the Year*. London: Angus & Robertson.

Shute, Carmel (1975) 'Heroines & Heroes: Sexual Mythology in Australia 1914–1918', *Hecate*, Vol. 1, No. 1: 7–22.

'Smallest Crowd for Years Sees Anzac Day March', *Argus*, 26 April 1954, 6.

Soutphommasane, Tim (2012) *Don't Go Back to Where You Came From: Why Multiculturalism Works*. Sydney: NewSouth Books.

Stanley, Peter (2010) *Bad Characters: Sex, Crime, Mutiny, Murder and the Australian Imperial Force*. Millers Point, NSW: Pier 9.

Stanley, Peter (2015) *Die in Battle, Do Not Despair: The Indians on Gallipoli*. Solihull: Helion & Company.

Stephens, David and Alison Broinowski (eds) (2017) *The Honest History Book*. Sydney: NewSouth Books.

Thomson, Alistair (1994) *Anzac Memories: Living with the Legend*. Melbourne: Oxford University Press.

Twomey, Christina (2013a) 'Prisoners of War of the Japanese: War and Memory in Australia', *Memory Studies*, Vol. 6, No. 3, 321–30.

Twomey, Christina (2013b) 'Trauma and the Reinvigoration of Anzac: An Argument', *History Australia*, Vol. 10, No. 3: 85–108.

Ward, Russel (1958) *The Australian Legend*. Melbourne: Oxford University Press.

Wilcox, Craig (2009) *Red Coat Dreaming: How Colonial Australia Embraced the British Army*. Cambridge: Cambridge University Press.

Wilson, Mary (1974) 'The Making of Melbourne's Anzac Day', *Australian Journal of Politics and History*, Vol. 20, No. 2: 197–209.

Winter, Jay and Emmanuel Sivan (1999) 'Setting the Framework', in Jay Winter and Emmanuel Sivan (eds), *War and Remembrance in the Twentieth Century*. Cambridge: Cambridge University Press.

Winter, Jay (2013–2016) *The Cambridge History of the First World War*, Volumes I to III. Cambridge: Cambridge University Press.

Wise, Nathan (2014) *Anzac Labour: Workplace Cultures in the Australian Imperial Force during the First World War*. Basingstoke: Palgrave Macmillan.

9 Dealing with the past

History, memory and the Northern Ireland Troubles

Ian McBride

In 1998 the Good Friday Agreement brought to an end 30 years of appalling political violence in Northern Ireland. The power-sharing structures of government established in Belfast have proved to be impressively resilient, in spite of periodic upsets. The peace process has enabled (overwhelmingly Protestant) unionists and (overwhelmingly Catholic) nationalists to co-exist peacefully with each other, and with their neighbours in Britain and the Irish Republic. For most outsiders Northern Ireland has become, once again, a dull if rather picturesque corner of Western Europe, whose puzzling inhabitants cannot quite let go of an ancient religious and political feud that nobody else quite understands.

Twenty-five or thirty years ago things were very different. The streets of Belfast and Derry were a depressingly familiar sight to television viewers around the world. Helicopters flew over the 'bandit country' of south Armagh, where it was unsafe for the British Army to travel by road. The names of small rural towns – such as Enniskillen or Omagh – instantly called to mind the terrible atrocities that occasionally punctuated Northern Ireland's routine patterns of rioting, assassinations and bombings. Today we seldom hear of them. Even for older generations, it takes a mental effort to recapture the sense of apocalypse that characterised the bleakest years of the Troubles. In 1972, which began with British soldiers killing thirteen unarmed demonstrators on 'Bloody Sunday', there were more than 10,000 shooting incidents and almost 500 people were killed – all this in a country the size of Yorkshire, with just 1.5 million inhabitants.

Inside Northern Ireland, meanwhile, it sometimes feels as if the Troubles never really ended. Students interested in the 'memory boom' will find here all the hard cases familiar from other 'transitional' societies. Investigation of the 'dirty war' fought by the British state has uncovered evidence of persistent collusion between the security forces and loyalist paramilitaries – Protestant extremists whose targets were usually randomly selected inhabitants of Catholic areas. The publicity surrounding public inquiries into state violence (most obviously Bloody Sunday) has reinforced the demand for official investigations into atrocities carried out by republicans: the Kingsmill massacre (1976) and the Omagh bomb (1998) are just two prominent examples. Northern Ireland has mourned its own 'disappeared': the painstaking identification and excavation of burial sites has now uncovered the remains of thirteen of the sixteen individuals killed and secretly buried between 1972 and 1985, mostly by the IRA (Irish Republican Army) ('The Disappeared of Northern Ireland').

The Troubles also generated their own *lieux de mémoire*, most obviously the high-security Maze Prison, the subject of recurrent controversy since the 360-acre site was transferred from the UK authorities to the devolved Stormont executive in Belfast in 2002. It was the death of ten republican prisoners on hunger strike, in 1981, that transformed Sinn Féin from the IRA's publicity agency into a political party with a substantial electoral base. As with many aspects of Northern Ireland, the very name of the Maze remains a source of contention. Former inmates refer instead to 'Long Kesh', the name of the internment camp upon which the notorious H-Blocks of the modern prison were constructed after 1976. When academics hedge their bets by speaking inclusively of 'the Maze/Long Kesh' they are signalling a wider uncertainty about whether those who served sentences there were terrorists or prisoners of war (Graham and McDowell 2007). And that uncertainly is perhaps the simplest way of encapsulating the difficulties faced by the Northern Irish in dealing with the past.

Remembrance in Northern Ireland often works by a process of accretion, so that the victims of violence during the 1970s or 1980s have been subsumed into rival cultures of commemoration reworked over several hundred years. 'History' was always at the centre of the Troubles, and the remembrance and re-enactment of past battles – the Battle of the Boyne (1690) for unionists or the Easter Rising (1916) for nationalists – has played a vital part in sustaining clashing identities. At the end of the last century there were 3,500 commemorative parades taking place annually. That makes one for every 500 inhabitants, or ten for each day of the year (Jarman 1997: 119). The vast majority of these are organised by the Orange Order, a large fraternal network dedicated to maintaining both the Protestant faith and loyalty to the British crown – two commitments that its members regard as essentially the same thing. Orange processions mark the anniversaries of seventeenth-century struggles, the period when the north of Ireland – Ulster – was first colonised by English and Scottish Protestants. But they also incorporate the collective traumas and trials of more recent times: remembrance of the carnage suffered by the Ulster Division at the Battle of the Somme emphasises the past sacrifices made by unionists, and – implicitly – their continuing claim to the protection of the British state.

'Memory work' is equally vital to Irish nationalism and republicanism. (In Ireland 'republicanism' signifies not only a goal – complete independence from Britain – but the conviction that only violent means or 'armed struggle' will achieve it.) Republican parades are often overtly militaristic. While the stereo-typical Orangeman wears a suit and a bowler hat, some republican marching bands are led by men in balaclava helmets. In practice they are effectively controlled by Sinn Féin, the political party that emerged from the Provisional IRA. Easter Monday remains the highpoint of the republican calendar, and the doomed rebellion of 1916 is still the paradigmatic act of nationalist resistance against British rule, even though Belfast's contribution to it was actually negligible. For both unionists and nationalists history is a morality tale, with contrasting lessons to be learned. The template for the Protestant predicament is the Siege of Derry (1689), when the walled Protestant city was relieved by the English after a siege of more than three months, encapsulating 'an endless repetition of repelled assaults, without hope of absolute finality or of fundamental change'. Nationalist remembrance, on the other hand, turns on a series of heroic defeats; its motifs are subjection and survival; and it celebrates 'the bearing of witness as against success' (MacDonagh 1983: 1, 13–14). These historical narratives, renewed and reinvented over centuries of contestation, assume that politics is a zero-sum game in which one side's deliverance means the other's defeat. Neither has much relevance to the anti-climaxes and compromises of the peace process.

Unionists now feel they are slowly but inexorably losing a war of ethnic attrition. In the May 2016 Assembly election, Unionist parties obtained 47.6 per cent of votes cast while the total figure for nationalists was 36 per cent.[1] The declining Unionist vote reflects the shrinking of the Protestant population from two-thirds to around 55 per cent of the total; indeed, Catholics now make up a majority of all age groups under 40. Unionism consequently remains locked into a holding pattern. To a curious outsider, the entrenched pessimism and leaden resentment of the Ulster Protestants may appear baffling. Republicanism as a revolutionary project has collapsed. Northern Ireland's constitutional position as part of the United Kingdom seems secure. The dismantling of the border and the reunification of Ireland seem no more likely today than in the 1960s. But these constitutional realities are offset by the general direction of political and cultural developments, which has seen the progressive empowerment of the nationalist community at the expense of unionists. The tone of public life in Northern Ireland – the flags and emblems it displays, its media and cultural policy – is increasingly Irish and correspondingly less British or 'Protestant'. The rebalancing of the public sphere extends to acts of remembrance too. While the British government naturally seeks to protect the reputation of its armed forces, it is now largely neutral in the ethnic clash between unionists and nationalists 'across the water'. Thus the most powerful actor in Northern Irish politics has demonstrated little interest in constructing an official narrative of the 'war' or trying to control the meaning of the disputed events whose anniversaries matter so much to the people of Belfast or Derry.

The Republican movement has become the most adept manipulator of collective memory on the island of Ireland. (The Republican movement is a term of art used to preserve the useful fiction that the Provisional IRA and Sinn Féin, whose members were largely interchangeable, were separate entities.) As we shall see, the violent campaign of the IRA was rejected by a majority of the Catholic population whose defenders they claimed to be. But Sinn Féin today portrays itself as the natural continuation of the peaceful civil rights campaign of the 1960s. The party still projects itself as the heir of earlier republican martyrs such as Wolfe Tone (1798) and Patrick Pearse (1916), situating itself in a long tradition of armed struggle against British rule. But republican groups have broadened their appeal by reframing their political demands in the newer discourse of human rights violations, often presenting themselves as victims of violence rather than insurgents.

The Bloody Sunday Justice Campaign, to take one prominent example, demonstrated a remarkable capacity to reinvent itself, successfully internationalising the elaborate rituals that grew up around the annual commemoration of the fourteen unarmed protestors killed by soldiers of the Parachute Regiment on 30 January 1972. At the same time, the prolonged campaign fought by the Bloody Sunday families was sometimes linked with other, more militant causes: the recovery of the remains of Tom Williams, the IRA man hanged for killing a Catholic RUC constable in 1942 (the Royal Ulster Constabulary was the armed police force of Northern Ireland between 1921 and 2001), or the call for an inquiry into the killing of three unarmed IRA members on Gibraltar in 1988 (Dawson 2007: 160, 183). This closer identification with physical-force resistance to British rule takes us a long way from the most famous image Bloody Sunday, that of Father Edward Daly waving his white handkerchief as he helped move the dying Jackie Duddy. The brutality of the Paras marked a turning point precisely because they were not shooting at IRA targets but firing indiscriminately: *ordinary* Catholic civilians realised that 'it could have been me' (Dawson 2005: 148).

To think of the Troubles as an 'ethnic' conflict, as many commentators have done, does not mean that inherited cultural differences spontaneously generate violence of their own accord. Over the centuries, competition between Protestants and Catholics has been about tangible, material things: the ownership of land, the allocation of jobs and housing, access to political power, the composition and conduct of the security forces, the existence and expression of territorial dominance in housing estates and farmlands. But unionists and nationalists practice 'ethnic' politics in the sense that their attempts to mobilise support are confined to their respective communities. Each side is divided within itself by social status, attitudes to clerical authority and secularism, beliefs about gender and matters of social morality. Each side also contains many bridge-builders who work hard to improve relations between the two communities. Moderate Protestants and moderate Catholics often have more in common with each other than with their more inflexible co-religionists. But the general political trend since the 1960s has been in the direction of greater polarisation. Members of the Northern Ireland Assembly created in 1998 are elected by a system of proportional representation in which moderate unionists and nationalists have the opportunity of transferring second-preference votes to one another; but in practice this seldom happens. Ideological divisions are contained within the two oppositional blocs. And these two blocs are cultural constructs. Indeed they are mnemonic constructs, shaped by symbols, rituals and the conflicting stories they tell about the past. In the aftermath of the Goodn Friday Agreement, the politics of memory has become war by other means.

What kind of conflict?

One influential guide to the Troubles comments that Northern Ireland is the subject of a 'meta-conflict'; that is, 'a conflict about what the conflict is about' (McGarry and O'Leary 1995: 1). The antagonism between unionists and nationalists has been described as an ethnic conflict, but also as an anti-colonial war or a terrorist campaign. The term 'Troubles', an enduring euphemism borrowed from older Irish conflicts and employed by large sections of both communities, encompasses a diverse spectrum of violent encounters. At the risk of simplification, we might pick out two basic patterns of conflict, which can be described as vertical and horizontal. The vertical pattern corresponds to the war between republican insurgents (the Provisional IRA is by far the most important group) and the security forces of the British state. It accounts for many of the deaths that resulted from gun-battles, sniper attacks, assassinations and ambushes. Of the 2001 deaths attributable to republican paramilitaries, more than half were members of the security forces. In fact, the IRA very rarely targeted Protestant civilians (Kowalski, 2016). The British Army meanwhile killed 117 republicans, and the principal objective of its long campaign, 'Operation Banner', was always to contain the IRA. The poorly armed and poorly organised loyalist paramilitary groups were by contrast a minor distraction. Many observers viewed this conflict as an anti-colonial struggle, a continuation of the IRA campaign of 1919–21 which established independence for the rest of Ireland. This is also how the Provisionals portrayed their own armed struggle. It is an interpretation embodied in the military terminology employed by republicans – of volunteers, OCs, active service units – and mimicked by their loyalist counterparts.

Republicans envisaged themselves as waging war against the British state. But the IRA campaign was activated and fuelled by street disturbances between working-class Protestant and Catholic communities. Patterns of residential segregation, rioting along territorial boundaries and localised bursts of ethnic cleansing or 'burning out' were all recurrent features of the history of Belfast since the 1830s. The sporadic rumbling of this horizontal violence was present during those periods of Irish history which appeared to be relatively calm at the level of high politics. As early as 1813 an Orange Order parade in Belfast precipitated a riot resulting in two fatalities. Disturbances followed in every decade between the 1830s and the 1930s. Orange processions frequently provided the spark, but other precipitating factors included elections, anti-Catholic preaching, a funeral procession and even on one occasion a Sunday school trip. By the 1880s these riots had already assumed highly ritualised forms. One Victorian writer recalled how he had learned 'the proper way to construct a street riot' in the town of Portadown in 1869; in later decades he charted the adaptation of the street-fighter's technology as kidney shaped cobbles gave way to 'square setts' and eventually to riveter's nuts from the Belfast shipyard (Moore 1914: 16, 22, 25, 45).

That the IRA should have been reborn in the streets running between the Shankill and the Falls Roads of West Belfast should not surprise us. Protestant and Catholic families lived there cheek by jowl. After the clashes of 1969 academics rediscovered a long history of Victorian and Edwardian riots concentrated along the same sectarian fault-lines. The most recent scholarly account of the early Troubles documents fully the communal tensions fomented by John McKeague's Shankill Defence Association, frequently labelled 'Paisleyites' at the time, although there was no substantial connection with the Reverend Ian Paisley, then embarking on a long and controversial career as fundamentalist preacher, street protestor and inciter of sectarian hatred. The stone-throwing and street-fighting orchestrated by McKeague escalated into full-scale rioting and the expulsion of Catholic families living in predominantly Protestant districts, creating the conditions in which disillusioned republican veterans like Billy McKee, Seamus Twomey and Joe Cahill were able to reactivate the IRA. If the loosely structured Protestant crowd was the initial aggressor, it was the armed interventions of this small group of diehards at Unity Flats in August 1969 and at St Matthew's Church in January 1970 that propelled the violence onto a more lethal plane (Prince and Warner 2012: 208).

In their attempts to manage the Northern Ireland problem, the two governments in London and Dublin have left the 'meta-conflict' to the locals. It is part of the historian's job, however, to test the concepts and categories employed by the protagonists, particularly where they depend on simplified or distorted representations of the past. Since the 1994 ceasefire our understanding of the character of political violence in Northern Ireland has been transformed by statistical analysis (Fay et al. 1999). The results have challenged common perceptions of perpetrators and victims in a manner that discomfits both unionists and republicans. Most notably, the examination of those killed reveals that republican paramilitaries have been responsible for more Catholic deaths than the British army and the local security forces combined – in spite of the IRA's self-image as the defender of nationalist communities. Most unionists, meanwhile, regarded Northern Ireland as a successful democratic polity in which ordinary people were under attack by terrorists. A subconscious tendency to equate the majority of ordinary, law-abiding people with the *Protestant* majority is perhaps evident in a detailed memorandum drawn up by FAIR (Families Acting for Innocent Relatives) in 2004:

> Here a violent terrorist minority sought to overturn the democratic wish of the majority and impose their political will through force. In the process they abused the rights of all and murdered with abandon. To equate that to a struggle for liberation and freedom is simply to accept the propaganda of the terrorist.
>
> (*Ways of Dealing with Northern Ireland's Past* 2005: II, Ev. 180)

This link was explicitly recognised in the 'Long March' of victims' groups and their supporters between Derry and Portadown in the summer of 1999, where the organisers' aims slipped unthinkingly from drawing attention to the 'forgotten victims' of the conflict to the broader project of securing 'parity of esteem for Protestant culture and heritage and for support for deprived unionist communities' (Finlay 2001: 17). In fact the Catholic minority (roughly a third of the population in 1969 rising to roughly two-fifths by 1998) accounted for a majority of all those killed, 1,548 people. If we exclude those victims who were not from the six counties, and those whose religious background cannot be identified, we find that 59 per cent were Catholic.

Table 9.1 Responsibility for deaths, 1966–99

	No.	*%*
Republican paramilitaries	2139	58.8
Loyalist paramilitaries	1050	28.9
British Army	301	8.3
Royal Ulster Constabulary	52	1.4
Ulster Defence Regiment	8	0.2
Other	80	2.2
Total	3630	100

Figures calculated from McKittrick et al. (1999, pp. 1475–6).

These statistics conceal significant local variations that have shaped perceptions of responsibility and victimhood. In the working-class nationalist areas of West and North Belfast we can find patterns of violence dominated by the 'vertical' struggle between the IRA and the security forces. In Ardoyne, for example, ninety-nine local people died during the conflict, most of them Catholics. Although twenty-six residents were killed by the state forces, more often than not in disputed circumstances, no one has ever been arrested or questioned about these deaths. A further fifty residents were killed by loyalist paramilitaries, who in some cases at least benefited from collusion with the state forces. It is easy to see how many people in North Belfast came to regard the Troubles as an attempt by the British state to coerce and control the nationalist people.

In many rural areas, by way of contrast, members of the local security forces greatly outnumbered civilians or paramilitaries among those who lost their lives. In the 'bandit country' of Newry and South Armagh, a stretch of hilly and mountainous terrain running along the border with the Irish Republic, 60 per cent of those killed belonged to the state forces and republican paramilitaries were responsible for 88 per cent of all deaths (Fay et al. 1999: 175). In many of these attacks family members were present and sometimes were injured or killed. The border towns of the west reveal a similar pattern. Castlederg, in County Tyrone, is a mixed town with just 3,000 inhabitants. *Lost Lives*, a remarkable compendium of all the victims of the Troubles, records that thirty people were killed in the area, of whom half were security-force personnel, most of them part-time soldiers of the Ulster Defence Regiment. The IRA were responsible for all but three of the total number. Five of their own members were killed when their bombs exploded prematurely; they 'executed' three alleged informers; they killed several civilians who had been mistakenly identified as security force personnel; one elderly woman died from heart attack when an IRA bomb exploded outside a Chinese restaurant. Most of the security force members were ambushed outside their own homes, or visiting relatives, or in the local shops where they worked during the day (McKittrick et al. 1999).

The most contentious element in the meta-conflict has been the role of the Provisional IRA. But attitudes to the IRA's campaign cannot be completely divorced from differences over the existence of Northern Ireland itself. Republicans were able to claim during the 1970s and 1980s that they could not 'join the democratic process' because an authentically democratic process had never existed in Northern Ireland. Sinn Féin's position is now constrained, however, by its participation in constitutional structures that do not provide any compelling reasons for thinking that a united Ireland is significantly closer than it was twenty or thirty years ago. Increasingly mainstream republicans justify their armed struggle by reference to the brutality of the British Army and the complicity of British intelligence agencies in loyalist assassinations, as opposed to the mere fact of British rule itself. Republicans have been unable to reverse the partition of Ireland, to undo the basic legal and constitutional framework of Northern Ireland, or even to have the criminal records of politically motivated prisoners expunged. At the same time, Sinn Féin routinely exploits its entrenched position in regional and local government to reiterate the moral justification for the IRA's armed struggle. Michael Gallagher, whose son Aidan was one of the twenty-nine civilians killed in the Omagh bombing on 15 August 1998, has complained that 'the word "terrorist" seems to have been removed from the dictionary that we used too often in Northern Ireland over the past 35 years' (HC, *Ways of Dealing with Northern Ireland's Past* 2005: II, Ev 185).

Republicans are perfectly aware that they never enjoyed the active support of most the nationalists they claimed to represent. But the self-image of the IRA volunteer as a soldier of the people is nevertheless rooted in communal experience. The Provisionals derived their mandate from the networks of sympathisers who gave them intelligence, shelter and food and who supported their protest within the prisons. They derived some comfort from the fact that many nationalists who rejected the armed struggle violence nevertheless shared the alienation and anger that drove it. It is impossible to quantify levels of popular backing for the IRA and very difficult or to interpret what little evidence we have. The most prominent nationalist politician during the Troubles was John Hume, leader of the SDLP, who consistently condemned the use of violence. In the 1984 European elections Sinn Féin ran a high-profile candidate, Danny Morrison, who received 13.3 per cent of first preference votes as compared to Hume's 22.1 per cent. This was perhaps as the closest thing we have to a nationalist poll on the relative attractions of moral and physical force. Research carried out in 1978 found that two-thirds of Catholics approved, to various degrees, with the statement that 'The IRA are basically a bunch of criminals and murderers' (Moxon-Browne 1981: 41–72).

Perhaps we can conclude that the IRA campaign enjoyed the active or passive support of somewhere between a third and two-fifths of nationalists. All serious scholarship stresses that the momentum of the Provisionals' campaign in Belfast was closely related to the aggression of the security forces, and in particularly of the British Army (English 2003: 140). Even in strongly nationalist areas of Belfast, however, attitudes were not static. In 1972–3 the sociologist Frank Burton found that around a third of the Catholics of Ardoyne were consistently pro-IRA with the local priests leading the critique of militant republicanism. In between these poles, the majority of residents tilted back and forwards, depending largely on the behaviour of the British soldiers (house searches, verbal abuse, physical violence and humiliation). Many local Catholics complained that the Provisionals, far from acting as defenders of their districts, were cynically using the local population as a shield, manipulating children and adolescents. There was some ill feeling too about punishment shootings and beatings inflicted on residents. On the other hand Burton emphasised that the Provisionals took care not to overstep the boundaries of tolerable behaviour: 'If the movement persistently violated community norms, doors would stop opening, billets would be harder to get, informing would rise and their isolation would increase' (Burton 1978: 109). Even in Ardoyne, ambivalence was probably more common than absolute positions on the morality of physical force.

What kind of peace?

The Good Friday Agreement recognised the importance of grappling with the legacy of violence, but the task of achieving truth and reconciliation was understandably subordinated to more urgent priorities. The Northern Irish political settlement is based on a *consociational* model of government, where parties participate in government together in proportion to their strength. It creates institutions that work around the entrenched antagonisms of the two main communities rather than attempting to overcome them. The most distinguished theorist of consociational politics is Brendan O'Leary, who has described the accommodation in Northern Ireland as 'a bargain derived from mutually conflicting hopes about its likely long-run outcome' (O'Leary 2004: 263). These mutually conflicting hopes could be sustained only because the external forces in London and Dublin who have driven the peace process forward have no desire to impose an official version of the past on the region's inhabitants.

The devolved structures created in 1998 constitute a repudiation of the simple majority-rule model of government which had been discredited under the old Stormont regime that existed between the 1920s and 1960s, when the Unionist Party held power continuously for fifty years. The new system institutionalises cross-community consensus as the basis of decision-making. This means accepting for the foreseeable future the existence of the communal division deplored by so many of the individuals and groups who actively tried to make Northern Ireland a more equal, tolerant and peaceful society. Elected members of the Legislative Assembly are required to register as unionist, nationalist or 'other'. Executive power is exercised by dual premiers appointed by parallel consent, that is, by the support of concurrent majorities in both the unionist and nationalist blocs. Other key decisions are reached by a 'weighted' majority procedure, that is, by at least 60 per cent of assembly members *including 40 per cent in each of the communal blocs*. Ministerial positions are then allocated according to the d'Hondt rule, a mathematical formula that enables the parties to nominate ministers in proportion to their strength in the assembly. The resuscitated Stormont government is the political embodiment of an entrenched stalemate rather than a mechanism for conflict resolution.

The drawback is that political stability derives from the hard bargaining of the political elites rather than any broader societal shift in attitudes. A stark demonstration of this situation can be derived from results in the first elections to the legislative assembly, held in June 1998. The adoption of the single transferable vote system created the possibility that moderates on either side might transfer their lower-order preferences across the divide in attempt to protect the Agreement against the extremes. The moderates were the Ulster Unionist Party and the Social Democratic and Labour Party, whose leaders, David Trimble and John Hume, were jointly awarded the Nobel Peace Prize. But the habits of communal solidarity proved resilient, with most voters transferring within their own ethnic bloc. The available evidence suggests that a relatively small number of SDLP votes (17 per cent) and Ulster Unionist votes (13 per cent) were cast in support of each other's candidates. By contrast 41 per cent of SDLP transfers went to Sinn Féin, with 56 per cent of Sinn Féin lower-preference votes going to the SDLP. The pattern on the Unionist side is even more revealing. The largest beneficiaries of transferred votes from the *pro-agreement* Unionists – candidates, that is, backing David Trimble – were in fact *opponents* of the peace process, including the Ian Paisley's hardline Democratic Unionist Party (31 per cent). And although the DUP fought the election on a belligerent 'No' platform, their bitter personal attacks on Trimble for caving in to 'IRA/Sinn Féin' did not prevent 44 per cent of their lower-preference votes – by far the largest single category – going to Trimble's 'Yes men' (Evans and O'Leary 2000: 89–90). Even during this brief honeymoon period, the traditional determination of the Northern Irish voter to keep 'the other side' out remained decisive.

Whereas all nationalists elected to the Legislative Assembly in June 1998 were supporters of the peace process, the unionists were split down the middle. What needs to be emphasised, however, is that divisions within unionism were not caused by unhappiness with the constitutional arrangements agreed at Good Friday – power-sharing plus cross-border bodies linking both parts of Ireland. The institutional links between North and South which absorbed so much attention in the all-party negotiations before Good Friday have since been viewed with remarkable indifference by unionists and republicans alike. In 1998, for first time, the vast majority of Irish people, North and South, effectively recognised the legitimacy of the partition of Ireland – albeit in a new, pluralist form. Sinn Féin ministers in the devolved executive engaged in an increasingly token opposition to the Union, as when Conor Murphy advised his civil service staff to refer to Northern Ireland as 'the North' or simply 'here' rather than use its official name (Bean, *New Politics of Sinn Féin* 2007: 174). Every single act of the assembly, as unionists point out, is an act of the British Crown – a judgement shared by dissident republicans. Instead, Protestant alienation was overwhelmingly focused on the early release of paramilitary prisoners, the reform of the RUC and the refusal of the IRA to decommission its weapons.

The importance of guns was not merely symbolic. The old Northern Ireland had been closely linked to its security forces – the RUC and the B Specials (a locally recruited part-time militia). But prisoners, policing and decommissioning were issues with fundamental implications for the clashing historical narratives cherished by unionists and republicans. By refusing to engage convincingly in the decommissioning process between 1998 and 2005 the republican movement made it impossible for David Trimble to survive as Unionist leader. The IRA's refusal to hand over its weapons also kept Sinn Féin at the centre of the peace process and left the SDLP struggling on the sidelines. This was not a risk-free strategy. Polls showed that Catholics were deeply divided over the early release of prisoners, with a third in favour, another third opposed and the remaining third somewhere in between. More than half of all Catholics surveyed believed that decommissioning should take place *before* the release of politically motivated prisoners (57 per cent) and before the admission to government of parties with paramilitary links (53 per cent) (Evans and O'Leary 2000: 93, table 14). But as decommissioning became the rallying cry of the Unionist parties – and, indeed, the key area in which the DUP sought to outbid the Trimble's moderates – it increasingly appeared to Nationalists that the real obstacle to peace was not so much the failure of the IRA to destroy its weapons as old-fashioned Unionist intransigence.

The Good Friday Agreement has therefore brought the political class together in a workable form of devolved government. In doing so, it defied the expectations of many of Northern Ireland's most experienced commentators. But it rests upon one central, constructive ambiguity. The question of the perceived legitimacy of the IRA's campaign is still bitterly divisive, often cutting through nationalist communities as well as exacerbating hostility between nationalists and unionists. This question was left unresolved by the 1998 agreement, which provided for the early release of politically motivated prisoners, but also required committed parties to renounce the use or threat of physical force for political purposes. As Sinn Féin has entered the political mainstream so too has the term 'IRA volunteer', once strictly avoided in the media, and the grouping together of the security forces and paramilitary organisations as 'ex-combatants'.

The core principles of consociational democracy provide that executive power should be shared across the two communities, that each community enjoys a measure of autonomy, particularly in cultural matters, that each benefits proportionally from public resources and each possesses the right of veto over major changes. It is very difficult to see how this check-and-balance model can be applied to the profoundly moral challenges of 'dealing with the past'. *Either* the IRA were terrorists *or* they were fighting a just war of national liberation. If the truth lies 'somewhere in the middle', we will need to invent a completely new political vocabulary to express that realisation. The consociational bargain has proved capable of managing the Northern Ireland conflict, but so far it has done nothing to resolve the conflict-about-the-conflict.

One way of illustrating this failure is to consider the lack of consensus among politicians and activists on how to define the 'victims' of the Troubles. In 2008 the executive was unable to agree on the appointment of a new Victims Commissioner, and decided instead to appoint four of them, rather in the spirit of the d'Hondt mechanism. They were Bertha McDougal, whose husband, a reserve police officer, was shot dead by the INLA (Irish National Liberation

Army) in 1981; Patricia McBride, whose brother Tony was killed in a shoot-out with the SAS near the Fermanagh border in 1984; the peace activist Brendan McAllister, director of Mediation Northern Ireland; and Mike Nesbitt, a former television news presenter who would go on to be leader of the Ulster Unionist Party. It was an admirably balanced team, representing both the shades of opinion in the region and the multi-faceted nature of the conflict. But a press release describing McBride's brother as an 'IRA volunteer' who was 'killed on active service' instantly alienated unionists, forcing the DUP to harden its position on 'dealing with the past'.[2] As the party's spokesman for victims put it:

> There has to be some moral line that you create here, because if you don't create that moral line what you say to future generations that, well actually it's okay to go out and kill people, it's okay to engage in criminal and terrorist activity because eventually you'll be almost absolved of it, and you yourself are a victim.[3]

The trouble with the truth

Official attempts to address the legacy of the Northern Ireland conflict began with the appointment in October 1997 of Sir Kenneth Bloomfield as the first Victims Commissioner. Bloomfield had previously been head of the Northern Ireland Civil Service and Governor of BBC Northern Ireland. He was a liberal, cosmopolitan unionist who had himself been the target of an IRA attack. Perhaps predictably, his report *We Will Remember Them* (1998) antagonised some of the most vocal elements within both unionism and nationalism. The political context for the creation of a Victims Commissioner was the public outrage caused by the phased release of paramilitary prisoners envisaged in the Good Friday Agreement. Hence Bloomfield's conclusion that 'victims must, at barest minimum, be as well served as former prisoners in terms of their rehabilitation, future employment, etc', and his recommendation that those killed or injured in the service of the community – that is, the security forces – should receive special consideration (*We Will Remember Them* 1998: 3.3, 8). This failed to satisfy some of the unionist victims' organisations. Meanwhile the report's relatively brief consideration of those killed by the security forces led to accusations that 'a hierarchy of victimhood' was being constructed: over the next decade Bloomfield was repeatedly attacked by organisations such as Relatives for Justice who lobbied for inquiries into state violence, with an increasing emphasis on allegations of collusion between the security forces and the loyalist paramilitaries.

Bloomfield's vision of a Northern Ireland Memorial Building, set in 'a peaceful location, amidst beautifully-landscaped gardens', inspired partly by the Hadassah Medical Centre in Jerusalem, with its 'extraordinary Chagall windows', suggested a level of decorum rather at odds with the unfolding debate on victimhood (*We Will Remember Them*, 7.13–18). The various proposals he considered – a memorial, an annual Reconciliation Day, a truth recovery process – were subsequently explored in a series of extensive consultation exercises and reports carried out by the Healing Through Remembering project (2002), the Northern Ireland Affairs committee of the House of Commons (2005) and the Consultative Group on the Past (2009) chaired by Lord Eames (former Anglican Archbishop of Armagh) and Denis Bradley (a former Catholic priest and journalist). The creativity, sensitivity and sheer hard work involved in these investigations contrasts sharply with the masterful inactivity of the politicians. The Eames–Bradley team crafted plans for a series of interlocking mechanisms to deal with sectarianism, the review of 'historical cases', a victim-centred mode of information recovery and 'thematic' inquiries into collusion and paramilitary activity. Their key recommendations have provided the basic template for government discussions ever since. In the short term, however, the painstaking research and reflection that went into the Eames/Bradley report was completely overshadowed by the Consultative Group's recommendation that relatives of those killed during the conflict – paramilitaries included – should receive a recognition payment of £12,000.

An examination of newspapers during the first fifteen years since the Good Friday Agreement also reveals the continuous low-level antagonism caused by the 'memory wars' at a local level. The memorialisation of the Troubles dead began soon after the IRA ceasefire. A number of republican memorials were denounced by unionists as offensive to those families who had suffered as a result of paramilitary violence. Perhaps the most dramatic case was the sculpture of a ten-foot masked INLA gunman in Derry City Cemetery, erected in honour of the hunger strikers Michael Devine and Patsy O'Hara. One Protestant pensioner threatened to exhume the remains of his parents from the cemetery and have them reburied elsewhere so that he would not have to pass 'this disgusting statue of a terrorist' every time he visited their grave.[4] The Equality Commission was asked to investigate complaints into two other Hunger Strike memorials in Dungiven and Dromore (Co. Tyrone), and a Celtic Cross dedicated to Colum Marks, an IRA man killed during a mortar bomb attack on Downpatrick RUC station. These bitter disagreements over republican memorials have been exacerbated by the demotion of the symbols of Britishness, particularly west of the Bann, where the political and demographic retreat of unionism has been most marked. Nationalists now occupy public spaces that unionists had monopolised under the first Stormont regime. Derry's Guildhall Square, once the preserve of the city's Unionist establishment, provided the stage for the dramatic broadcast of Prime Minister David Cameron's apology to the Bloody Sunday families. Even in Stormont buildings, the greatest monument to Unionist power, it is now possible to celebrate the life of IRA martyr Mairéad Farrell as an inspiration for contemporary Irish women.

Proposals for a truth recovery process have encountered similar obstacles, above all the difficult question of how to treat victims, like Mairéad Farrell, who have themselves been perpetrators of violence. At one end of the spectrum are those like FAIR, who believe that the only appropriate way to deal with the past is through the British criminal justice system. A number of the submissions made to Healing Through Remembering rejected talk of truth and reconciliation in language that implied entrenched hostility to the entire peace process and the compromises it required, including one recommendation that the best way to remember the victims of the conflict was to build more jails.[5] A much broader section of opinion, mostly but not entirely unionist, expressed fears that a truth process would be exploited by Republicans to rehearse the familiar justifications for armed struggle, and to 'condemn so-called British imperialism as the root cause of everything that is wrong with Northern Ireland society' (*Report of the Healing Through Remembering Project* 2002: 30). For these groups and individuals, it was vital that the remembrance of victims of the Troubles should exclude those who were killed whilst engaged in acts of terrorism, but should focus on the 'innocent' people 'who had no choices in their lives'.[6]

At the other end of the spectrum are the nationalist lobbying groups such as Relatives for Justice, the Ardoyne Community Project and Fírinne (Irish for truth), who have sought to expose the brutality and unaccountability of the state security forces. For these organisations the British criminal justice is not the solution but a large part of the problem. The following two statements, taken from memoranda drawn up for the Northern Ireland Affairs committee in 2004, make the point forcefully (*Ways of Dealing with Northern Ireland's Past* 2005: II, Ev 45):

> The British Parliament justified torture in Castlereagh and other police interrogation centres as referenced in various UN reports. They justified British soldiers murdering men, women and children on our streets. And worse still soldiers who murdered our loved ones were retained as serving soldiers within the ranks of the British Army. Their legislation facilitated daily harassment, house raids, physical and verbal abuse [Relatives for Justice and the New Lodge Six].

> It is important to note that a *de facto* amnesty has existed for the actions of the security forces since 1969. On the few occasions where soldiers have been convicted of murder for instance they have been granted early release from life sentences and allowed to rejoin the armed forces. At present two soldiers convicted of murder, Guardsmen Wright and Fisher, are serving soldiers. One has been promoted. Mrs Thatcher's claim that 'murder is murder is murder' has not been reflected in the actions of various governments to wrongdoing by the security forces [Pat Finucane Centre].

Between these polarised positions, what is most striking is the sheer diversity of responses to the problem of dealing with the past. The 108 submissions collected by Healing Through Remembering range from lengthy disquisitions with citations of Bourdieu or Derrida to the brief declaration that loyalist and republican paramilitaries deserved to 'Rot in Hell'.[7] Many of the clergy of all denominations have viewed both the Northern Ireland problem and its solution within a Christian framework in which constitutional preferences and national allegiances are muted or set aside. One of the most memorable statements came from a Presbyterian elder, who described how he used a marked-up copy of *Lost Lives* to pray every day for the victims of the Troubles.[8] Indeed spiritual commitments are clearly vital to some of the most prominent figures associated with Healing Through Remembering. Christian perspectives on forgiveness and reconciliation increasingly overlap with the psychological language of pain, closure, trauma and acknowledgement employed by a significant number of respondents, also generally free from overt political allegiances.

An extensive survey carried out in 2004 found that just over 40 per cent of respondents believed that a truth recovery process would help the people of Northern Ireland to come to terms with the past, with unionists notably more sceptical than nationalists. When given the statement, 'you wouldn't necessarily get the truth from a truth commission', however, a resounding 83 per cent agreed (Lundy and McGovern 2007: 328–9). Analysis of the South African experience (discussed by Tom Lodge in Chapter 10 of this book) reinforces the view that the truths uttered to truth commissions are likely to be selective, and that in many cases the tactical release of information rather than full disclosure is the likely result. In South Africa 'powerful groups and organisations have determined their own acceptable levels of truth through negotiation' (Stanley 2001: 531). The investigation of human rights violations was inevitably subordinated to political considerations: Chief Buthelezi's refusal to participate was tolerated, for example, by those anxious not to endanger the fragile relationship between the ANC and the Inkatha Freedom Party. The TRC abandoned attempts to obtain documents from the South African Defence Force, and the records of the Directorate of Special Tasks, the branch of Military Intelligence at the centre of the 'dirty war' in Angola, Mozambique, Lesotho and Zimbabwe, appear to have been shredded. Access to the ANC's own records was also severely limited.

The most compelling argument in favour of a truth recovery process has always been the palpable need of the bereaved to find out what happened to their relatives. Reading *Ways of Dealing with Northern Ireland's Past*, one encounters again the range of human responses to physical injury and emotional pain. Below are three female voices from the report (*Ways of Dealing with the Past* 2005: II, Ev. 75, 107, 112).

The first is Barbara Deane, a mathematics teacher who sustained multiple injuries in a bomb blast on Belfast's Ormeau Road in 1971, which resulted in the amputation of her right leg, 1,000 stitches and plastic surgery to her mouth and jaw.

> I had my hand on the red skirt when I became aware of a commotion behind me and turned to see a man with a gun. He put something down next to the wall beside the police station and I realised it was a bomb since it was lit. Calmly I asked him how long we had got – up until then there had been 20 minutes warning. He answered '20 seconds from when it was lit'. My memory is that I tried to marshal the others on the ground floor and as I emerged (last of them) I saw the police emerge and I went to towards them to direct them after the man. I hesitated then, because he was heading round the corner to where mother was sitting in the car. If I had dashed in the other direction I might have got away as some others did. As I turned he

was firing at them from the corner but I must have been looking down the barrel of his gun because I saw the intense light coming from it and thought 'Oh that is where the lost energy goes' – we had been doing sums in A-level maths about this. Afterwards someone told me that he had shot my ear almost off. . . .

I personally would have no problems with an amnesty but I know that some of the wider groups in the community might not feel like that. I just go on living; that is thrawn [i.e. stubborn] you see. I would not let them win by making me bitter.

The second is an Armagh social worker who, like a surprising number of people, was made a victim of the Troubles more than once. In August 1969 her father was shot dead by the B specials, one of the very first to die. Twenty-one years later she was injured in a land-mine explosion that killed three policemen and a nun on the outskirts of Armagh. One of the IRA bombers, released under the terms of the Good Friday Agreement, had returned to live in the town and now saluted her in the street.

He knows me personally, this man who had served 10 years for four murders and one attempted murder. For me, I would like at some stage to get in a room with him, sit down beside him and talk to him. I would like that to be facilitated in a way that would make it easy for me and make it equally easy for him. I do not want any apology from him but I would like him to hear my story and the impact that it has made on me and to hear, unlike the stories he has been told that he did not do me any harm, but I went on to live my life, have a nice home, have a nice job, have a nice car and a nice family, what he has put me and all my family through. For me he is a victim in that sense in that he does not really know what it has done to me. He sees it from his side. I would like to hear what his story is. I do not want an apology from him but I would like to hear his story.

Finally, 'Witness C' is the mother a thirty-four-year-old man shot dead in 1999, when Northern Ireland was supposed to be at peace. He was the target of a random sectarian attack carried out by a loyalist group calling themselves the Red Hand Defenders.

I reared my child to be a moderate and so when it came to my door I could not understand because I taught my children not to hate. As we were saying earlier on, only when it comes to your door do you understand. I said to an MP, 'When your daughter or son walks down a road and somebody shoots him in the back of the head then you can tell me you understand'. I just think we are used. . . . There are a lot of people that you do not hear about. There are a lot of Catholics who are not Sinn Fein supporters here. We are just ordinary people and you never hear our voices; you do not hear our voices.

Ways of Dealing with Northern Ireland's Past shows how a truth commission might help to recover the experiences of ordinary people who found themselves in very extraordinary circumstances after August 1969. It reveals how many individuals sought to maintain a moral space in which the pressures of communal solidarity could be weighed against other commitments. The same can be said for the numerous 'storytelling' projects and workshops that have set out to encourage and record testimonies from individuals and groups who have suffered in the conflict. Its advocates suggest that storytelling has a 'levelling effect': although we might disagree with narrator's political viewpoint we can nevertheless 'recognise and appreciate the human experiences of loss, trauma, disappointment, hope and triumph' (*Ways of Dealing with Northern Ireland's Past* 2005: II, Ev. 257).

This kind of latitude is probably an unrealistic aspiration for many of those damaged by the Troubles. Two academics from Queen's University Belfast who recorded the experiences of border Protestants in 2004–5 have described unforgettably the emotional intensity of storytelling, in this case concerning harrowing experience of IRA attacks. Listening to the story of one man, shot seven times with an Armalite automatic rifle in his home, and now partially paralysed, they were confronted by two local women who asked: 'Are you going to tell the truth? Do you know that this is a story of innocent victims murdered by butchers?' (Donnan and Simpson 2007: 18) The members of the Ardoyne Community Project equated 'storytelling' with fiction, preferring to publish their oral histories as *Ardoyne: The Untold Truth* (2002); the 'truth' in this case was 'very much bound up with a sense of bearing witness' and consciously opposed to what the residents viewed as the 'hierarchy of victimhood' established by Bloomfield (Lundy and McGovern 2006: 83). Nevertheless, the accumulation of individual testimonies is already helping historians to appreciate further the complexity of violence in Northern Ireland and the multi-dimensional nature of the conflict. In time it may also help us to understand that the inhabitants of Northern Ireland do not all come neatly stacked in two opposing piles labelled 'perpetrators' and 'victims', but that many played more than one role in the conflict still widely known as the Troubles.

Guide to further reading and online resources

There is now a large literature on the politics of memory in Northern Ireland. The first serious study of Troubles memory was Dawson (2007); the same author's essay on Bloody Sunday (Dawson 2005) was written before the publication of the Saville Inquiry report in 2010, but addresses one of the most controversial episodes of the Troubles and reminds us that underneath recent sites of memory there are much older imagined landscapes, equally contested. Other important facets of this topic include memorials (Graham and Whelan 2007), the gendering of memorialisation (McDowell 2008), the debate on truth recovery (Lundy and McGovern 2007) and memoirs of the Troubles (Hopkins 2013; McBride 2016).

Popular interpretations of the Troubles are shaped by contrasting cultures of commemoration among Protestants and Catholics that have existed in various forms for hundreds of years. For a long-term view see McBride (2001); some of the original and stimulating work on Irish memory has been by Guy Beiner (see, for example, Beiner 2007). The 'decade of commemorations', which has seen the Republic of Ireland reappraise its own origins in the Easter Rising of 1916 and associated events, has also encouraged important work, including Grayson and McGarry (2016).

Finally, Ó Dochartaigh (2016) provides an excellent introduction to the conflict in Northern Ireland; McGarry and O'Leary (1995) offers an indispensable analysis of interpretations of the Troubles. The heart-breaking record of those who lost their lives (McKittrick et al. 1999), remains in a class of its own.

Relevant websites

Conflict Archive on the Internet (CAIN) (http://cain.ulst.ac.uk)
The Bloody Sunday Inquiry (www.bloody-sunday-inquiry.org.uk)
Ways of Dealing with Northern Ireland's Past: House Of Commons Northern Ireland Affairs Committee Report (2005) www.parliament.the-stationery-office.co.uk/pa/cm200405/cmselect/cmniaf/303/303i.pdf
'The Disappeared of Northern Ireland' (http://thedisappearedni.co.uk)
The Report of the Healing Through Remembering Project, June 2002 (Belfast, 2002)
We Will Remember Them: Report of the Northern Ireland Victims Commissioner, Sir Kenneth Bloomfield KCB (Belfast, 1998)
House of Commons Northern Ireland Affairs Committee, *Ways of Dealing with Northern Ireland's Past: Interim Report – Victims and Survivors* (London, 2005)

Notes

1 For these purposes I have counted UKIP as part of the unionist vote but not the Conservative Party or Independent candidates. The largest party outside the unionist and nationalist blocs was the Alliance Party, which received 7 per cent of first-preference votes.
2 '"Volunteer" Row Rocks Victims' Commission', *News Letter*, 30 January 2008.
3 Jeffrey Donaldson, MP, interview with author, Westminster, 8 December 2010.
4 'Anger over Terror Statue in Graveyard', *Belfast Telegraph*, 2 March 2000; 'Pensioner's Anger over Terrorist Memorial', *Belfast Telegraph*, 3 March 2000.
5 I am grateful to Kate Turner and the staff of Healing through Remembering, Belfast, for permitting me to consult anonymised versions of the 108 submissions summarised in their 2002 report. Quotation from S039.
6 HTR, Belfast, 2002 submissions S024, S073.
7 HTR, Belfast, 2002 submissions: S082, 086, 020.
8 Ibid., S085.

References

Bean, Kevin (2007) *The New Politics of Sinn Féin*. Liverpool: Liverpool University Press.
Beiner, Guy (2007) 'Between Trauma and Triumphalism: The Easter Rising, the Somme, and the Crux of Deep Memory in Modern Ireland', *Journal of British Studies*, 46(2): 366–89.

Burton, Frank (1978) *The Politics of Legitimacy in a Belfast Community*. London: Routledge & Kegan Paul.

Dawson, Graham (2005) 'Trauma, Place and the Politics of Memory: Bloody Sunday, Derry, 1972–2004', *History Workshop Journal*, 59: 151–78.

Dawson, Graham (2007) *Making Peace with the Past? Memory, Trauma and the Irish Troubles*. Manchester: Manchester University Press.

Donnan, Hastings and Kirk Simpson (2007) 'Silence and Violence among Northern Ireland Border Protestants', *Ethnos*, 72(1): 5–28.

English, Richard (2003) *Armed Struggle: The History of the IRA*. Oxford: Oxford University Press.

Evans, Geoffrey and Brendan O'Leary (Jan. –Mar. 2000) 'Northern Irish Voters and the British–Irish Agreement: Foundations of a Stable Consociational Settlement?', *Political Quarterly*, 71(1): 78–101.

Fay, Marie-Therese, Mike Morrissey and Marie Smyth (1999) *Northern Ireland's Troubles: The Human Costs*. London: Pluto.

Finlay, Andrew (Dec. 2001) 'Defeatism and Northern Protestant "Identity"', *Global Review of Ethnopolitics*, 1(2): 3–20.

Graham, Brian and Sara McDowell (2007) 'Meaning in the Maze: The Heritage of Long Kesh', *Cultural Geographies*, 14(3): 343–68.

Graham, Brian and Yvonne Whelan (2007) 'The Legacies of the Dead: Commemorating the Troubles in Northern Ireland', *Environment and Planning D: Society and Space*, 25(3): 476–95.

Grayson Richard S. and Fearghal McGarry (eds) (2016) *Remembering 1916: The Easter Rising, the Somme and the Politics of Memory in Ireland*. Cambridge: Cambridge University Press.

Hopkins, Stephen (2013) *The Politics of Memoir and the Northern Ireland Conflict*. Oxford: Oxford University Press.

Jarman, Neil (1997) *Material Conflicts: Parades and Visual Displays in Northern Ireland*. Oxford: Berg.

Kowalski, Rachel Caroline (2016) 'The Role of Sectarianism in the Provisional IRA Campaign, 1969–1997', *Terrorism and Political Violence*. DOI: https://doi.org/10.1080/09546553.2016.1205979"10.1080/09546553.2016.1205979.

Lundy Patricia, and Mark McGovern (2007) 'Attitudes towards a Truth Commission for Northern Ireland in Relation to Party Political Affiliation', *Irish Political Studies*, 22(3): 321–38.

MacDonagh, Oliver (1983) *States of Mind: A Study of Anglo-Irish Conflict, 1780–1980*. London: Unwin Hyman.

McBride, Ian (ed.) (2001) *History and Memory in Modern Ireland*. Cambridge: Cambridge University Press.

McBride, Ian (2016) 'Provisional Truths: IRA Memoirs and the Peace Process', in Senia Paseta (ed.), *Uncertain Futures: Essays about the Past for Roy Foster*. Oxford: Oxford University Press.

McDowell, Sara (2008) 'Commemorating Dead "Men": Gendering the Past and Present in Post-Conflict Northern Ireland', *Gender, Place and Culture* 15(4): 335–54.

McGarry, John and Brendan O'Leary (1995) *Explaining Northern Ireland: Broken Images*. Oxford: Blackwell.

McKittrick, David et al. (1999) *Lost Lives: The Stories of Men, Women and Children who Died as a Result of the Northern Ireland Troubles*. Edinburgh: Mainstream.

Moore, F. Frankfort (1914) *The Truth about Ulster*. London: Nash.

Moxon-Browne, Edward (1981) 'The Water and the Fish: Public Opinion and the Provisional IRA in Northern Ireland', *Studies in Conflict and Terrorism*, 5(1–2): 41–72.

Ó Dochartaigh, Niall (2016) 'Northern Ireland', in Richard Bourke and Ian McBride (eds), *The Princeton History of Modern Ireland*, ch. 5. Princeton, NJ: Princeton University Press.

O'Leary, Brendan (2004) 'The Nature of the Agreement', in John McGarry and Brendan O'Leary, *The Northern Ireland Conflict: Consociational Engagements*. Oxford: Oxford University Press.

Prince, Simon and Geoffrey Warner (2012) *Belfast and Derry in Revolt: A New History of the Start of the Troubles*. Dublin: Irish Academic Press.

Stanley, Elizabeth (2001) 'Evaluating the Truth and Reconciliation Commission', *Journal of Modern African Studies*, 39(3): 525–46.

10 Truth and reconciliation in post-apartheid South Africa

Tom Lodge

Even today, government statistics divide South Africa's population into four main race groups: 40 million or so Bantu-language-speaking Africans, descendants of successive waves of migrants who moved at least two thousand years ago from Central Africa; 4.5 million whites who first started arriving in the seventeenth century; about the same number of 'coloureds', who trace their ancestry to indigenous Khoi-San hunter gatherers, the country's first inhabitants, and unions between them and white settlers and Indonesian slaves; and 1.2 million Indians, first brought to South Africa as indentured labourers in the 1860s. Historically, whites have been divided politically and culturally between Afrikaners, taking their name from Afrikaans, a Dutch-derived language that evolved among South Africa's original white settlers of Cape Town and the surrounding area, and English speakers who started emigrating to South Africa after the assumption of British imperial control in 1806. In defiance of British rule, groups of Afrikaners – the *voortrekkers* – began migrating northwards in 1836 to establish their own independent republics. These were subjected to a brutal British imperial invasion in the Anglo-Boer War of 1899–1902 and from the British colonies of the Cape and Natal and the former Afrikaner republics a Union of South Africa was established in 1910. From 1910 to 1994, the self-governing Union and later Republic of South Africa would be ruled by governments elected by the white minority. From 1948, these governments would commit themselves to a programme its leaders called 'apartheid'.

The Truth and Reconciliation Commission was established to address human rights abuses committed by defenders and opponents of apartheid and white minority rule during more than three decades of conflict between 1960 and 1994. In Afrikaans, *apartheid* means 'apart-ness'. The term began to be routinely employed by (Afrikaner) National Party politicians in 1943 and in 1948 the Party contested and won a general election by promising voters that it would implement a systematic programme of racial apartheid. At that time National Party politicians argued that their white English-speaking opponents were liberals, committed to racial equality. This was untrue. In 1948 South Africa was a segregated state and institutionalised racial discrimination against black South Africans was extensive. Black people – three-quarters of the population – had been denied freehold land-ownership from 1913. A small minority of black South Africans who had obtained voting rights were removed from the common roll in 1936. Local regulations governed their entry into cities and restricted where they could live. Both convention and laws limited black employment prospects. It was the case, though, that the wartime expansion of manufacturing encouraged black migration into cities and by the late 1940s blacks were competing with whites for semi-skilled factory jobs. White farmers found it increasingly difficult to find labour. An expanding trade union movement and new political militancy among communists and African nationalists signalled alarming challenges to white supremacy. In response, Afrikaner Nationalists would mobilise working-class whites, winning power in 1948.

Through the 1950s a national system of 'pass laws' extended controls over the movement and residential rights of the African population, incorporating black women into the system. Six hundred new labour bureaux would forcefully direct black workers to different employers. From 1950 official racial classifications as well as the prohibition of cross-racial sex and marriage addressed ideological concerns about racial miscegenation. Racial 'job reservation' proliferated and black workers were excluded from collective bargaining arrangements. Black traders and householders were excluded from the inner cities and on the urban peripheries the government embarked on a massive construction programme of state-owned housing in huge ghetto-like 'townships': Soweto, the most famous of these, was built mainly in the 1950s on the outskirts of Johannesburg.

By the end of the 1950s among apartheid hardliners there was increasing concern over the dependence of industry on black labour, accentuated by alarm over rising black militancy, inside and outside factory gates. Increasingly politicians and officials sought to tighten restrictions on black urbanisation. The Sharpeville massacre in March 1960, when police fired upon and killed at least 69 black anti-pass protestors, contributed to South Africa's international diplomatic isolation and reinforced white political intransigence. Late in 1960, for the first time, the National Party won a majority of white votes, beginning to make inroads into the English-speaking electorate, which was 40 per cent of the white population. Through the 1960s, apartheid social engineering would reach its fullest expression. Resettlements of hitherto urbanised black people would swell the populations of the rural 'native reserves'. Together with the evicted inhabitants of 'black spots', areas of black freehold landownership outside the reserves, more than three million people would move to already overcrowded and eroded ethnic 'homelands' between 1960 and 1975. Urban 'influx control' was implemented with increasing severity in the 1960s. Employers were expected to recruit an ever-increasing proportion of their workforce from migrant workers on annual contracts with no permanent urban residential rights. By 1970 the construction of family housing for blacks in cities had ceased and instead the government was accommodating more and more workers in huge single-sex barrack-like dormitories.

The main black political organisations were prohibited in the aftermath of the Sharpeville crisis. By 1963 their leaders were in prison or in exile, after both the African National Congress (ANC) and its militant rival, the Pan-Africanist

Congress (PAC), had attempted to sponsor armed rebellions. New anti-terrorist legislation removed *habeas corpus* entitlements and from 1962 police began using torture routinely in their investigations of suspected insurgents. Meanwhile the government began to pursue a traditional objective of apartheid ideologues: the promotion of different black ethnicities as 'self-respecting nations'. With the passage of the Promotion of Bantu Self-Government Act in 1959 the old native reserves were grouped into different ethnic clusters and each assigned a particular ethno-national identity. The Act provided for a progression through various stages of self-government allocating office and authority to the chiefs who had earlier helped to govern the reserves through a British colonial-style indirect rule system. Four of the reserves would eventually obtain notional independence: Transkei in 1976, Bophuthatswana in 1977, Venda in 1979 and Ciskei in 1981. All blacks irrespective of their wishes were supposed to be citizens of one or other of these statelets. To make the homelands more economically viable and to lessen the concentration of black workers in the major cities the government invested massively in a border industrial development policy.

The first official efforts to dismantle apartheid began in the late 1960s when South Africa's cultivation of diplomatic relations with African countries required exceptions to racial restrictions in up-market hotels and residential neighbourhoods in the capital cities. More serious modifications to apartheid happened through the 1970s with the erosion of racial job reservation in response to local skill shortages and the effective abandonment of much of the 'Bantu Education' syllabus after the 1976 Soweto schoolchildren's insurrection. The concession of collective bargaining rights to a burgeoning black trade union movement in 1981 represented a major reform. In 1986 the scrapping of influx control laws signalled the government's recognition that it no longer possessed the administrative capacity to block black urbanisation: police had been ignoring illegal African settlements in inner-city districts since the late 1970s.

From 1976 onwards through to 1994, confrontations between police and politically animated crowds were frequently extremely violent. A second source of politically motivated violence was the conflicts that developed between supporters of various political groupings: nearly 11,000 people were killed in hostilities between ANC loyalists and supporters of Inkatha, the ruling party of the KwaZulu homeland, between 1985 and 1994. ANC supporters viewed Inkatha members as the state's auxiliaries, and indeed the police did supply arms to Inkatha groups. Organised guerrilla warfare by trained and relatively disciplined ANC and PAC combatants from 1961 onwards was responsible for only a small proportion of the deaths attributed to politically driven killings between 1961 and 1994, which were about 30,000 in total. Victims of the conflict included suspected informers and other perceived collaborators with the authorities. Between 1985 and 1987 nearly three hundred of these people would be burned to death after tyres filled with petrol – 'necklaces' – were forced over their heads and set alight. The ferocity of the conflict between the ANC and Inkatha actually increased during the negotiations to end apartheid in the early 1990s: a development that ANC leaders blamed on supposed agent-provocateur activity by a third force which they believed to be sponsored by the government.

By the mid-1980s the scale of black anti-apartheid politics and the threat posed by international economic sanctions was sufficient to persuade National Party politicians to open negotiations with black leaders, releasing them from prison in 1989 and 1990 and inviting them home from exile. Serious constitutional negotiations began in December 1991 and were concluded with agreement on a transitional 'power sharing' constitution agreed finally in April 1994, only days before scheduled elections. A more definitive constitution would be negotiated by parliament sitting as a Constitutional Assembly between 1995 and 1996, incorporating many of the features of the interim document without its commitment to mandatory coalition government. Most of the remaining apartheid legislation was repealed before universal suffrage elections in 1994. The effects of apartheid are still evident, though: a persistent pattern of informal racial segregation in many residential areas and in important arenas of social life, very severe and still racialised social inequality, and extreme levels of violent crime believed to be the legacy of decades of disruption of family life and other communal institutions that reproduce social order.

Why was the Truth and Reconciliation Commission set up?

In South Africa's transition to democracy amnesty was indispensable. Negotiators agreed that there would be no reprisals for human rights violations undertaken as a consequence of apartheid laws or actions against them. The 1994 constitution stipulated that 'divisions and strife of the past' would be addressed in a conciliatory manner. 'Offences associated with political objectives' would be amnestied. For this purpose, the ANC's key legal thinkers, in particular Kader Asmal and Albie Sachs, advocated a truth commission inspired by Latin American experience. In several Latin American countries, notably Chile and Argentina, after their transition from harsh military dictatorships, truth commissions had been established with different purposes, though usually their functions were investigative and to recommend reparations.

Legislation enacted a Truth and Reconciliation Commission (TRC) with four objectives: investigation of 'gross violations' of human rights between 1960 and 1994; amnestying those disclosing involvement in politically motivated violations; identification of victims and the design of reparations, and a report to recommend ways of preventing future violations. The TRC enjoyed wide powers. No previous truth commission had granted amnesties. ANC leaders were convinced that amnesty had to be linked 'to restoring the honour and dignity of the victims' (Omar 1966: 25) through the disclosure of truth and payment of reparation and that if amnesty was managed in a separate process it would have lacked public legitimacy. Accordingly, the law endorsed the principle of publically accessible hearings.

President Mandela appointed Archbishop Desmond Tutu in November 1995 to chair the Commission. Head of the two million strong Anglican congregation,

Tutu was South Africa's most prominent church leader. Through the 1980s he had been a major figure in the campaign to mobilise economic sanctions against apartheid, though remaining politically independent of the ANC and often critical of its tactics. For Tutu's deputy, Mandela chose Alex Boraine. Boraine, once the Methodist Church's president and for twelve years a liberal MP, was a key lobbyist during the TRC's conception. Fifteen other commissioners were announced. They were intended to be people 'without high political profile' and this was the case despite the inclusion of two former Afrikaner parliamentarians. Seven of the commissioners were women, eight were African or black, two were coloured and seven were white. The commissioners included five lawyers, five medical workers (doctors, psychiatrists, a clinical psychologist and a nurse) and four clerics (including Boraine, an ordained minister).

Two key suppositions animated the commissioners. The first was that truth promoted reconciliation. In 1994, the Chilean truth commissioner Jose Zalaquett had advised the South Africans about what was needed to reconstruct 'moral order'. Reconciliation could be achieved either through punishment or forgiveness, Zalaquett proposed. Forgiveness, he suggested, was morally superior: 'this is stressed by all major traditions'. But a prerequisite for forgiveness was 'that wrongdoing is known, that it is acknowledged, that there is atonement' (Boraine et al. 1994: 11).

'Our hope', commissioner Wendy Orr recalled later, 'was that, in that telling, a sense of healing and catharsis could begin' (Orr 2000: 31). This hope was widely shared. Acknowledgement through truth could 'trigger catharsis' or spiritual purification, maintained Kader Asmal. Asmal's argument lent support to the notion that individual psychological healing could be reproduced collectively as Africans exercised their historical 'prerogative to be forgiving' in a 'civic sacrament of forgiveness' (Asmal et al. 1996: 48–49). This was certainly the commissioners' understanding of the function played by the public rituals over which they presided. As Alex Boraine noted, the first human rights violations hearings in the Eastern Cape city of East London were preceded by a church service which included 'the traditional enactment of purification, of repentance, or sorrow, of commitment' (Boraine 2000: 101). The service opened with the singing of a Xhosa hymn, 'The forgiveness of sins makes the person whole' (Krog 1998: 26).

The second idea was that compassionate 'restorative justice' accorded with popular preferences and the African cosmology of *ubuntu* in particular. The Commission's enactment had referred to *ubuntu* as the spirit animating a conciliatory settlement. As the Commission explained, restorative justice redefined crime as wrongdoing against people rather than a violation of the state, and instead of punishment it stressed restoration of both victims and offenders with the authorities 'facilitating' such resolutions. This judicial shift from adversarial confrontation would represent a revival of 'African traditional values' especially those associated with the concept of *ubuntu*, 'humaneness' and its maxim that 'people are people through other people' (TRC Report, Vol. 1, 1998: 112). For Desmond Tutu, though 'honouring *ubuntu* is clearly not a mechanical, automatic and inevitable process', its corollary, restorative justice, was certainly 'a characteristic of traditional African jurisprudence' in which the central concern is not retribution but instead 'the restoration of broken relationships' (Tutu 1999: 51). From this perspective, deployed by charismatic leadership, Alex Boraine argued, the 'politics of grace' represented in, for example, Nelson Mandela's symbolic gestures towards Afrikaners had the 'almost salvific power', it was believed, to 'make or break community' (Boraine 2000: 362).

The commissioners were assigned between three committees, each charged with one function: consideration of 'gross human rights violations' and the identification of victims, the planning of reparations and rehabilitation, and the administration of amnesty. These committees would be supported by what would grow into a substantial bureaucracy, for as many as 550 people would work in the TRC's four regional offices in Cape Town, East London, Durban and Johannesburg as well as in headquarters. Altogether the TRC was to spend by the end of 1998 a total of R70 million (at that time, US $15 million).

What did the Commission do?

The Commission held its first meeting shortly after the commissioners were appointed, on 16 December 1995 (a public holiday, the newly designated Day of Reconciliation, appropriately enough) in Archbishop Tutu's former official residence. The next few months were devoted to setting up the organisation so that the first human rights violations hearings could be held in East London, on 15 April 1996. The public violations hearings ended in August 1997 but statement taking from individual victims continued. Meanwhile the work of the Amnesty and Reparations Committees gathered momentum while the Research Department began analysing the information gathered from human rights violations victims. With the publication of a five volume interim report in October 1998, the TRC began to disband though the work of the Amnesty and Reparations Committees continued, supported by skeleton staff and the four regional offices until late in 2001. Parliament debated a 'national response' to the TRC's interim report in February 1999.

The Human Rights Violations Committee received most media attention. The Committee's procedures began with statement taking; specially trained 'statement takers' gathered information about abuses. After these encounters select 'deponents' testified at televised public meetings. Respectfully listening to victims' stories was viewed as a vital therapy, a process of 'validation of individual subjective experience of people who had previously been silenced' (TRC Report, Vol. 1, 1998: 112). Statement makers would not be cross-examined, neither before nor during public hearings, for the commissioners sought to make their 'interaction' with victims 'a positive and affirmative experience' (TRC Report, Vol. 1, 1998: 144). Instead, the Investigative Unit attempted to find 'corroboration' for the 'narrative truth' of each statement. Corroborated statements were handed over to the Reparations Committee.

The Violations Committee collected 21,000 statements. These referred to 38,000 incidents, 10,000 of them killings. 17,500 of the deponents spoke about violations experienced by other people; much of the evidence accumulated by the Commission was hearsay. As Tutu pointed out, 'when it came to hearing evidence from the victims, because we were not a criminal court, we established facts on the basis of probability' (Tutu 1999: 33). The public hearings were not so much concerned with establishing facts; rather they enacted ritual – essential in what the commissioners understood to be a process of local communal reconciliation – and, of course, they were to serve as 'a powerful medium of education for society at large' (TRC Report, Vol 1, 1998: 147).

The quasi-religious ceremony opening the hearings in the East London city hall in April 1996 set the tone. After an overture of hymn singing led by commissioner Bongani Finca, all stood with heads bowed while Archbishop Tutu prayed and the names of the dead who were to be subject of the day's hearings were recited. A big white candle inscribed with a cross symbolised the bringing of truth. Under the glare of television lamps and accompanied by hymn singing, the commissioners crossed the floor to the rows of victims to welcome them before returning to sit behind a table covered with white linen. These preliminaries deliberately evoked Christian liturgy associated with the extension of the sacrament, for the hearings were not simply about bearing witness; instead they were dedicated to the transcendence of individual experience and the reconstruction of community through the evocation of suffering and sacrifice. (Footage of the ceremony appears at the beginning of South African Broadcasting Corporation [SABC] TRC Episode 87, part 02.)

During many of the hearings, commissioners attempted to convert private experience into a common resource. Richard Wilson suggests that four stages were followed in this process. In the initial phase, commissioners' commentaries universalized individual testimony. For example, after listening in Klerksdorp to Peter Moletsane's account of his arrest and torture when he had tried to report the death of his uncle to the police, Archbishop Tutu told him: 'Your pain is our pain. We were tortured, we were harassed, we suffered, we were oppressed.' Tutu was not claiming personal experience of the treatment meted out to Moletsane, Wilson argues, instead 'he was constructing a new political identity, that of a 'national victim', a new South African self which included the dimensions of suffering and oppression'. Next, commissioners sought to emphasise that all suffering was of equal moral significance (Wilson 2001: 111–121). A white woman whose husband had been killed by guerrillas prompted Desmond Tutu to recollect that 'our first witness this morning (a black man, whose son had disappeared in 1985) also spoke of getting the remains of a body back'. It was wonderful, Tutu concluded, 'for the country to experience that – black and white – we all feel the same pain'. Several of the testimonies offered at the Klerksdorp hearings are available on YouTube (SABC TRC Episode 21, Part 02 and Part 03).

This 'sentimental equalization of all victims of war', a frequent feature of conflict resolution mechanisms, was sometimes resisted by audiences, though. Wilson refers to the consternation of the commissioners at the hilarity that greeted the story of a mother whose son's body was exhumed and set alight by 'comrades'. The body belonged to a leading figure in 'The Toasters', a criminal gang whose speciality was burning their opponents alive. After creating a moral equality of victims each one would then be invested with the heroic significance arising from their assigned roles in a teleology of sacrifice. In the commissioner's reactions to what they were told by witnesses, there was no room for the private or the accidental or the pointless. Sello Mothusi, shot and disabled by the police in 1986, insisted, to the visible irritation of the commissioners at the Klerksdorp hearings, that on the day of his shooting he was just on his way to the shops, undertaking an errand for his mother, that he was not involved in politics, that he had 'done nothing wrong'. This would not do. All suffering was meaningful and all its victims were public martyrs in a just war for liberation. Even the mother of the leader of the Toaster gang was told by commissioner Hlengiwe Mkhize 'that people like you struggling for freedom should be recognised' (Wilson 2001: 111–121).

The closing rite in this liturgy was redemptive. Commissioners would ask those who had offered testimony if they could forgive the perpetrators of the violations to which they had borne witness. Forgiveness and the renunciation of vengeance for certain commissioners represented the most important function of these hearings for, as Tutu subsequently explained, the loss of the entitlement to retribution was 'a loss which liberates the victim' (Tutu, 1999: 219). And indeed certain witnesses did seem willing to find in the TRC's proceedings a substitute for justice, as in the case of Carl Webber, mutilated in a bomb blast in an East London bar. Though he felt that 'justice should be done', even so he felt that with the TRC, there was 'the start of something new: something will happen, I've got a lot of faith' (SABC TRC Episode 01, part 07: 1:13).

In fairness to Tutu, he acknowledged that forgiveness had to be personal and had to be the outcome of a reciprocal process, most memorably when he 'begged' a visibly reluctant Mrs Winnie Madikizela-Mandela (the former wife of President Mandela) to express remorse for her responsibility for the killings and violence committed by her bodyguards (SABC TRC Episode 77, Part 02, 34:57). Most notably, in 1989, Mrs Mandela's bodyguards had killed a teenage activist, 'Stompie' Moeketsi Seipei, whom they accused of acting as a police informer. The extent to which Mrs Mandela herself was directly involved in this event remains contentious. At the TRC hearing, the best that Tutu could extract from her was a very stilted expression of regret. She may have been exceptional. Tutu insisted that the majority of perpetrators and witnesses experienced the kind of emotional release that supposedly results from such avowals of responsibility. And Wilson's choice of evidence may have been too selective, for not all witnesses needed the commissioners to induce them to speak about forgiveness. For example, Beth Savage, badly injured in a guerrilla attack on a golf club in King Williams Town told the hearing that she would like to meet her assailant, 'in an attitude of forgiveness and I'd hope he could forgive me too' (SABC TRC Episode 01, part 07: 1:41). But as well as providing such comfort and restitution to the individuals offering their testimony, the hearings were directed at achieving collective benefits. For with the making of private grief into public sorrow, forgiveness and renunciation were implicitly corporate all-embracing undertakings, 'rites of closure' as another academic observer of the hearings has noted (Bozzoli 1998: 171). These public hearings, then, were directed as much at the Commission's reconciliation mandate as its quest for truth.

Meanwhile, the Amnesty Committee undertook the review of the 7,127 applications that it received up to a deadline in September 1997. The applications needed to concern offences committed between 1960 and 1994. Amnesty procedures were legalistic. Applicants were represented by lawyers and both applicants and those who opposed applications could be cross examined. Amnesty judges initially wanted to conduct closed sessions and needed to be persuaded to allow hearings to be televised. To be granted amnesty, applicants had to prove their actions were politically motivated and they had to disclose all relevant information, including their chain of command. In December 2001, the Amnesty Committee announced the completion of its final case: of the total of 7,127 applications only 1,146 (16 per cent) had been successful. This is a very small fraction of the likely total of the perpetrators of the 38,000 or so human rights violations recorded by the TRC.

There was no obligation on amnesty applicants to express contrition let alone seek reconciliation. Hence Amnesty offered fewer opportunities for the kinds of spiritual uplift the commissioners encouraged during the violations hearings. Applications for amnesty were all too often accompanied by justifications or very qualified regret. Even when applicants apologised, judgments were often received with considerable bitterness amongst the relatives of political assassinations, as well as scepticism about the extent to which killers genuinely felt remorse. Andrew Ribeiro was the son of Pretoria doctors murdered by security force agents in 1986. In killing him, the agents hoped to inflame hostilities between two local rival anti-apartheid groupings, one of which the Ribeiros belonged to. After attending the amnesty application from his parents' killers, Andrew Ribeiro expressed a widely shared sentiment when he told a journalist that 'victims' wounds have been reopened and we have been left with more tears than before. Reconciliation should balance and in our case this hasn't happened'. In the case of his family, their unhappiness with the outcome would have been accentuated by the efforts of senior police and military commanders to exculpate themselves from any responsibility for the Ribeiros' murders (for their evidence see: SABC TRC Episode 69 Part 05).

Understandably, though, in their memoirs, commissioners emphasised testimony in which personal avowals of moral guilt elicited expressions of forgiveness. In the first-hand narratives of the amnesties the same conciliatory incidents again are repeatedly accorded emblematic significance. A dramatic early instance of public reconciliation was when a member of the Northern Transvaal Security Branch, Jacques Hechter, confessed his role in planning assassination attempts; after his testimony he and one of his intended targets, Reverend Smangiliso Mkhatshwa, were able to shake hands and subsequently Mkhatshwa was to invite Hechter and his accomplices to his church to say that they were sorry. A comparable instance of mutual empathy occurred at General Abubaker Ismail's hearing for his activities as head of the ANC's Special Operations Unit which was attended by survivors of the Pretoria Church Street bombing. In this incident, the ANC's first use of a car bomb, 17 people were killed outside the air-force headquarters as they emerged from work. At the time the ANC claimed that most of the casualties were military personnel. Ismail apologised to the civilians who had been hurt and a picture of him shaking hands with Neville Clarence, an air-force clerk blinded in the blast, appeared in every South African newspaper. Subsequently Clarence visited Ismail's home, and the two men, apparently, managed to develop a kind of friendship (Stanley 2001: 542).

More generally though, because testimony could be subjected to cross-examination, as Boraine concedes, 'the atmosphere of compassion and sensitivity of the Human Rights Violations Committee hearings was lacking' (Boraine 2000: 122). In any case, the notion of amnesty was not universally accepted. The Commission had to defend its work against court challenges including litigation by representatives of Steve Biko's family. Biko, one of the founders of the South African black consciousness movement had died in detention in 1977 after protracted beatings. The Commission denied his assailants amnesty. A more serious obstacle to the Committee's work was disengagement. Commissioners expressed disappointment at the reluctance of members of certain groups to apply for amnesty. Very few senior military personnel presented their cases before the Committee, encouraged no doubt by the state's failure in 1997 to obtain a conviction in its prosecution of General Magnus Malan for his complicity in the 1987 KwaMakhutha massacre in KwaZulu Natal. Here 13 people died in 1987 when Inkatha gunmen opened fire on the house of a prominent local ANC leader. Not all prosecutions were so unhelpful, however. Police applications for amnesty were much more forthcoming then from the soldiers, especially after top security police were named in the testimony the assassination squad commander Eugene de Kock presented to the Committee in his bid for indemnity following his conviction in 1996 (for police testimony at this hearing see: SABC TRC Episode 68, Part 2).

Meanwhile ANC applications for amnesty constituted about half the total but they only represented a small proportion of the people amongst the organisation's following who would have committed what the TRC defined as human rights abuses. One SACP member in Worcester, recalling various brutal killings by activists of suspected informers and drug dealers, toured the town with a loudspeaker announcing that he would wait in the church hall on a particular day to distribute amnesty forms: on the day he had specified he waited but no one came. It is possible that local residents may not have been aware of the possibility that they could still, in theory, be prosecuted for complicity in necklace murders committed ten years previously but it is also likely that they may have felt no particular sense of culpability (Garton Ash 1997: 34). The reality, though, is that most of the applications for amnesty were from supporters of liberation movements; fewer than three hundred soldiers and policemen applied for amnesty. At the victim hearings commissioners heard evidence on nearly 5,000 occasions when police used torture but the Amnesty Committee addressed only 90 cases involving police torturers (Malan 2008: 132).

The Reparations Committee's main efforts were directed at identifying who should qualify for any kind of restitution. During 1998 each of about 20,000 corroborated statements needed checking so that for each abuse of human rights a 'victim finding' could be reported. For a positive finding the violation would have to be gross, within the mandated period (1960–1994), politically motivated and corroborated. For each finding, the Committee produced a brief summary report on the circumstances of the violation, supposedly for inclusion in the final report, though in the end only a list of victims' names was published. With respect to each eligible victim they or their surviving relatives would be asked to complete a reparation application which would be used to assess the material impact of abuse. While this work was under way the Committee was also meant to prepare its recommendations for various kinds of reparation and restitution; the TRC itself had no resources of its own for this purpose and its role was limited to advocacy. By October 1998, when most of the Committee's members were discharged, 5,000 applications had been processed and the rest were to be reviewed by a skeleton staff retained until 2001. Reparations would eventually be paid by the government to the people named in the report, R15,000 each (about US$3,000), the equivalent of the housing subsidy awarded to low-income families: considerably less than the Commission had recommended. As troubling as the grudging scale of the compensation offered was its timing: several years after the first amnesties, so in effect perpetrators received benefits from the TRC well before victims (Gready 2010: 111). The government's Director General of Finance told commissioner Wendy Orr in 1997 that 'she had much more important issues on her desk' (Orr 2000: 227)

The historical narrative projected by the TRC

The TRC's report eventually extended to seven volumes. But despite its length the Report presented no major revelations for historians and often re-phrased and supplemented the findings of earlier official inquiries. The Report did provide a more comprehensive picture of the way in which the state security apparatus was organised in the 1980s than any other single source and it also supplied fresh insights into the history of some of the more shadowy state agencies such as the Bureau of State Security (BOSS) and its intelligence and 'covert action' successors, including bodies responsible for political assassinations. It also afforded more information about ANC guerrilla operations than available previously. Indeed, though the Commission agreed that apartheid constituted a crime against humanity and that liberation movements had fought a just fairly restrained war against criminal policies the report was nonetheless critical of the ANC, taking it to task for 'gross human rights violations' that extended well beyond the few 'scattered infringements' conceded by Kader Asmal (Asmal et al. 1996: 118–119). As might be expected, ANC leaders reacted angrily. Spokesperson Ronnie Mamoepa condemned the TRC's 'scurrilous attempts to criminalise the liberation struggle' (Tsedu 1998). More subtly, the SACP's Jeremy Cronin acknowledged that the report had 'reached important and correct conclusions' in its reference to a just war, but, he noted, the 'moral asymmetry' between the liberation movements and their adversaries was 'overwhelmed' by a 'gross human rights abuse' storyline in which any moral or contextual distinctions between 'perpetrators' were ignored (Cronin 1998).

In fact, the TRC's judgments of government officials including the former president, his predecessor and their colleagues were considerably harsher than its conclusions about the ANC. The state's security and law-enforcement agencies were responsible for most violations of human rights, including torture and assassinations. Senior politicians deliberately planned the killing of political opponents. However, more controversially, the Commission could find no evidence of senior politicians' or top bureaucrats' involvement in a 'centrally directed, coherent and formally constituted third force' engaged in agent provocateur activities between 1990 and 1994. Much of the 'internecine' conflict between supporters of rival black organisations during the negotiations was blamed by ANC leaders on a clandestine 'third force' of agent provocateurs, directed by National Party politicians and security officials, directed at inflaming political tensions. A third set of findings supplied extensive detail on abuses committed by Inkatha, and held Chief Mangosuthu Buthelezi 'accountable' for these 'in his representative capacity as the leader'.

Much of the criticism directed at the report focused on its methodological shortcomings. The testimony that constituted the primary source of evidence for the report's authors derived from victim statements; only a small quantity of the more stringently tested material from the amnesty hearings was available to them. Those amnesty applications that were available were mainly from policemen. With its primary dependence on victim testimony, the Commission was unlikely to generate significant insights into the causes of violence and the motivations of perpetrators and its explanations of why violations occurred were hardly incisive (see Posel 2002). Corroboration of victim statements seemed often to have been very cursory. TRC researchers encountered formidable obstacles in their pursuit of corroborative archival evidence much of which, in any case, appeared to have been destroyed or hidden from the Commission. Their initial use of a magistrate's search warrant to raid a military base in Cape Town elicited strong protests from military officials and hence it was agreed that the TRC would have access only to documentation which the military authorities were willing to release. The majority of victims who spoke to the Commission referred to events after 1984 and on earlier events the Report's treatment was perfunctory.

More importantly, the representation of many witnesses of their role as passive and even apolitical victims of outrages perpetrated upon them may have been misleading. It excluded the possibility that abused groups may have been both victims and perpetrators: as Cronin observed, 'millions of ordinary South Africans refused to be merely victims; they organized themselves for survival and struggle' (Cronin 1998). The Commission succeeded in collecting evidence on 14,000 killings, leaving at least another 12,000 deaths known to other investigations unexplored. One reason for this was that the IFP leadership had told its followers to boycott the proceedings and so IFP members were substantially underrepresented in victim hearings. Arguably for reasons of political expediency, the TRC decided not to subpoena Chief Buthelezi. Local warfare between Inkatha and ANC groups persisted after the election and in KwaZulu-Natal political violence had subsided only a few months before the TRC began its work. Compelling Inkatha's leader to testify would have risked the resumption of armed hostilities. Anthea Jeffries contends that the omissions in the evidence the Commission accumulated worked to Inkatha's disadvantage (Jeffrey 1999) though other readers have pointed out that relative availability of evidence could just as easily have implicated Inkatha's opponents. But more generally in apportioning blame, the Commission was working with an incomplete statistical base. Uncritical acceptance of victim testimony resulted in the reproduction in the report of conflicts between different accounts of the same events, most obviously when subsequent amnesty hearings sometimes exposed mistaken hearsay testimony with ANC perpetrators confessing to killings that victims had blamed on the police.

There are more favourable readings of the report as well as of the proceedings on which it was based. As Paul Gready notes, 'the reframing of testimony by commissioners at the hearings, constructing victims and witnesses in a more positive light and perpetrators in a more negative light than they themselves had done in their own self reporting is [an] . . . example of the TRC's role in the discursive redistribution of power' (Gready 2010: 75). For James Gibson, in their role as public historians, the Report's authors fulfilled the Commission's purpose. In his analysis he identifies three key elements in the 'truth' recounted in the Report. These were, respectively, that apartheid was a crime against humanity; apartheid was criminal not just because of individual actions undertaken in its defence, but because of deliberate outcomes of state policy, and that in the struggle against apartheid, both sides violated human rights. It is the last of these contentions that especially contributes to reconciliation, Gibson believes. This is because if South Africans refrain from viewing their conflict 'in terms of absolute good against absolute evil' and instead accept that there is evidence that both sides committed abuses they will generally become more dispassionate. It is easier to reconcile with people on the other side who committed gross abuses if one's own side is also tainted morally. Moral relativism promotes reconciliation, Gibson proposes (Gibson 2004: 76).

The political impact of the TRC

Is this right? Is there evidence to support Gibson's argument that the narrative the TRC unfolded helped reconcile South Africans politically? Did the TRC's history 'work'? Gibson's own evidence for supporting his argument was drawn from a massive survey of 3,700 South Africans embodying a cross-section of the population in 2000. Fieldworkers asked these people to agree or disagree with a series of statements about the past, statements that corresponded with the TRC's main historical propositions. In general, irrespective of race, most respondents felt apartheid was a crime. Most people amongst all groups felt that people on both sides of the conflict committed atrocities, though they generally attributed such actions to individuals, rather than to policy. Here public opinion only coincided partly with TRC 'truth', possibly a consequence of the prominence in the hearings given to individual actions as well as the scarcity and vagueness of testimony from senior politicians and upper echelons of the military. In the next stage of his argument, Gibson tried to show that these beliefs were shaped by the TRC's hearings. To do this he explores a range of correlations in his data and he found that more than any other variables, including race, class, interest in politics, group consciousness and level of education, knowledge of the TRC and confidence in its activities correlated with acceptance of the kind of historical understanding promoted by the TRC. From these correlations, Gibson concluded, 'it is plausible that the activities of the TRC contributed to truth acceptance' (Gibson 2004: 93), an acceptance of a complicated truth that he argued would help South Africans to reconcile.

Not all of Gibson's evidence was as reassuring. He tested his respondents' feelings about amnesty by incorporating into his questionnaire a set of questions that asked about a hypothetical situation in which a perpetrator of abuses, 'Philip', applies for amnesty. Respondents were asked to react to situations in which Philip was subjected to experiences that can be equated with the various substitutions for conventional justice that did in fact arise from TRC activities; restorative justice (in which Philip's victims experience the ameliorative effects of his apologies), procedural justice (victims can obtain official acknowledgement of the harm they have suffered), distributive justice (reparations) and retributive justice (in which the punishment is the stigma or shame that may be the consequence of confessions). Respondents tended to find that when Philip received all four kinds of treatment, amnesty was fairest, though most felt that amnesty was still unfair to victims. Compensation was most likely to affect positively people's assessment of fairness and the retributive element was the least significant. Gibson concludes that the extent to which TRC procedure did incorporate alternative forms of justice helped to compensate for the widespread perception that amnesty was unfair. We know, though, that through no fault of its own, the TRC succeeded only in obtaining token and belated reparations for victims.

Rather strikingly, at the inception of the TRC's activities in 1996 when people were polled about their views on amnesty, black South Africans were more likely to agree with the notion that perpetrators should receive legal immunity from prosecution (Market Research Africa 1996). Smaller proportions of white South Africans than among their black compatriots in 2000 agreed that 'it was their responsibility as citizens to contribute to national reconciliation' and only a small minority of whites, 18 per cent, believed that material compensation should be part of a process of reconciliation (Institute for Justice and Reconciliation 2000). Such reactions among whites suggest that many found it quite easy to dissociate themselves from the covert violations of a 'dirty war', a conclusion supported by the relatively low viewership among whites of the SABC's coverage of the TRC. Arguably a wider mandate that might have directed the TRC to explore the more general ways in which apartheid infringed human rights might have created an environment in which it would have been harder for whites to deny personal complicity as apartheid's beneficiaries (Mamdani 1998: 39–40).

Filmed testimony presented in the SABC's programmes as well as the anecdotal evidence supplied in the Commission's report and in the autobiographical accounts of several of the commissioners supply a considerable number of moving testimonies by TRC deponents that suggest that the process of telling their stories supplied relief and comfort, and as we have noted such sources supply equally compelling instances in which expressions of remorse elicited apparent forgiveness. One should be careful, though, in assessing the weight of such evidence. The number of conciliatory encounters between victims and perpetrators was small, and they were quite exceptional. Surveys and focus groups conducted well after the TRC have found that people who offered testimony tended to be less likely to feel forgiveness than the general public (Chapman 2007; Stein 2008). And most perpetrators who appeared before the Amnesty Committee, on both sides, adhered to their belief they were fighting for a just cause and did not feel compelled to express any personal guilt (Foster et al. 2005). And anthropologists' contemporary fieldwork in African townships raises serious questions about the extent to which the moral precepts of a gentle conciliatory justice really accorded with popular values (Wilson 2001; Ashforth 2005). Even so, at least in the short term, and with respect to those segments of public opinion that influenced the behaviour of political leaders, the TRC's version of history and its efforts to provide a form of redress seemed to work. At the very least they consolidated a public narrative about South African reconciliation that accorded with elite predispositions.

In this exercise, Nelson Mandela was a pioneer contributor with his publication of a carefully crafted autobiography just before the 1994 election, in which his magisterial and statesmanlike voice predominates and his belief in man's essential goodness ('all men have a core of decency') is a central theme in the text. In many of the key dramas recalled in his story, Mandela succeeds in eliciting such civility among his adversaries, even from the prison staff on Robben Island, the maximum security prison where most of the ANC and PAC leaders were confined from the 1960s. Of course in 1994, emphasising such moments was politically circumspect though earlier versions of his autobiography written in prison also feature considerate officials. The projection of Mandela's gentler personality is very much evident in the way he continues to be publically remembered. For example, a recent theatrical representation of his life invites us to share Mandela's 'self doubt and anguish' (Denselow 2016) over his wife's intemperate calls for insurrection. In fact, Mandela backed Winnie through the 1980s even to the extent of expressing support for a notorious speech she made in 1986 in which she seemed to be endorsing 'necklacing'; that is, the killing of informers with a petrol-soaked tyre. The persona of the kindly elder statesman is represented by the statues of Mandela that have now become ubiquitous features of every major South African city, in which different sculptors all seem to have taken their cue from Kobus Hattingh's 20-foot effigy in Sandton Square, Johannesburg's upmarket shopping centre, which Mandela himself endorsed with 'certificates of authenticity' for authorised copies (Savides 2014). In these sculptures a smiling Mandela is posed in the shuffling dance routine with which he accompanied the a-capella choral group Ladysmith Black Mambazo when they celebrated his inauguration: here he is always wearing his trademark 'Madiba' silk shirt, a design adapted from the batik Barong Tagalog presented to him during a visit to the Philippines. The earlier and younger images of bearded Mandela in military fatigues or in the traditional costume of a Xhosa prince no longer feature in this public iconography, and indeed a proposal in 1999 to reproduce Mandela's clenched fist salute as a gigantic megalith emerging from the sea outside East London's harbour was shelved.

Although it was very much Mandela's choice to construct his leadership around a public narrative of reconciliation, it was a narrative that resonated with the ANC's own past. As an authoritative 'insider' historian of the ANC has noted recently, the ANC has cultivated a consensual political tradition. In her three-volume chronicle of *The Congress Movement*, Sylvia Neame maintains that as a 'congress' the ANC's own structural character of embodying an alliance or a united front predisposed it to a politics of negotiation with the government. Hence from an early stage in its history 'the "round table" and national convention found a key place in the conceptions put forward by the ANC' (Neame 2015: volume 1, xvii), a conception revived by Mandela first in the 1960s and again of course in the 1990s. Congress President Zacharius Mahabane's proposal in 1923 for a constitutional convention put in place a strategic trajectory that the ANC would keep through its history. As Neame puts it, 'by 1923, the ANC had found its political location, which it was to maintain effectively from then on' (Neame 2015: volume 1, xxi).

Such backwards readings of the past are not confined to the movement's own Whiggish predisposition to view history as a progression towards enlightenment. In the late 1990s, parties of visiting university students at Pretoria's Voortrekker Monument would be taken by their guides through a newly revisionist reading of the 27-panel marble frieze in Gerard Moerdijk's Hall of Heroes. These tableaux recounted the triumphant story of the Voortrekkers' passage into the South African interior, their initial cordial reception by the treacherous Zulu King Dingaan and subsequent betrayal, and their final revenge at the battle of Blood River. But how the story can be understood depends on where one begins and the direction taken in inspecting the frieze (which can be viewed remotely on www.slideshare.net/frontfel/the-voortrekker-monument). As the guide demonstrated, if the viewing starts with the battle, and proceeds around the hall anti-clockwise, the final panels will feature Piet Retief clasping hands in friendship with the Zulu king. In this inversion, the guide may have been taking her cues from one the first ANC notables to make a public visit to the monument, ex-guerrilla Tokyo Sexwale. Sexwale requested journalists to photograph him standing by the entrance, gesturing to the carved Zulu assegai (spears) decorating the gates, while observing 'It was precisely the assegei at its height that turned the tide, Umkhonto we Sizwe, Spear of the nation, that opened the gates' (Hutchinson 2013: 21). Meanwhile, for local black South African municipal politicians there could be more prosaic reinterpretations of what the monument means. In the words of councillor Donise Khumalo: 'A person can always drive past and say it *was* one of the bastions of apartheid. Anyway, our black people provided the labour for building the thing' (Grundlingh 2001: 104).

Constructing consensual heritage

The Voortrekker Monument remains one of Pretoria's premier tourist attractions. And its 200,000 annual visitors are not limited to foreigners. A new curator appointed in 1999, ex-army general, Gert Opperman, 'worked hard to demythologise the site'. 'We have to become legitimate', he said, and he began organising tours from black schools in the vicinity. The monument, in his view, was no longer a sectional nationalist shrine and it should become 'a professional, hospitable organisation that welcomes all'. Appreciative officials doubled the monument's public subsidy: Opperman was doing an admirable job, according to Themba Wakashe, the deputy director at the Ministry (Nessman 2003). Meanwhile at one of the other three kopjes (hill tops) that fringe the city's southern portal, on Salvakop, the assembly of a new 'heritage destination' began in 2005. Today the 52-hectare Freedom Park surrounds the Sikhumbuto ('those who have passed on'), compound in which a winding 'Wall of Names' surround the sanctuary. There are at least 75,000 names on the wall and the list is periodically lengthened through public nominations. The names include Boer War generals, anti-apartheid leaders (including the novelist Alan Paton), Cuban soldiers and guerrilla combatants as well as the names of the people killed at Sharpeville in 1960. But the Wall of Names includes no soldiers from the guerrillas' adversary, the South African Defence Force, despite repeated representations from Border War veterans. Apartheid's defenders must rest content with their own Memorial Wall at Fort Klapperkop, on the crest of the third kopje. The inclusion of the Boer War generals on the Sikhumbuto roll elicited criticism, but the project's director, Wally Serote, was unmoved. As he explained, Africa perceived the Anglo-Boer War as an anti-colonial struggle (Du Preez 2003), a position the ANC had recently adopted in the centenary of the war, when local ANC Youth Leaguers and Umkhonto veterans assembled in commemorative parades. A similar consideration keeps in place the statue of Boer War and later first South African prime minister General Louis Botha outside parliament in Cape Town, despite public criticism (Adebajo 2016: 115).

A similarly circumspect balance characterised Mandela's and successive administrations' decisions about renamings. One of the first changes had to be Verwoerdburg, the settlement south of Pretoria that accommodates South Africa's main military facilities. The decision to rename it 'Centurion' was a tactfully respectful acknowledgment of the army's continuing local presence. D. F. Malan Drive in Johannesburg, named after apartheid's first prime minister, became Beyers Naude Drive; Naude, a Dutch Reformed theologian who had lived nearby was an early Afrikaner critic of apartheid. Meanwhile Verwoerd was again displaced, this time in Johannesburg, substituted with the Communist Party's martyred leader, Bram Fischer, another Afrikaner. Meanwhile, though, most of the main city names remain in everyday usage, including on road signs, despite the titles of the new 'metropolitan' entities that recall earlier local precolonial settlements. The new nomenclature was often deliberately uncontentious; as one newspaper columnist pointed out, 'people are encouraged to name places after birds and trees so that they can be all-embracing' (Mamaila 2003). In a similar vein, from 1994, a new set of public holidays attempted to universalise the appeal of an affirmative nation-building chronicle: 21 March, the anniversary of the Sharpeville massacre, became Human Rights Day; 16 June, the day of the Soweto uprising, Youth Day; and 16 December, the Afrikaner Day of the Vow (which commemorated the religious pledge the Voortrekkers made on the eve of the battle of Blood River; the date was also the more recent anniversary of Umkhonto's first operation) was now the Day of Reconciliation.

Even Johannesburg's Apartheid Museum, opened in 2001, draws on consensual representational strategies to memorialise traumatic but still contentious historical experience. There is the architecture of the museum itself, which, as Rankin and Schmidt have noticed, promotes 'empathy with those subjected to the regime's controlling manoeuvres' through mimicking its procedures through the building's 'manipulative' use of space (Rankin and Schmidt 2009: 79). This happens from the very beginning when visitors are randomly assigned tickets directing them through racially designated entrances, narrow gateways with security turnstiles. In this display, the precise taxonomy of objects takes second place to the evocation of experience. Even so, the exhibits themselves embody a didactic treatment that arguably orders the content to 'control for consensus' (Teeger and Vinitzky-Seroussi 2007: 59). For certain viewers this control is evident in a Marxist 'explanatory framework' that makes apartheid 'historically contingent' in which Afrikaners and Africans share a history or persecution. Nation-building consensus is also achieved through present-day legitimation, through the prominence accorded to Mandela 'even when the historical account does not call for it' (Teeger and Vinitzky-Seroussi 2007: 68). For, in the words of its website, the 'museum is a beacon of hope showing the world how South Africa is coming to terms with its oppressive past and working towards a future that all South Africans can call their own' (Apartheid Museum 2016).

More generally, the design and aesthetics of South Africa's new sites of public memory take their cues from Daniel Libeskind's commemorations of the Holocaust, in Berlin and elsewhere. These eschew realistic monumental sculpture to deploy more abstract and symbolic arrangements of light, shade, space and shape to prompt sensory engagement. One example of this is the Sharpeville Memorial Garden, where, within the cemetery where 69 of the massacre's victims lie buried, a stark field of 156 uniform raw-steel columns commemorate all the dead. Sharpeville's new memorial, completed in 2011, is bleakly beautiful, not consolatory: a landscaping of tragedy (see Figure 10.1). At the actual site of the massacre, though, next to the museum, in the grounds of the police station,

Figure 10.1 At Sharpeville Memorial Garden a procession led by Pan-Africanist
          Congress activists advances towards the 'steel flowers' which help frame
          the new Sharpeville Memorial precinct. Photograph courtesy
          GREENINC Landscape Architects, Johannesburg.

survivors of the massacre have chosen to remember their dead in a different
way. With the approval of the museum's curator, Sekwati Mokoena, in the open
space where the dead once lay, members of the local branch of Khulumani
now cultivate flowerbeds and rows of vegetables. Khulumani is a national organisation set up by deponents at the TRC. In Sharpeville its members are mainly
elderly survivors from the shootings. In their new garden they have reclaimed
what used to be a fearsome prohibited territory, establishing their own settlement
with the past.

Conclusion

Abstract symbolism and balanced political circumspection in official commemorations, as with the TRC's morally complex truth, may have been expedient and in
tune with public feelings twenty years ago. Without the possibility of amnesty,
there would have been no negotiated transition and the TRC was largely successful at the time in making impunity politically legitimate. Today's ANC leaders
continue to insist that Mandela was right in his efforts to persuade 'the Afrikaner
right wing to accept, if not embrace, the changes that need to take place', even
if this required concessions (Ramaphosa 2016). Even so, South Africa's political
consensus, the legacy of this negotiated settlement rests on fragile foundations.

As the architects of the Truth Commission warned, if material reparations for victims was to be a substitute for the punishment of their killers then they had to be meaningful and quick. As we have noted they were neither. Nor did abstention from the amnesty procedure attract penalties, at least not for a long time; only in February 2016 did prosecutions resume of officials charged with murders during the 'dirty war' of the 1980s, with the charging of four policemen who had failed to admit to the TRC their complicity in the murder of a woman whom they had detained as a suspected ANC courier (Burke 2016). In a setting in which overall social inequalities remain acute and continue to be racially codified, it is not really surprising that the first generation to grow up without any personal experience of apartheid reject the old pragmatic arguments about the necessary compromises with the past. In 2015 a protest by black university students developed into a national protest movement calling for 'decolonisation', targeting not just the higher education system but also the lingering wider inequalities left over from apartheid. It was not so odd that the students first directed their rebellion at a historical symbol, the statue of Cecil Rhodes on Cape Town's Table Mountain. The negotiated consensus constructed twenty years ago around South Africa's public history is now undergoing profound challenge.

Guide to further reading and online resources

Of all the truth commissions that have conducted investigations over the last two decades, the South African body is the most comprehensively written-up. Boraine's memoir (2000) is authoritative and, because it is almost an official history, quite dull. Closer to an inside story is Wendy Orr's less circumspect account (2000). The poet Antjie Krog's partly fictionalised autobiographical testament (1998) of her experiences as a journalist reporting on the hearings is unreliable in its historical details but vivid and compelling in its projection of the emotional impact of the evidence she encountered. The most elaborate effort to prove that the Truth and Reconciliation Commission helped to reconcile South Africans is Gibson's analysis of polling data (2004). Jeffrey (1999) and Posel and Simpson (2002) both supply critical assessment of the historical narrative in the Commission's report. Wilson (2001) argues that the Commission's guiding precepts were at odds with popular notions of justice and morality. Gready's more recent retrospective assessment of the Commission's impact argues its effects were limited by the narrowness of its focus.

For wider explorations of how modern public representations of South African past are shaped by politically inspired imperatives for reconciliation the most wide ranging treatment is Hutchinson's volume on South Africa's 'archives of memories'. Rankin and Schmidt (2009) and Teeger and Vinitzky (2007) offer more specialised insights into the messages underlying the aesthetics of museum architecture are also helpful in this respect.

You can explore this terrain yourself in several excellent websites. You can visit the Apartheid Museum at: www.apartheidmuseum.org/about-museum-0 (which includes pictures of many of the exhibits and a video tour). The best views of the

Voortrekker monument are at www.slideshare.net/frontfel/the-voortrekker-monument. The Freedom Park website – www.freedompark.co.za/elements-of-the-park/hapo.html – includes extensive imagery as well as useful explanations of its underlying philosophy of 'tolerance and inclusiveness'. The Institute for Justice and Reconciliation was established in Cape Town as a legacy body for the TRC and its website at www.ijr.org.za/ contains research reports that documents various reconciliation undertakings in South African and elsewhere in Africa since the TRC. Finally, you can watch various hearings at the TRC on YouTube

References

Adebajo, Adekeye (2016) *Thabo Mbeki: Africa's Philosopher King*. Auckland Park, Jacana.

Ashforth, Adam (2005) *Witchcraft, Violence and Democracy in South Africa*. Chicago: Chicago University Press.

Asmal, Kader, Louise Asmal and Ronald Suresh Roberts (1996) *Reconciliation Through Truth: A Reckoning of South Africa's Criminal Governance*. Cape Town: David Philip.

Bell, Terry (2001) *Unfinished Business: South Africa, Apartheid and Truth*. Redworks: Observatory.

Boraine, Alex (2000) *A Country Unmasked: Inside South Africa's Truth and Reconciliation Commission*. Cape Town: Oxford University Press.

Boraine, Alex, Janet Levy and Ronel Scheffer (1994) *Dealing with the Past*. Cape Town: Institute for Democracy in South Africa.

Bozzoli, Belinda (1998) 'Public Ritual and Private Transmission: The Truth Commission in Alexandra Township, South Africa 1996', *African Studies*, 57(2): 167–95.

Burke, Jason (2016) 'Trial Starts for 1983 Killing of ANC Courier', *Business Day*, 26 February.

Chapman, Audrey (2007) 'Truth Commissions and Intergroup Forgiveness: The Case of the South African TRC', *Peace and Conflict: Journal of Peace Psychology*, 13(1): 51–69.

Cronin, Jeremy (1998) 'Tutu's Report Tells a Truth, But Not the Whole Truth', *Sunday Independent*, 8 November.

Denselow, Robin (2016) "Mandela Trilogy Review", *Guardian*, 1 September, www.theguardian.com/music/2016/sep/01/mandela-trilogy-review-royal-festival-hall-nelson-cape-town-opera.

du Preez, Max (2003) 'Let's All Claim Our Common History', *The Star*, 8 May, 18.

Foster, Don, Paul Haupt and Marésa de Beer (2005) *The Theatre of Violence: Narratives of Protagonists in the South African Conflict*. Pretoria: HSRC Press.

Garton Ash, Timothy (1997) 'True Confessions', *New York Review of Books*, 17 July.

Gibson, James (2004) *Overcoming Apartheid: Can Truth Reconcile a Divided Nation?* Cape Town: HSRC Press.

Gready, Paul (2010) *The Era of Transitional Justice: The Aftermath of the TRC of South Africa and Beyond*. London: Routledge.

Grundlingh, A. M. (2001) 'A Cultural Conundrum? Old Monuments and New Regimes. The Voortrekker Monument as a Symbol of Afrikaner Power in a Post-Apartheid South Africa', *Radical History Review*, 81: 95–112.

Hammond, David (n.d.) *The Voortrekker Monument*. Cape Town: The Reformation Society, www.slideshow.net/frontfel/the-voortrekker-monument.

Hutchinson, Yvonne (2013) *South African Performance and the Archives of Memory*. Manchester: Manchester University Press.

Institute for Justice and Reconciliation (2000) *Reparation and Memorialisation*, newsletter inserted in newspapers, IJR, Cape Town, October.

Jeffrey, Anthea (1999) *The Truth about the Truth and Reconciliation Commission*. Johannesburg: South African Institute of Race Relations.

Krog, Antjie (1998) *Country of My Skull*. London: Jonathan Cape.

Malan, Yvonne (2008) *The Spectre of Justice: The Problematic Legacy of the South African Truth and Reconciliation Commission*, D. Phil. Dissertation, University of Oxford.

Mamaila, Khathu (2003) 'Resting Place for Our Heroes', *The Star*, 12 May.

Mamdani, Mahmood (1998) 'A Diminished Truth', *Siyaya!*, 3.

Market Research Africa (AC Neilson), Truth Commission, Report on Poll Conducted for *Business Day*, Johannesburg.

Neame, Sylvia (2015) *The Congress Movement*, 3 volumes. Cape Town: HSRC Press.

Nessman, Ravi (2003) 'Breaking Out of the Stone Laager', *The Star*, 8 May, 19.

Omar, Dullah (1996) 'Introduction to the Truth and Reconciliation Commission' in H. Russell Botman and Robin M. Peterson (eds), *To Remember and to Heal: Theological and Psychological Reflections on Truth and Reconciliation*. Cape Town: Human & Rousseau.

Orr, Wendy (2000) *From Biko to Basson: Wendy Orr's Search for the Soul of South Africa as a Commissioner for the TRC*. Saxonwold: Contra Press.

Posel, Deborah (2002) 'The TRC Report: What Kind of History? What Kind of Truth?' in Deborah Posel and Graham Simpson (eds), *Commissioning the Past: Understanding South Africa's Truth and Reconciliation Commission*, Johannesburg: Witwatersrand University Press.

Ramaphosa, Cyril (2016) 'Make a Positive Impact on the Lives of Others', *Sunday Times*, Johannesburg, 17 July.

Rankin, Elizabeth and Leoni Schmidt (2009) 'The Apartheid Museum: Performing a Spatial Dialectic', *Journal of Visual Culture*, 8(1): 76–102.

SABC, TRC Episode 01, part 07, www.youtube.com/watch?v=sY3LTX1yoDQ.

SABC, TRC Episode 21, Part 02, www.youtube.com/watch?v=hv8gMpCQ9xc.

SABC, TRC Episode 21, Part 03, www.youtube.com/watch?v=U5LxthKQ-jA.

SABC, TRC Episode 68, Part 02, www.youtube.com/watch?v=HuNsXWxBmp8.

SABC, TRC Episode 69, Part 05, www.youtube.com/watch?v=4TYBnYa4f5E.

SABC, TRC Episode 77, Part 02, www.youtube.com/watch?v=hd/WX7kRC18.

SABC, TRC Episode 87, Part 02, www.youtube.com/watch?v=qTvmbVJfQSo.

Savides, Matthews (2014) 'Missing Papers Frustrate Auction of Mandela Statute', *Sunday Times*, Johannesburg, 3 August.

Stanley, Elizabeth (2001) 'Evaluating the Truth and Reconciliation Commission', *Journal of Modern African Studies*, 39(3): 525–46.

Stein, Dan J., Soraya Seedat, Debra Kaminer, Hashim Moomai, Allen Hermann, John Sonnega and David R. Williams (2008) 'The Impact of the Truth and Reconciliation Commission of South Africa on Psychological Distress and Forgiveness', *Social Psychiatry and Psychiatric Epidemiology*, 43(62): 462–68.

Teeger, Chana and Vered Vinitzky-Seroussi (2007) 'Controlling for Consensus: Commemorating Apartheid in South Africa, *Symbolic Interaction*, 30(1): 57–78.

Truth and Reconciliation Commission of South Africa (1998) *Report*, 5 volumes, Juta & Co., Cape Town.

Tsedu, Mathatha (1998) 'Tutu Used his Casting Vote Against the TREC', *Sunday Independent*, 8 November.

Tutu, Desmond (1999) *No Future Without Forgiveness*. Johannesburg: Random House.

Wilson, Richard (2001) *The Politics of the Truth and Reconciliation Commission in South Africa*. Cambridge: Cambridge University Press.

11 History and memory in the American South

W. Fitzhugh Brundage

For many first-time visitors to the American South, one of the most striking features of the landscape is the prevalence of monuments commemorating white southerners who waged war against the United States during the American Civil War. In addition to the thousands of monuments that fill conspicuous civic spaces, the names of Confederate heroes adorn towns, streets, and highways. Since the 1960s, when legalized segregation and the systematic disfranchisement of African Americans in the region ended, southerners have debated the relevance and meaning of the region's inherited landscape and recalled past. These debates are symptomatic of the emergence of political and cultural pluralism in a region that has had little historical experience with the formal recognition or promotion of either. Although the American South was riven by marked regional, racial, economic, and political divisions throughout the nineteenth and twentieth centuries, white elites labored tirelessly to promote the perception of a "solid" South united by a cohesive regional culture in opposition to external threats. But this façade of a cohesive regional culture required ongoing struggle among southerners, and Americans more broadly, to define some social memories as authoritative and others as trivial fictions, to determine who exercised the power to make some historical narratives possible and to silence others.

Since the 1970s when southerners began to fashion a pluralist public culture they haltingly have adopted critical and inclusive accounts of their collective past that were inconceivable decades earlier. In growing numbers southerners understand that the hard edges of the past cannot be smoothed over by well-meaning talk and that confronting the region's traumatic history is more than boosterism or a therapeutic learning exercise. The persisting challenge that southerners now confront is what to do with the region's inherited commemorative landscape that perpetuates an exclusionary past, reinforces inequalities, and impedes the emergence of long-suppressed pluralism.

Some observers of the contemporary South may be tempted to dismiss periodic controversies there over heritage as shallow "identity politics" that divert attention and resources from more substantive problems that plague the region. But the stakes in the controversies that arouse the strongest passions and the widest interest are quite real. As has been true since the Civil War, claims to material resources, political power, and moral high ground are at the center of contemporary debates over the South's history. Although the future course of these debates cannot easily be predicted, there is ample reason to conclude that struggles over historical memory will remain conspicuous in southern public life. And how southerners choose to grapple with their disputed past will have enduring consequences for the region's civic culture and public institutions.

Although many aspects of the contest over historical memory in the American South are particular to the region, the broader parameters of the contest there resonate with struggles over the recalled past in other contemporary societies divided by region, ethnicity, and status. The American South, for example, is only one example of a society where white racial privilege remains mapped onto the landscape. In this regard the American South shares similarities with Australia and South Africa. Likewise, the region provides but one example of enduring contests over the teaching of a contested past; other examples range from modern Japan and Israel to China. The recent history of the recalled past in the American South, moreover, highlights ongoing struggles to expand and constrict public rhetoric so as to acknowledge, celebrate, or lament the region's contested heritage. Similar contests over public rhetoric abound from Poland and the Dominican Republic to the Netherlands.

Memory and the formation of a southern identity

The Civil War was both the defining event in and the inspiration for the region's commemorative landscape. The war gave the states that joined the Confederacy a collective identity that they had never previously possessed. Some white proponents of southern independence had toiled to foster a regional historical consciousness in the decades before the war but their efforts had been countered by others who insisted that the South was and should remain integral to the nation. Further evidence of the inchoate character of a southern regional identity was the adoption of familiar American symbols, especially George Washington, by the Confederacy (Faust 1988; Rubin 2005: 18–24)

The experience of the war itself, far more than the efforts of Confederate nationalists, was the catalyst for a new sense of regional identity. The scale of the defeat suffered and sacrifice made on behalf of the failed nation left many white southerners with an acute sense that they shared a history that set them apart from other Americans. The slaveholders' republic was not just defeated, it was crushed (Carter 1985: 6–23). To observe that the Civil War was, by orders of magnitude, the bloodiest war in American history does not do justice to its toll of death and human wreckage. There are estimates, or, better said, guesses that the Confederate dead numbered between 250,000 and 350,000. Confederate forces during the war totaled between 750,000 and 1.25 million. Thus, between one in five and one in three Confederate soldiers died during the war (McPherson 1988: 471–477).

Among the urgent needs in the postwar white South was a salve for ubiquitous human suffering and loss in the region. In addition to regaining a place in the Union, replacing slavery with a new form of labor, and rebuilding the region's economy, white southerners confronted the vexing challenge of making sense of a catastrophic war that achieved none of its avowed purposes. The impulse to reflect on the meaning of the tumult of the recent past was by no means distinct to white southerners. During the century after the Civil War assigning meaning to the conflict was a major preoccupation of American culture and public life.

When white southerners set about crafting their version of the past they embraced the aesthetic conventions and cultural assumptions that were widely held elsewhere in the nation and in Western Europe. They shared with many of their contemporaries in the Western world an expectation that historical commemoration should be to celebrate the heroic, exemplary, and distinctive attributes of a people, community, or nation. The cultural work of commemoration was unapologetically didactic; it was intended to teach unambiguous and eternal lessons that would undergird and preserve a group's sense of collective identity. In keeping with these ambitions, they employed familiar cultural forms to memorialize their past. For example, the common Confederate monument, which consists of a sculpture of a single nameless Confederate soldier standing atop a column, was most often purchased from northern foundries that also manufactured almost identical Union monuments. In many instances, northern artists actually produced Confederate memorials (Savage 1997; Brown 2004, 2015).

White southerners also shared with other late nineteenth-century Americans a belief that their historical experience was part of God's providential design. Given the conspicuous role of white clerics in defending the institution of slavery and championing the Confederate cause, the need to reconcile the war's outcome with God's will was inescapable. White ministers had no doubt that God's hand was evident in the South's defeat. Rather than interpret their defeat as evidence of God's wrath, white southerners instead concluded that they were latter-day Israelites of the Old Testament and that God had used the ungodly to chasten his chosen people. They re-asserted their submission to the divine order that would eventually deliver them (Wilson 1980; Snay 1993; Owen 1998: 93–113; Poole 2004: 37–56; Remillard 2011: 15–17, 95–103). The enduring contribution of southern white clerics was to sacralize the war and the Confederate warriors who fought in it.

Along with the clerics, the white southerners who took the lead in cultivating historical memory in the South after the Civil War, in most important regards, were indistinguishable from their counterparts elsewhere in the country. They were self-appointed activists who gathered together in voluntary groups and expected limited, and often received even fewer, state resources (Skowrenek 1982; Dawley 1991: 15–138; Cohen 2002). Campaigns to shape public memory, even by the most elastic definition of the term, rarely were topics of discussion within American administrative corridors and legislative chambers. Because public authorities and ruling elites embraced a narrow conception of state obligations, citizens looked to voluntary associations to meet needs that public officials were either incapable or indisposed to address (Kammen 1991: 101–282).

During the half century after the Civil War Confederate veterans were conspicuous among the groups who took a lead in crafting their region's recalled past.

Within a few years of the war's end, local benevolent associations with ties to veterans proliferated across Dixie. These small, closely knit organizations that performed both memorial and charitable work within their immediate communities. Gradually local veterans' groups affiliated into larger associations and in 1889, with the founding of the United Confederate Veterans in New Orleans, a truly regional organization committed to memorializing the Confederacy emerged (Davies 1955; Foster 1987; Janney 2013; Harris 2014).

The memory work of veterans was complemented by the activities of various groups of southern white women. Evidence of white women's organizational acumen emerged even before the collapse of the Confederacy. During the war, few southern towns had lacked Ladies' Aid societies, which raised money for war supplies, tended the wounded, and oversaw the burial of the dead. After the war, these same groups often took the lead in building Confederate cemeteries and honoring the men buried in them. In addition, a dramatic proliferation of women's literary associations and social reform groups occurred after the war. The rapidly swelling ranks of these societies were ideally positioned to be artisans of public culture, and collective memory in particular (Whites 2005; Janney 2008).

By the end of the century, white southern women were no more inclined to concede the privilege of being custodians of memory to men than were their counterparts in other parts of the country. The consolidation of white women's custodianship of white southern memory was a consequence of the broader organizational revolution underway among American women during the late nineteenth century. Just as voting and participation in the rituals of partisan politics were an essential part of contemporary male public identity, club activities likewise became for many southern and non-southern women an equally important

Figure 11.1 Clubwomen stand in the foreground of the dedication ceremonies in 1908 in the North Carolina state capitol for a plaque commemorating a protest by North Carolina women in 1773 against a British colonial tax. Source: *North Carolina Booklet VIII* (1908, public domain).

component of their public identity (Cox 2003; Brundage 2005; Morgan 2005; Whites 2005).

The truly distinctive facet of the white historical memory in the South during the century after the Civil War was the specific historical narrative embraced and promoted by many white southerners. White southerners fashioned their own image of the world and their place in it by establishing an accepted version of the past, a sort of genealogy of identity. Although the white southern historical narrative traced a chronology readily recognizable to other Americans, white southerners assigned importance to events within that narrative that diverged markedly from the significance ascribed to them by non-southerners. In addition to providing a singular ordering of the past, the dominant white southern memory, like the myth of Roland Barthes' *Mythologies*, addressed pressing concerns of identity, enabling a refashioning of the self-understanding of white southerners: "it purifies them, it makes them innocent, it gives them natural and eternal justification, it gives them a clarity which is not that of an explanation but that of a statement of fact" (Barthes 1972: 143).

This regional narrative dwelled on the emergence of the South's distinct civilization and on white southerners' struggle to defend their autonomy against jealous and hostile northerners. White southerners were quick to rebut what they perceived to be an exaggerated emphasis on New England's role in the American Revolution and subsequent rise of the republic. Through commemorative activities, white southerners sought to demonstrate that their ancestors had made an outsized contribution to the nation's founding and had a peerless record of loyalty to the republic (Baker 1995; Capps 1999).

At the same time that white southerners told themselves that the young republic was largely their handiwork, they traced the efforts of jealous northerners to destroy their region's civilization. The superiority of antebellum culture was a given. White southerners tirelessly contrasted the romance of the antebellum agrarian South with the tawdry, materialistic, and squalid culture of the urban North. After the Civil War, romantic renderings of the plantation South no longer had to contend with abolitionist attacks on the institution of slavery. Instead, white southerners were uninhibited in crafting nostalgic portraits of plantation lives told in quaint black dialect by aged former slaves (Taylor 1961; Clinton 1995; Cox 2011; Prince 2014).

According to conventional white southern lore, the Civil War, of course, had destroyed the idyllic plantation South. With the defeat of the Confederacy, the white and black civilizations that had given the region its unique charm and character were torn asunder. The white southern historical narrative culminated with the restoration of white political dominance and the wresting of power from northern Republicans and former slaves in the decade after the Civil War. White resistance to plans to "reconstruct" the defeated South demonstrated that the South was "a white man's country" and that it was folly to attempt to upend white supremacy there. The unmistakable lesson of the region's history was that the white South was united in its defense of regional autonomy and white supremacy (Baker 2007). That many white southerners invested themselves in propagating this narrative was hardly surprising. It, after all, presented the region's past in the most favorable possible light. It confirmed the honor and masculinity of white veterans. It provided an opening for white clubwomen to claim a civic role as defenders of regional heritage. And it offered white politicians a convenient way to yoke filiopietism and Confederate memory to the cause of white supremacy.

Counter-memories in the post-Civil War South

Given the prevalence of thousands of Confederate memorials that dot the southern landscape it is tempting to assume that this white southern memory went unchallenged. But the hegemony of this dominant white memory was always more appearance than reality. Indeed, white southerners were acutely aware that their recalled past was disputed both within and without the region. They also perceived that they faced long odds in their campaign to proselytize and preserve their regional memory.

White southerners had to contend with counter-memories from within their ranks. The glorification of the antebellum plantation South and the "Lost Cause" did not square easily with the historical experience of tens of thousands of white southerners. Many residents of the bayous of southern Louisiana, the piney woods of Mississippi, and the mountain hollows of the Appalachian Mountains displayed little nostalgia for a past during which plantation grandees had dominated the region's economy and public life (Inscoe 2008; Brundage 2009; Bynum 2010). There also were tens of thousands of white men who had avoided serving the Confederacy, had deserted the Confederate ranks, had fought in the Union army, or had remained committed to the Union throughout the war. For these white southerners, the conflict had been an unnecessary and unjustifiable tragedy that white southern elites had brought down upon the region. It was from among the ranks of these men that the Republican Party looked for support in the Reconstruction South and that a dissenting white historical memory threatened to take root (Janney 2013).

The most significant and enduring counter-memory to the dominant white historical narrative, without question, was that of southern African Americans. With the end of slavery, southern African Americans not only joined the ranks of the free but also gained the capacity to celebrate their history in ways that had been impossible during slavery. Blacks eagerly grasped this opportunity and worked during the half century after the war to establish a commemorative tradition that made sense of the past and accorded them a central role in it. When white southerners systematically set about codifying their heroic narrative and filling the civic landscape with monuments to it, they were conscious of a challenge from not only northern counter-narratives, but also from southern blacks. The mocking derision that white southerners showered on black commemorative spectacles and the frequency of legal and extralegal harassment directed against black revelers leave little doubt that whites understood that the rituals of black remembrance represented a form of cultural resistance. For all the efforts of southern whites, especially white women, to enshrine their historical understanding of slavery, the Civil War, and black capacities, black celebrations made manifest a forceful and enduring understanding of their own. Postbellum blacks, no less than whites, appreciated the power that flowed from the recalled past.

Pervasive racism reinforced the impulse of blacks to fashion a redemptive past. Whites constantly reminded blacks of their separateness. Along with common-place slights and discrimination, blacks had to withstand the viciously racist cultural milieu of late nineteenth-century America. Beginning during the ante-bellum era and reaching a climax at the century's close, American popular culture projected crippling images of African Americans. The inescapable affront of white racism provoked blacks to give collective voice to the trauma they endured. As an orator during a 1908 Emancipation Day event observed, white prejudice "is one of the means of making us distinctly a race with a common cause, a common purpose, and a common interest" (Brundage 2005: 58). United by their experiences as outcasts and collective resentment of their oppression, blacks yearned for an ennobling historical memory.

Whereas white southerners marshaled the full array of cultural forms at their disposal to give voice to their collective memory blacks had to make do with comparatively meager resources. Although poverty and oppression sharply circumscribed their efforts, blacks defiantly insisted upon the public expression of their memory. In their robust ceremonial life blacks most fully revealed their historical imagination. Public ceremonies, which became the preeminent forum in which blacks displayed their recalled past, enabled vast numbers of blacks to learn, invent, and practice a common language of memory (O'Leary 1999: 110–128; Blight 2001: 300–337; Kachun 2003; Brundage 2005; Clark 2005).

These exercises routinely filled the public spaces of the region. During the expansive ceremonies that black groups staged, men and women, dressed in elaborate regalia, preceded by a brass band, marched through the main streets of their communities until they reached a major civic landmark or church, where the ceremonial officers would reflect on the ceremonies and ministers would bless the occasion (Brown 1994; Feldman 1999; Johnson 2004). Especially impressive in magnitude and pomp were the celebrations presented in the region's large cities. There, the size and comparative wealth of black communities made possible spectacles that attracted thousands of onlookers. With banners that saluted Abraham Lincoln, abolitionists, and great blacks, organizers trans-formed commemorative celebrations into mobile living history exhibits that traced the evolution of African Americans from slaves to proud and progressive citizens (see Figure 11.2).

To counter white versions of the southern past, African American commemora-tors forthrightly called into question their central tenets. Blacks anxious to chart their race's history necessarily had to challenge the assumptions of white suprem-acy. In particular, black ceremonies were intended to affirm that African Americans, no less than any other race, displayed the capacity to progress through stages of development to "civilization." In the eyes of most southern whites, the lesson of history was obvious. To extend the entitlements of civilization, such as the right to vote, to blacks was to recklessly disregard the lessons of history. With whites

Figure 11.2 Crowds of Emancipation Day marchers and spectators filled the streets of Richmond, Virginia, ca. 1905. Source: Detroit Publishing Company Photograph Collection, Library of Congress. Courtesy Library of Congress.

concluding that they stood at the apex of human development and blacks at the opposite end of the evolutionary continuum, the implications for black Americans were clear (Bederman 1995; Gaines 1996; Adeleke 1998; Moses 1998).

Without fail, blacks used commemorative celebrations to puncture such white hubris. Orators often made a point of dismissing as ignorant the dominant image of Africa. Rather than a metaphor for barbarism, the continent, they insisted, had been the cradle of much that the world had come to define and salute as "Western civilization." Black orators proudly reclaimed the grand heritage of ancient Egypt from whites who chose to identify ancient Egyptians with Caucasians. They vouched that the technological and cultural innovations that made possible all subsequent civilization had emerged first in ancient Egypt and Africa. This reclamation of ancient Egypt represented a crucial first step in correcting crippling white distortions of history (Brundage 2005; Moses 1998: 47–50; Raboteau 1995).

The principal concern of black commemoration was to present a useable history for blacks in America. The marvels of ancient Egypt, the decline of Africa, and the enslavement of Africans were less important than the divine purpose assigned blacks in America. The explanation for the "fall" of Africans was simple. Rather than succumb to innate inferiority, Africans had given in to idolatry. But when God consigned Africans to slavery—their "furnace of affliction"—he did so in order that they could receive true "Christian civilization." The terrible suffering of slavery, then, had profound historical value because it was part of the providential design to transport their pagan ancestors to North America where they could assume their momentous role within a Christian civilization.

This providential interpretation of slavery placed the slave experience at the center of black commemorations. Although individual blacks were not eager to reopen the scars left by their enslavement, collectively they did not shy away from recalling it. Indeed, commemorative ceremonies remembered the slave experience in various ways. During the Emancipation Day ceremonies, for instance, a black child might evoke the trauma of slave auctions by reading the widely circulated lament "The farewell of a Virginia slave mother to her daughters sold to Southern bondage." Elsewhere, choirs performed spirituals and work songs associated with slavery. Organizers honored elderly slaves with conspicuous roles in the ceremonies and by distributing to them contributions donated by the audience. Black commemorations left no doubt that slavery had been an inhuman and debased institution. Instead black speakers dismissed romantic renderings of slavery and any suggestions that slavery had been an appropriate condition for African Americans. Ceremonies evoked the agony of slavery by lingering on the "centuries filled with sorrow, anguish, and degradation," "the terrible and trying ordeal of human bondage," "the greatest of all villainies," and "the blackest crime that ever disgraced America's dignity" (Brundage 2005: 93).

Blacks differed no less sharply with whites over the meaning of the Civil War. Southern whites, of course, strenuously defended secession and were acutely sensitive to any suggestion that the defense of slavery had motivated their failed rebellion. The black counter-narrative was equally unambiguous. Over and over again, speakers insisted that the Civil War had been God's punishment for slavery and that the plight of African Americans had been the catalyst for the nation's Armageddon. Rather than a tactical sleight of hand dictated by wartime pressures (as white southerners claimed), the Emancipation Proclamation was a redemptive act through which God wrought national regeneration. By so explaining the mystery of slavery, black orators insisted that the divine providence of history had worked (and might work again in the future) to elevate the African peoples. Emancipation anticipated some an even more profound, imminent, and millennial transformation in the status of black people (Fulop 1991; Hildebrand 1995).

Black paraders and orators intended their fervent identification with the nation to contrast sharply with the resentful sectionalism of white southerners. That the United States was a nation with a millennial destiny, and that blacks had an important role to play in it, was the central theme of the black commemorative tradition. The future of civilization in general and the black race in particular would be played out on this continent where blacks already discerned ample evidence of their rapid ascent up the ladder of civilization. Whereas most whites presumed that centuries would be required to elevate blacks above abject barbarism, blacks pointed to the exceptional strides they had made since slavery.

Evolving southern white attitudes about the Union and their place in it directly affected black commemorative activities. For several decades after the Civil War, most white southerners refrained from or openly repudiated any observation of the Fourth of July. But the comically brief Spanish–American War of 1898 reawakened frenetic nationalism even among former Confederates and southern whites displayed renewed enthusiasm for the anniversary of national independence (Silber 1993). Leading the efforts to revive white observance of the Fourth of July in many areas of the South were the Daughters of the American Revolution, a white women's patriotic society, and other white patriotic societies. In some southern cities, white groups prodded public officials to stage large patriotic festivities and parades that monopolized public spaces that blacks previously had used without challenge. As a consequence, blacks and their festivities were pushed to the margins of the civic landscape. This reassertion of white cultural authority over many patriotic celebrations, in combination with segregation, exacerbated the contest over public spaces and the remembered past in it. Disfranchisement added to the political significance of public celebrations of black history. For blacks who could no longer vote or who had never voted, commemorative holidays provided a forum in which to act politically and to give voice to political aspirations that contradicted any presumption of a cowed black populace.

Blacks continued to stage rousing public commemorations during the first half of the twentieth century, but with segregation sharply limiting their access to public spaces, they increasingly focused on creative use of the few communal spaces they controlled. Elementary and secondary public schools now emerged as one of the principal venues for the promotion of African American historical consciousness. Schools, more than perhaps any other institution, had the capacity to nurture historical awareness systematically and continuously. In one of the most profound ironies of the Jim Crow era, blacks used state and private resources to turn elementary and secondary schools into essential sites of collective memory that performed a role comparable to that of museums in the white community. Black professional historians, who supplied the scholarship and much of the energy that sustained the movement to incorporate "Negro history" into school curricula, sought allies among school teachers, who in turn reached the masses who would never attend college. Together, black historians and teachers rebutted historical fallacies about black Americans and argued for historical truths that would hasten racial equality (Brundage 2005: 138–182; Fairclough 2007).

That Jim Crow schools scattered throughout the South became vehicles for spreading history that contradicted white historical wisdom would have surprised and shocked many white southerners. Whites, of course, never intended that schools should promote black historical awareness. White legislators chronically underfunded black schools and stymied the work of black teachers and administrators. Confident in the control that white administrators exercised over black schools, most whites dismissed them as an expensive but harmless concession to misplaced black ambitions. Ultimately, whites failed to prevent blacks from creatively exploiting the modest resources that states made available for black education. Had the champions of white supremacy recognized this use of schools to nurture a black counter-memory, they undoubtedly would have agreed with Senator James Vardaman of Mississippi, who displayed uncharacteristic prescience when he forecast that "education is ruining our Negroes" (Baker 1908: 247).

The white southern historical memory that exerted such a powerful influence during the century after the Civil War had far-reaching consequences for the region, its white and black residents, and the nation. White southerners fashioned a collective memory that advanced a reactionary form of racial sectionalism. There was little scope for nuance or subtlety in their remembered past. It made white supremacy appear both inevitable and natural. It bolstered the legitimacy of the region's white political and economic elites, despite their support for secession, the Confederacy, and a war that claimed a dreadful human toll. Instead, the prevailing narrative absolved them of virtually any responsibility for the South's defeat while working to instill respect and awe for the region's dutiful white leaders who had founded the nation, established representative government, and purportedly provided steadfast public service. The unmistakable lesson of this past was deference to white social betters, reverence for established institutions, and fidelity to tradition (Marling 1988: 85–114; Lindgren 1993; Kammen 1991: 194–253; Bishir 1993).

Repeated over the decades, this historical memory of white southern victimhood had enduring utility. White politicos invoked it during the first half of the twentieth century whenever the national government or groups outside the South proposed any action that threatened entrenched regional interests. Hollywood movies that were not sufficiently deferential to white southern sensibilities, national legislation that threatened white privilege, federal programs that somehow undercut regional practices, or activists who displayed intolerable concern about southern race relations could all be easily fit into the larger narrative of uninformed or dangerous outsiders intent on destroying the "southern way of life."

Historical memory in the contemporary South

More than a century after the Reconstruction era whites bridled at blacks celebrating their freedom on the streets and byways of the region, public life continues to be interrupted by both familiar and new controversies over Confederate symbols, museum exhibits, historical monuments, and the naming of public thoroughfares. These clashes over the past show no signs of abating in the early twenty-first century. Yet, the segregated "solid" South has given way to the desegregated "Sunbelt" South, immigrants from Latin America and Asia have flocked to the region, personal incomes there now approach national levels, evangelical churches associated with the South have spread across the nation, and suburbanization has transformed huge swaths of the region into landscapes indistinguishable from those elsewhere. While some southerners continue to look to their heritage to define themselves and their region, ongoing demographic, economic, and social transformations in the South are nevertheless changing the tenor and character of the debates over the southern past.

The South's public spaces have emerged as prominent sites of controversy. Activists point to the persisting silences at the region's heritage sites and the preponderance of memorials to Confederate and white architects of white supremacy that clutter the region's landscape. The tussle over prominent monuments to Confederates in New Orleans is illustrative. Towering over three conspicuous spaces in the city are monuments to Confederate president Jefferson Davis and Confederate generals P.G.T. Beauregard and Robert E. Lee. Another monument celebrates a riot in 1874 by local white supremacists who staged an unsuccessful coup to remove the elected bi-racial state government. In recent decades the monuments, and especially the monument commemorating the white supremacist riot, had elicited periodic calls for their removal. In July 2015, after a white supremacist and Confederate enthusiast carried out a mass shooting in a historically black church in Charleston, South Carolina, some residents and public officials in New Orleans called for the end of the public display of Confederate symbols. New Orleans mayor Mitch Landrieu singled out the monument celebrating the 1874 riot and the statues honoring Robert E. Lee and other Confederate notables for removal. The New Orleans city council held public hearings to discuss the proposal and eventually voted to remove the monuments. But a coalition of historical preservationists and Confederate venerators challenged the decision to the remove the Confederate monuments (while offering no defense for the riot monument) in court. The legal controversy raises vexing issues of the ownership of the monuments, the authority of civic governments to both promote and suppress public speech by controlling public art, and the protection of the rights of citizens to enjoy historic public spaces. Outside of the courts debate flared over the appropriateness of "erasing" monuments and other public symbols that offend contemporary sensibilities. Some participants in the controversy call for the preservation *and* reinterpretation of the monuments; others contend that the monuments should stand as they are as reminders of, rather than memorials to, an unpleasant past. To remove them, the argument goes, will do nothing to revise the past. Yet others point out that even if the offending monuments are removed, the city and the state of Louisiana will still be crowded with countless memorials to the Confederacy. Whatever the final disposition of the monuments in New Orleans, the controversy underscores that the existing commemorative landscape in the South is no longer sacrosanct and is finally subject to possible revision.

Public schools have been another important site of contention regarding the region's past. The desegregation of the region's schools that began following the Supreme Court's *Brown* decision, which banned segregation public schools, occurred so slowly that southern officials and educators only gradually altered history curriculums to reflect the reality of integration. The history textbooks used in Virginia public schools from 1949 until 1973 are illustrative. In 1949 a state legislative commission proclaimed that students needed a thorough training in Virginia's history "to combat the trends toward statism" (or, in other words, communism). Unable to find professional historians who would produce books that were sufficiently anti-communist and celebratory of the preferred version of the state's history, elected officials themselves undertook extensive and heavy-handed editing of submitted texts.

The revised and now-acceptable texts reached Virginia's classrooms in 1957 and for the following decade and a half, students waded through them, learning that Virginia's Indians had been "sly and cruel," that "slavery made it possible for Negroes to come to America and make contacts with civilized life," and that Negro "servants" during the Civil War "had risked their lives to protect the white people they loved." The texts purposefully ignored the disfranchisement of blacks after 1902 because "there were enough hard feelings already." With mounting urgency during the late 1960s, blacks, joined by growing numbers of whites, criticized the textbooks as "out-and-out propaganda" that "glorified" the state's racist past and was "slanted toward a conservative political outlook." Organized opposition to the texts was a direct outgrowth of black political empowerment. As one critic of the texts pointed out, "There were few public attacks [on] history textbooks so long as the ideals they represented remained dominant." When the Virginia Council of Social Studies dismissed the texts as "ridiculous" and "reprehensible," the Virginia State Board of Education finally voted unanimously to discontinue their use after 1972. The board's decision won applause for ending, as one newspaper put it, an "embarrassing and degrading attempt by the state to package thought" (Brundage 2005: 282–283).

Although public school curriculums in Virginia and other southern states during the 1970s began to shed the conspicuous trappings of white supremacy, public schools in much of the region have not proven to be enduring catalysts for a new inclusive South. Instead the de facto resegregation of public schools in the South has culminated in public schools in most major southern cities that are either overwhelmingly white or overwhelmingly black. In rural areas, especially in the Deep South, meaningful integration often never occurred. So pronounced has been white flight to private academies that the racial divide between public and private schools in rural Mississippi, for example, is virtually complete (Boger 2005).

Because of this resegregation white and black students are not exposed to the same history curriculum. White students in private academies and African American and other students in public schools often have educational experiences that may be almost as different as those that their ancestors had during the era of legally segregated schools. Now that black students predominate in many public schools that previously served white populations, African American parents and students predictably insist that these schools should adapt to the overwhelmingly minority populations that they now serve. The renaming of public schools across the region is one conspicuous manifestation of this impulse. Black students and parents are loath to tolerate school names that continue to honor Confederate heroes, such as Robert E. Lee or Nathan Bedford Forrest, or prominent white supremacist politicians. Although some commentators have ridiculed the renaming of schools as meaningless grandstanding and "political correctness" run amok, it reflects a renewed sense of cultural custodianship among black parents and students for their schools (Brundage 2005: 274–284).

Even more jarring contrasts between inherited and emergent versions of the past are pronounced in contemporary southern tourism. The years between World War One and World War Two marked a watershed in the self-conscious commercialization of the southern past. Tourism translated historical memory in the South into commerce. Encouraging tourism became a pressing concern of white public officials' businessmen across the region. As southern tourism evolved, it increasingly became a commercially oriented celebration of the South's architecture, landscape, and history. By the 1930s the transformation of the southern past into a commodity, a process that would continue across the twentieth century, was well advanced in Charleston, St. Augustine, New Orleans, Williamsburg, Natchez, and other destinations (Greenspan 2002; Starnes 2003; Souther 2006; Stanonis 2006; McIntyre 2011; Cox 2012).

The tourist South became a stage upon which southerners presented the South both as they wanted to see it and as they imagined tourists wanted to experience it. Museums, preserved homes, and historic recreations provided settings in which southerners performed their "southernness" before eager audiences. Americans gravitated to these historical settings that offered a vivid intensification of experience and a magical suspension of time. The maturation of a regional industry that marketed quaintness and archaic traditions had enduring consequences for whites and blacks alike. Historical tourism was a project conceived of by whites for white consumers. With segregation precluding black patronage at most tourist facilities, African Americans were incorporated into southern tourism not as full equals but as domesticated "others" represented for public consumption. Tourists could enjoy the picturesque spectacle created by servile African Americans without needing to understand them. Indeed, an exaggerated concern for African Americans might have interfered with the tourist experience. To acknowledge the black past, at least as understood by blacks, would have raised knotty questions about the legacies of slavery as well as current race relations, thereby subverting the carefully nurtured images of gentility, romance, and nostalgia that sustained southern tourism (Brundage 2005: 183–226).

In the region's increasingly segmented contemporary tourist industry, many long-established sites continue to trade in the genteel and romantic "Old South" and offer retrograde interpretations that have changed little in decades. But such sites are now competing against sites that subvert familiar tropes of the region's past and attractions. Some southern institutions have begun to acknowledge the divergent memories of recent traumas that divide many whites and blacks and have even begun to address the thorniest questions about the region's past.

Until the 1980s southern museums of black history were small, obscure, and often ephemeral undertakings. African American interest in museums devoted to black history in the South was longstanding, extending back to the late nineteenth century and up through the black nationalist movements of the 1960s. But the organization and exhibition of major permanent collections was beyond the capacity of most local activists, who lacked access to the public funds and private foundations that sustained white museums (Eichstedt 2002).

The major black history sites launched in the South during the 1980s and 1990s were a testament to the influence of both the "new museumology" and newly gained black political power. The concern for the dispossessed and the attention devoted to the historical origins of inequality that characterized the new social history certainly made the African American past a rich new field for interpretation. Some museum specialists during the 1970s and 1980s eagerly reinterpreted their institutional missions in light of this new orientation. Simultaneously, the civil rights movement secured for blacks political rights that enabled them to prod elected officials to subsidize museums devoted to their heritage. Not surprisingly, the movement became the focus for the museums. These museums, including the National Civil Rights Museum in Memphis (1991), the Birmingham Civil Rights Institute (1992), the National Voting Rights Museum in Selma (1992), the Ralph Marks Gilbert Civil Rights Museum in Savannah (1996), and the Albany (Georgia) Civil Rights Museum (1998), were self-conscious efforts to institutionalize the links that both social historians and movement activists saw between historical awareness, black identity, and social change in the South. Arguably, the capstone for this long campaign was the founding of the National Museum of African American History in Washington, DC in 2016 (Honey 1995; Eskew 2003).

Perhaps the most ambitious campaign to acknowledge the region's traumatic history of racial oppression and to redress it has been the movement for compensation and formal apology. Calls for slave reparations to African Americans began with antebellum abolitionists and remained a topic of public debate during the late nineteenth century (Berry 2005). During the 1960s Whitney Young and other civil rights activists revived the issue when they urged the nation to launch a "Marshall Plan" for blacks. Appeals to moral justice and fair play provided the justification for these early proposals. More recently, proponents of reparations have grounded their litigation to recompense blacks for the illegal confiscation of their labor, property, and rights in contemporary understandings of civil rights. Reparation activists, however, have had little success. Civil rights laws may have created an opening for litigation, but conservative state and federal courts in the region have flatly denied legal claims for slave reparations, and the prospects for legal remedies against private firms, such as insurance companies, remain unclear.

Because of daunting obstacles to redress in the courts, some reparation advocates instead have turned to legislatures, where, because of black political empowerment, they stand a greater likelihood of securing a favorable hearing. With national contrition the goal, the slave reparations campaign is necessarily national, rather than regional, in scope. Indeed, reparations activists are especially keen to expose the extent to which the entire nation, and not just the slave South, was implicated in slavery and white supremacy. Consequently, the long history of white privilege in the South figures prominently in the justifications for slavery reparations, but the South itself has not been the focal point of the campaign. Drawing inspiration from various recent reparation schemes, including for Holocaust survivors whose assets were illegally confiscated and for

Japanese-American victims of forced relocation during World War Two, blacks in Congress have annually introduced a bill to establish a commission to study reparations for African Americans. Although the bill has never gotten out of committee during the past fifteen years, it remains a focal point for a substantial grass-roots campaign (Brooks 2003; Winbush 2003).

Reparations campaigns for African Americans have also emerged specifically in the South. In the most important reparations victory to date, the Florida legislature in 1994 acknowledged the failure of state authorities to suppress a 1923 race riot in the hamlet of Rosewood. Incited by trumped-up charges of black criminality, whites in the central Florida village marauded for days, destroying black property and murdering blacks. In light of the failure of public officials to protect life and property, state legislators approved more than $2 million in compensation for the riot's survivors and their descendants. In many regards the Rosewood reparations are unique; they compensate the victims of a specific event; the number of claimants was small; and the injustice was inflicted upon identifiable victims, as opposed to a broad, indiscriminate category of people (D'Orso 1996).

The creation of a pluralist public culture in the South has been halting and marked by periodic controversy. During the 1990s, especially in Georgia, controversy over the display of the Confederate battle flag spilled over into electoral politics and contributed to the ongoing consolidation of conservative white voters within the Republican Party, which aligned itself with the defense of southern white heritage. In South Carolina, the continuing display of the Confederate battle flag on the state capitol eventually prompted calls for tourists and groups to boycott visiting the state as long as the flag flew on state property. In the aftermath of a mass shooting of black churchgoers by a Confederate enthusiast and white supremacist in Charleston, South Carolina in 2015, Republican politicians in South Carolina responded by removing the Confederate battle flag from its position of honor at the state capitol. But otherwise the built landscape of Confederate monuments, street names honoring Confederates, and other physical reminders of white southern historical memory were left untouched there and in most areas of the South. With Confederate monuments increasingly the focus of controversy, elected officials in Louisville, Kentucky (2016), New Orleans (2017), Gainesville, Florida (2017), and a few other communities oversaw the removal of local monuments from public display. This "erasure" of southern white heritage provoked furious denunciations from white supremacists, white nationalists, neo-Confederates, neo-Nazis, and various other defenders of "white heritage." After a national rally by these groups, bolstered by self-declared militias, in August 2017 in Charlottesville, Virginia, to oppose the removal of a statue of Robert E. Lee from a city park, ended with bloodshed, the debate about Confederate symbols in public spaces intensified further. Scores of southern communities reacted to the tragedy in Charlottesville by removing monuments or planning to do so, but in several states these efforts were stymied by laws that prohibit the removal or alteration of monuments without approval of the state legislature. Legislators responsible for these laws in South Carolina (2000), Mississippi (2004), North Carolina (2015), Tennessee (2016), and Alabama

Figures 11.3 and 11.4 The Confederate memorial in Durham, North Carolina before and after protesters toppled the sculpture in August 2017. The desecration of the monument was a testament to the continuing divisiveness of Confederate symbols in the United States. (© Commemorative Landscapes of North Carolina project, used with permission.)

(2017) have insisted that they are intended to prevent the "erasure" of southern history but they have had the effect of freezing the current southern commemorative landscape with its surfeit of monuments and symbols honoring Confederates and architects of white supremacy.

Conclusion

Contemporary contests over historical memory in the American South have insured that historical inequities now are acknowledged in the region's public culture. When some southerners recall with nostalgia an age when a purportedly shared memory united their region, they reveal how little experience southerners have had according public recognition to competing historical memories. To the extent that any shared sense of the past ever united southerners it existed as much through coercion as consent. A pluralistic public culture in the region will emerge only through the strenuous expression and airing of public differences. The creation of a truly democratic civic culture that fully and appropriately acknowledges the South's contested past will necessarily require stamina, experimentation, and tolerance. Yet, at the same time, some narratives of the South's past are no longer defensible (if they ever were) and cannot withstand any standard of historical credibility. For example, slavery was not a positive good for the enslaved; white supremacy after the Civil War cannot be justified by alleged black barbarism; and the modern civil rights movement was not a front for communist subversion and godless atheism. These interpretations should be rebutted whenever and wherever they surface. They cannot contribute in any meaningful way to either deeper historical understanding or richer public debate. But such simplistic interpretations are less and less at the center of the controversies that roil the contemporary South.

Instead, now the complexities and contradictions of the South's history are often the points of contestation for black and white southerners. Slavery was an inhumane institution and yet both slave masters and slaves found ways to retain their humanity. How can this central facet of the history of slavery be discussed and rendered? The oppressiveness of the Jim Crow South was unquestionably soul-numbing, and yet blacks were never reduced, in the words of novelist Ralph Ellison, to "the sum of [their] brutalization" (Ellison 1967). How can this apparent paradox of modern southern history be presented? These and other nuances continue to challenge the efforts of southerners to refashion the historical memory of their region.

Guide to further readings and online resources

During the past two decades, historians have displayed a keen interest in historical memory in the American South. Some of the scholarship has its roots in older questions about southern "regional distinctiveness," which was a longstanding thread in the historiography of the region. Prominent examples of this scholarship, which accentuated how the recalled past of white southerners deviated from that of other Americans, include C. Vann Woodward, *The Burden of Southern History* (1968); George Tindall, "Mythology: A New Frontier in Southern History" (1974); and Rollin G. Osterweis, *The Myth of the Lost Cause, 1865–1900* (1973). During the 1980s the influence of sociology and anthropology was evident in two seminal works: Charles Reagan Wilson, *Baptized in Blood: The Religion of the Lost Cause, 1865–1920* (1980) and Gaines M. Foster, *Ghosts of the Confederacy: Defeat, the Lost Cause, and the Emergence of the New South, 1865 to 1913* (1987).

Since 1990 scholarship on southern regional memory has implicitly, and sometimes explicitly, addressed the topic with a broader comparative and theoretically informed perspective. A collection that typified this emerging work is W. Fitzhugh Brundage (ed.), *Where These Memories Grow: History, Memory, and Southern Identity* (2000). Important works have focused on the memory of the Civil War, including Kirk Savage, *Standing Soldiers, Kneeling Slaves: Race, War, and Monument in Nineteenth-century America* (1997); David Blight, *Race and Reunion: the Civil War in American Memory* (2001); Karen L. Cox, *Dixie's Daughters: The United Daughters of the Confederacy and the Preservation of Confederate Culture* (2003); W. Scott Poole, *Never Surrender: Confederate Memory and Conservatism in the South Carolina Upcountry* (2004); and Caroline E. Janney, *Remembering the Civil War: Reunion and the Limits of Reconciliation* (2013). Bruce E. Baker, *What Reconstruction Meant: Historical Memory in the American South* (2007) is a pioneering study of the historical memory of Reconstruction. An indispensable history of the origins of and controversies surrounding the Confederate flag is John M. Coski, *The Confederate Battle Flag: America's Most Embattled Emblem* (2005).

The role of gender in the articulation and dissemination of white memory has been explored by Cox, *Dixie's Daughters*; Joan Marie Johnson, *Southern Ladies, New Women: Race, Region, and Clubwomen in South Carolina, 1890–1930* (2004); and LeeAnn Whites, *Gender Matters: Civil War, Reconstruction, and the Making of the New South* (2005).

The historical memory of southern African Americans has been a focus of several important works, including Mitchell A. Kachun, *Festivals of Freedom: Memory and Meaning in African American Emancipation Celebrations, 1808–1915* (2003); and Kathleen Ann Clark, *Defining Moments: African American Commemoration & Political Culture in the South, 1863–1913* (2005). For a work that explicitly compares white and black memory see W. Fitzhugh Brundage, *The Southern Past: A Clash of Race and Memory* (2005).

Considerable scholarship on regional tourism and memory has emerged since 2000. Two of the best studies in this field are Karen L. Cox (ed.) *Destination Dixie: Tourism & Southern History* (2012); Anthony J. Stanonis, *Creating the Big Easy: New Orleans and the Emergence of Modern Tourism, 1918–1945* (2006); and Richard D. Starnes, *Creating the Land of the Sky: Tourism and Society in Western North Carolina* (2005).

Readers interested in exploring web resources related to the contested memory of the American South have a wealth of options. A cursory web search will identify literally hundreds of "Neo-Confederate" websites that promote white southern "heritage" while justifying and honoring the Confederate cause. The National Museum of African American History in Washington, DC has an exceptional collection related to southern African Americans: https://nmaahc.si.edu/. Similarly, the Library of Congress has extraordinary resources on virtually all aspects of southern historical memory: www.loc.gov/collections/. The web resources associated with the American Civil War Museum in Richmond, Virginia are especially interesting because the museum is committed to integrating the histories of the Confederacy, Union, and African American struggle for emancipation: https://acwm.org/. For a robust inventory of images, information, and primary sources relating to the diversity and evolution of commemorative monuments and sites in a single southern state, visit the Commemorative Landscapes of North Carolina site at: http://docsouth.unc.edu/commland/.

References

Adeleke, Tunde (1998) *UnAfrican Americans: Nineteenth-century Black Nationalists and the Civilizing Mission.* Lexington, KY: University Press of Kentucky.

Baker, Bruce E. (2007) *What Reconstruction Meant: Historical Memory in the American South.* Charlottesville, VI: University of Virginia Press.

Baker, Ray Stannard (1908) *Following the Color Line; an Account of Negro Citizenship in the American Democracy.* New York: Doubleday, Page & Company.

Baker, Thomas H. (1995) *Redeemed from Oblivion: An Administrative History of Guilford Courthouse National Military Park.* Greensboro: U.S. Department of Interior, National Park Service.

Barthes, Roland (1972) *Mythologies.* New York: Hill & Wang.

Bederman, Gail (1995) *Manliness & Civilization: A Cultural History of Gender and Race in the United States, 1880–1917.* Chicago: University of Chicago Press.

Berry, Mary Frances (2005) *My Face Is Black Is True: Callie House and the Struggle for Ex-slave Reparations.* New York: Alfred A. Knopf.

Bishir, Catherine W. (1993) "Landmarks of Power: Building a Southern Past, 1855–1915," *Southern Cultures* 1: 5–45.

Blight, David W. (2001) *Race and Reunion: The Civil War in American Memory.* Cambridge, MA: Belknap Press of Harvard University Press.

Boger, John Charles (2005) *School Resegregation: Must the South Turn Back?* Chapel Hill, NC: University of North Carolina Press.

Brooks, Roy L. (2003) "History of the Black Redress Movement," *Guild Practitioner* 60 (Winter): 1–12.

Brown, Elsa Barkley (1994) "Uncle Ned's Children: Negotiating Community and Freedom in Postemancipation Richmond, Virginia," PhD thesis, Kent State University.

Brown, Thomas J. (2004) *The Public Art of Civil War Commemoration: A Brief History with Documents.* Boston: Bedford/St. Martin's.

Brown, Thomas J. (2015) *Civil War Canon: Sites of Confederate Memory in South Carolina.* Chapel Hill, NC: University of North Carolina Press.

Brundage, W. Fitzhugh (ed.) (2000) *Where These Memories Grow: History, Memory, and Southern Identity.* Chapel Hill, NC: University of North Carolina Press.

Brundage, W. Fitzhugh (2005) *The Southern Past: A Clash of Race and Memory.* Cambridge, MA: Belknap Press of Harvard University Press.

Brundage, W. Fitzhugh (2009) "Redeeming a Failed Revolution: Confederate Memory," in William J. Cooper and John McCardell (eds.), *In the Cause of Liberty: How the Civil War Redefined American Ideals*. Baton Rouge, LO: Louisiana State University Press.

Bynum, Victoria E. (2010) *The Long Shadow of the Civil War: Southern Dissent and Its Legacies*. Chapel Hill, NC: University of North Carolina Press.

Capps, Michael A. (1999) *Moores Creek National Battlefield: An Administrative History*. Atlanta, GA: U.S. Department of the Interior, National Park Service, Southeast Regional Office, Cultural Resources Stewardship.

Carter, Dan T. (1985) *When the War Was Over: The Failure of Self-Reconstruction in the South, 1865–1867*. Baton Rouge, LO: Louisiana State University Press.

Clark, Kathleen Ann (2005) *Defining Moments: African American Commemoration & Political Culture in the South, 1863–1913*. Chapel Hill, NC: University of North Carolina Press.

Clinton, Catherine (1995) *Tara Revisited: Women, War & the Plantation Legend*. New York: Abbeville Press.

Cohen, Nancy (2002) *The Reconstruction of American Liberalism, 1865–1914*. Chapel Hill, NC: University of North Carolina Press.

Coski, John M. (2005) *The Confederate Battle Flag: America's Most Embattled Emblem*. Cambridge, MA: Belknap Press of Harvard University Press.

Cox, Karen L. (2003) *Dixie's Daughters: The United Daughters of the Confederacy and the Preservation of Confederate Culture*. Gainesville, FL: University Press of Florida.

Cox, Karen L. (2011) *Dreaming of Dixie: How the South Was Created in American Popular Culture*. Chapel Hill, NC: University of North Carolina Press.

Cox, Karen L. (ed.) (2012) *Destination Dixie: Tourism & Southern History*. Gainesville, FL: University Press of Florida.

Davies, Wallace Evan (1955) *Patriotism on Parade; The Story of Veterans' and Hereditary Organizations in America, 1783–1900*. Cambridge, MA: Harvard University Press.

Dawley, Alan (1991) *Struggles for Justice: Social Responsibility and the Liberal State*. Cambridge, MA: Belknap Press of Harvard University Press.

D'Orso, Michael (1996) *Like Judgment Day: The Ruin and Redemption of a Town Called Rosewood*. New York: G.P. Putnam's Sons.

Eichstedt, Jennifer L. (2002) *Representations of Slavery: Race and Ideology in Southern Plantation Museums*. Washington, DC: Smithsonian Institution Press.

Ellison, Ralph (1967) "A Very Stern Discipline," *Harper's* (March), 84.

Eskew, Glenn T. (2003) "Memorializing the Movement: The Struggle to Build Civil Rights Museums in the South," in Winfred B. Moore, Jr., Kyle S. Sinsi and David H. White, Jr. (eds.), *Warm Ashes: Issues in Southern History at the Dawn of the Twenty-First Century*. Columbia, SC: University of South Carolina Press, 363–72.

Fairclough, Adam (2007) *A Class of Their Own: Black Teachers in the Segregated South*. Cambridge, MA: Belknap Press of Harvard University Press.

Faust, Drew Gilpin (1988) *The Creation of Confederate Nationalism: Ideology and Identity in the Civil War South*. Baton Rouge, LO: Louisiana State University Press.

Feldman, Lynne B. (1999) *A Sense of Place: Birmingham's Black Middle-class Community, 1890–1930*. Tuscaloosa, AL: University of Alabama Press.

Foster, Gaines M. (1987) *Ghosts of the Confederacy: Defeat, the Lost Cause, and the Emergence of the New South, 1865 to 1913*. New York: Oxford University Press.

Fulop, Timothy E. (1991) "'The Future Golden Day of the Race': Millennialism and Black Americans in the Nadir, 1877–1901," *Harvard Theological Review* 84, 75–99.

Gaines, Kevin Kelly (1996) *Uplifting the Race: Black Leadership, Politics, and Culture in the Twentieth Century*. Chapel Hill, NC: University of North Carolina Press.

Greenspan, Anders (2002) *Creating Colonial Williamsburg*. Washington, DC: Smithsonian Institution Press.

Harris, M. Keith. (2014) *Across the Bloody Chasm: The Culture of Commemoration among Civil War Veterans*. Baton Rouge, LO: Louisiana State University Press.

Hildebrand, Reginald Francis (1995) *The Times Were Strange and Stirring: Methodist Preachers and the Crisis of Emancipation*. Durham, NC: Duke University Press.

Honey, Michael (1995) "Doing Public History at the National Civil Rights Museum: A Conversation with Juanita Moore," *Public Historian* 17 (Winter), 72, 76–7.

Inscoe, John C. (2008) *Race, War, and Remembrance in the Appalachian South*. Lexington, KY: University Press of Kentucky.

Janney, Caroline E. (2008) *Burying the Dead but Not the Past: Ladies' Memorial Associations and the Lost Cause*. Chapel Hill, NC: University of North Carolina Press.

Janney, Caroline E. (2013) *Remembering the Civil War: Reunion and the Limits of Reconciliation*. Chapel Hill, NC: University of North Carolina Press.

Johnson, Joan Marie (2004) *Southern Ladies, New Women: Race, Region, and Clubwomen in South Carolina, 1890–1930*. Gainesville, FL: University Press of Florida.

Kachun, Mitchell A. (2003) *Festivals of Freedom: Memory and Meaning in African American Emancipation Celebrations, 1808–1915*. Amherst, MA: University of Massachusetts Press.

Kamin, Ben (2012) *Room 306: The National Story of the Lorraine Motel*. East Lansing, MI: Michigan State University Press.

Kammen, Michael G. (1991) *Mystic Chords of Memory: The Transformation of Tradition in American Culture*. New York: Knopf.

Lindgren, James Michael (1993) *Preserving the Old Dominion: Historic Preservation and Virginia Traditionalism*. Charlottesville, VI: University Press of Virginia.

Marling, Karal Ann (1988) *George Washington Slept Here: Colonial Revivals and American Culture, 1876–1986*. Cambridge, MA: Harvard University Press.

McIntyre, Rebecca Cawood (2011) *Souvenirs of the Old South: Northern Tourism and Southern Mythology*. Gainesville, FL: University Press of Florida.

McPherson, James M. (1988) *Battle Cry of Freedom: The Civil War Era*. New York: Oxford University Press.

Morgan, Francesca (2005) *Women and Patriotism in Jim Crow America*. Chapel Hill, NC: University of North Carolina Press.

Moses, Wilson Jeremiah (1978) *The Golden Age of Black Nationalism, 1850–1925*. Hamden, CT: Archon Books.

Moses, Wilson Jeremiah (1998) *Afrotopia: The Roots of African American Popular History*. New York: Cambridge University Press.

O'Leary, Cecilia Elizabeth (1999) *To Die For: The Paradox of American Patriotism*. Princeton, NJ: Princeton University Press.

Osterweis, Rollin G. (1973) *The Myth of the Lost Cause, 1865–1900*. Hamden, CT: Archon Books.

Owen, Christopher H. (1998) *The Sacred Flame of Love: Methodism and Society in Nineteenth-century Georgia*. Athens, GA: University of Georgia Press.

Poole, W. Scott. (2004) *Never Surrender: Confederate Memory and Conservatism in the South Carolina Upcountry.* Athens, GA: University of Georgia Press.

Prince, K. Stephen. (2014) *Stories of the South: Race and the Reconstruction of Southern Identity, 1865–1915.* Charlottesville, NC: University of North Carolina Press.

Raboteau, Albert J. (1995) *A Fire in the Bones: Reflections on African-American Religious History.* Boston: Beacon Press.

Remillard, Arthur (2011) *Southern Civil Religions: Imagining the Good Society in the post-Reconstruction Era.* Athens, GA: University of Georgia Press.

Rubin, Anne S. (2005) *A Shattered Nation: The Rise and Fall of the Confederacy, 1861–1868.* Chapel Hill, NC: University of North Carolina Press.

Savage, Kirk (1997) *Standing Soldiers, Kneeling Slaves: Race, War, and Monument in Nineteenth-century America.* Princeton, NJ: Princeton University Press.

Silber, Nina (1993) *The Romance of Reunion: Northerners and the South, 1865–1900.* Chapel Hill, NC: University of North Carolina Press.

Skowronek, Stephen (1982) *Building a New American State: The Expansion of National Administrative Capacities, 1877–1920.* New York: Cambridge University Press.

Snay, Mitchell (1993) *Gospel of Disunion: Religion and Separatism in the Antebellum South.* New York: Cambridge University Press.

Souther, Jonathan Mark (2006) *New Orleans on Parade: Tourism and the Transformation of the Crescent City.* Baton Rouge, LO: Louisiana State University Press.

Stanonis, Anthony J. (2006) *Creating the Big Easy: New Orleans and the Emergence of Modern Tourism, 1918–1945.* Athens, GA: University of Georgia Press.

Starnes, Richard D. (ed.) (2003) *Southern Journeys: Tourism, History, and Culture in the Modern South.* Tuscaloosa, AL: University of Alabama Press.

Starnes, Richard D. (2005) *Creating the Land of the Sky: Tourism and Society in Western North Carolina.* Tuscaloosa, AL: University of Alabama Press.

Taylor, William Robert (1961) *Cavalier and Yankee: The Old South and American National Character.* New York: G. Braziller.

George B. Tindall (1974) "Mythology: A New Frontier in Southern History," in Patrick Gerster and Nicholas Cords (eds.), *Myth and Southern History.* Chicago: Rand McNally, volume I: 1–15.

Whites, LeeAnn (2005) *Gender Matters: Civil War, Reconstruction, and the Making of the New South.* New York: Palgrave Macmillan.

Wilson, Charles Reagan (1980) *Baptized in Blood: The Religion of the Lost Cause, 1865–1920.* Athens, GA: University of Georgia Press.

Winbush, Raymond A. (ed.) (2003) *Should America Pay? Slavery and the Raging Debate over Reparations.* New York: Amistad.

Woodward, C. Vann (1968) *The Burden of Southern History.* Baton Rouge, LO: Louisiana State University Press.

12 The politics of Holocaust memory

Adam Sutcliffe

No historical event is as laden with expectations of meaning as the Nazi genocide of European Jews during the Second World War. This mass killing, which did not emerge as a discrete and named focus of public memory until the early 1960s, has in recent decades become the primary benchmark of human barbarism, and the most frequently and earnestly invoked moral lesson from the past. Precisely what, though, does the Holocaust teach us? Coverage of the topic is legally enshrined as an educational requirement in many jurisdictions around the world, sometimes with its pedagogical purpose defined in detail. In the American state of Florida, for example, the Holocaust, which is the only curricular topic in non-US history mandated by the state legislature, must be:

> taught in a manner that leads to an investigation of human behavior, an understanding of the ramifications of prejudice, racism and stereotyping, and an examination of what it means to be a responsible and respectful person, for the purposes of encouraging tolerance of diversity in a pluralistic society and for nurturing and protecting democratic values and institutions.[1]

These are certainly laudable aims. However, it is far from self-evident how they should be realized in practice, or to what extent the slaughter of European Jewry should be singled out to transmit them. The more precise lessons to be drawn from this historical event have often been highly contested, particularly over attempts to apply them to adjudicate between political alternatives. The heavy moral freighting of the Holocaust has imbued its teaching, invocation and representation with a reflective intensity that has in many ways been highly productive. However, this atrocity has not yielded any straightforward, readily usable or universally accepted lesson for the future.

It was not until the 1960s that the Nazi extermination of European Jewry became internationally recognized as an important and distinct event in its own right, and as part of this process acquired its own name. The term 'Holocaust' was introduced into English as a translation for the Hebrew word *Shoah* (catastrophe, or destruction), which soon after the war became the established Israeli term for the genocide (Novick 1999: 133–4). Usually the word refers to the organized, targeted killing of approximately six million Jews by the Nazi regime during the

Second World War. However, because antisemitism was so central to Nazi ideology, the term is sometimes also applied to all Nazi persecution of Jews, from 1933 onwards. It is also sometimes used more broadly, to cover all Nazi killing of civilians, including Gypsies, the disabled, Poles and some other Slavs, Jehovah's Witnesses, homosexual men and left-wing activists. The definition of the term, its range of inclusion, and the classification and quantification of the exterminated people that it encompasses, has in many contexts been vociferously contested, politically sensitive, or awkwardly ambiguous (Novick 1999: 214–26; Snyder 2010: 409–14). At the centre of these definitional complexities is a question that also lies at the heart of debates over the memory of the Holocaust: the relationship of the victimization of Jews to that of other persecuted groups, both during the Nazi period and since.

The history of Holocaust memory

Astonishing though it may seem from the perspective of today's high level of Holocaust consciousness, until the beginning of the 1960s there was little public discussion of the Nazi extermination of the Jews. The general feeling in Europe was that the entire continent had lived through horror, of which the Nazi camps and mass killings were only a part, and that the focus should be on forward-looking reconstruction and recovery rather than on the past. There were also powerful geopolitical reasons not to dwell on recent history. The Iron Curtain now split Germany in two, and necessitated a rapid reorientation of adversarial energies, as for both sides in the emerging Cold War one of the two new Germanys was suddenly a key frontline ally. The early international processing of the Second World War was to a significant extent shaped by the war crimes trials in Nuremberg in 1945–6, which, seeking to re-educate rather than to overwhelm ordinary Germans, did not emphasize the extermination of Jews. Focusing mostly on leading Nazi criminals, the trials only superficially explored the depth and breadth of the genocide (Bloxham 2001: 93–181).

Before the 1960s there was little interest anywhere in the world in the particularity of Jewish victimhood during the war. In the nations of the West, a focus on the extermination of the Jews could not readily be assimilated into the predominant universalist and assimilationist value system of the period, which stressed communalities rather than differences between ethnic groups. For Jews in these countries, the main concern in these years was with 'fitting in': there was a general preference not to dwell on the antisemitism of the past, which, in America in particular, it seemed was finally being buried under the politeness and prosperity of post-war suburban life (Kushner 1994: 229–47; Novick 1999: 63–123). Holocaust survivors were not silent about their experiences: there was an early outpouring of written testimony, much of it in Yiddish or Polish, and also some notable memorialization and archiving initiatives. However, the wider public was largely unreceptive. It was not until the late 1950s, after the core phase of post-war recovery, that the slaughter began to be integrated into national historical cultures (Cesarani and Sundquist 2012: 1–38; Heuman 2015: 128–55).

In the new state of Israel there was also at first little desire to reflect on the Nazi genocide. The very limited ability of Jews to resist their mass killing induced feelings of shame, and the national focus was on laying the foundations for a very different future, in which Israeli Jews, in contrast to their forebears in Europe, were to be strong, proud and no longer a vulnerable anomaly in the world of nation-states. The approximately 250,000 survivors of the Holocaust who settled in Israel could not easily be assimilated into this national vision. Their presence, and the psychological scars that they still bore, were reminders of a traumatic past that the children of the pre-state Jewish settlement in Palestine (the *Yishuv*) mostly sought to forget and overcome. The Israeli 'Nazi and Nazi Collaborators Law', passed in 1950, was used during that decade almost exclusively to prosecute Holocaust survivors who were accused by other survivors of minor acts of collaboration with the Nazis. Over several years the nation was convulsed by the 'Kastner affair', triggered by the denunciation by a journalist of Rudolf Kastner, a senior Israeli civil servant who, in Hungary in 1944, had negotiated with Nazi leaders to secure the safe passage of a trainload of selected Jews from Budapest to Switzerland, in exchange for a ransom. Kastner's accuser was charged with libel by the Israeli state, but the judge, in 1955, substantially upheld his allegations. The case had major political reverberations, and two years later Kastner was assassinated in Tel Aviv, before being largely exonerated by the 1958 appeal verdict of the Israeli Supreme Court. Although the memory of the Holocaust was inescapable in Israel – the very existence of the state was indirectly dependent on it – its presence in the nation's early collective culture was raw, divisive and dissonant (Segev 1993: 153–86, 255–310; Zertal 2005: 5–90).

The first rise in international interest in the Holocaust was catalysed by the trial of Adolph Eichmann, one of the leading Nazi overseers of the genocide, in Jerusalem in 1961. In part to draw the country together after the Kastner trauma, the Israeli Prime Minister David Ben-Gurion ordered his Mossad secret service agents to capture Eichmann in Buenos Aires in 1960, and bring him to Israel to be tried under the 1950 law. The Eichmann trial attracted huge media attention, through which the term 'Holocaust' became established in English. The most influential reporting on the trial was by Hannah Arendt, a prominent philosopher and German Jewish refugee to America, who, struck by the ordinariness of the defendant, introduced the influential (though contested) concept of the 'banality of evil', interpreting the genocide as in large measure a bureaucratic crime perpetrated not by psychopaths but by normal people (Arendt 1963; Cesarani 2004: 343–56). Arendt also diffused more detailed knowledge of the Nazi genocide, drawing heavily on the pioneering historical research of another refugee to the United States, Raul Hilberg. In the late 1950s Hilberg had struggled to find a publisher; only in 1961, after the trial, did his seminal study, *The Destruction of European Jewry*, finally appear (Hilberg 1996: 91–120).

Ben-Gurion's staging of the Eichmann trial was directed at least as much to an international as to a domestic audience. Facing more assertive regional hostility after the Suez Crisis of 1956, spearheaded by the Pan-Arabism of the Egyptian President Nasser, Ben-Gurion sought to use the trial to promote Israel's legitimacy on the world stage, and to focus attention on the continued threat posed to the young nation – not by Nazis, but by the Arab nations that surrounded it. The 'nazification of the enemy', as the Israeli scholar Idith Zertal describes it, had already begun in the conflict of 1948, when the Zionists' Palestinian adversaries were frequently associated with the Germans. This rhetoric, with Nasser repeatedly equated with Hitler, intensified during and after the Eichmann trial and in the years leading up to the 1967 Six-Day War between Israel and its Arab neighbours (Zertal 2000, 2005: 91–127). Since the 1960s, Holocaust memory has been central to Israeli national consciousness. Yad Vashem, the national Holocaust memorial, museum and research centre on the outskirts of Jerusalem, has continually expanded since it first opened (for research in 1957, with a museum added in 1961). It is now the most visited museum in Israel, and a fixture on the itinerary of foreign dignitaries, offering a detailed and emotionally powerful encounter with the Nazi slaughter, culminating with the evocation of the Zionist state as the source of final transcendence and redemption (Hansen-Glucklich 2014: 57–75). No longer a source of shame, the Holocaust has become the linchpin of Israel's collective self-understanding and global self-representation as a country that is, in a unique sense, existentially vulnerable and imbued with moral indispensability and political purpose as a final refuge for a persecuted people.

In the United States, even more important than the impact of the Eichmann trial was the increased interest in the Holocaust among American Jews in the aftermath the 1967 war, which Israel won spectacularly. After 1967 there was a resurgence of American Jewish cultural confidence, in which an intensified identification with both Israel and the Holocaust played a central role. Changing domestic concerns were the key motor for this change. By the late 1960s the successful assimilation of Jews into the American mainstream, so eagerly sought in the 1950s, was causing alarm among many community leaders, who saw declining religious observance and very high rates of intermarriage as ominous for the Jewish future. After 1967 Israel became the focus of a more accessible form of Jewish engagement and expression, providing a source of pride, and, particularly at times such as 1973, when Israel managed to hold its territorial gains after a surprise attack by Egypt and Syria, anxious preoccupation. The memory of the Holocaust morally underwrote the argument for Zionism, and as such was inseparable from it. Additionally, the rise of ethnic consciousness during the 1960s, and, at the end of the decade, the fraying of what had been a strong bond of solidarity between blacks and progressive Jews in the early civil rights movement, contributed to a changed cultural environment in which the Holocaust took on a new significance. As the legacy of slavery was more clearly asserted by African Americans, white ethnic groups looked back, to some degree competitively, to their own memories of suffering in the Old World. For American Jews, the Holocaust placed their history at the fore of moral thinking about the past, and in the measurement of its horrors (Novick 1999: 127–203; Mintz 2001: 11–16).

In 1978, in response to the increased interest among American Jews in the Nazi atrocity over the previous decade, President Carter established a special commission charged with developing ideas for a major national memorial to the victims of the Holocaust. The debates that ensued were tense and at times vociferous, particularly over how to find the appropriate balance between commemorating the Jewish dead and incorporating broader conceptions of the scope and signifi-cance of the slaughter (Lilenthal 2001: 20–56). Nonetheless, when the United States Holocaust Memorial Museum (USHHM) opened in 1993 in a prominent site just off the Mall in the heart of Washington, DC, it quickly established itself as one of the most-visited educational and tourist sites in the nation's capital. As an institution supported by the federal government, the USHHM placed the Holocaust in the front tier of official national memory, blurring the boundary between 'America' and 'the World' in a hitherto unprecedented way. This has given rise to complex debates about the appropriate place in American memory, relative to the Holocaust, both of other episodes of mass violence around the world, and of the atrocities perpetrated on American soil. The histories of slavery and of the genocide of Native Americans found their place in Washington's museum core considerably later, and more mutedly.[2] In contrast to these two cases, at the USHHM Americans figure most prominently in a positive light, as uniformed liberators of the death camps (Bartov 1997: 70–5; Cole 2000: 146–71; Hansen-Glucklich 2014: 75–84).

By the late 1990s there were more than 100 museums and other institutions in North America dedicated to public Holocaust education (Rosenfeld 1997: 137–8). During the period between the end of the Cold War and the attacks of 9/11 there briefly flourished an optimistic belief that a peaceful and consensual 'end of history' might be within reach, with the United States serving as the benign policeman of a broadly cooperative liberal capitalist world order. This rose-tinted view of the future inflected the 1990s boom in American Holocaust memory, in which the US role in defeating Nazi Germany readily stood as the cornerstone of a moral vision of the lone superpower's place in the world. Some also criticized other aspects of the 'Americanization of the Holocaust', including the tendency to commercialize or sentimentalize the event, presenting it through slick and simplistically uplifting narratives. The most notable example of this was Steven Spielberg's *Schindler's List*, Hollywood's first major engage-ment with the Holocaust. This film met with mixed and internationally varied responses, but achieved considerable box office and critical success, winning seven Oscars in 1994 (Loshitzky 1997; Flanzbaum 1999; Novick 1999: 207–81; Cole 2000: 73–94, 172–88).

In Europe public attention was slower to focus on the Holocaust. The upheavals of the post-war years, and the ruptures and fears generated by the Cold War, to a large extent buried wartime memories, which most European populations were keen to leave behind. Surviving Jewish communities in Europe were in most places extremely reduced in numbers, and traumatized by their collective experiences. Even in countries not occupied by the Nazis, such as Sweden and Britain, Jewish communities were not very visible in the post-war years, and by the 1970s were greatly outnumbered by other ethnic minorities. In West Germany the focus in this period was on how to come to terms with the Nazi past, with liberals investing their hopes in the redemptive power of the republican procedures and institutions of the federal state, and controversy often hinging on the extent to which those who had been complicit with the Nazi regime could be nonetheless integrated into the reconstituted life of the nation (Moses 2007: 74–218). The Holocaust was not at the fore of these debates. In both East and West Germany engagement with the fate of the Jews was largely superficial, and was subordinated to the rival ideological frameworks that structured the economies and cultures of the two states (Herf 1997: 106–333; Sharples 2016).

Only in the second half of the 1980s, not long before the fall of the Berlin Wall, did the Holocaust emerge as the focus of a sustained public debate in West Germany. The complex *Historikerstreit* ('Historians' Quarrel') was triggered by President Reagan's visit to the German military cemetery at Bitburg, which included the graves of a number of troops from the Wafffen-SS, the elite military unit particularly closely linked with Nazi war crimes. The controversy hinged on whether the Holocaust, and other Nazi crimes, could be compared to those by other totalitarian regimes and even understood as a defensive reaction to Stalin's brutality, or, as the more left-wing side in the debate insisted, those arguments amounted to a dangerous attempt to whitewash recent German history. Reflecting on the debate, the German Jewish historian Dan Diner argued influentially that Germans and Jews remained locked in a 'negative symbiosis'. In contrast with the cultural flourishing of German Jewry in the late nineteenth and early twentieth centuries, widely idealized as a positive 'German Jewish symbiosis', Jews and Germans since Auschwitz remained negatively entwined, Diner argued, with their identities inescapably defined in relationship with each other (Diner 1990; see also Maier 1988; Moses 2007: 219–228).

In Poland, where three million non-Jewish citizens as well as three million Polish Jews (approximately 90 per cent of the pre-war total) were killed during the Holocaust, complex and traumatic memories were submerged within the ideological framework of the post-war communist state. In the official historical account of that regime, Jewish deaths were not remembered as a distinct category, but were subsumed within the totality of national Polish victimhood at the hands of the Nazis. In 1968, seeking to deflect pressure for reforms from a student protest movement, the communist government mobilized this deeply rooted nationalist narrative of the primacy of Polish suffering, declaring itself the victim of a 'Zionist plot' instigated by agents of West Germany and Israel. Approximately 20,000 Jews were expelled from Poland, leaving only a tiny community behind (Steinlauf 1997: 62–88). Discussion of the Jewish past opened up tentatively during the 1980s, and when communism collapsed in 1989 the clash between the dominant memories of Jews and Poles leapt to the fore of public controversy. In July of that year, the newly free Polish press was fascinated and outraged by the high-profile attempt of rabbi from New York to uproot a large cross that stood before a Carmelite convent at Auschwitz. Supporters of the rabbi were deeply offended by the presence of a Christian cross towering over this site of Jewish extermination, while for many Catholic Poles his protest was an unacceptable and alien intrusion into a religious sanctuary (Steinlauf 1997: 122–44).

Polish confrontation with the past has been more recently spurred by the work of the historian Jan Gross, whose book *Neighbours* (2001) explores in detail the massacre in July 1941 of the Jews of the Polish village of Jedwabne by their non-Jewish civilian neighbours. Drawing attention to the role of ordinary Poles in the Holocaust, Gross's work has posed challenging questions about Polish antisemitism and selective memory, and continues to provoke intense debate and controversy (Gross 2001; Zimmerman 2003; Polonsky and Michlic 2004). Although there is broad agreement among scholars, in Poland and elsewhere, on the history of the Holocaust in its geographical heartland, the communication of this consensus to public audiences, in Poland and also internationally, remains challenging (Engel 2009).

Public controversy over who should bear responsibility for the Holocaust has also raged elsewhere, most notably in response to the Harvard scholar Daniel Goldhagen's *Hitler's Willing Executioners* (1996), which ascribed the Holocaust to the deep-seated and age-old 'eliminationist antisemitism' of most ordinary Germans. Although widely critiqued by historians as simplistic or worse, Goldhagen's book was a major public success, particularly in Germany, where his argument seemed to resonate with the anxieties and generational conflicts of the newly reunified nation (Eley 2000). By the early years of the new millennium the remembrance of the Holocaust was highly institutionalized across the Western world, with interest spreading also in countries with little or no historical Jewish settlement. The enshrining of the Holocaust as a cornerstone of twenty-first-century global historical memory is emblematized by the United Nations designation, since 2005, of 27 January – the anniversary of the liberation of Auschwitz – as 'International Holocaust Memorial Day'. In the UK this memorial date had already been established in 2001, though scholars of the Holocaust were divided on whether this would be helpful, and the annual commemorative events have in some years been the focus of controversy over the extent to which other genocides and killings should also be recognized (Cesarani 2000; Stone 2000; Pearce 2014: 133–64). Does this annual jostling and ceremonial suggest a routinization of Holocaust memory in the early twenty-first century? The attacks of 11 September 2001 created a new 'anchor event' of modern atrocity, while the passing away of the final survivors of the Nazi death camps also marks a significant transitional phase. However, public and scholarly interest in the Holocaust shows no sign of dimming. The Nazi genocide continues to spur new reflections and debates, and is today as crucial a point of reference as ever.

Thinking through the Holocaust

Is the Holocaust unique? When are comparisons with other mass killings appropriate and illuminating, and when are they illegitimate? These issues have been hotly contested, particularly in the 1990s, when the argument that the slaughter of European Jewry should be treated as an exceptional event, essentially beyond comparison, was attacked by, among others, scholars of the Armenian, Gypsy, and Native American genocides (Rosenbaum 1996). The Ottoman extermination of over a million Armenians and other Christian minorities in Turkey during and after the First World War in many ways foreshadowed the Nazi extermination of Jews during the Second World War, while the killing of close to a million people, mostly ethnic Tutsis, in Rwanda in 1994 was conducted at a rate many times faster than the Holocaust, and with a much higher level of civilian participation. All significant events are in some way unique, but it seems clear, at least to experts on genocide, that there is no key dimension of analysis according to which the Jewish Holocaust stands alone (Jones 2011: 254–5). Only Jews were targeted by the Nazis for thorough elimination – but the Roma (Gypsies) of Europe were also subjected to genocidal killing. Over the past two decades, as the field of genocide studies has burgeoned, comparison has been recognized as an extremely valuable interpretive tool, and insights developed by scholars of the Holocaust have been widely used to illuminate other genocides. However, the unique prominence of the Holocaust across the world has at times impeded these comparisons and cross-fertilizations, as many other genocides struggle to reach an equivalent level of recognition and attention. Comparisons with the Holocaust often meet with resistance, and in public debate they can be highly charged and sensitive.

Within European history the study of the Holocaust has produced a trans-formative jolt in how we think about the recent past (Stone 2003). This slaughter emerged in the heart of Europe, from a country intimately associated with the continent's high culture and Enlightenment values. For the sociologist Zygmunt Bauman, the Holocaust must be understood not as an atavistic rejection of modernity (as many interpreters of Nazism have insisted), but as a product of modernity, enabled by its bureaucratic systems and its ordering mentality, according to which the Jews could readily be seen as an intrusion in the European garden of nations, and therefore due for efficient 'weeding' (Bauman 1989: 88–93). Taking in a sense the opposite view, the historian Dan Diner has emphasized the unfathomable irrationality of the Nazi slaughter, which was pursued even at the expense of the German war effort. This irrationality, he argues, presents us with a historical 'limit case', testing the boundaries of the explicability of human behaviour (Diner 2000: 117–37). The usual rules of conduct in the writing of history – to be as detached and objective as possible – have also been challenged by the moral weight and visceral horror of this particular subject matter. In many ways and to a unique extent, reflection on the Holocaust has prompted profound questioning about the shape, meaning and methodologies of history.

In the spring of 2000 some of these questions made front-page news, as international attention was focused on a court case at London's Old Bailey ubiquitously but inaccurately referred to as 'the Irving trial'. The primary defendant in this case was in fact the American historian Deborah Lipstadt, the recent author of an academic study on Holocaust denial in which she had exposed, as a leading example of this phenomenon, the lies and distortions circulated by the British author David Irving (Lipstadt 1993). Claiming that his reputation as a historian had been besmirched, Irving sued Lipstadt and her publisher for libel. Although he had very few supporters, the outcome of the ensuing trial was highly uncertain, because according to British libel law the burden of proof was on the defendants to demonstrate that the allegations made against him were true, and that Irving had deliberately and indefensibly twisted historical evidence in order to exonerate Hitler, in keeping with his antisemitic and neo-fascist beliefs. After a forensic courtroom dissection of Irving's work by the leading historian Richard J. Evans, and expert testimony from several other scholars, the judge ruled in favour of the defendants, to widespread public relief (Guttenplan 2001: 273–86).

In the eyes of many, the implicit defendant at this trial was the writing of history itself, as a practice capable of distinguishing clearly between truths and falsehoods. This was certainly the view of both Evans and Lipstadt, who depicted the trial in these terms in their published accounts of the proceedings (Evans 2001: 1–39; Lipstadt 2005). Both historians had already expressed their concerns about the rise of postmodernism, which they, along with a good number of their colleagues, regarded as a dangerously relativist perspective that imperilled the empirical craft of the historian. For Lipstadt, the popularity of postmodern theory, which she saw as casting into question all absolute truths, had contributed to the creation of a climate conducive to Holocaust denial (Lipstadt 1993: 7, 215–19). These arguments placed the trial on the frontline of one of the most vociferous intellectual battles of the turn of the millennium, with some of their supporters casting Evans and Lipstadt as the defenders not just of the accurate representation of the Holocaust but of our belief in truth itself.

The key challenge of the Holocaust to the practice of history is that it poses with particular acuity two demands that are in tension with each other. On the one hand, the empirical truth of these events must be established in full detail – particularly in the face of attempts to deny those facts. However, the enormity of genocide also demands a response beyond the facts: an ethical response, and perhaps also an emotional one. A cool and disengaged response to the Nazi genocide is almost impossible, and approaching it in this way, strictly according to the norms of empirical history, seems both banal and morally inadequate (Ankersmit 2001: 176–98). There is no straightforward way to integrate the demand for factual mastery and comprehension with the equally compelling demand for a human, non-analytical response to mass murder that does not reach resolution through empirical knowledge. The web of ideas described as 'postmodern' can usefully be considered as tools for thinking through these issues – and it is therefore not surprising that the Holocaust has figured very prominently in postmodern thought (Eaglestone 2005). These debates do not, though, undermine the basic distinctions between sense and nonsense, or between honesty and deception, which, in the case of David Irving, Richard Evans and other historians were able to establish very clearly (Guttenplan 2001: 217–34). Rather than demonstrating the need for historiography to be straightforwardly empirical, then, the issue of Holocaust denial more profoundly highlights the complexity of our responses to genocide, as historians, individuals and societies (Eaglestone 2001).

In 2006 Irving himself stood trial in Austria, and was sentenced to three years imprisonment for Holocaust denial, which in many European countries is illegal. These laws mark the exceptional status of the Holocaust in European collective memory. However, like Holocaust Memorial Day, they have also sometimes become a focus for the contestation of that status. The enshrining of the Holocaust as an event demanding unique treatment in public life inevitably generates unwelcome controversies, as the existence of particular rituals and taboos tempt some to challenge and transgress them. These official structures of Holocaust memory may also be problematic for another reason: by providing the reassurance of a 'correct' mode of remembrance, they can inhibit more profound and unsettling reflection. The orchestration of sentimental tears can lead, according to the philosopher Gillian Rose, to a too-easy 'Holocaust piety', in which the mystification of the Nazi genocide, and the catharsis provided by stage-managed representations and commemorations of it, distances us from the event, and protects us from asking harder questions about its relationship to the world in which we live today (Rose 1998). Visitors entering the USHHM, for example, are given an 'identity card' booklet of a potential Holocaust victim of their own gender, the pages of which they are invited to turn as they progress through the exhibition, discovering that person's fate at each stage (ultimately, just over 50 per cent survive). This device has been very popular with museum visitors, but it has been critiqued for focusing on identification with victims, rather than inviting more challenging reflections on our human similarity to Holocaust bystanders and even to perpetrators (Cole 2000: 161–4; Lilenthal 2001: 187, 304–5).

The appropriateness or otherwise of particular responses, and the strategies used to guide these responses, is a central concern for those who present the Holocaust to students or to the public. In recent decades Holocaust education has developed into a significant field in its own right, with its own scholarly literature, training courses and methodological debates (Totten and Feinberg 2016). The desire to draw usable lessons from the past is, as noted at the start of this chapter, the core motivation of public and pedagogical encounters with this historical episode. Many if not most visitors to Holocaust museums, monuments and atrocity sites around the world hope that in some way their experience will improve them as people, and so contribute to the building of a world in which a similar horror is less likely to recur. The importance of memory as an abstracted amulet protecting against repetition is often endorsed through reference to the famous 1939 quotation from Adolf Hitler: 'Who talks nowadays of the annihilation of the Armenians?' (Jones 2011: 149–50). History, however, does not provide us with unambiguous guidelines or alerts for the future. The question of how to memorialize and publicly present the Holocaust, without reducing the event to overly simple messages, has prompted extremely probing reflection on the nature, potential and pitfalls of public memory.

This challenge has been faced most succinctly in the design of public memorials to the Holocaust. The traditional architectural idiom of imposing columns, arches and plaques has generally seemed inadequate to this task. There has therefore been a search for a new visual language that is appropriate to the enormity of the event, elicits a response that is both reflective and powerful, and is meaningful to a wide range of different constituencies. This search has been particularly probing in Germany, where the traces and absences left by the Nazi exterminations must be rendered visible amid the particularly complicated layering of earlier and later German history. Reacting against the tendency of official monuments to be politically consoling or cathartic, artists and architects in Germany have sought to design monuments that are persistently provocative and unsettling. In contrast to the monumental bombast of the Nazis and their forerunners, numerous 'counter-monuments' to the Holocaust have been constructed in Germany. These urban interventions irrupt unexpectedly into the urban fabric and create a jarring clash with everyday normality: a striking example is the posting, in a residential neighbourhood of Berlin, of excerpts from antisemitic Nazi laws restricting, for example, the hours during which Jews could shop or the park benches on which they could sit (see Figure 12.1) (Young 1993: 27–48, 2000: 90–151). Following

Figure 12.1 Sign near the Bayerischer Platz, Berlin: 'Jews must hand in their radio sets. 23.9.1938'. Photograph courtesy of Anna Maerker, 2017.

Figure 12.2 Memorial to the Murdered Jews of Europe, Berlin, with the dome of the Reichstag in the background. Photograph courtesy of Anna Maerker, 2017.

the reunification of Germany in 1990, and the decision to re-establish Berlin as its capital, there was a protracted debate over how the Holocaust should be memorialized in the reconstructed core of the city. The chosen design, consisting of over 2,500 concrete slabs on a very large site in the central governmental and tourist district, is in a sense also a counter-monument, in that it is offers no readily legible cues to guide the responses of the visitor. The unsettling openness of the site is fundamental to its power as a memorial (see Figure 12.2) (Young 2000: 184–223; Dekel 2009).

The Nazi concentration and extermination camps themselves are today the most morally freighted *lieux de mémoire* in Europe. Whereas Pierre Nora conceived this concept to designate sites of significance in the heritage of a national community (in his own work, France), Auschwitz and the other major camps are sites of transnational and transcultural memory par excellence. The camps have different meanings for different constituencies and national identities: in Israel they play a central role, with a group trip to the death camps in Poland a standard and highly emotive rite of passage for teenagers (Feldman 2008). The long and rich history of Jewish life in Poland, and its modest revival in recent decades, remains overshadowed by these locations. This poses the challenge of how to hold alongside the death camps the non-mournful memory of Polish Jewish history and attention to its continuance in the present and future (Lehrer 2013: 54–90). Each site of mass death also poses particular challenges to curators and visitors, relating to issues such as the superimposition of different episodes of violence on the same site, or the surrounding and sometimes the covering of zones of horror by the regeneration of the natural landscape (Rapson 2015: 6–12).

Textual and psychological reflections on the Holocaust have been no less fertile than those relating to space. A great deal of attention has been given to the highly varied and sometimes searing testimony of Holocaust survivors, and to the interpretive challenges posed by this material. The recounting of memories always combines empirical recall with feelings and forgetting. This mixture is often particularly complicated in the case of survivors, whose traumatic experiences may well have transformed their most intimate sense of self and worldview, and therefore also the very fabric of their written and oral testimony (Langer 1991; LaCapra 2001: 86–113). The brittleness of these memories – with their varied uncertainty, incompleteness, rawness, and psychological after-effects – is often transmitted to the next generation, and even beyond. The inheritance of traumatic memories by the children of Holocaust survivors has been influentially theorized by Marianne Hersch as 'postmemory' – a concept that has been widely extended and used in other contexts (Hirsch 1996). The Holocaust has also stimulated a wider interest in psychological approaches to the past, in particular to understand the actions and mindsets of perpetrators and bystanders (Hughes 2015).

All these areas of inquiry have provided considerable stimulus to historians of other atrocities and genocides, who have faced similar interpretive challenges, and have often found concepts first developed in relation to the Holocaust, such as 'postmemory', extremely useful. More broadly, the Holocaust can at times usefully function as a 'screen memory' onto which other historical traumas can be projected. This process, the literary critic Michael Rothberg has influentially argued, often productively facilitates the discussion of other episodes of mass violence, including those of colonialism and slavery (Rothberg 2009: 1–29). It is certainly the case that remembrance is not a zero-sum contest. However, despite these cross-fertilizations, it remains the case that memories can and do compete with each other for attention and identification, and also for public funding and support. This competitive element is particularly important in relation to the politics of memory, as the past is persistently marshalled in support of particular perspectives and causes in the present. The intense engagement in Europe and North America since the end of the Cold War with the history and legacies of the Holocaust has been enormously intellectually fecund. However, these debates must also be situated in their historical context, taking full account also of the political role of Holocaust discourse, both in the second half of the twentieth century and in the recent past up to the present.

The Holocaust today

Our new millennium has been characterized by a strong desire in Europe and other Western countries to enshrine a common understanding of the lessons learned from the Nazi atrocity. This commitment animated the prominent Stockholm International Forum on the Holocaust in January 2000, which established high-level intergovernmental cooperation in Holocaust education, remembrance and research. Its culminating 'Stockholm Declaration' affirmed the participants' 'commitment to plant the seeds of a better future amidst the soil of a bitter past'. This eight-point statement is the foundational text of the International Holocaust Remembrance Alliance, which was founded in 1998 and currently has 31 member states (Allwork 2015).[3] There has also been an attempt, in part in response to the institutionalization of the Holocaust also beyond the West, to rethink the significance of its remembrance at a global level. For the sociologists Daniel Levy and Natan Sznaider, the Holocaust is central to a new 'cosmopolitan memory', dissolving the significance of nation-state borders. In an unprecedentedly complicated and seemingly unstable world, they see the moralized memory of the Holocaust as key to the establishment of new connections and solidarities, in response to 'the need for a moral touchstone in an age of uncertainty' (Levy and Sznaider 2006: 18). In a similar vein, the cultural anthropologist Sharon Macdonald has argued that the Holocaust today provides a cosmopolitan 'moral forum', while according to the social theorist Helmut Dubiel the Holocaust has become the foundation for a globally transnational political ethic of solidarity (Macdonald 2013: 188–215; Dubiel 2003).

How well founded is this optimism? It is far from clear that the memory of the Holocaust has strengthened internationalist engagement in the recent past. According to Samantha Power – at the time an academic, and later elevated to serve as President Obama's ambassador to the United Nations – debates in the United States about whether to intervene in the conflict in Bosnia (1992–5) repeatedly invoked the Holocaust not as a spur but as a brake to action, on the grounds that massacres by Serbs, although deplorable, were not comparable to the Nazi genocide (Power 2002: 247–328). In 1994 – the year of *Schindler's List*'s Oscar triumph, when Holocaust consciousness was surging in Europe and North America – there was no meaningful mobilization to prevent the slaughter in Rwanda. Despite the widespread desire for lessons from the Holocaust to be drawn and applied in other contexts, this aspiration does not seem to have been achieved in practice.

Nowhere is the rhetorical use of the Holocaust more inflamed and pervasive than in the Israeli–Palestinian conflict. This has been incisively analysed by Avraham Burg, a former Speaker of the Knesset and now one of the most prominent voices on the Israeli left, in his pointedly titled book *The Holocaust is Over*. The memory of the Holocaust, and the fears and aggressions incited by its place in Israeli politics, is, Burg has argued, a key barrier to the establishment of a lasting peace in the Middle East (Burg 2008: 11–26, 201–42). The Holocaust is repeatedly drawn into the politics of the region and of the conflict in emotive and instrumental ways. To cite just two recent examples: there was widespread outrage when, in October 2015, the Israeli Prime Minister Benjamin Netanyahu falsely claimed that the genocide of the Jews was first suggested to Hitler by the Palestinian Grand Mufti of Jerusalem, and again the following month when he linked European Union policies on the labelling of products from West Bank settlements with the Nazi persecution of Jews.[4]

Palestinian collective memory has also been profoundly influenced by the Holocaust. As the historian Gilbert Achcar has shown, the dispossession of 1948 – the *Nakhba* – was shaped in Palestinian consciousness, against a backdrop of continual conflict with Israel over land and resources, as 'our Holocaust' (Achcar 2010: 220–31). This has been condemned by some as an appropriation of Jewish memory. Thinking within Rothberg's paradigm, however, it is just one example of the 'multidirectional memory' phenomenon. The memory of the Holocaust has been repeatedly drawn into the propaganda war that is an increasingly bitter and keenly contested aspect of the Israeli–Palestinian conflict. This tussle is debated intensely across the world, and in this millennium it has become enmeshed with an even more charged debate: the antagonism, in the eyes of some, between supposedly 'Western' values and those ascribed to Islam. The elevation of Holocaust memory as central to cosmopolitan citizenship is often extremely problematic in this context, as those who do not express themselves in accordance with its norms are then readily deemed to be lacking in, and possibly impervious to, the required standards of historical sensitivity and civility. Confusion and ignorance over aspects of the past, including the Holocaust, will never be entirely banished – and, more specifically, receptivity to Jewish victimhood at the hands of the Nazis is likely sometimes to be diminished among those who identify closely with the suffering of Palestinians, and feel that this suffering is not also given due recognition. For Muslim communities in the West particularly, the unwillingness of majority non-Muslim opinion to recognize these factors is exacerbating a widespread sense of cultural marginalization.

In his recent book *Lessons of the Holocaust*, the distinguished Holocaust historian Michael Marrus has given voice to a widespread fatigue with pedagogical optimism, asserting that the 'principal lesson of the Holocaust is . . . beware of lessons' (Marrus 2016: 160). He emphasizes the traditional historians' task of 'getting it right', and argues for a renewed emphasis on empirical accuracy as a bulwark against what he regards as the sometimes hasty, inappropriate or glib tendency to draw moral lessons from the Nazi genocide. In contrast, the prominent Yale historian Timothy Snyder has in his latest book extended the admonitory power of the Holocaust to new terrain. Snyder argues that the Nazis' expansionist and exterminatory policies were driven by a fear that Germany would lose out in a battle with its imperial rivals for scarce resources, and that this provides us with a stark warning of what might ensue if we fail to correct our current path towards environmental catastrophe (Snyder 2015: 319–43). There are temptations for historians both in staying above the fray and in maximizing the public impact and resonance of their work. However, there are dangers in both strategies. Freighting the Holocaust with continually renewable and adaptable moral meaning can induce scepticism, and can also over-sacralize the event, reinforcing its separation from the general course of history. If historians retreat from debates over the significance of the Holocaust, though, they will leave open terrain for others to project their own possibly tendentious or dangerous interpretations.

The stakes here are too high for scholars to stand aloof from the uses that are made of their work.

Far from becoming the moral focus for a transnational and cosmopolitan solidaristic consensus, the politics of Holocaust memory seem if anything to be more contested than ever. Past controversies at the national level continue to resonate, particularly in Germany (Port 2017). At the same time, thinking about the Holocaust is now increasingly international, and complicatedly interwoven with the wider controversies of our time: not only the unresolved conflict between Israelis and Palestinians, but also the sometimes adversarial assessment of antisemitism and Islamophobia as social and political problems, and the broad relationship of the West to the rest of the world. For some the pervasive invocation of the Holocaust today serves mainly to reinforce Western smugness and arrogance: according to Enzo Traverso it serves as a 'civil religion' according to which Western democracies measure their moral virtues and judge those of other states (Traverso 2016: 113). In contrast, others fear that the memory of the Holocaust has been weakened because it has become so ubiquitous. Alvin Rosenfeld has lamented 'the domestication of the Holocaust', which he fears is diminishing the collective sense of outrage in response to it, and may even be leading us toward the possibility of 'a second Holocaust' against Israel (Rosenfeld 2011: 12, 271–80).

Holocaust memory remains an extraordinarily rich resource of nuanced thinking and excellent scholarship, with the potential to be a major resource for valuable reflection and learning. However, it will only fulfil its pedagogic potential in our globalized world if it is approached in a context that is attentive to the varied perspectives of different communities, and confronts with honesty the challenges and controversies that are inherent to this subject. Sensitive explorations of difficult collective memories must always be attentive to the raw emotions these may still nourish in the present. They must also consider the complex contestations between competing perspectives on the past, and the impact upon this of material differences of power between adversarial groups both in the past and the present (Moses 2011; Moses and Rothberg 2014). These factors are all highly applicable in this case. The memory of Holocaust has always been, and remains, political. Any serious engagement with the topic must recognize this, and consider carefully the various contexts that have shaped our changing perspectives on the genocide over the past seventy years. We must also consider the political context of the present, in which we are actors.

Guide to further reading and online resources

The literature on the Holocaust, and its representation and remembrance, is immense. The best brief historical overview of the genocide remains Marrus (1987), while two useful readers are helpful starting points: Gigliotti and Lang (2005) is strong on the event itself, while Levi and Rothberg (2003) offers an excellent range of extracts from key theoretical readings. The commissioned essays by experts in Stone (2004) offer an incisive overview of the historiography of the Holocaust up to that date.

Novick (1999) is a key study of American Holocaust memory, which prompted much debate. More recent books by Zertal (2005), Pearce (2014) and Sharples (2016) offer thoughtful overviews for Israel, the United Kingdom and Germany respectively. The work of Young (1993 and 2000) is foundational on Holocaust memorials, while the seminal essay by Hirsch (1996) introduces the concept of 'postmemory'. Rothberg (2009) has been extremely influential on recent comparative and transnational work on Holocaust memory, while Snyder (2015) and Marrus (2016) offer contrasting and strongly argued perspectives that bring the debate up to the present.

There is a wealth of online material available at the websites of the leading museums and memorials dedicated to the Holocaust around the world. An extensive but incomplete global database of institutions of Holocaust memory can be found at www.memorial-museums.net

The most useful websites are those of:

Yad Vashem, in Jerusalem: www.yadvashem.org.il

The United States Holocaust Memorial Museum, in Washington, DC: www.ushmm.org

Memorial to the Murdered Jews of Europe, in Berlin: www.holocaust-mahnmal.de/en

Auschwitz-Birkenau Memorial and Museum, in Poland: www.auschwitz.org/en/

Holocaust Memorial Day Trust, in the UK: www.hmd.org.uk

Notes

1 Florida Statute 1003.42, section 1 (g), available at the 'Online Sunshine' website: www.state.fl.us.
2 The Smithsonian National Museum of African American History & Culture was opened by President Obama in September 2016: https://nmaahc.si.edu.
3 Further information, including the full text of the Stockholm Declaration, is available at the organization's website: www.holocaustremembrance.com.
4 'Anger at Netanyahu Claim Palestinian Grand Mufti Inspired Holocaust', *Guardian*, 21 October 2015; 'E.U. Move to Label Israeli Settlement Goods Strains Ties', *New York Times*, 11 November 2015; 'EU Envoy: Comparing Labeling to Holocaust Cheapens Memory', *Times of Israel*, 18 November 2015.

References

Achcar, Gilbert (2010) *The Arabs and the Holocaust: The Arab–Israeli War of Narratives*. London: Saqi.
Allwork, Larissa (2015) *Holocaust Remembrance between the National and the Transnational: The Stockholm International Forum and the First Decade of the International Task Force*. London: Bloomsbury.
Ankersmit, F. R. (2001) *Historical Representation*. Stanford, CA: Stanford University Press.
Arendt, Hannah (1963) *Eichmann in Jerusalem: A Report on the Banality of Evil*. New York: Viking.

Bartov, Omer (1997) 'Chambers of Horror: Holocaust Museums in Israel and the United States', *Israel Studies* 2: 66–87.

Bauman, Zygmunt (1989) *Modernity and the Holocaust*. Cambridge: Polity.

Bloxham, Donald (2001) *Genocide on Trial: War Crimes Trials and the Formation of Holocaust History and Memory*. Oxford: Oxford University Press.

Burg, Avraham (2008) *The Holocaust is Over: We Must Rise from its Ashes*. Basingstoke: Palgrave Macmillan.

Cesarani, David (2000) 'Seizing the Day: Why Britain Will Benefit from Holocaust Memorial Day', *Patterns of Prejudice* 34: 61–6.

Cesarani, David (2004) *Eichmann: His Life and Crimes*. London: Heinemann.

Cesarani, David, and Eric J. Sundquist (2012) *After the Holocaust: Challenging the Myth of Silence*. Abingdon: Routledge.

Cole, Tim (2000) *Selling the Holocaust: From Auschwitz to Schindler, How History is Bought, Packaged and Sold*. New York: Routledge.

Dekel, Irit (2009) 'Ways of Looking: Observation and Transformation at the Holocaust Memorial, Berlin', *Memory Studies* 2: 71–86.

Diner, Dan (1990) 'Negative Symbiosis: Germans and Jews After Auschwitz', in Peter Baldwin (ed.), *Reworking the Past: Hitler, the Holocaust and the Historians' Debate*. Boston: Beacon Press, 251–61.

Diner, Dan (2000) *Beyond the Conceivable: Studies on Germany, Nazism and the Holocaust*. Berkeley, CA: University of California Press.

Dubiel, Helmut (2003) 'The Remembrance of the Holocaust as a Catalyst for a Transnational Ethic?', *New German Critique* 90: 59–70.

Eaglestone, Robert (2001) *Postmodernism and Holocaust Denial*. Cambridge: Icon.

Eaglestone, Robert (2005) *The Holocaust and the Postmodern*. Oxford: Oxford University Press.

Eley, Geoff (ed.) (2000) *The "Goldhagen Effect": History, Memory, Nazism – Facing the German Past*. Ann Arbor, MI: University of Michigan Press.

Engel, David (2009) 'On Reconciling the Histories of Two Chosen Peoples', *American Historical Review* 114: 914–29.

Evans, Richard J. (2001) *Lying about Hitler: History, Holocaust and the Irving Trial*. New York: Basic Books.

Feldman, Jackie (2008) *Above the Death Pits: Beneath the Flag: Youth Voyages to Poland and the Performance of Israeli National Identity*. New York: Berghahn.

Flanzbaum, Hilene (ed.) (1999) *The Americanization of the Holocaust*. Baltimore, MD: Johns Hopkins University Press.

Gigliotti, Simone, and Berel Lang (eds) (2005) *The Holocaust: A Reader*. Oxford: Blackwell.

Gross, Jan (2001) *Neighbors: The Destruction of the Jewish Community in Jedwabne, Poland*. Princeton, NJ: Princeton University Press.

Guttenplan, D. D. (2001) *The Holocaust on Trial*. London: Granta.

Hansen-Glucklich, Jennifer (2014) *Holocaust Memory Reframed: Museums and the Challenges of Representation*. New Brunswick, NJ: Rutgers University Press.

Herf, Jeffrey (1997) *Divided Memory: The Nazi Past in the Two Germanys*. Cambridge, MA: Harvard University Press.

Heuman, Johannes (2015) *The Holocaust and French Historical Culture, 1945–65*. Basingstoke: Palgrave Macmillan.

Hilberg, Raul (1996) *The Politics of Memory: The Journey of a Holocaust Historian*. Chicago: Ivan R. Dee.

Hirsch, Marianne (1996) 'Past Lives: Postmemories in Exile', *Poetics Today* 17: 659–86.

Hughes, Judith M (2015) *The Holocaust and the Revival of Psychological History.* New York: Cambridge University Press.

Jones, Adam (2011) *Genocide: A Comprehensive Introduction*, 2nd edn. Abingdon: Routledge.

Kushner, Tony (1994) *The Holocaust and the Liberal Imagination.* Oxford: Blackwell.

LaCapra, Dominick (2001) *Writing History, Writing Trauma.* Baltimore, MD: Johns Hopkins University Press.

Langer, Lawrence L. (1991) *Holocaust Testimonies: The Ruins of Memory.* New Haven, CT: Yale University Press.

Lehrer, Erica T. (2013) *Jewish Poland Revisited: Heritage Tourism in Unquiet Places.* Bloomington, IN: Indiana University Press.

Levi, Neil, and Michael Rothberg (eds) (2003) *The Holocaust: Theoretical Readings.* Edinburgh: Edinburgh University Press.

Levy, Daniel, and Natan Sznaider (2006) *The Holocaust and Memory in the Global Age.* Philadelphia, PA: Temple University Press.

Lilenthal, Edward T. (2001) *Preserving Memory: The Struggle to Create America's Holocaust Museum.* New York: Columbia University Press.

Lipstadt, Deborah E. (1993) *Denying the Holocaust: The Growing Assault on Truth and Memory.* London: Penguin.

Lipstadt, Deborah E. (2005) *History on Trial: My Day in Court with a Holocaust Denier.* New York: HarperCollins.

Loshitzky, Yosefa (ed.) (1997) *Spielberg's Holocaust: Critical Perspectives on "Schindler's List".* Bloomington, IN: Indiana University Press.

Macdonald, Sharon (2013) *Memorylands: Heritage and Identity in Europe Today.* London: Routledge.

Maier, Charles (1988) *The Unmasterable Past: History, Holocaust and German National Identity.* Cambridge, MA: Harvard University Press.

Marrus, Michael R. (1987) *The Holocaust in History.* London: Penguin.

Marrus, Michael R. (2016) *Lessons of the Holocaust.* Toronto: University of Toronto Press.

Mintz, Alan (2001) *Popular Culture and the Shaping of Holocaust Memory in America.* Seattle, WA: University of Washington Press.

Moses, A. Dirk (2007) *German Intellectuals and the Nazi Past.* New York: Cambridge University Press.

Moses, A. Dirk (2011) 'Genocide and the Terror of History', *Parallax* 17: 90–108.

Moses, A. Dirk, and Michael Rothberg (2014) 'A Dialogue on the Ethics and Politics of Transcultural Memory', in Lucy Bond and Jessica Rapson (eds), *The Transcultural Turn: Interrogating Memory Between and Beyond Borders.* Berlin: De Gruyter, 29–38.

Novick, Peter (1999) *The Holocaust in American Life.* Boston: Houghton Mifflin.

Pearce, Andy (2014) *Holocaust Consciousness in Contemporary Britain.* New York: Routledge.

Polonsky, Antony, and Joanna B. Michlic (eds) (2004) *The Neighbors Respond: The Controversy over the Jedwabne Massacre in Poland.* Princeton, NJ: Princeton University Press.

Port, Andrew I (2017) 'Historical Scholarship and Politics in the Public Sphere: Reexamining the Causes, Consequences and Controversy of the *Historikerstreit* and the Goldhagen Debate: A Forum with Gerrit Dworok, Richard J. Evans, Mary Fulbrook, Wendy Lower, A. Dirk Moses, Jeffrey K. Olick, and Timothy D. Snyder', *Central European History* 50: 375–403.

Power, Samantha (2002) *A Problem from Hell: America and the Age of Genocide*. New York: Basic Books.

Rapson, Jessica (2015) *Topographies of Suffering: Buchenwald, Babi Yar, Lidice*. Oxford: Berghahn.

Rose, Gillian (1998) 'Beginnings of the Day: Fascism and Representation', in Brian Cheyette and Laura Marcus (eds), *Modernity, Culture and the Jew*. Stanford, CA: Stanford University Press, 242–56.

Rosenbaum, Alan (ed.) (1996) *Is the Holocaust Unique? Perspectives on Comparative Genocide*. Boulder, CO: Westview Press.

Rosenfeld, Alvin H. (1997) 'The Americanization of the Holocaust', in Alvin H. Rosenfeld (ed.), *Thinking About the Holocaust: After Half a Century*. Bloomington, IN: Indiana University Press, 119–50.

Rosenfeld, Alvin H. (2011) *The End of the Holocaust*. Bloomington, IN: Indiana University Press.

Rothberg, Michael (2009) *Multidirectional Memory: Remembering the Holocaust in the Age of Decolonization*. Stanford, CA: Stanford University Press.

Segev, Tom (1993) *The Seventh Million: The Israelis and the Holocaust*. New York: Hill & Wang.

Sharples, Caroline (2016) *Postwar Germany and the Holocaust*. London: Bloomsbury.

Snyder, Timothy (2010) *Bloodlands: Europe Between Hitler and Stalin*. New York: Basic Books.

Snyder, Timothy (2015) *Black Earth: The Holocaust as History and Warning*. London: Bodley Head.

Steinlauf, Michael C. (1997): *Bondage to the Dead: Poland and the Memory of the Holocaust*. Syracuse, NY: Syracuse University Press.

Stone, Dan (2000) 'Day or Remembrance or Day of Forgetting? Or, Why Britain Does Not Need a Holocaust Memorial Day', *Patterns of Prejudice* 34: 53–9.

Stone, Dan (2003) *Constructing the Holocaust: A Study in Historiography*. London: Valentine Mitchell.

Stone, Dan (2004) *The Historiography of the Holocaust*. Basingstoke: Palgrave Macmillan.

Totten, Samuel, and Stephen Feinberg (eds) (2016) *Essentials of Holocaust Education: Fundamental Issues and Approaches*. New York: Routledge.

Traverso, Enzo (2016) *The End of Jewish Modernity*. London: Pluto.

Young, James E. (1993) *The Texture of Memory: Holocaust Memorials and Meaning*. New Haven, CT: Yale University Press.

Young, James E. (2000) *At Memory's Edge: After-images of the Holocaust in Contemporary Art and Architecture*. New Haven, CT: Yale University Press.

Zertal, Idith (2000) 'From the People's Hall to the Wailing Wall: A Study in Memory, Fear and War', *Representations* 69: 96–126.

Zertal, Idith (2005) *Israel's Holocaust and the Politics of Nationhood*. Cambridge: Cambridge University Press.

Zimmerman, Joshua D. (ed.) (2003) *Contested Memories: Poles and Jews during the Holocaust and its Aftermath*. New Brunswick, NJ: Rutgers University Press.

13 LGBT histories and the politics of identity

Laura Gowing

On 7 November 1698, Edward Rigby propositioned William Minton at the George Tavern in Pall Mall with a call to history. To Minton's doubts as to what precise deeds he was suggesting, he responded 'It's no more than was done in our Fore-fathers time; our Saviour called St John the handsome apostle for that reason . . . Is it not what great men do? The French King did it, and the Czar of Muscovy made Alexander, a Carpenter, a Prince for that purpose.' The biblical reference reiterated blasphemous words attributed to Elizabethan playwright Christopher Marlowe, the activities of the French King circulated in popular rumour, but Rigby, a ship's captain, claimed to have seen Peter the Great through a ship's porthole (Dabhoiwala 2012: 129–30) That most of this story was then published in a journalistic account must have aided its diffusion into the history of the streets.

In the tea parties of 1820s Yorkshire, Anne Lister used her careful reading of homosexuality in the classics to subtly determine whether the women she met shared her erotic interests. One, she noted, 'has read the Sixth Satyr of Juvenal. She understands these matters well enough' (Lister 1988: 268). References to the Latin poets in conversation served to signal her own sexual knowledge, and she flirted by referring to Sappho, Achilles and Tiresias (Clark 1996: 39).

For both Rigby and Lister, as for countless others, glimpses of a queer past informed and inspired their queer present, in the face of cultural repression, criminal prosecution or social concealment. But while Rigby's story was immediately published in the trial proceedings of the Old Bailey, Lister's conversations were kept secret in her coded diary until its translation and publication in the 1990s, when scholars expressed both delight and scepticism at what one back-cover blurb described as 'a veritable Rosetta Stone of lesbian life in the early nineteenth century' (Lister 1992). In both stories, we see the pivotal role a sense of the past might play in defining and expressing sexuality and in legitimating desire against the currents of social norms. Both also joined in creating a collective memory that validated the unspeakable desires of the present.

The relationship between LGBT (lesbian, gay, bisexual and transgender) history and politics is intimate. Every one of those terms is laden with memory; each category, and many other conceptions of sexual identity and community not included in them, has its own relation with a past of oppressions, suppressions, pleasures and liberations.[1] Moreover, the tacit or explicit exclusion of histories of lesbian, gay, bisexual or transgender people, and the lack of discussion of sex, gender and sexuality more generally, has been a key part of the ways that institutions and discourses of public history reinforce power structures. While the last twenty years has witnessed both a burgeoning of manifestations of LGBT history and a scrutiny of its terms, the literature on public history and memory has done little to incorporate its challenges. This chapter examines first the theories and models that have shaped LGBT history in the public and academic world. It goes on to analyse some of the ways LGBT public history has been produced in relation to political exigencies, community dynamics, and desires both collective and individual, by looking at law, monuments, heritage and collective memory. It concludes by looking to the future of the queer past.

Identity and history

The subject that LGBT history represents is itself a vexed one. For if the modern politics of sexuality has any common ground, it is to work towards undoing fixed identities, towards allowing a freedom of sexual expression and activity and experience. Sexual labelling has often been a vehicle of repression. But for much of its lifetime gay politics has drawn strength from an essentialist understanding of sexuality, and has invoked a history that essentializes, rather than challenges, categories of sexuality. Looking for signs of recognizable modern sexual identities has been a crucial way of repairing the losses and repressions, the pages torn out and documents destroyed, that impoverish the queer archive. The sexologists of the late nineteenth century, notably Havelock Ellis, deployed a history of heroic same-sex love going back to the ancient world, and recognizable transculturally (Ellis and Symonds 1897). Such a history would testify to homosexuality as a natural category of sexual behaviour or identity, and hence justify more liberal treatment. The same broadly essentialist understanding of sexuality was at the heart of much political support for toleration for most of the twentieth century, too. But, from the 1970s on, sexuality began to be understood as a social construction, whose manifestations varied by time and place. The search for gay ancestors was no longer legitimated by the project of history; and the deconstructive approach, which stressed the historic development of the modern category of homosexuality, seemed less politically useful. In 1993 some of the results of the UK's national survey of lesbian and gay history, aimed at filling in the gaps in the Mass Observation archive, were published under the title *Proust, Cole Porter, Michelangelo, Marc Almond and me*. It's a title that is both reductive and expansive: only by a great leap of historical imagination can most of these men be imagined to inhabit the same sexual and conceptual universe. But that leap is a critical one for lesbian and gay history, both in the public realm and in the scholarly world.

Historians have called into play a variety of terms to imagine same-sex relations in the past. Historicizing the terms of sexuality is crucial: the modern meaning of sodomy, for example, is quite different to the much looser medieval understanding, and to the variety of meanings that were attached to it by American colonists in the seventeenth century. At the same time, deploying terms like 'lesbian' to identify women in the distant past who might more likely be read as companions or cross-dressers offers a strategy for playful identification (Hayward 2016). This approach insists, usefully for our purposes, on LGBT history's relevance for the present, and it also foregrounds ideas of 'identification' or 'projection' that emphasize the psychological impact of the history of sexuality. Bisexuality, though, despite its apparent relevance for the sexual lives of very many people in the past, has been surprisingly absent both from academic and public history, and this points up the dilemma of identification: most people in the past whose deeds or lives might fit into the broad rubric of LGBT history could well be described by more than one of these flexible terms.

In the 1990s, academic historians of sexuality increasingly took up the theoretical concept 'queer'. Activists, particularly in the UK and the US, were turning away from a politics grounded in identities. 'Queer' reclaimed an abusive term as a call to liberation, memorializing a rejecting past in a call to pride: its use was itself an intervention in LGBT history. It also offered a single, expansive word with which to challenge 'heteronormativity' – the established norms of sex, gender and sexuality. Scholars, too, used the term to rethink normative categories (Jagose 1996). Yet the very strengths of 'queer' as a theoretical term, and as a call to action, can make it uncomfortable for history in the public realm. Its legacy of abuse raises unpleasant memories still; its generational resonances vary wildly.

Queer theory is also a utopian project. At its heart is the deconstruction of the idea of fixed sexual identity that provided the foundation for so much lesbian and gay history. Furthering feminism's project of deconstructing fixed gender identities, queer theory argued for the expansive, indeterminate meanings of sexuality and gender. Even this utopianism has a historic dimension. Separating sexuality from identity makes excellent sense for erotic and amatory connections before modern definitions of homosexuality and heterosexuality were established by sexologists in the nineteenth century. It also offers a way of putting 'otherness' into the histories of sexuality, so as to reveal, for example, the ways in which heterosexuality was not always normative – such as in medieval monastic cultures. Equally useful may be the perspective that pre-modern histories offer in which sexuality is simply nothing to do with identity; that it involves acts, not selves, in a world in which selfhood and identity are in any case less individualist and more embedded in family, work and community than they later became. (Karras 2005)

Most challengingly for historians, queer history has also been understood as a methodology: something that shapes how history is done, as well as who its subjects are. Scholars and activists work to 'queer' identities, disciplines, eras, archives and institutions. Queerness, Lee Edelman argues, 'can never define an identity; it can only ever disturb one' (Edelman 2004: 17). Hence, queer can usefully destabilize not just the categories and norms of the history of sexuality, but the terms of historical method. The history of sexuality need not fit into periodizations such as 'early modern' or 'nineteenth century'. More provocatively scholars have used the idea of 'queer temporality' to challenge historicism itself. Historians have followed Foucault's notion of 'genealogy', which offers to critically examine the discourses that help construct bodies and sexualities through the inscription of power, rejecting linear development in favour of complex relationships and paradoxes (Foucault 1978). Looking for spectres and ghosts has helped resolve (or complicate) the issue of lesbian invisibility in the record of the past. Efforts like these engage creatively with the emotional charge of 'the queer desire for history' (Dinshaw 2007). This affective charge is a complex one. Queer criticism uses past negativity for a positive political agenda, in a strategy of reverse discourse (Butler 1993). Yet the historicity of the term queer also memorializes shame, scandal and loss (Love 2009).

The creative relationship of queer history with temporality and with the emotional investment in sexuality and its performance has rich potential for history and memory. But adopting these insights to queer public history is a challenging project. With its legacy of abuse, 'queer' remains a less likely term for museums and other institutions to use, and in the UK and US has been mostly confined to small exhibits, such as the Museum of London's small *Queer Is Here* exhibition (2006). Its derivation from the global north can have a colonizing effect (Hayward 2016). As both methodology and definition, though, its approach can be fruitful for public history work. Bob Mills suggests that 'translating queer history into the language of public culture will involve a contestation of the very norms in which museums and other 'popular' history narratives are currently embedded' (Mills 2006: 261). Queer museums, he argues, should prioritize interrogation, appropriation and interaction, over fixed categories and grand narratives. Such an approach draws, too, on feminist interrogations of the museum, which challenge the ways that meaning is produced in the museum context, attempting to unravel existing ideas of male/female and masculine/feminine boundaries (Porter 1996: 107). Queer history might also inspire institutions to decentralize heterosexuality, to question its naturalization in exhibits from the prehistoric period forwards (Levin 2010). All these approaches would support queer history's capacity to challenge the bigger frame of public history and memory, as well as offering a series of minoritizing stories.

Mills's analysis of some of the LGBT public history in the UK also notes that the 'T' in LGBT is too often an empty letter (Mills 2006). Transgender history offers most obviously another way of completing the queer past. If transgender is read as the transgression of gender, or a journey away from an assigned gender role, its history is capacious, ranging – in the title words of Leslie Feinberg's *Transgender Warriors* – 'from Joan of Arc to RuPaul' (Feinberg 1993). Transgender can be a more fruitful category than lesbian, gay or queer for some historical figures and stories. Prosecutions of sex between women in sixteenth-century Europe, for example, fixed on the impersonation of a man, rather than the act of lesbian sex, which was not often legally proscribed as sodomy was. The history of the modern transgender movement has a narrower focus, but its commonly recognized starting point, with the sexology of Magnus Hirschfeld and the earliest gender reassignment operations, reveals the overlapping origins of the categories of homosexuality and transsexuality.

But while incorporating 'transgender' into 'LGBT' and its associated acronyms suggests that transgender is another, often more historically appropriate, kind of identity, its implications are methodologically bigger. Like 'queer', 'transgender' can be argued to function as a modality as much as a category: it can offer a way of thinking. Critiquing the erasure of transgender stories from some celebrated episodes of queer history, scholars have suggested that a transgender public memory project could excel at forcing gender onto the agenda, by moving beyond the binary; at foregrounding the body in queer history; and at disrupting normativity (Stryker 2008; Dunn 2015). All these, of course, have also been aims for other strands of LGBTQ history: perhaps one message is the resilience and creativity of queer history in all its varieties in response to changing political norms.

None of these terms are straightforward for academic historians, and they should not be so for public history or for memory. They work best not as distinct categories but as overlapping ways of 'reading' the sexual past. Together they can constitute an interrogative force, a curatorial insistence on removing not just the presumption of heterosexuality, but the constraints of modern categories of sexuality and gender. In what follows, we will look at some of the manifestations of LGBTQ history in public and as memory to see how these readings of sexual politics play out in monuments, museums, places and practices.

Law and the arc of history

In much lesbian and gay public history, one narrative has prevailed: the story of repression leading to liberation. Amongst the events that have taken the spotlight, the riot at New York's Stonewall bar in 1969 is most prominent in the UK and North America. Recently and problematically memorialized on film, Stonewall is also invoked in the name of numerous campaigning groups, including the UK's leading LGBT lobbying group, and its timing is remembered in the annual Pride celebrations worldwide. The Stonewall history became a collective memory that provided focus for contests about political strategy, and in that process differences around race, gender and politics were erased in favour of a narrative of co-operation (Bravmann 1997). Yet Stonewall was just one of many protests against the policing of gay bars, and it was remembered precisely because a collective political decision determined that it merited the status of a defining moment (Armstrong and Crage 2006). That convenient story has helped, in some political contexts, to secure political change as well as individual and collective identities.

For the earliest gay movements, a call to gay history was part of the legitimacy of their message: gayness had to have been always already there, and the evolving gay history of ancient Greece provided forebears as well as contrast. But by the 1970s, many gay political movements were looking to critique the normal, rather than to fit into it: the Gay Liberation Front in Britain and the US had as its rallying cry the call for sexual freedom, for gays and lesbians to critique the 'normal' rather than to adopt it. At the same time, a more politically straightforward historical narrative retained its usefulness. Late twentieth-century America, in a political climate where individual states retained laws criminalizing sex between men, offers a useful case study of the interaction between law and public history. The historical narrative of same-sex sex could be critical to legal challenges to such laws.

The right of individual states to uphold anti-sodomy laws had been supported by the US Supreme Court in the case *Bowers v. Hardwick* (1986). Sodomy, it had been determined, was 'a criminal offence at common law and was forbidden by the laws of the original thirteen states': it was taken to include oral sex. This understanding of same-sex sex as criminal harked back to ideas imported from English common law in the seventeenth century. That interpretation of English common law was, of course, highly debatable, and it was unsuccessfully challenged twelve years later, in *Lawrence v. Texas*, a complaint on privacy grounds against the state of Texas's prosecution of a man for consensual sex with another man. But when this case eventually reached the Supreme Court in 2003, a different reading of history prevailed. Despite the continuing interest in old English law, the Supreme Court was persuaded that the legal prohibition of sodomy in seventeenth-century England amounted to a specific, local issue, not a moral condemnation of homosexuals and homosexual acts. This time, the court listened to the testimony of academic *amicae* (friends of the court) on the historical meaning of homosexuality and its legal treatment. George Chauncey, historian of gay America, was amongst them. The *amicae* argued that the idea of 'the homosexual' was foreign to the early settlers and lawgivers, as it was to English common law. Rather, the crime of sodomy criminalized a variety of non-procreative sexual acts. Their brief demonstrated convincingly that the idea of the homosexual was not a historical constant, but the product of nineteenth-century ideas and twentieth-century laws by which, for example, bars and restaurants were forbidden from serving homosexual men, the federal government from employing them and Hollywood from including gay characters in movies. So the anti-sodomy law's use against homosexual men was demonstrably modern, not traditional. Making homosexuality historically contingent was a sea change in the arguments that activists had offered up to lawmakers.

Lawrence v. Texas did indeed result in the anti-sodomy law not just of Texas, but other states, being struck down. The historians' case for homosexuality as a historically constructed category – an active attempt to intervene in public memory – was one part of the jigsaw of circumstance and pressure that made this possible. So was another idea offered to the judiciary by historians: the arc of progressive change. The historians' case for decriminalization had also argued that there had been a radical change in public attitudes towards gay people in the last generation, demonstrating that the apparatus of anti-gay discrimination had been dismantled in the last third of the twentieth century, and that many cultural and political authorities embraced gay rights. Recent history and tradition reflected an expanding and more inclusive moral vision of the reach of liberty. Prejudice had become un-modern and un-American. This, George Chauncey wrote, allowed the judiciary to see themselves as 'actors in a sweeping historical 'drama' – an unfolding narrative of liberation (Chauncey 2008: 33). Moreover, Chauncey suggests, history's reinvention of the narrative of the gay past was itself helpful, enabling judges to see themselves as revising past decisions based on new scholarly knowledge.

In the Britain of the last ten years, too, public political rhetoric has tended to align modern democracy with aspirations to equality. This idea of the arc of history has sometimes been co-opted to the reverse effect too. The trajectory of colonial law is implicated in both cases. The former Zimbabwean President Robert Mugabe's attack on homosexuality as a Western invention that will destroy the moral fabric of Africa sits alongside similar pronouncements from leaders in Gambia, Liberia and elsewhere, sometimes explicitly identifying homosexuality with colonialism, and its decriminalization with foreign intervention. In fact, the criminalization of same-sex sex was part of the colonial project. This was particularly true in British colonies, France having decriminalized sex between men in 1791. Section 377 in India's penal code criminalizes consensual homosexual sex with a prohibition on 'carnal intercourse against the order of nature with any man, woman or animal'. When this clause was under challenge in 2003, India's Ministry of Home Affairs defended it as a response 'to the values and mores of the time in the Indian society'; tolerance, it was claimed, was a feature particular to Britain and the USA. The same Section features in Malaysia's penal code, and in both cases is a direct result of colonial-era legislation, rather than a reflection of any other traditions. Section 377, in the words of Human Rights Watch, 'became a model anti-sodomy law for countries far beyond India, Malaysia, and Uganda. Its influence stretched across Asia, the Pacific islands, and Africa, almost everywhere the British imperial flag flew' (Human Rights Watch, 2008: Introduction). Legislation like this, and protest against it, calls on memory. At issue are two key challenges. One, to the nature of law: what precisely did colonial laws address? In the US case, a historicization of what sodomy actually meant in the 1600s helped make change possible. Second, to the idea of 'tradition': the narrative of repression to liberation turned out to be a self-fulfilling narrative in the US and the UK, but American evangelical churches have taken the same narrative as a basis to push criminalization across Africa, creating a narrative in which anti-gay laws are taken to be 'traditional'.

The public discourse around same-sex marriage has called on history in a different way, but also one that required the apparently timeless to be radically rehistoricized. By the time marriage equality appeared as a serious political aspiration in Western Europe, North America and Australasia in the late 1990s, there was already a growing body of historical knowledge about the celebration of same-sex unions in the Christian churches of the past, ranging from sworn brotherhoods in the Orthodox church to the burial of two women in the same grave in Westminster Abbey. The work of John Boswell in this field reached the American press just as public debate on the feasibility of lesbian and gay marriage was coming to the fore. In June 1994 Garry Trudeau's 'Doonesbury' comic strip presented readers across America with a character relating Boswell's argument – 'His research turned up liturgies for same-sex ceremonies that included liturgies, communion, and kissing to sanctify union' (Trudeau 1994). Several newspapers dropped the strip in response, and Trudeau was criticized in editorials as, in one Catholic paper's words, 'an apologist for homosexuality'. In the UK, particular press attention was given to Cardinal Newman, buried in the same grave as his lifelong friend in 1890. Alan Bray's work on sworn friendship described centuries of same-sex intimacy honoured by the Christian church (Bray 2003). Bray's complex story of friendship, rather than sex, was glossed in the *Guardian* newspaper as 'Church has "long blessed gays"' but its message for scholars was a good deal more historicist than Boswell's relatively straightforward identification of a recognizable gay past (*Guardian* 2001). Neither of these stories of the Church's past, however, had much apparent impact on its contemporary approach: in 2016 the Anglican communion remains deeply divided on same-sex marriage. Just as the prompt to rethink the historical meaning of sodomy did, the recovery of a story of religious blessings for a wider set of relationships probably added some fuel first to the argument for civil partnerships, which were introduced in the UK in 2005, and later to equal marriage. More broadly, the idea that marriage was not an unchanging institution gained support. Twelve years after the landmark decision in *Lawrence v. Texas*, the US Supreme Court passed the appeal of *Obergefell v. Hodges*, ruling states' opposition to same-sex marriage unconstitutional: part of the evidence was another amicus brief describing the long changing history of marriage, from unions of two families through arranged marriages and coverture (Perry and Michel 2015). Again, public and most of all judicial opinion seems to have been won over largely by the simple narrative of the 'arc of change' towards enlightenment: but beneath that story lies the complexity of the narratives of lesbian and gay identity that have been told and retold over the years.

Monuments and symbols

Can there be gay '*lieux de mémoire*'? Pierre Nora's concept describes places or objects that have become part of a community's memory. There are few explicitly lesbian or gay monuments. In the wake of the devastating mortality of the AIDS crisis, the AIDS Memorial quilt offered a personally crafted intervention into the culture of national memorials (Blair 2007). Commemorating well-known individuals raises concerns about the whole place of sexuality in the public sphere. Monuments are suggestive, more than explicit. Danny Osborne's 1997 monument to Oscar Wilde in Dublin's Merrion Square positions a colourful statue of the author, lolling on a boulder that is set in triangular relation to two pillars, one featuring a male torso and one a pregnant figure of Wilde's wife Constance. Wilde's gaze is fixed firmly on neither (Dunn 2014). Wilde has been persistently identified as a gay icon; the monument arguably makes better sense of him by offering a less static identification, reflecting something of Wilde's nineteenth-century persona and also resonating with an anti-essential queerness – or perhaps actually bisexuality, which is rarely ever discussed in relation to queer memory. This subtlety is less apparent in official treatments of the statue. Dublin City Council's account of the monument makes no mention of Wilde's sexuality at all, yet twice uses the heavily coded word 'flamboyant' (Dublin City Council 2016).

The commemoration of Alan Turing, the British computer pioneer and code-breaker whose prosecution and punishment for homosexuality and subsequent suicide in 1953 led, eventually, to an official pardon in 2013, is itself a story of transformed memory, for his history is not one of heroic rebellion or outspoken sexual dissidence. A statue of him at the University of Surrey, near the town where

Figure 13.1 Alan Turing memorial statue, University of Surrey, June 2016. (©
Katherine Hubbard.)

he lived, remembers him carrying books, and makes no explicit reference to his
sexuality. But statues have their own lives. The day after the massacre at the gay
nightclub Pulse in Orlando, Florida, in 2016, Turing's statue in Surrey was draped
with a rainbow flag and adorned with flowers, an unlikely yet utterly apposite
act of identifying memory which has become part of the university LGBT
community's rituals.

The most explicit memorials of gay history have been established in eventual
response to the Nazi persecution of homosexual men. Monuments have been
built in Germany, Israel, Australia and the Netherlands. Other attempts are still
ongoing. A guide to France's *'lieux de mémoire'*, listing wartime battlefields, war
graves and monuments, includes one gay entry, which is really a virtual one: the
Mémorial de la Déportation Homosexuelle in Paris is not an actual memorial but
an association working to protect the memory of the deportation by establishing
plaques of remembrance and naming streets after Pierre Seel, the only French
survivor to have spoken publicly of his experiences (Doussot 2012: 117).

The Nazi persecution of gay men took a long time to be publicly remembered;
the first memorial, known as the Homomonument, was created in Amsterdam in
1987, though its planning began in 1979 after wreaths commemorating gay
victims were removed from official war monuments. The Homomonument is
an integrated part of city space, composed of three rose granite triangles with
10-metre sides, with a plaque commemorating 'all women and men ever oppressed
and persecuted because of their homosexuality' and calling for 'permanent

vigilance'. Each triangle points in a meaningful direction: one to the central Dam square, for the present; one to the Anne Frank House, for the past; one to the oldest surviving lesbian and gay community organization, for the future. More than, for example, the enclosed letter-box type structure of Berlin's monument to homosexual victims of Nazi persecution, the 'Homomonument' of Amsterdam offers both an urban feature at which to rest, meet or celebrate, and, in the words of its designer, Karin Daan, a podium from which to fight. Easily found fortuitously, it demands and provides explanation, making it a far-sighted intervention into public history, even as the identity categories it names seem to pass into history.

Figure 13.2 The Memorial to Homosexuals Persecuted under Nazism, Berlin. Photograph courtesy of Anna Maerker, 2017.

Figure 13.3 The Homomonument, Amsterdam. Photograph courtesy of the author.

The Homomonument's primary visual connection involves a symbol that, when it was created, seemed to be on the road to becoming the universal symbol of the 'lesbian and gay movement'. The internationalization of the pink triangle as gay symbol was part of the hard-fought position of lesbian and gay history in the 1970s and 1980s, whose tensions remain visible today. The pink triangle symbolized gay men as victims of the Holocaust, when it had been used on the clothing of men in the camps imprisoned for their homosexuality. This was a story that had taken generations to emerge. In the immediate post-war period it had no meaning: homosexuality was still against the law in most European states and remained so in Germany. French deportee Pierre Seel remembered his return to Alsace in 1945: 'I was already starting to censor my memories . . . Liberation was only for others' (Seel 2011: 88). Some survivors of the camps were actually re-imprisoned for homosexuality after being liberated at the end of the war. Despite years of campaigning, victims were not offered government compensation until 2000. The continuing repression was due in part to the silences of the post-war years in Germany, and the disinclination of the German activists of the 1960s to root newly confident gay communities in a history of trauma and oppression. In 1972 Heinz Heger's memoir of a gay man's life in a concentration camp, *The Men with the Pink Triangle*, brought this history into the public realm. The relationship between Jewish and gay memory proved potentially painful. Martin Sherman's 1979 play *Bent,* inspired by Heger's book, which brought the story to a wider public gay audience, ended with a scene that shocked many for its apparent equation of the killing of gays with that of Jews. Some political campaigns for gay liberation made explicit reference for the need to present gays as victims, and the invocation of the phrase 'lowest of the low' to describe the place of homosexuals in concentration camp hierarchy evoked a deeply troubling sense of competing oppressions (Jensen 2002: 331).

The pink triangle came to play a prominent and contested role in lesbian and gay imagery. It was sold as a lapel pin, and featured in the background to many political campaigns, particularly in the UK, mainland Europe and North America. Black triangles began to be used, more problematically, to represent lesbianism in the form of the victimization of 'antisocial' women in the camps: the needs of 1980s identity politics visibly overwrote what was known of Holocaust history. Pink and black triangles became a key symbol in lesbian and gay public life; by the early 1990s they featured on the wall décor of London's Lesbian and Gay Centre, and 'pink' became a widely recognized marker for gay venues, newspapers and businesses. In this way, evolving design put a repressive part of gay history at the heart of emerging gay identity. AIDS transformed the triangle again. Activist group ACT-UP took the slogan SILENCE=DEATH – a reversal of a whole era when silence had meant survival – and laid it over an inverted pink triangle. The pink triangle had become a mnemonic object whose use, like other cultural devices of memory, helped formulate both community memory, and personal identity in a politicized frame (Cubitt 2007: 148).

Incorporating lesbian and gay memory into the memorialization of the Second World War itself continued to be controversial: until 1987 wreaths in the forms of pink triangles were banned from London's Cenotaph ceremony. In 1999, a coalition of British lesbian and gay organizations sponsored a Queer Remembrance parade to follow after the official ceremony on 11 November, remembering 'the queer contribution to defeating Nazism' and protesting against the Royal British Legion's exclusion of the partners of lesbian and gay veterans from their Remembrance Day parade.

Alongside the triangle as symbol ran a more celebratory version of lesbian and gay history, alluding in particular to an ideal of the classical Greek past. From the 1970s, the labrys – a double-headed axe – was adopted as a lesbian symbol to Scythian Amazon warriors and to a mythical Minoan past of matriarchal communities. Earlier still, the Greek lambda was used by New York's Gay Activists' Alliance from 1970s, and formally adopted in 1974 by the International Gay Rights Congress: while one explanation was its role as the sign used by physicists for kinetic energy, it too also visibly referenced the ancient world and the long-standing power of classical myth for lesbian and gay identity. Historical symbols of identity, with which many were deeply uncomfortable, seem to have run their course with the decline of sexuality's identity politics. The rainbow flag that has come to represent LGBTQ communities and Pride now is explicitly ahistorical, designed deliberately to include.

Queer museums

What would a queer museum look like? Collecting policies and donor sensitivities have long imposed barriers to explicit discussion of sexuality in the museum sector; LGBT history has often been confined to small exhibitions and community venues. Increasingly, though, institutions have been concerned to explicitly address the diversity of the communities they aim to reach. In London's mayoral election in 2004, all the main candidates seized on the proposal made by long-time gay activist Peter Tatchell of a gay museum, as a way of demonstrating the city's openness. Tatchell's proposal harked back to the work done by members of the Gay Liberation Front in the 1970s to uncover a history that seemed hidden, and erased: 'Unlike other communities', he wrote in the *Guardian* newspaper, 'we had no families, and no stories of tragedies and triumphs to pass from genera-tion to generation. Queers were a people without any sense of a collective past' (Tatchell 2004). Tatchell's story of that past included Renaissance homosexual culture, campaigners for sexual liberation in the late nineteenth century and victories of the twentieth century. In the event the museum was created only as an online archive, Proud Heritage, and LGBT museum work in the UK has been more prominent through site-specific installations and interventions, such as Sean Curran's 2015 installation of videos of Shakespeare's sonnets performed by LGBTQ readers in Sutton House, a Tudor property in East London owned by the National Trust, or temporary exhibitions in honour of LGBT History Month. Tatchell's words address one of the particulars of queer memory: its potential disconnect from family memory, which has often occluded the people and things that mattered to queer people. LGBT stories demand other vehicles of transmission to reach from the personal to the collective. Archives and muse-ums carry a correspondingly heavy weight, noted by Joan Nestle, one of the founders of New York's Lesbian Herstory Archives:

> Always our message has been 'You, the women listening and watching, are our Lesbian herstory. You must send the photo, copy the letter, make the tape. You must cherish the courage of your own days, of your ways of loving, and not be intimidated by the thought of being part of a people's memory.'
> (Nestle 1990: 91)

Yet, as lesbians and gays have expanded the notion of family, the family archive can be a more complex, hospitable place than these fears suggest, as witnessed in the film made by Quentin Crisp's great-nephew to celebrate the familial side of his great-uncle's life – far from the 'solitary homo' of Crisp's self-presentations (Cook 2014: 87–90).

The museum context also raises questions of identification: who should be identified as lesbian, gay, bisexual or transgender, and on what grounds? Academic approaches to queer history can involve multiple terms and identifications (such as Judith Bennett's 'lesbian-like' as a way of understanding affectional and erotic relations between women in the pre-modern era: Bennett 2000). The careful negotiations of identity that are provided by scholarly apparatus are less easy to manage in the context of museum display, but the relative novelty of LGBT museum work has coincided with a new commitment from major museums to social justice. Interpretative frameworks are moving away from the didactic, leaving more space for imagination and queer potential. Queer routes round museums and interactive social events are amongst recent innovations.

One of the most accessible ways of writing the marginalized into public history has been through the calendar. Women's History Month, Black History Month and LGBT History Month have all offered a means of turning erasure into reparation and celebration, and they also deliberately address a wider public audience. However, a month of reparation can easily collude with another eleven months of wilful ignorance, and the 'history' in all these months does not often offer much substantive help to the project of rethinking historical narratives and assumptions. Famous figures and narratives of liberation predominate, and 'black' is often taken not to include or overlap with 'LGBT'. LGBT History Month includes events in libraries, galleries, bars and theatres, and in the UK it is also markedly distant from scholarly input. For its first several years (beginning in 2005), the brochure and website tended to feature a familiar genre of biographical history, with features on famous gay, lesbian and transgender people. More recently it has presented a more confident, challenging tone, with a thematic agenda, though the historical aspect remains light. In 2016 its materials included a wallchart featuring a wide variety of individuals and event from the nineteenth century to the present, from the birth of the poet Jackie Kay to the abolition of the death penalty for buggery in 1861, and ending with the Marriage (Same Sex Couples) Act of 2013.

There are good historical reasons for this approach. LGBT History Month in the UK essentially uses history as a tool: it offers a relatively neutral way to make room for LGBT issues in a curriculum where they have often been stifled. From 1988 to 2003, Section 28 of the Local Government Act effectively proscribed any discussion of homosexuality in local authority settings, including schools and many museums. One key phrase of the legislation bears repetition: 'a local authority shall not promote the teaching in any maintained school of the acceptability of homosexuality as a pretended family relationship'. It also, more generally, banned local authorities from 'intentionally promoting homosexuality'. This phrasing, aimed at securing the future from queer assaults on the 'normal' family, also secured the normalizing of the past, ensuring that museums (two-thirds of which were local authority funded), galleries and schools all felt largely unable to deal with lesbian and gay history or culture. The very capacity to talk about sexuality and history together in educational environments was still revolutionary when LGBT History Month was initiated in 2005; the popular *Sun* newspaper complained that 'sexual preferences . . . are a private matter, not a badge to be worn nor a propaganda weapon with which to influence young minds' (Mills 2008: 47). Here, the phrase 'sexual preferences' as an alternative to 'sexuality' is itself a weapon, typically adopted as a way of privatizing sexuality, and a response that continues to be used to undermine the inclusion of sexuality in curricula at all levels. Disciplinary regimes at various levels use power to structure bodies into 'sexuality': a public history that reflects their operation, as well as the freer play of sex and gender, is political and potent. Stories of the famous are still a useful tool in an educational world where sexuality often remains difficult to discuss.

Focusing on things, rather than people, offers another way forward. In 2008 the British Museum introduced a tour of its 'queer' objects which takes an approach much more closely related to academic interpretations of LGBT issues. Its online version is headed 'The evidence for same-sex desire and fluid ideas of gender has often been overlooked in the past, but museums and their collections can allow us to look back and see diversity throughout history'. The words queer and same-sex are used to mark out 'fluid' understandings of sex, gender and sexuality, rather than searching for recognizable identities; the result is an inquiry, rather than a narrative. The British Museum's approach to sexuality echoes much recent museum work in interrogating in preference to narrating. It problematizes assumptions, as well as locating objects that could be said, broadly, to suggest queerness: a gender-changing Babylonian goddess, or an African masquerade mask (Parkinson 2013). This approach works particularly well for times and places where sexual orientation, in the identity-forging sense, was a less significant interpretive force. It also goes some way to meeting the challenge posed by Robert Mills:

> Transforming the question 'Who is queer' into *why* and *how* one finds queerness historically or culturally might be a means of responding to the gaps and omissions that condition museum practice, and of ensuring that the meaning-making structures of the museum are themselves subjected to evaluation and critique.
>
> (Mills 2008)

How to extend this kind of interrogative approach into a more permanent feature of museums remains a challenge. The heritage industry's increasing interest in issues of LGBT equality, spurred on by legislation such as the UK's Equality Act (2010), is still rarely translated into permanent structures; as well, online tours and separate leaflets offer a convenient route for visitors to find a queer way round the museum, without being confronted by sexuality where it is not expected. If queer public history is really to challenge norms, perhaps the next step should be a more forceful, permanent presence.

Place and memory

The losses sustained by the queer paper archive, and the resonance of social space for LGBT life, give particular resonance to a history of place. Historic houses like Sissinghurst, home of writer Vita Sackville-West, are invested with a well-known history of their queer owners; the very earliest lesbian groups encouraged visits to sites of lesbian heritage, creating a secret, shared history. Lesbian and gay history has often involved a clash between the project of identification, seeking out similarity in the past, and the understanding of historical otherness, emphasizing the social construction of sexuality. Alison Oram's analysis of what visitors do in historic houses suggests these different ways of using the past are two sides of one coin. Visitors looking for reflections of themselves and their lives in the past are necessarily cognizant of the past's otherness: similarity is always accompanied by alterity. Visitors intent on a queer reading also often have to work against the ambivalences or silences in curatorial presentations, as they project their own needs onto the building, its furniture and its past occupants. The projections in which they engage, Oram suggests, help form selfhood (Oram 2011). The dissonances of both historic houses, and their interpretations, disrupt heteronormative assumptions. Of course, the meaning of that disruption is itself in flux: the idea of queer domesticity that seemed disruptive and challenging twenty years ago might now be read as affirming the homonormativity of the era of marriage equality.

The collective spaces of lesbian and gay culture have always been transient. In London and other major cities, commercial pressures have rebounded particularly harshly on long-established gay pubs and other queer spaces. In response to this, an audacious campaign to protect one such space provides a fascinating case study and model for the future. English Heritage (now Historic England) actively encouraged this kind of application as part of a broader attempt to recognize LGBT heritage alongside that of other 'minority' groups. The Royal Vauxhall Tavern, at risk from private developers, was listed in 2015, a status that protects historic buildings. It is the only building in the UK to have been listed specifically for its LGBT significance. The case made for this listing is an instructive one. The RVT, as it is often known, was described in the listing case as 'the country's oldest continuously operating site of LGBT socialising'. This neat framing encapsulates many of the issues of memory and place with which we have been concerned. The RVT, now a solitary terraced building standing by a busy urban roundabout, is indeed the repository of long queer histories. The difficulty in substantiating these are finessed in Ben Walters's report for Heritage England, which, rather than chasing down specific lesbian or gay identities, characterizes the tavern as a site of 'social and cultural transgression', suggests that its fabric might incorporate iron columns from the original eighteenth-century Vauxhall Gardens, and locates a criminal record for Princess Seraphina, a cross-dressed laundress of the 1730s, whose neighbours recalled her borrowing women's clothes to wear to the Vauxhall masquerade. The social spaces of the LGBT past, as this document notes, have been poorly memorialized: this is a challenge to queer collective memory and to social history more generally (Walters 2015: 11). The current fight to preserve some of those places, under threat in so many cities, is also a battle to create and preserve the kind of collective memory whose absence has been so marked. The cartoonist Baz's 'Tales of the Tavern', presented online as part of the 'RVT Futures' campaign, uses comic art to create an appropriately episodic, patchy queer history for the Vauxhall Tavern, depicting moments in the venue's history from 1861 to 1995. 'They leave a lot unsaid and unseen', he writes, '. . . and that makes viewers think quite hard without actually realising it.' Baz's cartoon for 1988 retells a legendary story of Freddie Mercury taking Princess Diana to the tavern in drag – a tale that connects gender and class transgressions,

Figure 13.4 Bazcomics, 'Tales of the Tavern – 1988', 2015. (© Bazcomics, bazcomics.com.)

a perfect fit for the history today's RVT is claiming for itself in order to secure a place in London's queer future.

The lesbian and gay memory project has always had a virtual dimension to it, countering the heteronormative world of solid monuments and permanent memorials. The *Pink Plaque Guide to London* (1986) offered a palimpsest of imaginary pink plaques memorializing lesbians and gays of note, to overlay London's long-established blue plaques. None were ever created, so the book provided instead an alternative virtual heritage story with which to walk the streets. Feminists had long used historical walks to create an alternative history of houses, streets, people and communities (Davin 1991). Lesbian and gay walking tours did the same thing for lesbian and gay heritage, preserving stories and serving a community function at the same time. Interviewed in 2013, the tour leaders of London's weekly gay history walk (run from a community centre in Soho) described how they had revised the tour's emphasis away from 'salacious' stories of gay men's bars, towards a longer history of 'people who we can identify as LGBT in the Soho area', going back to molly houses and the Chevalier D'Eon, to 'give gay people a better perspective on their identities' (Resonance FM 2013). Roots and diversity matter to this use of history for community: it also bespeaks a continuing investment in the way places can buttress 'identities' and, by implication, emotional health. In other places smartphone apps have been developed to provide an interface between people and place. In Brighton, writer Rose Collis's Pink Plaques app offers a literally virtual equivalent to heritage plaques, featuring sites of collective memory and political action as well as more biographical ones.

The digital dimension has offered LGBT heritage another approach to creating collective memory by preserving specific memories. Here, though, the battle for visibility and recognition is fought on a rather different ground. Like so much public LGBT history, digital maps depend on crowd-sourcing. They draw from enthusiasm, commitment and random voluntary contributions. In 2014, the government body Historic England announced funding for one such project. With local and central government cuts accompanying a legal obligation to greater inclusion, digital responses are a seemingly ideal solution. 'Pride of Place: England's LGBTQ Heritage' aims to 'put LGBTQ heritage on the map'. Its range is enormous: entries range from a Roman burial of a male skeleton with feminine jewellery, identified as a potential cross-gendered 'gallus', in Catterick, to the South London Women's Centre. Strikingly, it is the community places that, at first glance, take up the most entries. Precisely that history of sociability, of collective gay life, is what contributors have chosen to mark, ahead of the more standard biographical fare of plaques and monuments. It includes, too, a whole range of stories that come broadly under the category of LGBTQ heritage: personal stories of gay neighbours, tributes to community organizations, rumours of the sexuality of famous or private figures in the past, and reminiscences of community rounders games (Historic England 2016).

Run by academics and researchers at Leeds Beckett University, Pride of Place enables everyone to map their past. Of necessity, the criteria of 'LGBTQ heritage' is capacious, and the references are unverified. For historians, the question of authenticity and credit is immediately raised: while referencing is possible, it is by no means necessary. This approach gives the map a popular, even arbitrary character that immediately challenges the authority claims of much academic history. It also allows it to steer a safe course between the genealogical tracking of 'lesbians', 'gays' and other categories in the past, and a complete undoing of categories. If anything, in fact, it offers a set of sources and evidence, rather than a complete story. But its main pleasure is surely that it offers a creative way of making a mark on the past: of knowing oneself remembered. Not just inter-activity, but taking part in creating the historical record, must be one of the keys to success for digital projects. In the USA in 2016, the National Park Service was running a similar initiative with the line 'It is important that we all see ourselves, now and in the future, in the story of America' (National Park Service 2016:1) This kind of memory work draws on the emotional power of the queer archive, which has been characterized as recuperative and affective: LGBTQ archive work offers the potential to both mourn and recoup some of the losses, repressions and excisions of the historic archive (Cvetkovich 2003; Morris 2007). Archives that specifically collect on the experience of LGBTQ people of colour are demonstrably crucial to creating a representative public history, as well as performing political work themselves. London's rukus! Black LGBTQ archive came into being as part of an arts and performance organization, collecting material to prevent the loss of memories of black LGBT activism in the UK, and to make the categories 'black' and 'queer' connect: its founders cite as inspiration Stuart Hall's idea of the living archive, interrupting a settled field, as well as his words 'making difference work'. Its subsequent rehousing in London's official archive, the London Metropolitan Archives, deliberately involved a community of young volunteers new to the archival world (X 2010; rukus! 2016).

The legacy of digital projects is essentially virtual. They live, and will be passed on, in individual memories, if not in a reliable archive (the internet is littered with broken links and abandoned sites of virtual gay heritage). Inevitably this risks a less secure history than one manifested in public monuments. It also means that the memory thus created is for and by a community: people are unlikely to come across queer history online fortuitously. And so it may change personal stories, but perhaps less so, public narratives.

London's queer scene has offered up another way of producing a collective memory of the social: through bringing the lost archive to social events them-selves. For the last twenty years Duckie, a 'post-queer performance and events collective', have run a residency at the Royal Vauxhall Tavern, featuring cabaret, burlesque and promenade performances that draw eloquently on queer history. One of their earliest performances, in 1999, was of a Vauxhall Promenade, attempting to re-create the long history of Vauxhall Pleasure Gardens and the queer lives that were part of the area. Most recently Duckie's performances have included oral history on stage, with a forum of recollections of the 1950s lesbian Gateways club, followed by a night re-creating and celebrating the Gateways, and a re-enactment (with study weekend and costume workshop) of Lady Malcolm's

Servants Ball, an almost forgotten event between the wars whose attendees notoriously included domestic servants, cross-dressers and male prostitutes. Duckie's archival research often throws up an even queerer world than anyone expected, stressing the fault-lines of identity and the crossing of social and sexual boundaries. Making queer nightlife itself a historical project recognizes fully the individual memory underpinning collective memory; it also refuses passive consumption of a commodified past, but demands projection and participation. Judith Butler theorized gender as a performance; here, gender and sexuality can also be a performance of history (Butler 1993).

The future of the queer past

In many places and in many ways, LGBTQ public history is flourishing as never before, though its permanent place in national and social stories remains uncertain. We have seen three key ways in which sexuality and history entwine in the public realm. Narratives of the gay past have provided the foundation for political campaigns for equality: a sense of history's potential to be written has been actively fruitful of political gains. Objects of memory, from monuments to symbols, have embodied identity stories whose significance is continually changing. And creative archiving is a critical arena for both making a queer past, and living with it. In all these manifestations of history and memory, it is the dissonances of LGBTQ history that provide lasting resonance: multiple voices, competing stories and methodological challenges promise to give the queer past new life. A focus on social justice and equality tends to frame LGBT public history as a way of serving particular constituencies and audiences, offering redress and reparation. But queer history takes aim at the whole spectrum of history-making. A queer critique of history and memory might engage the very practices and categories by which museums make meaning. And a queer memory could mean challenging the ways that 'memory', both public and personal, is structured around 'the normal'.

Guide to further reading and online resources

Literature on LGBT public history has mostly focused on the areas of museums and social justice; monuments; and the queer archive. Alongside Levin (2010) and Mills (2006), the journals *GLQ* and *Radical History Review* provide a starting point for further research in these areas. Bravmann (1997) was the first scholarly work to examine lesbians' and gays' engagement with the past. Issues of terminology are explored in Hayward (2016)'s interviews with leading scholars.

Useful online resources include:

LGBT History Month http://lgbthistorymonth.org.uk/ and the site's Twitter/
    Facebook feeds
http://notchesblog.com/ re(marks) on the history of sexuality
www.unstraight.org/ The Unstraight Museum, 'dedicated to LGBTQI history in
    all its forms'.

http://rictornorton.co.uk/ – one of the longest-established gay history sites,
which made original eighteenth-century sources available and also features
debates about essentialism v. social construction

Acknowledgements

Thanks to Matt Cook and Louise Gray for their comments and Katherine Hubbard
for her picture of Alan Turing.

Note

1 This chapter generally tries to reflect the changes in terms and acronyms over
time, but uses 'LGBT' most often. The most expansive current version would be
LGBTQI (lesbian, gay, bisexual, transsexual, queer, questioning, intersex).

References

Armstrong, Elizabeth A. and Suzanna M. Crage (2006) 'Movements and Memory:
The Making of the Stonewall Myth'. *American Sociological Review* 71(5):
724–51.
Baz, 'Tales of the Tavern'. Future of the Royal Vauxhall Tavern: www.rvt.community/
tales-of-the-tavern/ (accessed 19 July 2016).
Bennett, Judith M. (2000), '"Lesbian-Like" and the Social History of Lesbianisms'.
Journal of the History of Sexuality 9(1/2): 1–24.
Blair, Carole, and Neil Michel (2007) 'The AIDS Memorial Quilt and the
Contemporary Culture of Public Commemoration'. *Rhetoric and Public Affairs*
10(4): 595–626.
British Museum (2008) 'Same-Sex Desire and Gender Identity'. www.britishmuseum.
org/explore/themes/same-sex_desire_and_gender.aspx (accessed 12 July 2016).
Bravmann, Scott (1997) *Queer Fictions of the Past: History, Culture, and Difference.*
Cambridge: Cambridge University Press.
Bray, Alan (2003) *The Friend.* Chicago: Chicago University Press.
Butler, Judith (1993) 'Critically Queer'. *GLQ: A Journal of Lesbian and Gay Studies*
1(1): 17–32.
Castle, Terry (1995) *The Apparitional Lesbian: Female Homosexuality and Modern
Culture.* New York: Columbia University Press.
Chauncey, George (2008) 'How History Mattered: Sodomy Law and Marriage
Reform in the United States'. *Public Culture* 20(1): 27–38.
Clark, Anna (1996) 'Anne Lister's Construction of Lesbian Identity'. *Journal of the
History of Sexuality* 7(1): 23–50.
Cook, Matt (2014) *Queer Domesticities: Homosexuality and Home Life in Twentieth-
Century London.* London: Palgrave.
Cubitt, Geoffrey (2007) *History and Memory.* Manchester: Manchester University
Press.
Cvetkovich, Ann (2003) *An Archive of Feelings: Trauma, Sexuality, and Lesbian Public
Cultures.* Durham, NC: Duke University Press.
Dabhoiwala, Faramerz (2012) *The Origins of Sex: A History of the First Sexual
Revolution.* Harmondsworth: Penguin.

Davin, Anna (1991) 'Standing on Virginia Woolf's Doorstep'. *History Workshop Journal* 31: 73–84.

Dinshaw, Carolyn, Lee Edelman, Roderick A. Ferguson, Carla Freccero, Elizabeth Freeman, Judith Halberstam, Annamarie Jagose, Christopher Nealon and Nguyen Tan Hoang (2007) 'Theorizing Queer Temporalities: A Roundtable Discussion'. *GLQ: A Journal of Lesbian and Gay Studies* 13(2–3): 177–95.

Doan, Laura (2013) *Disturbing Practices: History, Sexuality, and Women's Experience of Modern War*. Chicago: University of Chicago Press.

Doussot, Michel, et al. (2012) *Guide des Lieux de Mémoire 2013*. Paris: Petit Futé.

Dublin City Council (2016) 'Oscar Wilde Memorial Guide'. www.dublincity.ie/DublinArtInParks/English (accessed 14 July 2016).

Dunn, Thomas R. (2014) '"The Quare in the Square": Queer Memory, Sensibilities, and Oscar Wilde'. *Quarterly Journal of Speech* 100(2): 213–40.

Dunn, Thomas R. (2015) 'Historical Trans-Cription: Struggling with Memory in Paris Is Burning'. In Jamie C. Capuzza and Leland G. Spencer (eds), *Transgender Communication Studies: Histories, Trends, and Trajectories*. Lanham, MD: Lexington Books.

Edelman, Lee (2004) *No Future: Queer Theory and the Death Drive*. Durham, NC: Duke University Press.

Elliman, Michael, and Frederick Roll (1986) *The Pink Plaque Guide to London*. London: Gay Men's Press.

Ellis, Havelock, and John Addington Symonds (1897) *Sexual Inversion*. London: Wilson & Macmillan.

Feinberg, Leslie (1996) *Transgender Warriors: Making History from Joan of Arc to Rupaul*. Boston: Beacon Press.

Foucault, Michel (1978) *The History of Sexuality: The Will to Knowledge: The Will to Knowledge v. 1*. Translated by Robert Hurley. New York: Pantheon books.

Guardian (10 August 2001) 'Church has "long blessed gays"'.

Hayward, Claire, et al. (2016) 'Queer Terminology: LGBTQ Histories and the Semantics of Sexuality'. *NOTCHES*, 9 June. http://notchesblog.com/2016/06/09/queer-terminology-lgbtq-histories-and-the-semantics-of-sexuality/.

Historic England (2016) 'Put LGBTQ Heritage on the Map': https://historicengland.org.uk/research/inclusive-heritage/lgbtq-heritage-project/ (accessed 20 July 2016).

Human Rights Watch (2008) *This Alien Legacy: The Origins of "Sodomy" Laws in British Colonialism*. 17 December. www.hrw.org/report/2008/12/17/alien-legacy/origins-sodomy-laws-british-colonialism (accessed 31 October 2017).

Jagose, Annamarie (1996) *Queer Theory: An Introduction*. New York: New York University Press.

Jensen, Erik N. (2002) 'The Pink Triangle and Political Consciousness: Gays, Lesbians, and the Memory of Nazi Persecution'. *Journal of the History of Sexuality* 11(1/2): 319–49.

Karras, Ruth Mazo (2005) *Sexuality in Medieval Europe: Doing unto Others*. New York: Routledge.

Levin, Amy K. (2010) 'Straight Talk: Evolution Exhibits and the Reproduction of Heterosexuality' in Levin (ed.), *Gender, Sexuality and Museums: A Routledge Reader*. London: Routledge.

Lister, Anne (1988) *I Know My Own Heart: The Diaries of Anne Lister, 1791–1840*. Edited by Helena Whitbread. London: Virago.

Lister, Anne (1992) *I Know My Own Heart: The Diaries of Anne Lister, 1791–1840.* Edited by Helena Whitbread. New York: New York University Press.

Love, Heather (2009) *Feeling Backward: Loss and the Politics of Queer History.* Cambridge, MA: Harvard University Press.

Mills, Robert (2006) 'Queer Is Here? Lesbian, Gay, Bisexual and Transgender Histories and Public Culture'. *History Workshop Journal* 62: 253–63.

Mills, Robert (2008) 'Theorizing the Queer Museum'. *Museums & Social Issues* 3(1): 41–52.

Morris, Charles E. (2007) *Queering Public Address: Sexualities in American Historical Discourse.* Columbia, SC: University of South Carolina Press.

National Lesbian and Gay Survey (1993) *Proust, Cole Porter, Michelangelo, Marc Almond and Me: Writings by Gay Men on Their Lives and Lifestyles.* London; New York: Routledge.

National Park Service (2016) 'What Can You Do to Get Involved with the LGBTQ Heritage Initiative?': 1. Available at www.nps.gov/subjects/lgbtqheritage/upload/GetInvolvedFinalversion.pdf (accessed 13 July 2016).

Nestle, Joan (1990) 'The Will to Remember: The Lesbian Herstory Archives of New York'. *Feminist Review* 34(1): 86–94.

Oram, Alison (2011) 'Going on an Outing: The Historic House and Queer Public History'. *Rethinking History* 15(2): 189–207.

Parkinson, R. B. (2013) *A Little Gay History: Desire and Diversity Across the World.* London: British Museum Publications.

Perry, David M. (2015) 'A New Right Grounded in the Long History of Marriage'. *The Atlantic*, 26 June. www.theatlantic.com/politics/archive/2015/06/history-marriage-supreme-court/396443/.

Porter, Gaby (1996) 'Seeing through Solidity: A Feminist Perspective on Museums'. *The Sociological Review* 43(1), supplement: 105–26.

Resonance FM (2013) Interview by Clayton Littlewood, 16 April.

rukus! – The Collections – City of London (2016): www.cityoflondon.gov.uk/things-to-do/london-metropolitan-archives/the-collections/Pages/rukus.aspx (accessed 19 July 2016).

Sandell, Richard, and Eithne Nightingale (eds) (2012) *Museums, Equality and Social Justice.* Abingdon: Routledge.

Seel, Pierre (2011) *I, Pierre Seel, Deported Homosexual: A Memoir of Nazi Terror.* New York: Basic Books.

Stryker, Susan (2008) 'Transgender History, Homonormativity, and Disciplinarity'. *Radical History Review* 2008(100): 145–57.

Tatchell, Peter (2004) 'Inside the Gay Museum'. *Guardian*, 8 June.

Trudeau, Garry (1994) 'Doonesbury'. *Washington Post*, 8 June.

Walters, Ben (2015) 'Supporting statement for an application to have the Royal Vauxhall Tavern added to the National Heritage list for England'. Available at www.rvt.community (accessed 21 January 2016).

X, Ajamu, Topher Campbell and Mary Stevens (2010) 'Love and Lubrication in the Archives, or Rukus!: A Black Queer Archive for the United Kingdom'. *Archivaria* 68: 271–94.

Index